THE AMERICAN EXPERIENCE IN VIETNAM

THE AMERICAN EXPERIENCE IN VIETNAM

REFLECTIONS ON AN ERA

THE EDITORS OF BOSTON PUBLISHING COMPANY

ZENITH PRESS

This edition published in 2014 by Zenith Press, an imprint of Quarto Publishing Group USA Inc., 400 First Avenue North, Suite 400, Minneapolis, MN 55401 USA. First edition, *The American Experience in Vietnam* by Clark Dougan and Stephen Weiss, published in 1988 by Boston Publishing Company, Inc. Much of the narrative text of this edition and the historical research that informs it is based on the first edition.

The information in this book is true and complete to the best of our knowledge. All recommendations are made without any guarantee on the part of the author or Publisher, who also disclaims any liability incurred in connection with the use of this data or specific details.

We recognize, further, that some words, model names, and designations mentioned herein are the property of the trademark holder. We use them for identification purposes only. This is not an official publication.

Zenith Press titles are also available at discounts in bulk quantity for industrial or sales-promotional use. For details write to Special Sales Manager at Quarto Publishing Group USA Inc., 400 First Avenue North, Suite 400, Minneapolis, MN 55401 USA.

To find out more about our books, visit us online at www.zenithpress.com.

ISBN-13: 978-0-7603-4625-9

Library of Congress Cataloging-in-Publication Data
The American experience in Vietnam / the editors of Boston Publishing Company. --
 [Zenith press edition].
        pages cm
   Earlier edition has statement of responsibility: Clark Dougan, Stephen Weiss and the editors of Boston Publishing Company ; pictures selected by Kathleen A. Reidy.
   Includes bibliographical references and index.
   ISBN 978-0-7603-4625-9 (hc w/jacket)
   1. Vietnam War, 1961-1975--United States. 2. Vietnam War, 1961-1975--Pictorial works.
I. Dougan, Clark. American experience in Vietnam. II. Boston Publishing Company.
   DS558.D66 2014
   959.704'3373--dc23
                    2014013529

Zenith Press
Editorial Director: Erik Gilg
Project Manager: Madeleine Vasaly
Art Director: James Kegley
Layout Designer: Kall Design

Boston Publishing Company
Publisher: Robert George
Managing Editor: Carolyn Medeiros
Senior Writer and Photo Researcher: Nick Mills
Senior Editor: David Shapira
Research Assistant: Michele Tezduyar

On the cover: An unidentified soldier from Bravo Company, 4th Battalion, 31st Infantry Regiment, Americal Division, during a firefight in the Hiep Duc Valley, 1969.

Opposite page: A young Marine private waits on the beach during the Marine landing at Da Nang.

Printed in China

10 9 8 7 6 5 4 3 2 1

CONTENTS

PUBLISHER'S NOTE

THE BIG PICTURE

I arrived in Da Nang, South Vietnam, in August 1969 as a first lieutenant in the US Marine Corps trained to fly the A-6 Intruder, a state-of-the-art all-weather jet aircraft widely considered to be the most capable combat aircraft the US had deployed to Vietnam. As long as I could remember, I had wanted to fly airplanes, particularly jets. It had taken more than two years of rigorous, competitive training to achieve my goal. Even so, when I left Cherry Point, North Carolina, for Vietnam, I knew very little about the war I was about to join.

Once in-country, I flew 118 combat missions over the next year. Most of my flights occurred at night, providing close air support for US Marine infantry fighting in the heavily vegetated, mountainous regions of I Corps; we also provided air cover for the Army's 101st Airborne Division. Close air support is a Marine pilot's primary mission, but we also flew missions far to the north, more than a thousand miles round trip, patrolling the borders of China and North Vietnam in search of truck convoys carrying supplies and munitions to the battlefields in South Vietnam. As a Marine pilot I also spent time with the Marine infantry in the bush coordinating air-ground operations, and with the Navy's Combat Information Center aboard the aircraft carrier USS *Ranger* stationed just off the coast.

My brother, Ken, also served in Vietnam. He was a Marine infantryman with 3/3/M on the Rockpile, Con Thien, and on Mutter's Ridge during the Tet Offensive in 1968. Ken endured some very difficult times during the height of Tet in areas that were hotly contested. He returned home from Vietnam only to die a young man from the effects of Agent Orange. His son was born with hydrocephalus, a birth defect likely caused by the chemical. My generation's Vietnam experience, I learned, would not end with us; it would be passed to future generations as well.

These very different roles and experiences that my brother and I encountered gave me an unusual perspective on the war, along with a mix of very strong emotions, primarily frustration. Whereas most US troops saw only a narrow slice of the fighting in one particular region of the country, I saw the war from the air, the ground, and the sea, in the north as well as the south. Witnessing the war in this way, I soon began to draw my own conclusions— we had been assigned an impossible task. The enemy's supply lines were too scattered, its ground forces too difficult to find and fix, and its stationary military targets too limited in number to be effectively interdicted from the air. Most of North Vietnam's supplies came from beyond its borders, mainly the Soviet Union and China. There was a steady source of supplies flowing down a vast network of roads to an enemy that was difficult to distinguish from the local population we were expected to protect.

One mission in particular seemed to epitomize the futility of it all. I had flown up to the Chinese border on an Operation Barrel Roll mission in search of truck convoys rolling across China's border bound for North Vietnam and onto the Laotian branch of the Ho Chi Minh Trail. I managed to hit two trucks. I had flown a multimillion-dollar jet—the most technologically advanced aircraft in the American arsenal—on a thousand-mile round-trip bombing

Corporal Ken George, Mike Company, 3rd Battalion, 3rd Marines, on the Rockpile, July 1968.

Lieutenant Robert George, Da Nang, December 1969.

Marines of Mike Company, 3rd Battalion, 3rd Marines, on patrol near Con Thien, 1968. This photo was taken by Ken George.

run, and all that I accomplished was to destroy two trucks. Meanwhile, hundreds, if not thousands, of other trucks rolled across the border driving along impossible-to-detect dirt roads protected by six-thousand-foot karst mountain ranges and large amounts of Soviet anti-aircraft artillery. There appeared no way to prevent the southward flow of supplies and munitions—in short, there seemed no way to help our Marines on the ground fighting a well-equipped and determined enemy hidden in the triple-canopy jungles of I Corps. I began to feel that the war was unwinnable.

The mind copes in many ways. I stopped looking at the big picture and the politics of it all. Instead, I looked at the little picture; I focused on helping the "kids" in the jungle, as we often referred to the younger ground troops, by giving them the best air support we could, either as pilots or as forward air controllers. Give them the support they needed, get them home safe, and then get ourselves home safe: that became the mission. And the fact that my brother had been one of those kids, though we were not allowed to serve in-country at the same time, only intensified that feeling.

But the "big picture" was always there, lurking in the background—especially when we came home. The country was deeply divided over the war, though it wasn't always easy to know who was on which side or even what the sides were. I remember one incident that occurred soon after I returned to the US. My wife, Pam, had flown to meet me in Laguna Beach, California, where some of us were housed in a civilian motel because of overcrowding at the El Toro Air Base. We went to a local bar. After a while, I began to feel uncomfortable because I was one of the few short-haired men in the place— a telltale sign I was in the military. So we went back to the motel to look at some slides I had taken in Vietnam (this being the first time I was able to see the undeveloped film I had mailed home). Then there was a knock at the door, and when I opened it, a long-haired hippie was standing in front of me. He had been looking through the gap in the curtains, which we had intentionally closed, and asked if the pictures projected on the wall were of Vietnam. I assumed we were about to have a confrontation. Instead, he asked if he could come in. "I just got back from there myself not too long ago."

After my tour in Vietnam, which ended on July 15, 1970, when my eardrums were blown flying a close air-support mission for the 101st Airborne during Operation Ripcord, I joined the Marine Reserves and gained some experience in public affairs, starting off my career in publishing. I began by publishing periodicals, then books, and did reasonably well back in those days when book publishing was in its heyday.

In the late 1970s, I sold my company to Harcourt Brace Jovanovich, where I accepted a position as vice president of marketing. During those years, like many Vietnam veterans, I rarely mentioned my service in the war. But one day while I was meeting with Bill Jovanovich, it slipped out. Before I could explain my involvement—or try to explain it away—Bill interrupted me and said, "You don't have to apologize for going." He told me his son had gone, too, and there was nothing to be ashamed of. I never apologized again for my service in Vietnam, though I still wrestled with a lot of suppressed emotions about the war and its aftereffects that had built up over the years. But these feelings would become a driving force for me professionally and, without question, shaped what would become my life's work. At the time, I didn't know that I would end up publishing twenty-seven books on Vietnam. I only knew that I was searching for answers, and I learned that thousands of other veterans were, too.

In 1979, I left HBJ and resumed my career as an independent publisher. At Harcourt I had worked with the Italian publisher Rizzoli on a couple of continuity book series—books linked by a common theme that could be marketed to a list of subscribers—and I began toying with the idea of publishing a series on the Vietnam War. At that time, only four years after the fall of Saigon, many people I consulted didn't believe there would be an audience for such a series. In fact, most Americans were so weary of the topic it seemed as if the entire country had entered a period of collective amnesia about the war. I did, however, encounter one person who thought my idea might work—Robert Wolff, Coolidge Professor of History at Harvard University. I also conducted market research that suggested some potential, although some copywriters refused to work on a project about Vietnam.

Following the market tests, I asked Bob Wolff to serve as editor of the new series, he took an early retirement from Harvard, and together we began to move ahead with the series I titled *The Vietnam Experience*, to be published under the imprint of Boston Publishing Company.

When Bob Wolff died unexpectedly in 1980, before the first volume was in print, I enlisted Robert Manning—former European bureau chief for *Time* magazine, former assistant secretary of state in the Kennedy administration, and longtime editor of the *Atlantic Monthly*—to edit the series. We hired a team of young writers, most of them academic historians fresh out of grad school, along with photo editors and researchers, and set to work on what we originally envisioned as a twelve-book series. It would eventually grow to twenty-five.

We sent our writers and researchers into government and military archives and presidential libraries to examine documents that in many instances had not been seen, or declassified, since the end of the war. They interviewed government officials and battlefield commanders along with ordinary veterans from every branch of the American military. And they supplemented this primary research by consulting a vast range of published sources, from newspapers and magazines to memoirs and scholarly monographs. The result was one of the earliest comprehensive histories of the war, described by the *New York Times* as "the definitive work on the Vietnam War."

The first three volumes of the series, which traced the history of US involvement in the conflict from 1945 through the Kennedy years, sold modestly. But following the November 1982 dedication of the Vietnam Veterans Memorial in Washington, D.C., interest in the series spiked, and sales quickly followed, particularly after Time-Life Books signed on to market and distribute the series. *The Vietnam Experience* ultimately attracted more than seven hundred thousand subscribers, who collectively purchased more than eleven million books. It was apparent that many people, vets or not, still wanted to know "How?" and "Why?"

After the series came to a close, I commissioned two of the writers, Clark Dougan and Stephen Weiss, to write a single-volume history of the Vietnam War that encapsulated the work we had done over the previous eight years. That book, published in 1988 under the title *The American Experience in Vietnam*, was in many ways the capstone of the series we had launched in 1979. The book you are about to enjoy is based on that edition, revised and expanded by Nick Mills, another writer on the original series and himself a Vietnam veteran and combat photographer.

—Robert George,
President, Boston Publishing Company

A TIME TO REFLECT

The original edition of this book was essentially a history, a recounting of events—one of many written about the Vietnam War. Now, fifty years after US Marines landed at Da Nang—the beginning of the all-out US effort to prevent a Communist takeover of South Vietnam—our perceptions of the conflict have been altered by time and by dramatic events elsewhere in the world. The US has fought three more wars, in the Persian Gulf, Iraq, and Afghanistan, and engaged in other conflicts in places like Grenada, Panama, and Mogadishu.

When work began on the project that would become the original edition, just a few years after the last US troops left Saigon, Vietnam was still fairly fresh in the minds of many Americans. The Vietnam Veterans Memorial—the Wall—had been completed just six years earlier and was still controversial to some veterans. Today, the Wall is almost universally hailed as a masterpiece and a fitting tribute to the more than fifty-eight thousand Americans who died in Vietnam or from injuries suffered there.

The world has moved on. The United States now has diplomatic and economic ties with Vietnam. Vietnam was all but inaccessible when this book was first published; today, it hosts millions of tourists every year, including many Americans, returning veterans among them. What they see is a stunningly beautiful and diverse place, with few visible traces of what the Vietnamese call the American War. Virtually everything the half-million-strong US military force built in Vietnam is gone, having been demolished, the materials repurposed and the sites obliterated by Vietnam's rapid economic development. The Vietnamese population is young; more than 85 percent of the country's 92.4 million people were born after 1960. Most Vietnamese know about the war only through their history books. The people are industrious and entrepreneurial, and very friendly to American visitors, even—perhaps especially—to the former soldiers who once fought them in bloody and devastating battles and rained so much death and destruction on their cities, towns, and hamlets.

The time is right for this new perspective on the Vietnam War; indeed, this reflection. *The American Experience in Vietnam: Reflections on an Era* is not just another "order of battle" history, though it does recount the major military operations, heroic firebase defenses, and bloody mountaintop battles. We cannot forget those, but *reflection* must be the operative word for this fiftieth-anniversary edition.

Vietnam suffered much at the hands of the Americans, but it had a much longer history of suffering under the yoke of occupiers. China occupied Vietnam for a thousand years; the French for over sixty. Even Japan occupied Vietnam, though briefly. We can now appreciate Ho Chi

Lieutenant Nick Mills (right) with Lt. Marty Katz, both of the 221st Signal Company (Pictorial), aboard an Army river patrol boat near Vung Tau, December 1968.

The days before e-mail: a Marine at Mutter's Ridge writes home, 1968.

Minh's lifelong struggle to win Vietnam's independence. He appealed to three US presidents for help but was rebuffed, in part because he carried the label of Communist. But his brand of communism was pragmatic and nationalistic; once the Americans left and Vietnam was united, the Vietnamese fought brief wars with China to the north and Cambodia to the south, laying to rest the so-called domino theory that postulated a solid Red bloc of East Asian states if Vietnam were to fall to the Communists.

Vietnam's harsh postwar era, during which tens of thousands of Vietnamese were herded into "re-education camps," slowly gave way to a reopening of the doors to the world. A former South Vietnamese army officer who spent ten years in a re-education camp following the NVA's final victory traveled back to Vietnam with me in 2003. Khanh Nguyen was apprehensive about how he might be treated on his return, but his fears proved groundless as we traveled by car and domestic airline from deep in the Mekong Delta to Hanoi. Khanh had emotional reunions with many members of his extended family along the way, including a nephew who met us at Da Nang airport in a new SUV, negotiating deals on his cell phone as he drove us around.

When I visited Hanoi during that trip, I found my way from my four-star hotel, the Hanoi Opera Hilton, to the notorious prison that Americans knew as the "Hanoi Hilton." It didn't look like a prison. With its plain façade and the words *Maison Centrale* above the entrance, it might have been a French restaurant. But this was where captured US servicemen, most of them pilots whose planes had been shot down during bombing raids over North Vietnam, were held for years in harsh conditions. The *Maison Centrale* has shrunk since the end of the war, a good two-thirds of it having been razed to make way for a residential tower. But enough is left, now serving as a museum, to give a visitor some idea of what it might have been like to be imprisoned there. As one might surmise from its French name, the prison predated America's war in Vietnam by many decades; it was built in the late nineteenth century by the French to imprison, torture, and often execute (the centerpiece of the museum's exhibits is a guillotine) captured Viet Minh fighters, who warred for decades to drive the French from Indochina. In 1954, just before the French surrendered at Dien Bien Phu, the prison held some two thousand inmates, stuffed into a space built for less than half that number. To be sure, some exhibits recall the years of the American War—Sen. John McCain's flight suit has been on display—but the focus of the museum is the much longer occupation of Vietnam by the French and their cruel treatment of Viet Minh prisoners.

Just as it is in Vietnam, the war is ancient history to today's American students. Veterans are in their sixties and seventies. Wounds have healed, families have been raised, and memories have softened. Few Americans today, even Vietnam veterans, think of Vietnam as the enemy. We have too many other enemies to focus on. And Americans have a history of friendship with former enemies—witness our relationships with Japan and Germany, two of our staunchest allies in the world today. Today's recounting of "the American experience in Vietnam" must be tempered by the events of the intervening years.

It is said that more books have been written about the Vietnam War than about any of America's other wars—an ever-growing collection of around thirty thousand, by some counts. Some great journalists and photojournalists cut their teeth in Vietnam, and the press played a key role in shaping our perceptions of the conflict. It was the first war in which reporters and photographers had largely unrestricted access to the battlefields, a freedom that the US military has been at pains to limit ever since. Some military minds still blame the media for "losing the war," but most reporters supported the war in the early years and the coverage was mostly positive until the 1968 Tet Offensive, when many Americans at home began to realize—as reporters such as David Halberstam, Neil Sheehan, and others had known from the beginning—that their military leaders and the president had been less than truthful about the success of the US military effort.

It was also the first American conflict covered extensively by television, though it was not as extensive as some people think they remember. The Vietnam War was not "live" on TV every night; technology had not yet developed to the point where reporters in the field could do live shots on the evening news, and there was little footage of actual combat. Still, television gave Americans a window into the war that had not been possible in earlier conflicts. (Motion picture footage was shot in World War II, but it didn't appear on TV the night after it was filmed because there was no TV broadcasting, only newsreels shown in movie theaters.) Film shot in the field in Vietnam could be shown on American television in a matter of hours—after being flown out of Vietnam, processed, and edited—or at most, a couple of days.

More importantly, though, there was no military or government censoring of the footage. Morley Safer's 1965 story, aired on the *CBS Evening News*, of Marines burning a cluster of hamlets at Cam Ne would not have been broadcast had it happened during World War II. After the story aired, the military lashed out at Safer, and President Johnson called CBS president Frank Stanton to complain. This was one of a number of stories from Vietnam, on television and in the newspapers, that may have fueled antiwar sentiment in the United States. As Safer said years later on the PBS series *Reporting America at War*, Americans at home "saw American troops acting in a way people had never seen American troops act before, and couldn't imagine." In the aftermath of the Cam Ne story, the military and the Johnson administration briefly discussed imposing censorship on the press in Vietnam but concluded it would be unworkable.

Robert George, a former Marine Corps pilot who flew many missions in Vietnam and the publisher of the original, groundbreaking twenty-five-volume series *The Vietnam Experience* (to which I contributed one volume, *Combat Photographer*), asked me to update the first edition of this book because he wanted the perspective of a veteran who could add personal stories. I also wanted to add the stories of other veterans who had returned to Vietnam years after the war and of veterans who had found ways to give back—to their fellow Vietnam veterans, to the veterans of more recent wars, and to the burgeoning nation of Vietnam, still recovering from the many years of war fought on its soil.

The original text, written by my friends, the historians Clark Dougan and Stephen Weiss, remains the solid foundation of this new edition, and Clark gave generously of his time and expertise to keep me from straying off the historical track. I hope that what I have added does justice to their work and to the many who served and sacrificed in that long and difficult war.

—Nick Mills,
Senior Writer

Long patrols in the rain-soaked jungles of Vietnam led to "jungle rot" and other foot problems. Powder and dry socks were a grunt's best friend.

THE ROOTS OF INVOLVEMENT

Endings and Beginnings

One more day. If Charlie McMahon and Darwin Judge could have survived one more day, their names would not be engraved in history as heartbreaking footnotes to the story of the Vietnam War. But there they are, two names on the Wall, distinguished by the date of their deaths: April 29, 1975, making them the last two American servicemen killed in Vietnam. The two young Marines—Corporal McMahon would have turned twenty-two in eleven days; Lance Corporal Judge was nineteen—had been in Vietnam for just a week when a North Vietnamese rocket struck their checkpoint outside the US Defense Attaché's office at "Pentagon East," the sprawling US command center at the big Tan Son Nhut Air Base just outside of Saigon, where they were pulling guard duty as thousands of Americans and Vietnamese were being evacuated from Vietnam.

In the final days of the Vietnam War, a Vietnamese refugee family tries to push their scooter onto Highway 1 outside Saigon as they flee the advancing North Vietnamese, days before the fall of Saigon in April 1975.

MASTER SERGEANT CHESTER M. OVNAND, US ARMY
Photo on loan from Vietnam Military Lore © 1988 Bows & Co.

MAJOR DALE R. BUIS, US ARMY
Photo on loan from Vietnam Military Lore © 1988 Bows & Co.

Photos of US Army military advisors Master Sgt. Chester Ovnand (left) and Maj. Dale Buis (right) are displayed at a ceremony at the Vietnam Veterans Memorial Wall in Washington, D.C., on July 8, 2009, commemorating the fiftieth anniversary of their deaths. They were the first American servicemen to die in the Vietnam War.

Just weeks earlier, the North Vietnamese Army (NVA) had begun a lightning drive south toward Saigon, steamrolling the opposing South Vietnamese forces, many of whom had abandoned their posts and fled, leaving their weapons and even their uniforms behind in a desperate effort at survival. In late March, the old imperial capital of Hue fell, and Da Nang was taken on March 29—Da Nang, where exactly ten years earlier, the landing of US Marines marked the start of American ground combat operations in South Vietnam. In late March 1975, no one was coming ashore at Da Nang; rather, there was a mass exodus, as civilians and soldiers alike scrambled to board any available watercraft that could carry them to the safety of waiting ships chartered by the US Military Sealift Command. As many as twenty thousand military and civilian personnel were evacuated to the ships. One Boeing 727 flown by World Airways landed at Da Nang to try to evacuate women and children, but some panicked South Vietnamese troops fought their way onto the plane, which eventually took off with around three hundred people on board. Now, a month after capturing Da Nang, the North Vietnamese were within a few miles of Saigon, poised to take the biggest prize and claim total victory. At Tan Son Nhut, US Air Force transport planes had been taking off around the clock with capacity loads of passengers: American military and civilian personnel, South Vietnamese military personnel, and civilians who had been working for the Americans, and flying them to the safety of US bases in the Philippines or Guam. At 4:00 a.m., the North Vietnamese launched a rocket attack on Tan Son Nhut, sending more than 150 rockets into the big complex. One of the rockets struck a US Air Force C-130 cargo plane waiting to take refugees on board, destroying the plane and halting the airlift. And one of the rockets scored a direct hit on the checkpoint manned by McMahon and Judge.

Later in the day of April 29, the few remaining Americans in Vietnam, including Ambassador Graham Martin, scrambled aboard a helicopter on a Saigon rooftop and flew to the safety of the ships of the US 7th Fleet waiting offshore. The day after, April 30, 1975, North Vietnamese Army tanks smashed through the gates of the presidential palace and claimed victory over South Vietnam. The Vietnam War was over. The new Vietnamese government declared April 30 Reunification Day.

Charles McMahon and Darwin Judge were the last American servicemen to die in the Vietnam War, but the case for the first American soldier to die there is open to debate. Some argue that it was US Army Lt. Col. Peter Dewey, who was shot on September 26, 1945, by soldiers of the Viet Minh, Ho Chi Minh's army, who apparently thought Dewey was French. Lieutenant Colonel Dewey was in the Office of Strategic Services—the OSS, precursor of today's CIA—and he had gone to Saigon to assess the situation there after the surrender of Japan, which had occupied Vietnam during World War II. Ironically, the OSS had been working closely with the nationalist leader Ho Chi Minh, who had been supplying the Americans with intelligence on the Japanese, and Dewey supported the Viet Minh's objective of keeping the French from reestablishing colonial rule of Vietnam after the war.

Those factors complicate Dewey's status as the first American soldier to die in Vietnam. He was killed by the Communist Viet Minh, but by what we might now call "friendly fire," because he was actually on Ho Chi Minh's side, as was the administration of President Franklin Roosevelt. Roosevelt's opposition to French colonialism in Indochina, as well as the US collaboration with Ho Chi Minh during World War II, seemed to promise a lasting friendship between the two peoples. On September 2, 1945, three weeks before Dewey's death, other US Army officers had stood on a reviewing stand in Hanoi and listened to a band playing "The Star-Spangled Banner" as Ho proclaimed his country's freedom in words borrowed directly from the American Declaration of Independence, and US aircraft flew overhead in salute. It was Ho's finest moment, the culmination of a lifetime struggle for a unified, independent Vietnam—but the moment didn't last, and Ho Chi Minh would not live to see his dream fulfilled. Yet on that heady day in 1945, it was unthinkable that fourteen years later, Americans and Vietnamese would be dying at each other's hands.

Flash ahead to a hot July night in South Vietnam in the summer of 1959. The few Americans in the country at that time were not worrying too much about death.

At a small South Vietnamese army camp in Bien Hoa, a village about twenty miles east of Saigon, six American advisors—US Army personnel who were part of the US Military Assistance Advisory Group—were absorbed in the first reel of a movie, *The Tattered Dress*, starring Jeff Chandler and Jeanne Crain. They did not hear the shadowy, black-clad figures who crept out of the darkness surrounding their mess hall. They did not see them

Retired US Army Capt. Nathaniel P. Ward IV (left) and retired Army Maj. Sam Ratcliffe stand with a wreath in honor of Major Buis and Master Sergeant Ovnand, both of whom were killed when their compound in Bien Hoa, just north of Saigon, was attacked.

ready a French submachine gun in the rear window or push two rifle muzzles through the pantry screens. They did not realize anything was wrong at all until Master Sgt. Chester Ovnand turned on the lights to change the reel. Suddenly, automatic-weapons fire exploded through the room. The high-caliber shells slammed into the startled Americans, spinning one man around and knocking two others from their seats before Maj. Jack Hellet snapped off the lights and the gunmen fled, or all six men might have died. In the bloody confusion of the mess hall lay Capt. Howard Boston. Badly wounded, he would survive.

But for Master Sergeant Ovnand and Maj. Dale Buis, the night would go on forever.

Ovnand, from Texas, was forty-four, and a couple of months away from retirement. Buis, thirty-eight, from California, had arrived at Bien Hoa only two days before.

In the time between the deaths of Major Buis and Major Sergeant Ovnand and the deaths of Corporal McMahon and Lance Corporal Judge, 58,721 Americans lost their lives to the Vietnam War, along with 183,528 South Vietnamese army soldiers, an estimated 925,000 North Vietnamese soldiers and guerrillas, 415,000 South Vietnamese civilians, and as many as 65,000 North Vietnamese civilians.

How, and why, did it all happen?

A Long History of Occupation

Around 100 BC, Chinese warriors invaded the northern provinces of what is now Vietnam, and China dominated the country for roughly a thousand years. It could be argued that the Vietnamese people's desire for independence was born during that millennium, and it grew until, in 938 AD, the Vietnamese hero Ngo Quyen drove out the Chinese. For the next several centuries, Vietnam expanded slowly southward, finally encompassing the Mekong Delta region in the eighteenth century. But by that time, civil wars were tearing the country apart, and Vietnam was for the first time divided by north and south. China, taking advantage of the civil strife, reoccupied parts of the north.

Enter the French. A Jesuit missionary, Alexandre de Rhodes, arrived in 1620, the same year that a boatload of English pilgrims landed at Plymouth Rock in America. Through Father De Rhodes, the French established Europe's first ties with Vietnam, and in the late eighteenth century another French cleric engineered the 1787 Treaty of Versailles, which promised French assistance to Prince Nguyen Anh to conquer Vietnam's

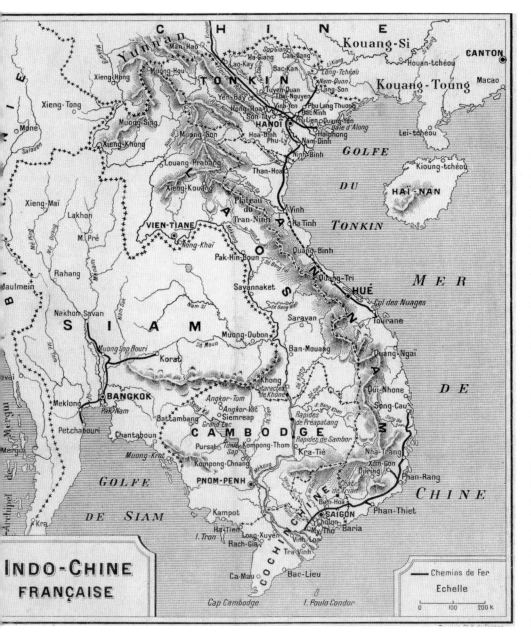

French Indochina as it appeared in 1910, including Cambodia and Laos. The French created a three-part federation of Tonkin in the north, Annam in the center, and Cochin in the south. To the west is Siam, now Thailand.

feuding warlords and reunify the nation. The French king, Louis XVI, had troubles of his own, however, as the French Revolution was afoot, and he was only able to offer a small number of French soldiers. But that proved to be enough to tip the balance, and Nguyen Anh managed to capture Saigon, unify Vietnam, and rule as Emperor Gia Long well into the nineteenth century, when another sort of French ruler, Napoleon III, formed his own designs on Vietnam. In 1858–1859 Napoleon's forces captured Saigon and Da Nang, and in 1884–1885 French forces drove China out of northern Vietnam. In 1887, French Indochina was formed, including not only Vietnam but Cambodia as well. Laos was added in 1893 after the brief Franco-Siamese War. But long before the maps could be redrawn, Vietnamese resistance to French rule had begun.

Three years after the French claimed "Indochina" for their own, in the little village of Hoang Tru, a boy named Nguyen Sinh Cung was born.

He would change his name several times. When he was ten, his father, a Confucian scholar and imperial magistrate, renamed his son Nguyen Tat Thanh, "Nguyen the Accomplished," in recognition of the boy's scholastic achievements. In Paris, around 1920, Nguyen took yet another name, Nguyen Ai Quoc, "Nguyen the Patriot." In 1940, serving as an advisor with the Chinese Communist forces that would eventually take over the country, Nguyen took the name that stuck: Ho Chi Minh, "He Who Enlightens."

Ho Chi Minh

The life of Ho Chi Minh is the thread that bound the United States to Vietnam, as allies and enemies, for many decades. He petitioned three American presidents to help him get the French out of Vietnam, worked with American intelligence services during World War II, borrowed liberally from the American Declaration of Independence in his rhetoric, and finally fought the Americans until he died, in 1969, in pursuit of his lifelong goal of a unified, independent Vietnam. He was a Communist from an early age, but in the broad view, his communism seemed "small c" and more pragmatic than rigidly ideological. He lived in the Soviet Union and in Red China, and when he finally came to power in North Vietnam, he ruled with a firm and sometimes brutal hand, but he never seemed interested in the world Communist movement. Vietnam was his world, and if the democratic West would not help him achieve it, the Communist East would. And if, in the eyes of the Cold Warriors of the West, Vietnam became a fallen domino, it was also the final domino: the *bloc* stops here. After the Americans left, the Soviets, who had sent three thousand soldiers to advise and train (and perhaps fight alongside) the North Vietnamese, became Vietnam's principal ally and maintained a military presence until the Soviet Union collapsed in 1991, but Vietnam never became the USSR's minion. Or China's. In 1978–1979, Vietnam invaded Cambodia, ousting the Beijing-backed Khmer Rouge and ending the Pol Pot nightmare, in the process earning China's outrage. The Vietnamese were denounced by Chinese leader Deng Xiaoping as "the hooligans of the East."

The man who eventually would become the symbol of Vietnamese communism, the mortal enemy of the United States, and later, in death, be revered as the Father of the Nation, was a bright child. He learned, from his father, Chinese and Vietnamese writing as well as the requisite French at a *lycée* in Hue. His first political act is thought to have been participation in a peasant anti-tax demonstration in Hue when he was seventeen. At twenty-one, with his educational opportunities limited in Vietnam because his father had been fired from his government post for an abuse of power, he shipped out of Saigon on a French steamer, working in the galley, and arrived in Marseilles in late 1911. Rejected for study at the French Colonial Administrative School—think what might have happened, or not happened, had he become an administrator of French colonial rule in Vietnam!—Nguyen decided to work his way around the world on ships, and for the next several years visited the United States, Britain, and France. He lived in the US in 1912–1913, and again in 1917–1918, and worked at several jobs, including a stint as a baker at Boston's venerable Parker House Hotel. Between those visits he sailed to Britain, where he odd-jobbed, mainly in restaurants, before crossing the English Channel to France, where his political education really began.

North Vietnamese nationalist leader Ho Chi Minh, born Nguyen Sinh Cung, pictured circa 1950.

By the time Nguyen arrived in Paris, probably in 1919, there was a sizeable Vietnamese community in France. Within that community, a nationalist movement had bubbled up, and Nguyen joined it, quickly becoming one of the movement's leaders and taking a new name: Nguyen Ai Quoc. At the Versailles peace talks at the close of World War I, Nguyen and the nationalists petitioned US president Woodrow Wilson and other Western leaders to force an end to French colonial rule in Indochina. This was the first time that the man who would become Ho Chi Minh brushed up against the US government, though he did not leave much of an impression. The nationalists' plea was ignored, which served to fortify Nguyen's patriotic resolve. His Paris activities may not have moved the West, but they did not go unnoticed in Vietnam, where he became a symbol and a rallying figure for the anticolonial movement.

In the years between the world wars, Nguyen Ai Quoc became a founding member of the French Communist Party and traveled to Moscow, where he spent a year studying and working for the Communist International (Comintern). In 1924, he went to Canton, China, where he gave lectures to young Vietnamese revolutionaries. He remained in China until 1927, when Chiang Kai-shek's anti-Communist coup forced him to leave. For the next decade, he was constantly on the move—he returned to Moscow and then went to Paris, Germany, Switzerland, and Italy. In 1928, he moved to Thailand and then went to India, Shanghai, and Hong Kong, where he was arrested, possibly at the request of the French, in 1931. The British authorities in the Crown Colony resisted French demands for Nguyen's extradition, then falsely reported his death and allowed him to slip away to Italy, where he worked for a time in a Milan restaurant (purportedly, a portrait of him still hangs on a wall there), but he was suffering from tuberculosis, and he spent several years in the Soviet Union recovering. He returned to China, where communism was in its ascendancy, working with Mao Zedong's army, in 1938—the year Hitler's Germany seized Austria and set its sights on the rest of Europe. In China, Nguyen Ai Quoc began calling himself Ho Chi Minh.

World War II

Hitler invaded Poland on September 1, 1939. Two days later, Britain and France declared war on Germany. Eight months later, on May 10, 1939, Germany invaded France; France surrendered on June 22, placing its new, pro-Axis Vichy government in charge of France and her territories, including Indochina.

By then, Japan and China had been at war for two years. Japan had long coveted China's resources, including its seemingly inexhaustible supply of human labor, and had sent its armies in to try to seize them. In 1937, Japan captured Nanking, the Chinese capital, and began a six-week rampage of slaughter and rape that left as many as three hundred thousand Chinese civilians and disarmed soldiers dead.

The Nationalist Chinese government was supported by the US and France, who funneled war supplies to China through the Vietnamese port of Haiphong. In 1940, Japan invaded northern Vietnam to shut off the Allied pipeline to China, but left the Vichy government in place. The following year, with the rubber-stamp approval of the Vichy government, the Japanese placed forces in southern Vietnam and created the bases that served as

A Japanese officer gives his weapon up to allied forces during the Japanese surrender in Indochina, August 1945. Ho Chi Minh had led guerrilla actions against the Vichy French and Japanese occupiers. When the Japanese surrendered, he proclaimed Vietnam's independence.

springboards for Japanese assaults on the Philippines, Malaysia, and other Pacific territories. In July 1941, President Roosevelt asked the Japanese to withdraw from Indochina, and began an oil embargo of Japan that threatened to cripple its military machine. On December 7, 1941, the Japanese bombed Pearl Harbor and the US entered the war.

Ho Chi Minh returned to Vietnam in 1941 to lead the Viet Minh in the fight for independence, which now had two adversaries, the French and the Japanese. He led many guerrilla actions against the Vichy French and the Japanese occupiers, reportedly with clandestine support from the American OSS, given in return for the intelligence on the Japanese that the Viet Minh could supply. In March 1945, the Japanese jailed the Vichy French administrators and took sole possession of Vietnam. Five months later, after Hiroshima and Nagasaki, Japan surrendered and World War II ended. In September, Ho Chi Minh seized the moment to proclaim Vietnam's independence, declaring, "All men are created equal. The Creator has given us certain inalienable rights: the right to Life, the right to be Free, and the right to achieve Happiness. . . . These immortal words are taken from the Declaration of Independence of the United States of America in 1776."

But Ho's declaration carried no weight in the postwar world. The French reestablished their authority in Indochina. Had President Roosevelt lived, he might have been able to prevent France's reoccupation of Indochina; he was no fan of colonialism and supported independence. But Roosevelt was dead and the world was a vastly changed place, now dominated by two great powers, the US and the USSR, and two competing ideologies that would face off for decades in the Cold War. Ho and the Viet Minh resumed their long war of independence against the French and, ultimately, the Americans.

The death of Roosevelt and the onset of the Cold War left a new American president facing problems larger than Vietnamese independence. Alarmed by the threat of Soviet expansionism, determined to maintain cordial relations with a key European partner, and having been persuaded that Ho Chi Minh was a creature of Moscow, Harry Truman did not oppose the restoration of French sovereignty in Indochina. When war broke out between France and Vietnam in 1946, the United States adopted decidedly pro-French "neutrality," declining requests for direct military aid but providing France with sufficient economic assistance so that Paris was able to fund the war out of its own pocket. The French had little success in subduing the Viet Minh. But Indochina remained a peripheral issue for the Truman administration until 1949, when the fall of Nationalist China precipitated a crucial change in US strategy. Fearing that another Communist success would have "critical psychological, political, and economic consequences" for the Western alliance, Truman abandoned American neutrality and committed the United States to a French victory. In early 1950, a US Military Assistance Advisory Group (MAAG) arrived in Vietnam to funnel military aid to France's expeditionary army. By 1952, the United States was paying more than a third of the cost of the war; two years later, it was 80 percent.

Truman's Indochina policy was adopted in its entirety by President Dwight Eisenhower, who believed his predecessor had erred only in allowing France too much leeway. Using more than $1 billion of increased funding as leverage, Washington insisted the French make greater efforts to win Nationalist support and adopt a more aggressive strategy. But nothing could arrest the steady deterioration of the military situation. In March 1954, the Viet Minh surrounded twelve thousand French troops at Dien Bien Phu. When France requested American help, Eisenhower warned that the loss of Indochina would set off a chain reaction felling other nations in the region "like a row of dominoes." But the administration was not prepared to act alone and found no support in Congress for intervention. On May 7, after a fifty-five-day siege, the French garrison at Dien Bien Phu finally surrendered.

Attention immediately shifted to Geneva, where an East-West conference had just begun to discuss the Indochina problem. Buoyed by their victory, the Viet Minh demanded an immediate withdrawal of foreign troops and a comprehensive political settlement. But China and the Soviet Union persuaded Ho Chi Minh to accept temporary partition of Vietnam at the seventeenth parallel with elections to reunify the country in two years. A million anti-Communist Vietnamese, many of them Catholic, fled to the South; some fifty thousand people, many of them Viet Minh guerrillas and their families, moved to the North. The United States prepared to take over the defense of Laos, Cambodia, and the nascent state of South Vietnam, which few observers expected to survive the year.

The new nation's leader, Ngo Dinh Diem, was an experienced administrator and ardent nationalist. But he faced a devastated economy, a lack of trained civil servants, a million refugees, and dozens of armed sects hostile to his government. Diem was a Catholic in a predominantly Buddhist country—a factor that would contribute to his downfall. But in the early years, with US help and a stubborn persistence, Diem not only survived but triumphed. In September 1955, in a declaration that reflected both his internal strength and the backing of his American patrons (President Eisenhower was adamant that the US not recognize the Geneva accords), Diem denounced the accords and refused to participate in the reunification elections scheduled for the following year. Many historians believe that if the elections had been held, Ho Chi Minh would have received 80 percent of the vote.

Once Diem had consolidated his regime, Washington launched an experiment in nation-building that took on the atmosphere of a crusade. From 1955 to 1961, the United States provided South Vietnam with more than $2 billion in aid. Along with the flood of American money came American engineers,

President Dwight Eisenhower (left) and Secretary of State John Foster Dulles (second from left) greet President Ngo Dinh Diem of South Vietnam at Washington National Airport, 1957.

doctors, agriculturalists, social scientists, military advisors, and public administrators to rebuild the South Vietnamese armed forces, reshape the South Vietnamese economy, and reorganize the South Vietnamese government. By the late 1950s, more than 1,500 Americans were building roads, planting crops, training bureaucrats, and dispensing medicine all across South Vietnam under the supervision of the largest US mission anywhere in the world.

US officials called it a "miracle," but their rhetoric outstripped reality. Although the United States was spending $85 million a year on training and equipment, the Army of the Republic of (South) Vietnam (ARVN) suffered from serious manpower shortages and command deficiencies. Although American aid prevented economic collapse and gilded life for the urban elites in Saigon, little was spent on industrial development or to improve the living conditions of the rural peasants who constituted 90 percent of the population. And although American advisors clothed South Vietnam in the trappings of democracy, Diem presided over a ruthless, authoritarian regime that steadily alienated popular support for his government.

Diem lost ground particularly in the countryside, where his suppression of traditional village government, an ineffectual land-reform program, and a penchant for public executions by guillotine created a receptive audience for revolutionary alternatives. In 1957, Viet Minh cadres who remained in the South after partition resumed political agitation in the villages, their efforts soon escalating into a systematic campaign of terror and assassination against local government officials. In January 1959, North Vietnam formally endorsed the resumption of armed struggle in the South and soon after began constructing the network of roads and trails that would become the

Ho Chi Minh Trail. Over this route, Hanoi sent weapons and advisors to assist the insurgents who, in December 1960, coalesced under the banner of the National Liberation Front. By the time John F. Kennedy took office at the beginning of 1961, the military situation had become critical.

Along with the immediate crisis, the young American president had inherited a national commitment. By insisting on the vital importance of Southeast Asia to America's security, Presidents Truman and Eisenhower had made it virtually impossible to retreat from the region. Moreover, Soviet threats to blockade Berlin and the failure of an American-sponsored invasion of Cuba (known as the Bay of Pigs invasion) made it imperative in Kennedy's mind that the United States demonstrate its resolve in Vietnam. At the same time, the experience of the Korean War made him deeply reluctant to deploy American troops on the Asian mainland. Nor would their presence alone guarantee victory. The survival of the Diem government ultimately depended on its willingness to address the social and economic needs of South Vietnam's peasant majority, something it had so far refused to do. Yet without a credible threat of withdrawal, Washington had no leverage to enforce its demands for reform.

Confident of his ability to maintain control of US involvement and unwilling to accept the costs of pulling out, Kennedy opted for a middle course between retreat and direct military intervention. Warding off pressure to introduce combat troops, the president substantially increased the amount of US aid and the number of American advisors. Any consideration of a larger US military presence depended on evidence from Saigon that the government intended to put its house in order.

President Kennedy meets with Secretary of State Dean Rusk (left) and Secretary of Defense Robert McNamara (right), two of his chief foreign policy advisors.

Thich Quang Duc, a Buddhist monk, burns himself to death on a Saigon street on June 11, 1963, to protest the alleged persecution of Buddhists by the South Vietnamese government.

The influx of American men and weapons took the Communist guerrillas by surprise, but the continuing inadequacy of the South Vietnamese army enabled the insurgents to regain the initiative. Washington's attempts to change the direction of the Saigon government also met with failure. Diem instituted token economic reforms to appease the Americans while simultaneously enacting new measures of political repression. The inevitable crisis erupted in the summer of 1963 when militant Buddhists challenged the government with massive street demonstrations and fiery self-immolations. After months of upheaval, a group of South Vietnamese army generals began preparations that culminated on November 1 with the overthrow of the Diem government. During the coup, Diem and his brother Ngo Dinh Nhu were assassinated.

Although Washington had approved Diem's removal, his murder shocked Kennedy and brought to the surface his growing doubts about the course he had taken. When he had assumed office, there were 875 US servicemen in Vietnam. Now there were more than sixteen thousand. Since 1961, millions of dollars had been spent and 109 Americans had lost their lives. Yet the United States was further than ever from its goal of a secure and independent South Vietnam. In mid-November 1963, the president ordered a "complete and very profound review" of American policy in Vietnam. Whether or not Kennedy could have reversed the momentum of US involvement nearly two decades in the making, he never got the chance to try. One week later, John F. Kennedy was dead.

Darwin

If you invented a character like Darwin Lee Judge, people would say that he was too good to be true. A compact, handsome kid with sky-blue eyes, he grew up amid cornfields, hog farms, and churchgoing folks in a town that was founded by the father of Hall of Fame baseball player Cap Anson.

Marshalltown, Iowa, sits smack in the middle of the Hawkeye State. A thousand or so of the town's twenty-seven thousand residents work at the JBS plant, packing Iowa hams. Darwin's older sister, Lori Desaulniers, said Darwin was "the baby of the family—so we babied him!" But he turned out to need no babying.

As a kid, Judge got a paper route, as his brother Loren had done, delivering the *Marshalltown Times Republican*. He played second base for his Little League team—he had good hands, they said—and he made all-star twice. He played guitar in his youth group at the Hope United Methodist Church. He carried groceries for customers at Clifton's. He became an Eagle Scout. As a high school senior, he built a tall grandfather clock that stood in the home of his parents, Henry and Ida Judge, until they died; the clock is now in the Marshalltown home of Darwin's sister Lori.

Right after high school, Judge and three other Marshalltown boys enlisted in the Marine Corps together. Jonathan Lake, one of the four, said that during boot camp, Darwin was "more attentive" than the others and never once was reamed out by the drill instructor. Judge graduated first in his class at boot camp, and as a reward he was sent to the elite Marine Embassy School and assigned to the Marine Security Guard Battalion—the Marines who guard American embassies around the world. Judge and Charlie McMahon, also a graduate of the Embassy School, had been sent to Vietnam in late April to help secure the American Embassy, but when help was needed at Saigon's Tan Son Nhut Air Base to guard the withdrawal of the last few US diplomats from the country in the chaotic days before it fell to the North Vietnamese, Judge and McMahon went there together.

During that frantic week, Darwin Judge became a hero to a fellow Marine guard. Doug Potratz was trying desperately to get his

US Marine Corps Lance Corporal Darwin L. Judge of Marshalltown, Iowa.

wife and three-year-old daughter, Becky, aboard an evacuation aircraft, but he was struggling to get their names on a manifest. Lance Corporal Judge knew the system. He found two open slots on a manifest, then took the little girl from Potratz and put her on his back—"piggy-back style," Potratz said—sprinted off, and put her and Doug's wife on the plane that took them safely out of Vietnam. Potratz stayed until April 30, and was evacuated from the roof of the US Embassy. Becky Potratz went on to graduate with honors from the University of Southern California. She said if it hadn't been for Darwin Judge, she might still be in Vietnam.

Charlie

Charles McMahon Jr. was a big kid with Irish good looks and natural charm, a born leader with something of a wild streak, according to his boyhood pal George Holland. They grew up in Woburn, Massachusetts, nine miles north of Boston. Woburn

Continued

US Marine Corps Corporal Charles McMahon of Woburn, Massachusetts.

was once a leather manufacturing town. The Woburn High football team is nicknamed the Tanners; they won the Eastern Massachusetts Division 1 Super Bowl in 1975, a few months after McMahon died in Vietnam. If he had survived one more day, he might have been at the game with Holland and his other high school buddies.

Charlie McMahon and George Holland were ten when they met at the Boys Club of Woburn. They both loved swimming and became lifeguards at the club's pool, and then swimming directors, and McMahon became president of the club's community service group, the Keystone Club. McMahon had leadership ability. "He was a pied piper," said Holland. "People just followed Charlie." During high school, McMahon and Holland got summer jobs as lifeguards at New Hampshire's popular Hampton Beach, and

McMahon would bring Labor Day traffic to a halt by jumping off the Hampton Beach bridge "for the fans," he would say.

McMahon joined the Marines after high school, planning to train as an MP and then come home to join the Massachusetts State Police, said Holland, who also joined the Marines and served four years in the Corps. "He loved the Marines as much as anybody I ever saw in the Marines." After Holland enlisted, when they were both home on leave, McMahon told Holland, "Bring your dress blues," so that when they went out for dinner they would be recognized as Marines. "He was so proud to show the world who he was," said Holland. He loved the Boys Club, too. Holland recalled the time when McMahon was stationed in California and was going to miss the Club's annual banquet for the first time. McMahon and another Marine got a car and drove fifty-six hours straight right across the country, so that McMahon could attend the banquet, in full MP regalia, nightstick and all. Less than a month before he died, McMahon, like Darwin Judge, had graduated from Marine Embassy School, at the top of his class. His orders had been cut; he was going to the US Embassy in Peru after home leave. On the 17th of April, he left Woburn, thinking that he would soon be in Lima, Peru. But en route, his orders were changed. He flew to Hawaii. He was headed for Vietnam.

Coming Home

In the panic and chaos of April 29 and 30, 1975, the bodies of Charlie McMahon and Darwin Judge were left behind, and wound up in a Seventh Day Adventist hospital in Saigon. But they were not forgotten.

In the months after the Paris Peace Accords were signed in 1973, US senator Edward "Ted" Kennedy of Massachusetts had maintained communication with high-ranking officials in both the Saigon and Hanoi governments. Kennedy began efforts to repatriate the remains of McMahon—who was, after all, a constituent—and his fellow Marine, Judge. In December, the Provisional Revolutionary Government in Saigon informed Kennedy that the bodies would be returned. On Sunday, February 22, 1976, Kennedy aides Jerry Tinker and Dale Dehaan flew from Bangkok, Thailand, to Saigon. A few hours later, they flew back to Bangkok with two flag-draped metal caskets bearing the remains of Darwin L. Judge and Charles

McMahon Jr. From Bangkok, they flew to Travis Air Force Base in California. From there, McMahon's casket was placed aboard an American Airlines flight to Boston. It was escorted by his uncle, Francis McMahon, an Air Force master sergeant. Judge's casket was flown to Des Moines, Iowa, where it was met by a contingent of Marines, who escorted it to Marshalltown for burial.

On March 6, at 11:00 a.m., traffic came to a halt in Woburn center as the bells of the First Congregational Church tolled, slowly, for Marine Cpl. Charles McMahon Jr. Across from the church, two hundred people stood in silence. Charlie McMahon's casket was borne into the church by Marine pallbearers and placed before the altar. A young man in Marine dress blues, in a wheelchair, was carried into the church by fellow Marines and placed before the casket. Scott McMahon had joined the Marines two months after his big brother Charlie's death. He lost both legs in an auto accident at Camp Pendleton in California.

After the service, Charles McMahon was buried in the soldiers' lot of Woodbrook Cemetery, across from Woburn High School. A Marine detail fired three rounds into the air in salute. Three buglers played taps, the long, sad notes drifting across the cemetery as hundreds of mourners stood silently around the grave. The six Marines holding the flag over McMahon's casket folded the flag and handed it to Marine Capt. Michael Maloney, who presented it to Edna McMahon, Charlie's mother.

Charles McMahon was the last of 1,423 Massachusetts serviceman killed in Vietnam, the thirteenth from Woburn.

Darwin Judge was the last of 856 Iowa boys killed in Vietnam; twelve were from Marshall County.

On the night of April 29, 1975, a Marine casualty officer in dress blues rang the bell at Henry and Ida Judge's home. Ida called her daughter Lori and told her to come over right away. The next day, Lori Judge's boyhood friend Ken Locke was working at Clifton's grocery store where Judge had worked, when he heard the news on the radio. "I went into the back room and sat down on some boxes and cried like I had never cried before," Locke said.

When Darwin Judge's body arrived home, mourners filled the gym of Marshalltown High School, where he had graduated the year before. He was buried in Rose Hill Memorial Gardens cemetery, with a Marine honor guard.

In the final day of his life, Darwin Judge became a hero to Doug Potratz for rescuing his three-year-old daughter. But he had been a lifelong hero to Ken Locke. They had been Cub Scouts together. Locke was much the taller of the two, but it was he who looked up to Judge, who was "much more mature" than his peers and "someone to model yourself after," said Locke.

For years after Judge's death, Locke wanted to do something to properly honor his friend, who had never been given a burial with full military honors, or even awarded a Purple Heart. "I love my country, but I'm not so sure we have done what we should do to say thank you" said Locke. He started rounding up Marines from Judge's unit.

On April 30, 2000, the twenty-fifth anniversary of the Fall of Saigon, hundreds came to the Rose Hill Cemetery to pay their respects at a burial service with full military honors, attended by seventeen Marines who had served in Saigon along with Darwin Judge and Charlie McMahon. The former Marines had traveled to Marshalltown from all over the country—one came from as far away as Saudi Arabia. After the burial, they gathered around the Vietnam War Memorial on the grounds of the Iowa Veterans Home, where Judge finally got his Purple Heart and other military awards. Iowa governor Tom Vilsack and Mayor Floyd Harthun proclaimed it Darwin Judge Day in Marshalltown and in the state of Iowa. Doug Potratz spoke, recalling Judge's rescue of Becky and his wife. Ken Locke told the gathering, "May we never forget that freedom has a price."

At the gravesite, Locke overheard a Marine say, "Why did it have to be the good ones?"

Then, in a small park near the Veterans Home—Darwin L. Judge Memorial Park—two young spruce trees were planted, one representing Judge and the other representing Charlie McMahon.

The memories of Darwin Judge and Charlie McMahon are kept alive by the Fall of Saigon Marines Association, which annually awards the Lance Corporal Darwin L. Judge Scholarship "to Eagle Scouts who are Seniors at Marshalltown High School and are active in their church and have provided community service," and by the Corporal Charles McMahon Jr. Memorial Scholarships, awarded to outstanding members of the Boys and Girls Club of Woburn, Massachusetts.

CHAPTER ONE

THE ROAD TO WAR

President Lyndon Baines Johnson assumed power on November 22, 1963, in the wake of the most shocking national event since the Japanese attack on Pearl Harbor. "Everything was in chaos," Johnson would later recall. "We were all spinning around and around, trying to come to grips with what had happened, but the more we tried to understand it, the more confused we got." Uncertain of his legitimacy in the eyes of the American people, the new president clothed himself in President Kennedy's mantle, vowing to carry forward the work his martyred predecessor had left undone—protecting the civil rights of African Americans, ameliorating the hardships of the poor, and defending South Vietnam from the threat of Communist aggression.

With apparent disregard for the columns of US Marines on the road, South Vietnamese natives walk the center lane. The Marines are on a reconnaissance mission west of the Da Nang Air Base.

The growing conflict there was extremely vexing to Johnson, who was much more comfortable in the realm of domestic politics and saw Vietnam as an unwelcome distraction. As he would later say, "that bitch of a war" came between him and "the woman I loved—the Great Society," but he fully appreciated its political significance, both for himself and the Democratic Party. "I am not going to lose Vietnam," he told Ambassador to Vietnam Henry Cabot Lodge less than forty-eight hours after Kennedy's death. "I am not going to be the president who saw Southeast Asia go the way China went."

Johnson's rhetoric reflected his shrewd appreciation of the national mood in the aftermath of Kennedy's death, but his commitment to Vietnam had deeper and more important roots. There were, to begin with, the lessons of Munich and the geopolitical imperatives of the Cold War, which presented the world as communism versus democracy. Like many of his generation, Lyndon Johnson remembered all too vividly what appeasement of Hitler had purchased in 1940. Behind Hanoi's bellicosity, Johnson saw the aggressive hand of a Communist China intent on dominating the entire Southeast Asian peninsula. Should the United States fail to meet this challenge, Johnson believed, it would not only cost the South Vietnamese their freedom but also have "profound consequences everywhere."

If Vietnam was a trial of US credibility and resolve, it was also a personal challenge. For all his mastery of domestic politics, the new president had little experience in foreign policy, a point made repeatedly by those in the press who doubted his capacity to handle the complex problems of international affairs. His sensitivity on this issue led him to retain Kennedy's top foreign policy advisors—men like Rusk and Secretary of Defense Robert McNamara—who had their own stake in South Vietnam's survival.

Compounding matters was the sense of crisis enveloping Southeast Asia at the end of 1963. In Indonesia, the mercurial President Sukarno had gone from flirtation with Peking to open war against the pro-Western government of Malaysia. In Cambodia, Prince Norodom Sihanouk had renounced American aid and called for an international conference to guarantee his nation's neutrality. The same theme was trumpeted by President Charles de Gaulle of France, who challenged American influence in southern Asia with a proposal for the neutralization of South Vietnam.

Meanwhile, the military junta that took power in Saigon after the coup that deposed Ngo Dinh Diem was not able to either fill the political vacuum left by Diem's death or cope with the upsurge of fighting that wracked the countryside. On December 21, Robert McNamara returned to Washington after a brief inspection tour with a grim report of political turmoil, administrative paralysis, and military reverses at every hand. Unless the situation was stabilized immediately, warned the secretary of defense, the fate of South Vietnam would be "neutralization at best and more likely a Communist-controlled state."

Secretary of Defense Robert McNamara (left) confers with Secretary of State Dean Rusk at the White House, July 1965.

Concerned for his own political standing and the credibility of America around the world, determined to show his critics he could deal with the crisis he had inherited, Johnson responded by vigorously affirming his government's intention of resisting communism in Southeast Asia. He expressed his resolve in terms of America's global responsibilities. "Our strength imposes on us an obligation to assure that this type of aggression does not succeed," Johnson wrote in February 1964. Neutralization was unworkable, withdrawal unthinkable.

For all that, the new president proceeded with restraint during his first year in office. One reason for the measured pace was Johnson's reluctance to employ American military power on a large scale so far from home. No more than Kennedy or Eisenhower did he relish the prospect of US troops engaged in battle on the Asian mainland. Nor was Johnson certain how the Soviets or Chinese would react to the appearance of American combat forces in the region. Moreover, American assumption of responsibility for the war might seriously undercut South Vietnam's will to defend itself.

Even more important were the potential domestic repercussions of greater US involvement in Southeast Asia. Any significant American escalation would endanger the administration's legislative program and jeopardize Johnson's bid for election in November. Johnson was not only unwilling to let this happen, he saw no reason for it. Preoccupied with establishing his leadership and taking advantage of the moment to push major civil rights and antipoverty bills through Congress, the president balanced commitment with caution, putting off difficult decisions for as long as possible—1964 was, after all, an election year, and Johnson did not want to rock his own boat any more than necessary in an election year.

Thus, for all the upheavals of the previous six months, the spring of 1964 witnessed little apparent change in the course of US policy. After a review of the options available to him, Johnson authorized the deployment of additional US military advisors and an enlargement of the economic assistance package to Saigon. The emphasis, however, remained squarely on the South Vietnamese, with new plans for an increase in the size of the ARVN, intensification of the pacification program, and stepped-up military operations against the Viet Cong (VC).* "The only thing I know to do," Johnson told Sen. William Fulbright in March, "is more of the same, and do it more efficiently and effectively."

Yet hidden from public view were important changes that, like the heightened rhetoric of US commitment, contained a momentum of their own. Concerned over reports of increased infiltration of men and supplies flowing south, the administration approved a program of clandestine operations into Laos and North Vietnam. Pressed by McNamara for concrete steps to counter the continuing military decline on the ground, the president authorized contingency planning for retaliatory air strikes north of the demilitarized zone (DMZ). Determined to demonstrate American resolve, Johnson privately warned Hanoi that continued support for the insurgency could bring the "greatest devastation" to North

---

*The term *Viet Cong* was an American creation. Viet Minh was a nationalist organization, albeit Communistic, but using *Viet Cong* (Vietnamese Communist) gave the US intervention in Vietnam more credibility as a fight against global communism.

Vietnam. Taken as a whole, these measures revealed a fundamental shift in perspective, a growing belief in Washington that direct action against North Vietnam could somehow achieve what US policy had failed to accomplish in the South.

For the time being, the counterinsurgency war in the South continued, with the US more deeply involved than ever. Over the next nine months, the number of American military advisors increased from sixteen thousand to twenty-three thousand, among them naval officers working with the fledgling Vietnamese navy, and nearly one hundred US Air Force pilots flying combat-support missions for ARVN offensives as well as training Vietnamese pilots. The US Army was also becoming increasingly engaged in the shooting war. By the end of 1964, American Special Forces Civilian Irregular Defense Group (CIDG) teams had established forty-four camps throughout South Vietnam. Many of them were located along the Laotian border, enabling the Green Berets and their Montagnard allies to monitor traffic along the Ho Chi Minh Trail, but also making them more vulnerable to Communist attack. From 1960 through 1962, thirty-two US military personnel lost their lives in South Vietnam. During 1963 that figure climbed to seventy-seven, and in 1964, deaths from hostile action totaled 137. While the numbers were still low, the trend was disquieting.

But US servicemen were not the only Americans struggling to contain the Communist guerrillas. In the late spring, Frank Scotton, a junior field operator with the United States Information Service, unveiled the first People's Special Forces group—six-man teams of armed Vietnamese civilians trained to fight local insurgent bands on their own terms. By August, the program had been taken over by the Central Intelligence Agency (CIA), which also provided arms and funding for Vietnamese Counter-Terror Teams and sponsored Radio Freedom, a ten-thousand-watt station based in Hue that sent propaganda broadcasts to North Vietnam.

Alongside these "public" activities was an expanding program of US-directed covert operations. Some were run by the US Military Assistance Command, Vietnam (MACV), such as Project Leaping Lena, which sent eight-man squads of Vietnamese commandos on long-range reconnaissance patrols into Laos, or Project Delta, in which ten-man "Hunter-Killer Teams" made up of American and Vietnamese Special Forces soldiers penetrated enemy-controlled territory within South Vietnam. The most dramatic covert activities, however, were carried out by the innocuously named Studies and Observation Group (SOG), a highly classified unit controlled directly by the Pentagon. SOG teams entered Cambodia, Laos, and even North Vietnam to gather intelligence on enemy activities, snatch prisoners for interrogation, and interdict infiltration. SOG also sent Vietnamese PT boats against North Vietnamese coastal installations in a series of raids code-named Operation 34-Alpha.

Unfortunately, the dispatch of additional advisors, the expansion of covert operations, and an increase of $125 million in aid were not able to arrest the steady decline of Saigon's military and political fortunes. The junta that had deposed Diem was itself overthrown two months later by a group of younger officers under the leadership of Gen. Nguyen Khanh. Although Washington lent Khanh vocal public support, the new government was no more successful than its predecessor in extending its authority into the countryside. A US report issued on April 1 estimated that the Viet Cong controlled between 40 and 60 percent of the rural population. Even in areas that Saigon could claim as its own, a lack of trained officials, bureaucratic lethargy, insufficient resources, pervasive corruption, and the sometimes

Staff Sergeant Howard Stevens, Special Forces advisor to a Montagnard strike force, reads his mail at Phey-Shuron, a camp built in the central Vietnam highlands. Stevens was part of a twelve-man team making soldiers of Koho tribesmen in the jungle mountains west of Da Lat.

brutal behavior of government soldiers undermined the new pacification program and prevented the implementation of ambitious development plans drafted by the Americans.

Although Khanh proved inept at rallying public support, his main problem was the steadily worsening military situation. In December 1963, as Viet Cong units roamed at will over large sections of the South Vietnamese countryside, the central committee of the Vietnamese Communist Party met in Hanoi to approve a new strategy for the southern insurgency. Hoping to discourage the US and bring down the Saigon government, North Vietnam funneled increasing amounts of war materiel to its southern allies, who began to take to the field armed with mortars, machine guns, and recoilless rifles.

Unable to solve the problems that surrounded him, Khanh called upon his countrymen to "March North," a cry echoed immediately by Gen. Nguyen Cao Ky. The flamboyant young commander of the Vietnamese air force publicly announced that his pilots had already been training for just such a mission. "We are ready," Ky told the press, resplendent in a black flight suit and lavender scarf. "We could go this afternoon. I cannot assure that all of North Vietnam would be destroyed, but Hanoi would certainly be destroyed." Although Maxwell Taylor, the new American ambassador to Vietnam, privately reprimanded both South Vietnamese leaders for their provocative remarks, many Washington officials had by this time come to much the same point of view.

Head of the new military junta government in South Vietnam, Air Vice Marshal Nguyen Cao Ky (left) confers with his newly appointed defense secretary, Brig. Gen. Nguyen Hiu Co, after the "directorate" was formed.

Indeed, pressure for direct US military action against the North was coming at Johnson from all directions. As early as January, the Joint Chiefs of Staff (JCS) recommended the commitment of US combat forces to South Vietnam, an invasion of Laos to hinder infiltration, and the bombing of key targets in North Vietnam. Although Secretary of Defense McNamara rejected escalation for the time being, he persuaded the president to authorize planning for a bombing campaign against the North. By June, as the situation in Vietnam worsened, both outgoing Ambassador Lodge and the newly appointed commander of MACV, Gen. William C. Westmoreland, were calling for vigorous American military action to bolster South Vietnamese morale. Chief among their proposals were air strikes against Laos or North Vietnam.

Frustration over Saigon's inability to put its own house in order, the existence of a major unused air capability, and President Johnson's reluctance to risk American ground combat units had fashioned a growing consensus within the administration for the application of air power against North Vietnam. By midsummer, planning for a program of "graduated overt pressure" against the North was well advanced, along with drafts of a congressional resolution supporting US policy in Southeast Asia and providing authorization to the president for whatever military action he might deem necessary. In Johnson's mind, such a resolution was simply "part of the normal contingency planning effort. I continued to hope that we could keep our role in Vietnam limited." Events in the Gulf of Tonkin in August, however, suggested that within the administration the momentum toward full military involvement was almost irresistible.

Among the covert operations approved by the president during the spring were electronic surveillance missions, code-named DeSoto and conducted by US destroyers off the coast of North Vietnam. These patrols had gone on for several months without incident when, on the night of August 2, the USS *Maddox* was attacked by three North Vietnamese PT boats near the island of Hon Me in the Gulf of Tonkin. After a twenty-minute engagement, the *Maddox* drove off the attackers with the help of four jet fighters from the aircraft carrier USS *Ticonderoga*. Assuming that the North Vietnamese had confused the *Maddox* with an unrelated 34-Alpha raid against Hon Me two days earlier, Johnson declined to retaliate. Lest his restraint be misinterpreted by Hanoi, however, the president ordered the patrols to continue with the addition of a second destroyer, the USS *Turner Joy*, the provision of air cover, and explicit authorization to respond with force to any attack in international waters.

Two nights later, on August 4, as the two ships plowed through heavy seas sixty miles from the North Vietnamese mainland, the *Maddox* radioed that the destroyers were under attack by North Vietnamese gunboats. In fact, on an "inky black night" that one seaman described as "darker than the hubs of Hell," no one aboard either ship actually saw the enemy craft, firing their guns instead at sonar and radar contacts of questionable reliability. After a brief engagement, the destroyers reported they had repulsed the North Vietnamese without sustaining any casualties or damage. But several hours later, the commander of the *Maddox* reassessed the situation, indicating that "freak weather effects" as well as an "overeager" sonarman may have accounted for the apparent torpedo attacks and enemy contacts.

Navy jets are scrambled from the deck of the USS *Ticonderoga*, August 2, 1964.

Emphasizing that there had been "no actual visual sightings," he concluded that the entire action "left many doubts" and suggested a complete evaluation before any further action was taken.

By the time these second thoughts reached Washington, however, Johnson had already decided on a swift retaliatory strike. Discounting the uncertainty of the men on the scene in favor of North Vietnamese radio intercepts that appeared to confirm an engagement, and relying on assurances by Adm. U. S. Grant Sharp, commander-in-chief, Pacific Fleet (CINCPAC), that "the ambush was bona fide," Secretary of Defense McNamara recommended that the air raids proceed. At 11:37 p.m. on the evening of August 4, some thirteen hours after the first reports reached Washington, Johnson went on television to inform the American people that US jets were already in the air. The carrier-launched attacks, code-named Pierce Arrow, struck patrol boat bases and oil storage depots at Quang Khe, Vinh, Phuoc Loi, Hon Gai, and the Lach Chao Estuary, sinking twenty-five PT boats and destroying an estimated 10 percent of North Vietnam's total petroleum storage capacity.

The following day, the president submitted to Congress a resolution authorizing him to take "all necessary measures to repel any armed attacks against the forces of the United States and to prevent further aggression." Asserting that the peace and security of the region were "vital" to the national interest, the measure further committed the US, "as the president determines, to take all necessary steps, including the use of armed force, to assist any member or protocol state of the Southeast Asia Collective Defense Treaty requesting assistance in defense of its freedom." On August 7, after less than ten hours of debate, Congress delivered the mandate the president wanted. Although Alaska senator Ernest Gruening attacked the resolution as a "predated declaration of war," and Sen. Wayne Morse of Oregon warned his colleagues they were circumventing the Constitution, the Senate overrode their objections by a vote of 88–2. The margin in the House was 466–0.

An oil painting depicting the Gulf of Tonkin incident. In foreground is the USS *Maddox*.

The strain of battle is shown on the face of US Army Sgt. Philip Fink, an advisor to the 52nd Vietnamese Ranger battalion. The unit had borne the brunt of recapturing the jungle outpost of Dong Xoai from the Viet Cong, June 1965.

The events in the Tonkin Gulf proved to be a watershed of vast proportions. By seizing the opportunity afforded him, Johnson won a resounding congressional endorsement for his policies. His firm but restrained handling of the crisis earned him broad popular support, neutralized the hawkish Republican presidential nominee, Sen. Barry Goldwater, and paved the way for Johnson's overwhelming electoral victory in November. Yet, in time, both he and the nation would pay a heavy price for his victory.

The Southeast Asia Resolution raised the level of US commitment, linked American prestige more firmly than ever with the fate of South Vietnam, and virtually compelled Washington to respond to future North Vietnamese provocations. The air attacks themselves had shattered the barrier against taking the war to the North, making further escalation of the conflict that much easier. And if the administration had punished the North Vietnamese, America had also paid a price. Anti-aircraft fire during the raids brought down two US aircraft and damaged two more. One of the pilots ditched his plane in the ocean and perished. The other, Lt. Everett Alvarez of San Jose, California, became the first American pilot taken prisoner by the North

Vietnamese (see sidebar, page 244). Although Alvarez would languish in a Hanoi prison for the next eight years, he was not alone. The United States, too, had become a hostage of the war.

During the fall of 1964, however, political considerations of various sorts enforced restraint. With the presidential election fast approaching, Johnson emphasized his desire to limit American involvement. "We seek no wider war," he declared repeatedly, assuring campaign audiences that American boys would not be sent to do the fighting that Asian boys should be doing for themselves.

Nonetheless, the pressure on Johnson to expand the war mounted steadily. In mid-September, with both the US Air Force and Marine Corps urging extended air attacks against the North, Ambassador Taylor reported to the president that sharp increases in hardcore Viet Cong strength had reduced the area of government control in the South to no more than 30 percent of the country.

More than anything else, however, what propelled the United States toward war in the spring of 1965 was the continued disintegration of the Saigon government and the threatened defeat of the South Vietnamese army at the hands of the Viet Cong. Combined with reports that North Vietnamese regular units had entered the country, the political instability that had once been the principal obstacle to escalation now became the most persuasive argument for it. Without the psychological shot in the arm that a strike against the North would provide, argued Johnson's advisors, no anti-Communist South Vietnamese government could survive.

On February 6, Viet Cong units launched mortar attacks on a US base at Pleiku, killing several US personnel, handing the administration the opportunity it sought. "We have kept our guns over the mantel and our shells in the cupboard for a long time now," exclaimed an angry President Johnson. "I can't ask American soldiers out there to continue to fight with one hand behind their backs." One day after the Pleiku attacks, US planes struck North Vietnamese targets in Operation Flaming Dart. When the Communists struck the quarters of American enlisted men in Qui Nhon on February 10, Johnson ordered an even heavier series of bombing raids. "They woke us up in the middle of the night, and we woke them up in the middle of the night," said a grim-faced president. "They did it again and we did it again." But the time for "tit-for-tat" reprisals had ended. On February 13, convinced that Hanoi was "moving in for the kill," Johnson approved a program of graduated, sustained air attacks against North Vietnam, code-named Rolling Thunder. Johnson and McNamara had placed limits on the bombing: no strikes within thirty-six miles of Hanoi or within twelve miles of the port of Haiphong, and no airfields would be targeted. The restrictions infuriated some military commanders who felt that Haiphong and the North Vietnamese airfields should have been the first targets to be bombed. Targets were selected by the Joint Chiefs in Washington, not by commanders in the field.

After a series of delays, the operation finally got underway on March 2 when US Air Force fighter-bombers struck an ammunition depot at Xom Bang thirty-five miles north of the DMZ. But the North Vietnamese had been planning for air assaults, and its anti-aircraft batteries downed six American planes during the raid. Five of the pilots were rescued, but one was lost. The second Rolling Thunder mission did not take place for nearly two weeks, in keeping with Johnson's desire for a "limited air action." The thinking of the administration was that the strikes would show the Hanoi regime what US air power could do to more significant targets if the North didn't back off, but the meager results of these first strikes, plus pressure from the Joint Chiefs for more substantial blows and ominous reports of a worsening military situation within South Vietnam, induced the president to authorize an expanded effort against North Vietnamese lines of communication as far north as the twentieth parallel. During April, American and South Vietnamese pilots flew a total of 3,600 sorties in what had become a sustained bombing campaign. Now the targets had military significance—rail lines, bridges, river ferries, ammo depots, radar installations, and even military barracks. In May, the number of sorties climbed to four thousand and US planes began flying "armed reconnaissance" missions to attack targets of opportunity, with decision-making power residing in the cockpit.

As the intensity of the bombing was ramped up, the North Vietnamese air defenses were beefed up, from around 1,500 anti-aircraft guns at the beginning of Rolling Thunder to five thousand guns, including surface-to-air missiles (SAMs) and radar-guided weapons a year later. By the end of 1965, 170 US aircraft had been lost, including eleven to SAMs. In 1966, the North Vietnamese launched more than 1,900 SAMs, which downed thirty-one more US planes, and a North Vietnamese MiG fighter scored its first kill, shooting down an Air Force F-4 Phantom from the 433rd Tactical Fighter Squadron.

Just as Rolling Thunder was getting underway in the North, a historic threshold was crossed in the South. Fearing Viet Cong retaliation for the air strikes, Westmoreland requested two Marine infantry battalions to defend the vital US air base at Da Nang. Although a staunch advocate of bombing, Maxwell Taylor expressed grave reservations about the dispatch of ground forces, questioning the suitability of American combat troops for an Asian guerrilla war and the difficulty of "holding the line" once the first step had been taken. Despite Taylor's warnings, Washington went ahead. Preoccupied with the first stages of the air campaign against the North, the administration treated Westmoreland's request as a minor detail, a "one-shot affair to meet a specific situation." Westmoreland and his Vietnamese counterpart, Gen. Nguyen Van Thieu, who had by then become the most prominent of South Vietnam's military leaders, agreed that the Marine landing be as inconspicuous as possible. However, when the 3,500 troops of the 3rd Battalion, 9th Marine Expeditionary Brigade splashed ashore near Da Nang City on the morning of March 8, 1965, they were greeted by Vietnamese girls who draped leis around their necks, a gaggle of sightseers, and four American soldiers holding a sign that read, "Welcome, Gallant Marines." Westmoreland was furious.

The beach landing was the prime photo op of the day, but as the 3rd Battalion was wading ashore, the 1st Battalion arrived dry-shod, disembarking from US Air Force C-130 transport planes from Okinawa. But whether by sea or air, when the Marines' boots hit the sands of Red Beach and the tarmac of Da Nang Air Base, it signaled a key turning point for the US role in South Vietnam. American combat troops were now on the ground.

Opposite page: A young Marine private waits on the beach during the Marine landing at Da Nang.

Marines storm ashore at Da Nang. They are among the first combat troops on the ground in the Vietnam War.

Viet Cong prisoners are led to a helicopter landing zone for evacuation to the regimental collection point.

Arguments over the wisdom of sending US troops to South Vietnam had been, if not raging, burning steadily since the French collapse at Dien Bien Phu in 1954. Then, Gen. Matthew Ridgway, who knew a thing or three about fighting a land war in Asia, campaigned strenuously against President Eisenhower's desire to come to the aid of the French in Indochina. Ridgway, who in World War II had become one of the most distinguished officers in American history, had also commanded the 8th Army in Korea, retaking Seoul from the Communist forces. He then succeeded Gen. Douglas MacArthur as supreme U.N. commander in Korea after President Truman had sacked MacArthur, and pushed the Chinese and North Korean forces back to a line just north of the thirty-eighth parallel, where the war was stalemated until the signing of the armistice in July 1953. After leaving Korea in 1952, Ridgway succeeded General Eisenhower as supreme allied commander in Europe, and in 1953, now-President Eisenhower appointed Ridgway US Army chief of staff. When Eisenhower contemplated American intervention in Indochina, Ridgway convinced the president that victory there would require huge numbers of US troops, and Eisenhower dropped the idea.

General Maxwell Taylor, who had served under Ridgway in World War II and succeeded him in Korea, served as President Kennedy's primary military advisor and was appointed chairman of the Joint Chiefs of Staff by Kennedy in 1962 before serving as ambassador to South Vietnam under President Johnson. In 1961, Taylor recommended to Kennedy that US ground troops be sent to Vietnam—despite his own warning, in a cable revealed in the Pentagon Papers, that "we can ill afford any detachment of forces to a peripheral area of the Communist bloc where they will be pinned down for an uncertain duration," and if "the first contingent is not enough to accomplish the necessary results, it will be difficult to resist the pressure to reinforce."

Taylor was right on both counts, but spectacularly wrong on another. He opined that, for American troops, "South Vietnam is not an excessively difficult or unpleasant place to operate." That, plus his assessment that the troops would boost South Vietnam's morale and raise the prestige of the US internationally—both wildly optimistic forecasts—led Taylor to recommend sending eight thousand American troops to South Vietnam "at once." He later told historian Arthur Schlesinger, who had been a special advisor to President Kennedy, "I don't recall anyone who was strongly against, except one man, and that was the president," who held the conviction that "US ground troops should not go in." But over the next two years, Kennedy dispatched sixteen thousand military personnel to South Vietnam, "advisors" who were known to cross the line between advising and active combat support.

Once ashore, the 3/9 Marines took up positions on the edge of the sprawling Da Nang Air Base, which was becoming an increasingly vital asset. Located just eighty-five miles south of the DMZ, the base housed the Vietnam air force's 41st Wing, which had launched its first strikes against North Vietnam on February 8 using A-1 Skyraiders provided by the US. The base would soon become a joint operating airfield when US combat and logistical aircraft made it their home as well. By the height of the war in 1968, Da Nang Air Base was one of the busiest airports in the world, handling fifty-five thousand takeoffs and landings a month—sixty-seven thousand including helicopter operations. Its warplanes flew north-of-the-border bombing missions and provided tactical air support for ground combat operations, and the base served as a diversionary airfield for emergency landings by Thailand-based American bombers—a fairly common occurrence.

While the first wave of Marines played a defensive role at the Da Nang Air Base, the second wave, 1,500 troops of the 2nd Battalion, 3rd Marine Regiment was sent out to establish firebases on hilltops in the countryside. These Marines became the first official US offensive troops of the war; their mission was to patrol a wide area outside of the base to secure roads and prevent Viet Cong mortar attacks on the airfield. First Lieutenant Del Williams, H (Hotel) Company, 2nd Platoon, landed at Da Nang on April 10 and was sent to Hill 312 overlooking the village of Le My, on the Cu De Song River.

A Marine from 1st Battalion, 3rd Marines, moves a Viet Cong suspect to the rear during a search-and-clear operation held by the battalion fifteen miles west of Da Nang Air Base.

Marine Lt. Del Williams's first look at a tropical jungle was not in Vietnam, but in the Philippines. It was standard procedure for the Marines to expose their troops to a variety of environments in which they might one day have to fight, so new Marines did the West Pacific–West-Pac–tour, starting on Okinawa. Then they underwent cold weather training on the frozen slopes of Japan's Mount Fuji, jungle training under the high canopies of the steaming Philippines rain forest, and nighttime submarine-to-shore amphibious assault exercises in Thailand, using small rubber rafts.

"After that exercise, we were given four days of shore leave in Thailand," said Williams, from his home in Kentucky, where he retired after a career as a lineman, part of that with the Tennessee Valley Authority. "Then we boarded ships and headed back to Okinawa." At least, that was the plan. Williams was assigned to lead 2nd Platoon, Hotel Company, 2nd Battalion, 3rd Marine Regiment, and decisions had been made in Washington, D.C., that would reroute his ship to the South China Sea, sending Williams and his battalion into the history books.

Clarence "Del" Williams was born and raised in Georgia cotton country, in the town of Manchester. His dad, a farmer, insisted that all of his kids graduate high school. After earning his diploma, Williams joined the Marines, and he spent his first six years as an enlisted man, rising to the rank of sergeant. He was picked for Officer Candidate School at Quantico, Virginia, and instead of stripes on his sleeve, he began wearing the gold bar of a second lieutenant. He had made first lieutenant by the time his troop carrier, the USS *Linnoway*, and her sister ships, the *Washburn* and the *Guston Hall,* set course for Vietnam.

"We were ordered to proceed to fifty miles off the coast," said Williams, "and stand by."

Then, on the morning of April 10, a warm, sunny day, the ships steamed closer to shore. "We thought, 'Oh, shit, here we go!'"

US Marine Corps 1st Lt. Clarence "Del" Williams with his squad on Hill 312 near Da Nang, April 1965. Left to right: Sgt. Howard W. Brinning; Staff Sgt. James P. Summers; Williams; Lance Cpl. Ivan R. Lott; Navy Corpsman HN Charles Hayes.

said Williams. "We didn't know what to expect when we landed." They had learned in training that the enemy "worked in the dark, knew the countryside, and wore no uniforms, making it impossible to tell a Viet Cong from a rice farmer."

The Marines loaded their M14 rifles but left the firing chambers empty. They scrambled down the nets and took their positions in the landing craft, which headed for the beach. A hundred yards from dry land, the boats stopped and lowered their ramps, and Williams and his Marines plunged into the crotch-deep water and waded ashore. While Battalions 1/9 and 3/9 were holding defensive positions inside the wire at the air base, 2/9 had a different mission: they would be the first American combat troops to conduct offensive operations in Vietnam.

That same day, April 10, the first of fifteen F-4B fighter planes of Marine Fighter Attack Squadron 531 landed at Da Nang, becoming the first land-based Marine Corps jet fighters of the war.

As the hot sun began drying their fatigue uniforms, Williams's company formed up on the beach and began an eight-mile march west to Hill 312 (hills were designated by their elevations, in meters) overlooking the village of Le My, on the Cu De Song ("song" means "river" in Vietnamese). It wasn't long before they wished they were back in the cool waters off Red Beach; the men were now drenched with sweat. They reached the hill in midafternoon with enough daylight left to begin digging foxholes, hacking down and burning the scrub brush to clear fields of fire, and setting up a defensive perimeter. Lieutenant Williams assigned his automatic weapons, machine guns, and listening posts.

Hill 312 offered a panoramic view of the river valley, and Hotel Company did nothing but enjoy that view for a week or so—when they weren't filling sandbags, building bunkers, and improving their living conditions, which were spartan at best. They had taken no hostile fire. "We were told that there were no known enemy forces in the area," said Williams. "The worst thing about our situation was that we weren't able to take showers for a month. Things got pretty ugly."

The job of the 2/9, which occupied three hilltops around Da Nang Air Base, was to prevent mortar attacks on the base. With Operation Rolling Thunder underway, protecting the planes based at Da Nang became extremely important. But sitting in foxholes on hilltops wasn't going to prevent mortar attacks, so on April 17, the troops of the 2/9 began patrolling. There were three bridges over the Cu De Song, one made of iron, and upriver, two others of wood. The Marines set up positions at all three. Daily patrols kept the roads clear, at least in daytime. The patrols were a provocation to the VC, who began harassing the Marines with sniper fire. Some nights, two or three VC would probe the hilltops' defenses, drawing fire and melting away in the dark. On May 10, after a patrol was ambushed, killing a scout, elements of Hotel Company and two other companies mounted

a search-and-clear operation against the village of Le My, which was known to be held by the Viet Cong. That's where the Marines met their first serious opposition.

"That was the first time things got nasty enough to be called combat," Williams recalled. "We took a lot of casualties, many of them from booby traps and antipersonnel mines." It was the first significant US combat operation in Vietnam.

Williams showers on a bridge over the Cu De Song. Williams built the shower himself.

For General Westmoreland and the Joint Chiefs, the deployment of the Marines was only the first stage in a troop buildup of much vaster proportions. Having come to the conclusion by mid-March that the only way for the United States to avert disaster in South Vietnam was "to put our own finger in the dike," the MACV commander recommended the commitment of two US Army divisions. Westmoreland also proposed that American troops not be limited to defensive coastal enclaves, as Taylor wanted, but engage in offensive operations against enemy units in the Central Highlands.

Although frustrated by the limited results of the bombing campaign and angry over a VC attack on the US Embassy in Saigon on March 29, Johnson was still reluctant to become too deeply embroiled in the ground war. He was concerned, however, that a lack of decisive action might precipitate the long-feared South Vietnamese collapse. Johnson forged a compromise between Taylor and the Joint Chiefs that was formalized in a national security action memorandum dated April 6. The new policy called for a continuation of the bombing campaign against the North, the deployment of two additional

At Hill 312, pictured with C-rations, are members of 2nd Platoon, Hotel Company, 2nd Battalion, 3rd Marines, Pfc. Edward J. Walker (left) and Pfc. Charles W. Ward.

CHAPTER ONE

One day after the "grunts" hit Red Beach, a Marine tank rolled ashore followed by dozens of artillery pieces—105mm and 155mm howitzers—and with the big guns came twenty-year-old Pfc. Robert L. Barker.

Bob Barker grew up in South Carolina. He joined the Marines the day after his eighteenth birthday and was trained as an artilleryman. He made private first class right out of basic infantry training, a grade that he was locked into for many months. "I tried everything to get rank," Barker said, "but nothing worked until I got to Vietnam, where promotions came fast."

In late 1964, Barker got orders to ship out for Okinawa on the USS *Vancouver*, an "amphibious transport dock," built to carry a thousand troops and their equipment and having the means to put them ashore. After steaming from port to port in the Pacific for weeks, the *Vancouver* took up station off Da Nang on February 8. A month later, after two false starts, the *Vancouver* dropped anchor in Da Nang harbor and the first US combat troops went ashore on Red Beach, in rough seas that delayed the landing by several hours.

"We didn't know what to expect," said Barker. "All we knew was that Vietnam was a dangerous place." Reputation meant nothing on that day, however, as the Marines were welcomed by Vietnamese girls, a flock of journalists, and various onlookers.

It was a short drive to the Da Nang Air Base, where Barker and his crewmates set up their guns inside the perimeter, at the most remote end of the runway. "We were never fired on," Barker said, "and about the only fire missions we did were H and I [Harassment and Interdiction]. We had several FO [Forward Observer] teams in small aircraft and helicopters, and we'd fire where they told us to."

A month after Barker arrived in Vietnam, the 2/3 Marines were put ashore at Da Nang to take up positions on hilltops outside of the air base, and soon began patrols through the villages and hamlets in the area. A couple of months after that, as ground combat heated up, Bob Barker's guns left their fixed positions inside the wire and became air-mobile. Helicopters ferried the guns two-by-two to makeshift hilltop firebases where they fired combat support missions.

"We had a reinforced battery," Barker said, "consisting of six 105s, two 155s, and two mortars. Ammo was resupplied by truck

Private First Class Bob Barker in Vietnam.

if possible, or by helicopter during monsoon season when the roads were too muddy to drive. Or sometimes the ammo was parachuted to us."

The war was heating up, and the artillery batteries were often attacked by the enemy. "Some of our neighboring batteries were overrun by the VC," said Barker, "and I had a great fear of that, but it never happened to my battery."

At the end of his twelve-month tour, Barker signed up for another six months. In his eighteen months in Vietnam, all within fifty miles of Da Nang, he reckons he pulled the lanyard on eighty-five thousand to ninety thousand rounds. His only injury? "I'm virtually deaf," he said. "The noise of those guns was unbelievable, and the Marines gave us nothing to protect our ears."

Back in the US, he served out his hitch at Fort Bragg, North Carolina, leaving the Marines as a sergeant. He then joined Bell South in Atlanta as a lineman, retiring at the end of 2012 with "nothing but positive memories" of his service in Vietnam.

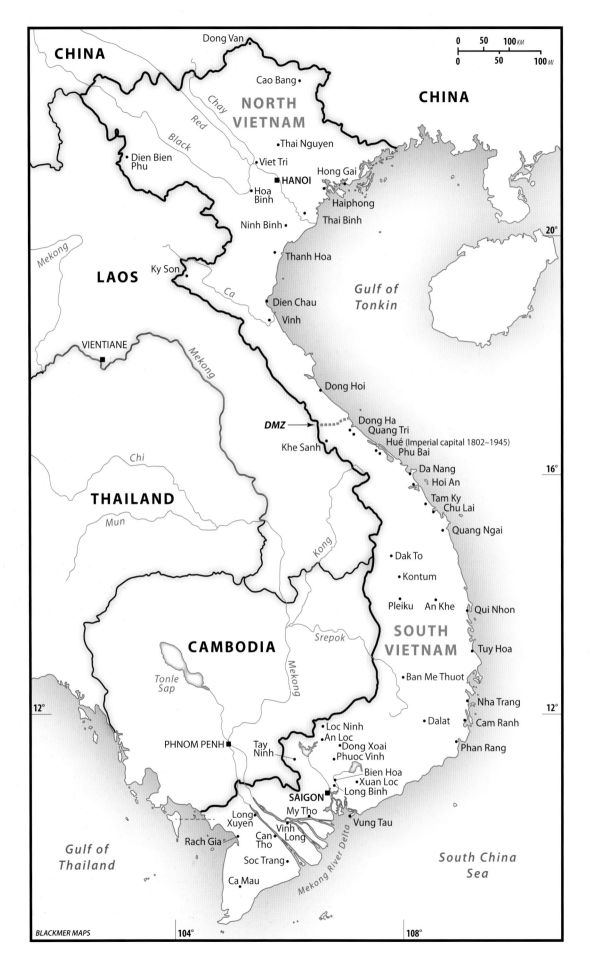

US Marines ride through sand dunes on amphibious vehicles in I Corps, 1966.

Opposite page: Vietnam as it was when the American Marines came ashore in 1965. The six-mile-wide Demilitarized Zone (DMZ) was created after the French defeat at Dien Bien Phu in 1954.

Marine combat battalions to South Vietnam, and an increase of some twenty thousand men in US military support forces. Although the new troops would continue to be confined to enclaves around major US bases, the president also approved a "change of mission" for all Marine battalions deployed to Vietnam, permitting offensive operations within fifty miles of their base areas. Three weeks later, under continued prodding from Westmoreland and the Joint Chiefs, Johnson approved the deployment of nine more battalions, bringing total US troop strength in Vietnam to eighty-two thousand men.

The full implications of these decisions, which marked a major step toward large-scale involvement in the ground war, were carefully concealed from the public. During the deliberations that produced the new policy directives, Johnson told reporters, "I know of no far-reaching strategy that is being suggested or promulgated." When the Marines' new mission of conducting combat operations was accidentally mentioned in a government press release two months later, the administration issued a heated denial, opening a "credibility gap" that would torment Johnson for the remainder of his presidency. The obvious expansion of the war, however, was enough to provoke vocal protest, including a march on Washington that attracted twelve thousand college students. Johnson attempted to disarm his critics by sending spokesmen to university campuses and authorizing a five-day bombing pause in early May. The temporary halt produced no response from Hanoi but did help the administration push through Congress a $700 million appropriation to support military operations in Vietnam.

To the president's dismay, however, neither the new deployments nor the additional funding were enough to reverse the deteriorating military situation. At the end of May, the Viet Cong launched their spring-summer offensive with regiment-size attacks in Quang Ngai Province that within a week had killed more than one thousand of the government's best troops. In mid-June, the offensive moved into War Zone C northwest of Saigon, where tactical ineptitude and a lack of leadership contributed to the savage mauling of still more South Vietnamese units. By the end of the month, MACV estimated that five ARVN regiments and nine separate battalions had been rendered "combat ineffective" as a result of the fighting. The new American commitment also seemed to have little effect on stabilizing the chaotic South Vietnamese political scene from which General Khanh had been ousted in February in favor of a civilian government, itself to be overthrown on June 12 by a group of young officers under the leadership of Generals Ky and Thieu.

A Vietnamese woman weeps over the body of her husband, killed in fighting between the ARVN and VC, 1965.

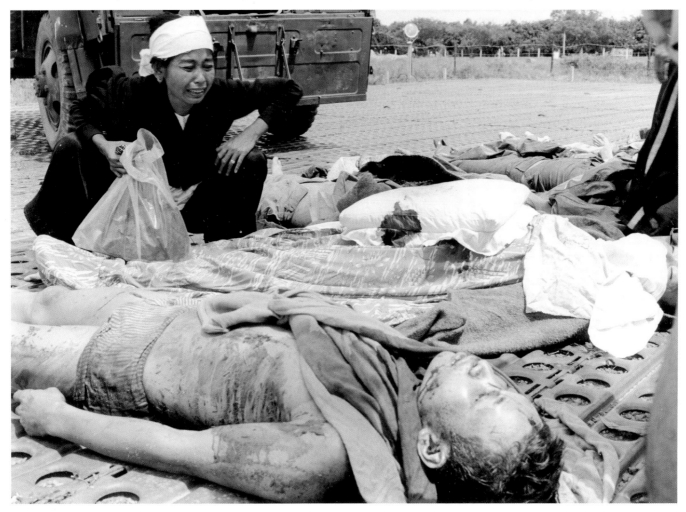

The unexpected ferocity of the Viet Cong offensive and the staggering casualties sustained by the South Vietnamese led Westmoreland and the Joint Chiefs to propose an intensification of the air war against North Vietnam, a drastic expansion of American ground forces in the South, and the adoption of a new offensive strategy. MACV's request in early June for an additional 150,000 men precipitated a month of intense discussion in Washington, constituting the last major review of US policy on Vietnam until the spring of 1967.

The military was convinced that the size and posture of US forces in Vietnam were not getting the job done. "You must take the war to the enemy," argued Gen. Earle Wheeler, JCS chairman. "No one ever won a battle sitting on his ass."

Their entreaties were seconded by Ambassador Taylor, whose reluctance to use American ground forces in general combat had been overcome by the strength of the VC offensive and by national security assistant Walt Rostow, who urged a full-scale air assault on North Vietnam's industrial infrastructure. Among Johnson's advisors, only Undersecretary of State George Ball, already skeptical about the impact of air power, opposed this new commitment of US ground forces, expressing grave doubts about Washington's ability to force Hanoi to the bargaining table and profound concerns over the eventual costs of escalation.

Secretary of Defense McNamara also warned the president that the war would be protracted and costly, testing the endurance of Americans as much as Vietnamese. Nonetheless, after a visit to Saigon in early July, McNamara recommended the deployment of an additional one hundred thousand men.

By the end of the month, Johnson had reached a decision. The enclave strategy was scrapped in favor of aggressive operations aimed at the gradual attrition of the enemy. The president approved Westmoreland's request for the use of B-52s in South Vietnam, agreed to a gradual intensification of the bombing in the North, and publicly announced the immediate deployment of fifty thousand men, with more to be sent later. Finally, he would seek from Congress an additional $ 1.7 billion military appropriation to fund the increases.

With these July decisions, Johnson had fully committed the US to the defense of South Vietnam. Yet the president had not authorized a mobilization of the reserves as sought by the Joint Chiefs. He had not declared a state of national emergency or asked Congress for an increase in taxes as McNamara urged; he was taking the "guns and butter" approach, though to send what would become a half-million-man army to war at the same time the US was in a Cold War arms race would put severe strains on the economy. Nor had Johnson informed the nation that he had privately authorized the incremental dispatch of an additional one hundred thousand men, raising US troop strength in Vietnam to more than 225,000. And he had not made his decisions known to the American people in a formal address, choosing instead the subdued forum of an afternoon press conference. Unwilling to face the consequences of withdrawal, yet fearful that the war would destroy the domestic reforms of his "Great Society," the president determined to do "what will be enough, but not too much." The US would fight in Vietnam, but it would do so with a minimum of domestic disruption. Or so he thought. On July 28, 1965, President Lyndon Johnson told the American people that their sons and daughters were going to war in Vietnam. "We did not choose to be the guardians at the gate, but there is no one else," declared the president. "We will stand in Vietnam."

Thus did Lyndon Johnson lead the American people into what would become the nation's longest war.

Focus: ARVN

After the departure of French troops in April 1956, the United States Military Assistance Advisory Group (MAAG) assumed full responsibility for rebuilding the South Vietnamese army. Over the next four years, as the US provided equipment, streamlined command arrangements, and conducted training programs, MAAG slowly increased its advisory corps from 350 to nearly 700. The outbreak of armed insurgency and the arrival of a new administration in Washington, however, rapidly transformed this relatively low-key effort into a sizable commitment. Alarmed by the deteriorating prospects of the Diem government, President Kennedy sharply increased all forms of military assistance to Saigon. At the end of 1961, MAAG strength stood at 2,067. Twelve months later, there were more than 11,000 US military personnel in Vietnam. Among them were several thousand American soldiers acting as advisors to every level of the South Vietnamese army. Working with their Vietnamese counterparts, the advisors reviewed intelligence reports, helped plan operations, set up communications, and arranged for supplies.

ARVN soldiers disembark from a helicopter in the Mekong River Delta in August 1962 as an American crewman looks on.

On a mission in the delta, ARVN soldiers move past a hut they set afire after discovering Viet Cong propaganda inside.

Getting used to Vietnam was tough enough—the strange language, the alien culture, the ripe smell of *nuoc nam* fish sauce (which the Vietnamese seemed to pour on everything they ate), the mind-numbing heat. But the job itself was even more demanding, especially at the lower levels where advisors accompanied the ARVN into the field to coordinate artillery and air support and assure medical assistance. Although they had no command authority, the Americans were sometimes forced to take upon themselves the burden of leadership when faltering soldiers threatened to panic.

To the Vietnamese they made a striking picture, these tall, confident Americans. Striding through the bush in their sweat-soaked uniforms and faded green baseball caps, carrying World War II carbines in their hands and .45-caliber pistols strapped to their sides, the advisors were the combat pioneers of the American enterprise in Vietnam, the handful of men who blazed the path that thousands would soon follow.

Many of the new advisors who arrived in-country as part of the buildup of the American assistance program in 1962 were assigned to the 7th ARVN Division, whose troops patrolled the watery world of the Mekong Delta. A vast, shimmering plain stretching south from Saigon to the Ca Mau Peninsula, the delta was twenty-six thousand square miles of rich, alluvial rice lands crisscrossed by irrigation canals and the tributaries of the Mekong River. The region had been under the influence of the Viet Minh since before World War II. Their Viet Cong successors operated out of the hundreds of villages that clustered along the canal banks and from bases concealed in the impenetrable swamps and thick forests that dotted the coast. Hunting them down, discovered one advisor, was "like trying to identify

tears in a bucket of water." After three years of mounting violence, the contest in the delta between the Communists and the ARVN was not being won by the government troops.

Like their adversaries, the vast majority of ARVN soldiers grew up in rural villages, the sons of peasant farmers. Likewise, they had little if any formal education, and like the guerrillas, they would serve for the duration or until they were no longer able to fight. Unlike the Viet Cong, however, they were usually assigned to a unit far from home. Although some wives followed their husbands and settled near ARVN camps, most enlisted men saw their families no more than once a year. Also unlike the Communists, their lack of education meant they had little chance of escaping the lowest rungs of army life, surviving as well as they could on a salary of $11 a month.

Extended absences without leave and outright desertion were common. But for the most part, they accepted their circumstances philosophically. Generally neglected by their officers, given little idea of what they were fighting for, the ordinary ARVN soldiers displayed a courage and endurance that won the respect of the Americans. When asked what had been his most lasting impression of Vietnam, one US advisor replied: "I think it would be the almost limitless ability of the Vietnamese soldier to bear suffering and pain without complaint. I've never heard a wounded Vietnamese cry, never heard a tired one complain." For their part, ARVN troops admired the bravery and skill of the advisors, prizing individual Americans as an endless source of food, cigarettes, and other small favors. They also understood that they had a better chance of decent treatment when the Americans were around than they did from their own commanders.

As a group, the ARVN officer corps differed in almost every respect from the men they led. The well-educated sons of wealthy, urban Vietnamese families, most had received their appointment as the result of patronage. The beneficiaries of family or political connections, they used their positions to line their pockets with money siphoned from unit budgets or extorted from local farmers. The ultimate products of a traditional, class-bound society, they looked down on the peasants they commanded and on the young Americans whom they sometimes treated with an obsequious condescension, all the more irritating for its partial validity. "They are too new at the game," observed one ARVN colonel archly, "but they can learn."

The advisors wondered whether the Vietnamese really wanted American advice and complained that too much of the burden had been placed on them to "get along." Most of all, the Americans were dismayed to find that many ARVN officers had no more enthusiasm than the enlisted men for the difficult task of subduing the Viet Cong.

Yet month by month, American men and machines changed the face of war in the Delta. Caught off-guard, the Viet Cong suffered one stunning defeat after another. As the government extended its control into insurgent areas, Communist defections grew, while the rate of new recruitment dropped sharply. So grave were the new problems facing their armed forces that the National Liberation Front even considered abandoning delta strongholds they had held for thirty years.

By the end of the year, many Americans were enthusiastic about the prospects for driving the Communists out of the delta entirely. It seemed as though all the Vietnamese needed was a little leadership. "These people may not be the world's greatest fighters," said one advisor, "but they're good people, and they can win a war if someone shows them how."

William Westmoreland was born on March 16, 1914, in Spartanburg, South Carolina, in comfortable circumstances—his father had done well in Spartanburg's principal industry, textiles, and in banking. Young William was, it seemed, born to wear a uniform, born to lead. Boy Scout, Eagle Scout, Citadel cadet, West Point cadet, combat artillery officer in World War II, all the way up through the Army's ranks to four-star general, commander of all American forces in Vietnam, and finally Army chief of staff. He received the Boy Scouts of America's highest honor, the Silver Buffalo Award, a distinction he shared with fourteen US presidents. At West Point, he graduated first in a class that included his eventual successor as US commander in Vietnam, Creighton Abrams, and was awarded the Pershing Sword, given to the academy's outstanding cadet. In World War II, he saw action in France, Germany, Italy, and North Africa, and he was appointed chief of staff of the Army's 9th Infantry Division in 1944.

Twenty years later, Secretary of Defense Robert McNamara told President Lyndon Johnson that Westmoreland was "the best we have, without question," and in June 1964, Westmoreland took charge of the Military Assistance Command in Vietnam (MACV). A few weeks later, on August 4, the Gulf of Tonkin incident—the phantom attack on a US destroyer by North Vietnamese patrol boats—served as the catalyst for the congressional resolution that gave Johnson broad powers to make war in Southeast Asia. In the months and years that followed, Westmoreland saw his command mushroom from a few thousand advisors to more than a half-million troops.

Westmoreland's strategy in Vietnam boiled down to one brutal, bloody principle: attrition. Take the fight to the enemy wherever he is and kill his soldiers until his losses become unsustainable and he quits. He had no patience for long-term strategies such as "pacification" or "hearts and minds"—he was all about body counts, which he was famously accused, in a CBS News report, of inflating.

But the general never really understood his enemy, or the Vietnamese people. He once dismissed his North Vietnamese counterpart, Gen. Vo Nguyen Giap, as a small-unit fighter trying to wage a big war, and he didn't understand Giap's willingness to send so many of his troops to the slaughter—a half-million by the end of 1968. "An American commander losing men like that would hardly have lasted more than a few weeks," Westmoreland told *George* magazine. Had Westmoreland forgotten his history? Well over a half-million Americans died in the Civil War, and that war's generals' motivation was similar to Giap's—they were fighting to save their country. And in the filming of the 1974 documentary *Hearts and Minds*, Westmoreland told shocked filmmaker Peter Davis, "The Oriental doesn't put the same high price on life as

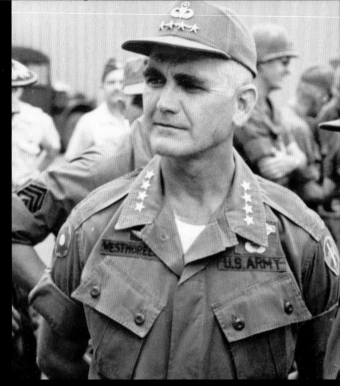

General William Westmoreland in Vietnam, 1967.

does a Westerner . . . they don't care about life and human dignity." Westmoreland's comment was juxtaposed over footage of the funeral of a South Vietnamese soldier as a sobbing woman tries to climb into the grave with the coffin.

In 1982, CBS aired a report titled, "The Uncounted Enemy: A Vietnam Deception," which accused Westmoreland of deliberately understating the strength of the Viet Cong in 1967. Westmoreland sued for libel, but settled out of court for an apology, apparently convinced by his attorneys that he would lose the case.

Westmoreland believed to the end of his life that the US did not lose the war so much as it failed to meet its commitment to South Vietnam. He believed in the domino theory and that US support for South Vietnam had kept the other dominoes from falling—a proposition that's now in the realm of the "What if . . . ?" game. It is worth noting that among the dominoes, only Laos has a Communist government, and after the unification of Vietnam, Hanoi sent its army into Cambodia, not to establish a Communist government but to oust the nightmarish Pol Pot regime.

In mid-1968, a few months after the Tet Offensive, Westmoreland was replaced as MACV commander by his West Point classmate Abrams. The change of command had the appearance of faulting Westmoreland's performance, but Westmoreland and Johnson said it had actually been planned in 1967. Westmoreland became Army chief of staff, a position he held until his retirement in 1972. He died in 2005 at the age of ninety-one, and was buried in West Point Cemetery.

General Vo Nguyen Giap, nearly as much as his mentor, Ho Chi Minh, was the face of the enemy for the Americans who fought against his forces.

Giap was born in 1911 or 1912 in Quang Binh Province. His father, a rice farmer, was an educated man and a passionate nationalist who taught his children to resist the French; Giap joined an underground resistance movement when he was fourteen. He studied law and political economics and taught history until 1941, when Ho Chi Minh picked him to lead the Viet Minh in Vietnam's struggle against Japanese occupiers during World War II—and then against the French, who reestablished control over Vietnam after the war.

In 1954, Giap's forces laid siege to the French stronghold of Dien Bien Phu, near the border with Laos. After eight weeks of fighting, the French surrendered, ending their long colonial occupation of Indochina. The fight to keep Vietnam had cost the French ninety-three thousand soldiers; the Vietnamese, by some estimates, lost at least three hundred thousand—but they won.

When Vietnam was divided north-south after the French decamped, President Dwight Eisenhower refused to sign off on the Geneva plan for an election that might have unified Vietnam, and Giap and his Viet Minh continued their fight, this time against the South Vietnamese army and their new backers, the Americans.

The 1968 Tet Offensive launched by North Vietnamese and Viet Cong forces resulted in huge losses for both the VC and NVA, and Giap was seen as having failed because the South Vietnamese population did not rise up and join the Communist side, as he had hoped. Although he had overseen execution of the offensive, he had initially resisted the plan, which was more or less forced on him by a group of hardline generals. Nonetheless, Giap could see victory in the defeat. The Tet Offensive undermined the American public's faith in the war and its leaders, both military and civilian. Until Tet, Giap later said, the Americans "thought they could win the war, but now they knew they could not."

Giap was removed from his military command in the aftermath of the 1972 Easter Offensive, which ended in defeat, but he remained minister of defense and oversaw North Vietnam's eventual victory over the South in 1975.

General Vo Nguyen Giap in Hanoi, 1994.

Giap outlived his friend and mentor Ho Chi Minh by forty-four years. When he died in 2013 at the age of 102, his body lay in state in Hanoi before being flown to his home province, where thousands of mourners, many holding portraits of the old general, lined the highway to pay last respects.

One Vietnam War veteran told the BBC's Le Nguyen that the people of Quang Binh were proud that Giap had chosen to be buried in his birthplace. "It is our great happiness to be close to him," said Phan Thanh Cong.

CHAPTER TWO

AMERICA TAKES OVER

Raising an Army

Neither the arrival of the Marines in March nor the Rolling Thunder bombing campaign had any appreciable effect on Viet Cong gains in South Vietnam. Pressed by the Joint Chiefs to commit far greater numbers of troops to the conflict, President Johnson in late July 1965 ordered the immediate deployment of the 1st Cavalry Division, a doubling of draft calls, and expansion of the target list for US bombers. Johnson was also urged to mobilize the reserves, which he refused to do, but he asked for congressional authorization for a 340,000-man increase in all US armed forces. His request initiated the largest military buildup in US peacetime history. Six months after the president's announcement, the number of US military personnel in South Vietnam had jumped from 81,000 to 250,000. Within two years, that figure almost doubled.

Troopers from the Americal Division make an air assault into the Central Highlands of Vietnam. They are flying in UH-1 Hueys from the 161st Assault Helicopter Company.

To get the numbers of troops he needed to fight the war in Vietnam, President Johnson turned to the Selective Service System (SSS)—the draft. When the Marines landed at Da Nang in March 1965, there were slightly more than twenty-nine thousand US military personnel in Vietnam. During the next twenty-one months, US soldiers, sailors, Air Crewmen, and Marines poured into the country in ever-increasing numbers. Many came courtesy of the Selective Service, which by the end of 1965 was processing up to forty thousand men a month. Primarily the sons of lower-middle-class or working-class families unable to get the still-liberal college deferments, these men were funneled into expanded training bases all over the country, then rapidly shipped to Vietnam.

When President Kennedy decided to dispatch thousands of advisors to South Vietnam, millions of young American men began to feel their local draft boards breathing down their necks. All male US citizens are to this day required to register for the draft within thirty days of their eighteenth birthday.

Unless he qualifies for one of some thirty exemptions, ranging from student deferments to physical disabilities, the registrant is classified 1-A: "Available for unrestricted military service." When Kennedy told the SSS director, Gen. Lewis B. Hershey, that married men with children should be at the bottom of the list, many men married and hastily fathered children. They were called "Kennedy husbands."

To handle the sudden demand for fighting men, the US Air Force, Navy, and Marines all expanded their training facilities. But the buildup had the greatest impact on the Army. Ordered by the Pentagon to create three new 7,500-man infantry brigades and more than seven hundred smaller units, the Army expanded half a dozen bases and opened new facilities all around the country. By the end of the year, six Army basic-training centers—Fort Ord, California; Fort Dix, New Jersey; Fort Jackson, South Carolina; Fort Polk, Louisiana; Fort Gordon, Georgia; and Fort Leonard Wood, Missouri—were teaching nearly thirteen thousand recruits, in overlapping eight-week training cycles, how to fight and survive in the jungles of Southeast Asia.

Whether they signed DD Form 4—ENLISTMENT CONTRACT: ARMED FORCES OF THE UNITED STATES—or received a letter headed "Greeting:" the beginnings were all the same. A bus or a train took them to a place like Marine boot camp at Parris Island, South Carolina, or one of the many Army training centers, the lively young men growing strangely silent as they neared their destination. "There was no conversation now, no sound but the mechanical grate and whine of the bus itself," remembered one recruit years later. "Nervous anticipation—raw fear of the unknown—made thought impossible." Then the bus stopped, the train coasted to a halt, and the doors folded open on a new world.

At some reception centers, the new arrivals were met by brass bands. The next greeting they received was apt to be a good deal less friendly. It usually came from a large man in a wide-brimmed, forest-ranger hat whose title was drill sergeant, whose face was scowling, and whose voice carried unmistakable conviction when it growled, "You're all mine now!" The routine of the next few days varied from place to place, but everywhere included orientation lectures, haircuts, shots, more lectures, blood tests, forms to fill out, talks by chaplains and Red Cross representatives, more orientation sessions,

A US Army drill sergeant during basic training at Fort Dix in New Jersey, 1963.

US Army draftees participate in physical training during their first week of basic training at Fort Dix, 1963.

fingerprinting, TB tests, form letters to write home, and a small reference booklet that covered everything a soldier needed to know, including "Pay due a serviceman at time of death." Along the way, the new recruits were issued boots, uniforms, field gear, rifles, and bedding. They learned how to salute, how to hold a cotton ball for their blood test, and how to make a bed to military specifications.

Training the Troops

In the mid-1960s, the Army was undergoing a renaissance in the ranks led by Army Chief of Staff Gen. Harold K. Johnson. Convinced that modern warfare required a modern soldier, Johnson wanted his men to think for themselves. "You can't just stand there and yell 'Hurry it up,'" he once admonished a drill instructor. "The American soldier has to be led, not pushed."

The Marines remained wedded to an older tradition, however. Like thousands of others, Bill Ehrhart's first sight of a Marine drill instructor was unforgettable, as he recounted in *Vietnam-Perkasie: A Combat Marine Memoir.* "The DI who got on that bus was eight-and-a-half-feet tall. And he was ugly. Standing there with his hands on his hips, he looked like a cross between Paul Bunyan, Babe the Blue Ox, and Godzilla." The ear-shattering bellow that came from his mouth, recalled the suddenly terrified recruit, sounded like the voice of God. "'There's four columns of yellow footprints painted on the deck in front of those steps over there!' roared the DI. 'When I give the word, you filthy pigs have three seconds to get outta this bus and plant yourself on one of those sets of yellow footprints. You will not talk. You will keep your head and eyes front at all times. You will do everything you're told instantly, and you will do nothing else. I'll kill the first cocksucker that fucks it up. You scuzzy shitbirds are *mine*, ladies! And I don't like you. Now, MOVE! *Do it! Do it!*'"

Not that the much larger number of men welcomed into the Army had it easy. Despite such novelties as automatic dishwashers and potato-peeling machines in K.P., their training was in many ways tougher than ever. Compared to the eight to twelve weeks of military instruction given during World War II, soldiers heading to Vietnam underwent a minimum of four months of training divided into basic and advanced courses, some of it on subjects unimaginable only a decade earlier.

Once initial processing was completed, the new recruits were divided into 250-man companies and shipped off to basic-training centers. Over the next eight weeks, the Army provided them with 352 hours of instruction. Some of it took place in classrooms where instructors lectured on military courtesy and sanitation. But the trainees spent most of the time preparing their minds and bodies for war.

Crawling out of their bunks at 5:15 or 5:30 in the morning, they filled the days with calisthenics, close-order drill, and marching, always marching, whether they were Marines or Army soldiers. They learned about "Jody"— the undrafted guy back home whose exploits were their cadence calls:

> Ain't no use in goin' home
> Jody's got your girl and gone.
> Ain't no use in goin' back
> Jody's got your Cadillac.

"Whenever I think back to those days at Basic School," wrote former Marine Philip Caputo, "the recollection that first comes to mind is always the same: a double file of green-clad men, bent beneath their packs, are tramping down a dirt road. A remorseless sun is beating down. Raised by our boots, a cloud of red dust powders the trees alongside the road, making them look sickly and ashen. The dust clings to our uniforms, runs in muddy streaks down our sweating faces. There is the rattle of rifle slings and bayonet scabbards, the clattering of mess kits bouncing in our haversacks. Our heads ache from the weight of steel helmets, and the cry 'Close it up, keep your interval, close it up' is echoing up and down the long column."

When they dropped their packs, the young recruits were introduced to their rifles. "A soldier's weapon is his best friend," intoned the instructors who made sure their charges not only could shoot their rifles but also knew how to take them apart and put them back together again. And woe unto the recruit who referred to his M14 rifle as his "gun." After the requisite push-ups, he would be ordered to recite loudly,

> This is my rifle [pointing to his M14],
> This is my gun [pointing to his crotch].
> This is for killing [rifle],
> This is for fun [crotch].

Senior writer Nick Mills relates the story of his enlisting as an Army officer during the Vietnam War.

General Hershey often said that for every man drafted, three or four were "scared" into enlisting. I was one. Enlistment offered some advantages, such as choice of branch. While most draftees were ticketed for the Army, or to a lesser extent, the Marines, recruiters for the Air Force and Navy could cherry-pick the most qualified enlistees. But even those who enlisted in the Army were offered choices, and an enlistee who qualified for Officer Candidate School (OCS) could choose the Signal Corps, or Transportation, or Quartermaster, where direct combat would be less likely. Draftees were placed into one of the three combat arms, where the Army needed them most: infantry, artillery, or armor.

In September 1964, I had just graduated from Boston University and was living with my parents at their home in Maine when I received the letter I had been waiting for: I had been accepted to train for a Peace Corps project in Colombia, starting in January of the following year. In the weeks before the start of training, I took a job as a staff announcer at WLBZ radio in Bangor. By that time I knew a little bit about what was going on in Vietnam, but I didn't think it would affect me—maybe the Vietnam thing would blow over by the time I had done a two-year hitch in the Peace Corps. I had taken my pre-induction physical, and was classified 1-A, but I had managed to convince myself that I would not be called up, and that the Peace Corps would somehow exempt me from military service. Then came the letter: "GREETING: You are hereby ordered for induction into the Armed Forces of the United States . . ."

Naturally, I panicked. But by that time I had worked in radio for several years, having started my broadcasting career at WRKD in Rockland, Maine, (where my draft board was located) at the age of fifteen, so I was accustomed to calling public officials and interviewing them. I looked up the Maine office of the Selective Service System and dialed the number. I was eventually put through to the colonel in charge of the office, and I told him my situation. "Go into the Peace Corps," he said. "I'll take care of your draft board." I wish I remembered his name, because I owe him a lot. I went into the Peace Corps. My draft board seethed over the colonel's interference in their business, and for the next two years they grudgingly gave me deferments—six months at a time. Every six months I had to write them to say that, yes, I was still in the Peace Corps and would be there until January 1967.

Congressman Alexander Pirnie (center) reaches into a container of draft numbers as others look on, including Selective Service Director Lt. Gen. Lewis Blaine Hershey (left) and Deputy Director Col. Daniel Omer (right), at the Selective Service Headquarters during the nationwide draft lottery in 1969.

By that time, I had a wife; another Peace Corps volunteer and I had married in Bogota, Colombia. When we finished our tours and arrived back in the US, my wife and I drove to Rockland on a snowy day in early February for a hearing with my draft board. The board members had not showed up because of the snow. The only person in the office was the board's secretary. "It doesn't matter," she said. "They're gonna draft you." I practically raced out of the office, turned the car around, headed down to Portland, and presented myself to the Army recruiter. A battery of tests showed that I was qualified for Officer Candidate School. The recruiter tried hard to persuade me to select one of the combat arms, but all of my experience, education, and training had been in communication. I chose the Signal Corps, and my ticket was punched for basic training at Fort Dix, New Jersey; Advanced Individual Training (infantry) at Fort McClellan, Alabama; and Signal OCS at Fort Gordon, Georgia.

On one of the saddest and scariest days of my life, at the last possible hour I kissed my wife goodbye and boarded a bus at New York's Port Authority terminal for the ride to Fort Dix—the first leg of a long journey that would impel me inexorably toward the jungles of Vietnam.

There were classes in grenade throwing and hand-to-hand combat, pugil-stick fights, and bayonet training (*"What's the spirit of the bayonet?" "TO KILL!"*). There were exercises in mock combat with real bullets whizzing a few inches over a man's head as he crawled through the mud under strands of barbed wire. Near the end of basic, the men were taken out on bivouac to learn how to live in the field and eat C-rations.

Through it all, the veterans with the stripes on their sleeves tried to teach the new recruits how to get back in one piece from "the boonies." Never stand in groups, or one incoming round could get you all. Do not give or re-turn salutes—Charlie likes to shoot the officers. When you hear a loud noise, hit the deck, do not try to run for a bunker. Sleep as close to the ground as you can, under the ground if possible. And the one rule that summarized all the rules for survival in a war zone: "Keep your ass down."

Slowly, steadily, the regimen of training began to mold the former ci-vilians into soldiers. Chubby recruits lost their baby fat. The marching, running, low-crawling, pushups, and repetitions of the "daily dozen" exer-cises toughened them physically. The endless barking of the drill instruc-tors disciplined their reactions. They saw the realities of interdependence and the necessity of teamwork. Those who failed any portion of the course "recycled" that segment until they got it right. When everything worked, a

Recruits train in hand-to-hand combat under the watchful eye of an instructor, 1967.

Army trainees crawl under barbed wire during their eight-week course in basic training at Fort Dix, 1967.

group of individuals became a machine that theoretically would respond as a single unit in the face of danger and do as their leaders ordered. Finally, after passing the Army's exhaustive Physical Combat Proficiency Test, recruits graduated from basic training.

Army recruits went on to Advanced Individual Training (AIT). There they learned additional skills based on their aptitudes and interests. Some received further training as clerks or cooks, typists or truck drivers. Others underwent a nine-week course in one of a variety of combat arms specialties. These ranged from artillery to tanks to helicopters, but also included the most basic specialty of all—infantry tactics.

AIT was designed in part to refine skills first mastered in basic training, but the primary goal was to give novice soldiers the experience of Vietnam before they had to face the real thing. To do so, the Army constructed replicas of VC hamlets—"staffed" with "enemy" soldiers and complete in detail down to the last tunnel and punji stick—then set combat "problems" for the trainees to deal with. They learned how to detect enemy booby traps and place claymore mines, how to set ambushes and establish listening posts outside night defensive perimeters, how to jump from hovering helicopters into "hot" LZs and flush enemy guerrillas into predesignated "killing zones." Particular attention was devoted to patrolling and ambush and counter-ambush techniques, along with the intricacies of camouflage. As an officer lectured one class in methods used by the VC to conceal themselves, a hidden soldier carrying a machine gun jumped from a hole only a few feet in front of the startled recruits.

At the end of AIT, the recruits were considered qualified for combat. "When they leave here," said a training officer at Fort Polk's AIT center, "they are ready to fight." And many soon found themselves in Vietnam. But some men chose to extend their training into more exotic specialties. There was airborne, where men "slept four and five hours a night and then got up and ran everywhere," remembered one parachutist. "Everything—home, letters, concerns, friends—everything faded under the weight of exhaustion" until the rigors of practice jumps from 250-foot towers and the fear of their first real jumps made them forget how tired they were. Then there was Ranger training, where the schedule made airborne look like a piece of cake: 3:30 a.m. wake-ups, twelve-minute-mile runs with hundred-pound field packs, perilous descents down ice-covered cliffs, and low-level night parachute jumps into impenetrable cypress swamps.

The long weeks of preparation gave young men the endurance they would need to hump mile after mile in searing, mind-numbing heat. It taught them how to read a map, how to fire a mortar, what to do when someone shot at them, and what to do when they or a buddy got shot. Their training nurtured pride in themselves and loyalty to their comrades. Equally important, it transformed the way they looked at the world around them. Landscape was no longer scenery, it was terrain. The little man in the black pajamas was no longer quaint, he was the enemy.

Training the Officers

The elite institutions for the training of America's military leaders are the academies: the US Military Academy on the Hudson River, known simply as West Point; the US Naval Academy in Annapolis, Maryland; the Air Force Academy in Colorado Springs, Colorado; and the US Coast Guard Academy in New London, Connecticut. (Though the Coast Guard's role in Vietnam is often overlooked, four Coast Guardsmen were killed in action and one died later of wounds received in action.) But each of the service academies graduated fewer than a thousand commissioned officers each year; far more of the US military's officer corps earned their bars through the various Officer Candidate Schools (OCS). Before the massive troop buildup for the Vietnam War, there were only two Army OCS programs operating: Infantry at Fort Benning, Georgia, and Field Artillery at Fort Sill, Oklahoma. But with demand running high, between 1964 and 1973, in order to meet the demand for junior officers, the Army ran eight branch-specific OCS programs.

Opposite page: The US military command divided South Vietnam into four zones, called Corps Tactical Zones (CTZ), each with its own military administration and command. The zones were designated by Roman numerals: I Corps (spoken as "Eye Corps"), II Corps (Two Corps), III Corps (Three Corps), and IV Corps (Four Corps).

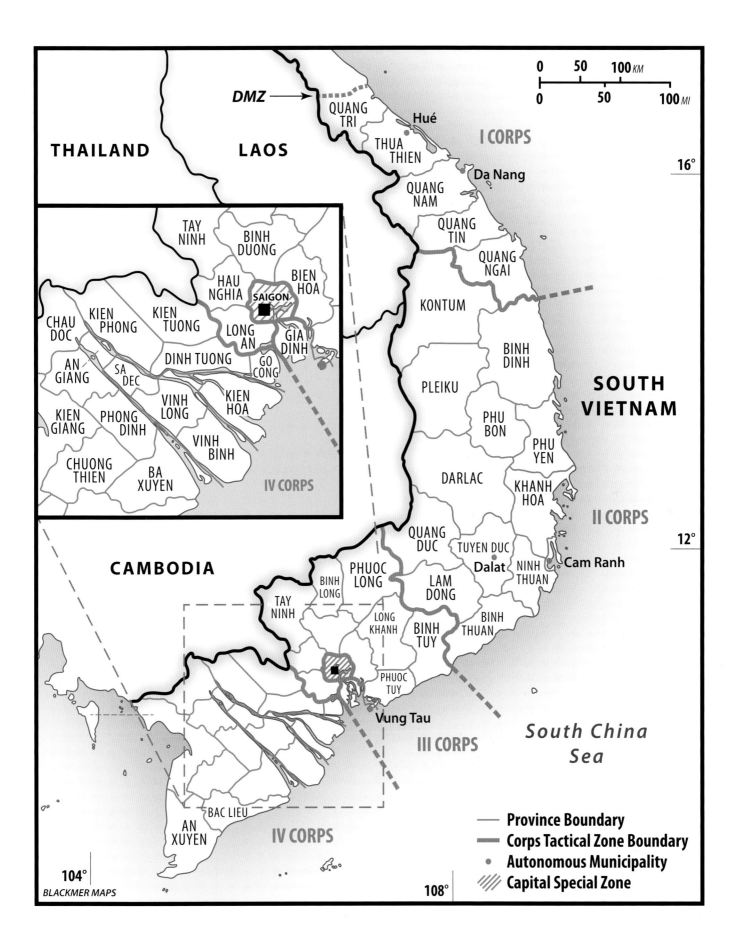

THAILAND

LAOS

DMZ →

QUANG
TRI

Hué

I CORPS

THUA
THIEN

Da Nang

16°

QUANG
NAM

QUANG
TIN

QUANG
NGAI

TAY
NINH

BINH
DUONG

HAU
NGHIA

BIEN
HOA

SAIGON

KONTUM

CHAU
DOC

KIEN
PHONG

KIEN
TUONG

LONG
AN

GIA
DINH

BINH
DINH

SOUTH
VIETNAM

AN
GIANG

SA
DEC

DINH TUONG

GO
CONG

PLEIKU

KIEN
GIANG

PHONG
DINH

VINH
LONG

KIEN
HOA

PHU
BON

PHU
YEN

CHUONG
THIEN

BA
XUYEN

VINH
BINH

IV CORPS

DARLAC

KHANH
HOA

II CORPS

12°

CAMBODIA

QUANG
DUC

TUYEN DUC

Dalat

Cam Ranh

NINH
THUAN

BINH
LONG

PHUOC
LONG

LAM
DONG

TAY
NINH

LONG
KHANH

BINH
TUY

BINH
THUAN

PHUOC
TUY

Vung Tau

South China
Sea

III CORPS

BAC LIEU

AN
XUYEN

IV CORPS

— Province Boundary
━ Corps Tactical Zone Boundary
• Autonomous Municipality
▨ Capital Special Zone

104°

BLACKMER MAPS

108°

At the war's peak, Fort Benning's Infantry OCS program alone turned out seven thousand officers a year; a smaller number came out of the Marine Corps OCS program at Quantico. During the war, approximately 4,600 Army and Marine lieutenants were killed in action, and it was often said, only partly in jest, that an infantry lieutenant in Vietnam had a life expectancy measured in minutes. Graduates of the OCS programs emerged from months of physically and mentally challenging training with their fatigue uniform collars adorned with small gold bars that symbolized their readiness to lead an infantry platoon or a tank platoon, set up a remote signal site, command a firing section of an artillery battery, or perform any of the scores of leadership roles in the field or in rear areas.

In-Country

When "we marched into the rice paddies on that damp March afternoon," Marine Lt. Philip Caputo later wrote, "we carried, along with our packs and rifles, the implicit conviction that the Viet Cong would be quickly beaten." Certain that its goals were legitimate, confident that the application of American military power would swiftly drive the enemy from the field, the United States went to war in 1965 with an almost casual assumption of victory.

So pervasive was this optimism that little attempt was made to tailor American strategy to the realities of the situation in Vietnam. As a result, US policy was filled with uncertainties and questionable assumptions. The dispatch of troops was meant to halt the Communist onslaught and compel negotiations, but no one in Washington made any serious attempt to determine just what level of force would be necessary to accomplish those ends. Meanwhile, the introduction of large numbers of American units pushed the indigenous military into the background, steadily diminishing ARVN's ability to shoulder the burden of their nation's defense. Further confusing matters was President Johnson's sensitivity to adverse public reaction. Fearful of domestic unrest, he sought a quick end to the war. Yet, equally concerned that an overly aggressive pursuit of victory would draw in China or the Soviet Union, he imposed limitations on his military commanders that made their missions more difficult to achieve.

For its part, the military never fully accommodated itself to Washington's restrictions. Nor did US commanders adjust their vision to a revolutionary struggle in which political victories were always more important than military triumphs. Instead, MACV employed regular forces in a conventional war of attrition against an unconventional enemy in an unfamiliar setting. When that strategy failed to produce adequate results, when more and more men were sent to hold the line, the early optimism of 1965 degenerated into a bitter frustration that threatened to tear the nation apart.

Exemplifying this strategic confusion was the air campaign against North Vietnam. The initial bombing raids were designed to meet the political need for a quick, negotiated settlement of the war. The administration was confident that US air power would force the North Vietnamese to cease their support of the southern insurgency and that this could be achieved without significant loss of American lives. When the initial attacks failed to cow Hanoi, however, the goal of the air assault shifted. The primary task became a military one—to halt the flow of reinforcements and supplies to the South

US Air Force F-4 Phantom jets, used in Operation Rolling Thunder, fly in formation over South Vietnam, 1966.

where US ground troops were engaged in battle with Communist forces. Whether air power was suitable for either task would remain a subject of debate long after the war was over.

After the fruitless five-day bombing pause in mid-May, Rolling Thunder resumed in earnest, long-range US Air Force fighter-bombers striking inland targets while carrier-based Navy aircraft operated along the coast. By September, American warplanes were flying almost four thousand sorties a month against military bases, supply depots, and infiltration routes in the southern half of North Vietnam. At Johnson's insistence, major targets within the Hanoi-Haiphong restricted zone initially escaped the aerial onslaught. As the ground war below the DMZ intensified, however, the Joint Chiefs argued that air power could not prevent the flow of men and materiel south as long as these areas remained off-limits. In June 1966, the president finally approved a full-scale assault against the North's vital petroleum, oil, and lubricants (POL) storage facilities and transportation network.

While American aircraft blasted tank farms and railroad yards on the northern outskirts of Hanoi, other American pilots flew interdiction strikes along the Ho Chi Minh Trail in southern Laos. Code-named Tiger Hound, this multiservice operation utilized modern reconnaissance jets and leftover attack aircraft from World War II, propeller-driven observation airplanes, and high-flying B-52s. During the first five months of 1966, Tiger Hound attacks destroyed thousands of structures and trucks, dozens of bridges, and hundreds of anti-aircraft positions along the major enemy infiltration route into South Vietnam.

The tempo of air raids over the North increased steadily during the summer to a peak of twelve thousand sorties in September. Two months later, under continuing pressure from the military, Johnson enlarged the target list even further to include key railroad yards on the outskirts of Hanoi. By the end of 1966, the United States had flown more than 105,000 sorties over the North. The 165,000 tons of bombs delivered by American warplanes since the beginning of 1965 had destroyed nearly 350 fixed structures and thousands of railroad cars, motor vehicles, and watercraft.

Estimates of the economic and military damage done to North Vietnam exceeded $200 million, yet the air attacks cost the United States more than $1.5 billion and the loss of 489 aircraft. Nor had the bombing appreciably affected the course of the war. Much that had been destroyed was replaced by increased aid from China and the Soviet Union. What could not be replaced was rebuilt by armies of civilian workers. In January 1967, a CIA analysis concluded that Rolling Thunder had been unable to cripple the North Vietnamese economy, weaken the North's military establishment, or significantly impede the flow of supplies to the South. The US command argued that the disappointing figures were the direct result of Washington's graduated and limited application of American air power. Others, like Secretary of Defense Robert McNamara, had begun to believe that no amount of bombing would break the will of the North Vietnamese. Whatever the causes, the failure of the air campaign meant that US troops would play far more than a stopgap role. By the beginning of 1967, the war on the ground in South Vietnam had long since become an American fight.

By the beginning of 1966, US troop strength in Vietnam had grown to 250,000, including nearly 160,000 soldiers and Marines comprising twenty-two Army and thirteen Marine infantry and tank battalions. But the pace of deployment scarcely slackened—the 1st Marine Division went to Chu Lai in January; the 25th Infantry Division to Cu Chi in March; the 4th Infantry Division to Pleiku in July; the 196th Infantry Brigade to Tay Ninh in August; the 11th Armored Cavalry Regiment to Long Binh in September; the 9th Infantry Division, slated for duty in the Mekong Delta, in December; the 199th Infantry Brigade to Long Binh, also in December. At year's end, US ground combat strength had grown to fifty-nine Army and twenty-four Marine infantry and tank battalions.

To meet their logistical needs, Army engineers constructed four major deep-water ports, rebuilt South Vietnam's highway system, and greatly expanded that nation's air transport facilities. Meanwhile, the 1st Logistical Command headquartered in Saigon became one of the largest army organizations in the world. But there was more to logistics in Vietnam than military supplies. Convinced that the maintenance of morale was of prime importance, Westmoreland not only limited each soldier's tour of duty to 365 days, he also attempted to provide his men with "all the comforts of home." Even the troops in the field could expect regular hot meals—with ice cream flown in by helicopter for dessert.

For all that, Vietnam remained an alien place for most of the young Americans who served there, a beautiful but strange land of shifting

The skeleton of a burned Marine F-4 Phantom jet fighter rests on the tarmac at Da Nang Air Base after being hit by enemy rockets while taxiing to the refueling area. Both crewmen perished in the fire.

Weariness and uncertainty are reflected in the weathered faces of a Vietnamese couple in the Le My refugee camp.

topography, climatic extremes, and enigmatic people. In the south was the delta, a watery world of flat rice fields, impenetrable mangrove swamps, and isolated forests. North of Saigon, the emerald green fields dwindled to a narrow strip along the rocky coast, the area of cultivation limited by the sparsely populated mountain forests of the Central Highlands. Still farther north, the high plateau gave way to the rugged peaks and plunging waterfalls of the Truong Son Mountains, a steep wilderness of dense rain forests rising as high as eight thousand feet above sea level.

Less varied than the land, the weather of Vietnam was dominated by the annual cycle of monsoons. During the summer, drenching torrents of rain created a perpetual humidity that rotted clothing, mired everything on the ground in mud, and made flying treacherous. In the winter months, the rain was replaced by scorching heat, a veritable furnace that took a man's breath away and turned the winter mud into clouds of gritty red dust.

Almost as impenetrable as the heat was the peasant population of the Vietnamese countryside. "My time in Vietnam," recalled one infantryman, "is the memory of ignorance. I didn't know the language. I knew nothing about the village community. I knew nothing about the aims of the people—whether they were for the war or against the war." Instead of grateful "natives" eager to be "liberated," US troops frequently encountered indifference and suspicion. Even worse, there was often no way of distinguishing who was friend and who was enemy, no way of telling by how they acted or what they wore, who was a farmer and who was a guerrilla, until it was too late.

Despite the overwhelming advantage the Americans had in raw fire-power, the Viet Cong and NVA proved elusive and deadly adversaries. Dispersed into platoon-size units that would consolidate only for carefully planned attacks, the enemy avoided contact except at their own initiative. The elaborate preparations made by US units prior to an operation and the effectiveness of the Communist intelligence network made surprise almost impossible for the Americans to achieve. When enemy troops were cornered, they fought stubbornly, standing their ground even under the most punishing artillery and air strikes. In populated areas, Viet Cong guerrillas frequently fired on American troops from within villages, prompting return fire that rarely found its target but often destroyed civilian property and killed or wounded innocent villagers. In the uninhabited border regions, well-trained, heavily armed regular troops of the NVA challenged the Americans in an escalating series of ferocious encounters that by the end of 1965 were already claiming heavy casualties on both sides.

While the White House maintained tight control over the bombing of North Vietnam, Westmoreland was given considerable freedom to develop and execute the ground war in South Vietnam. The strategy he formulated was divided into three parts. First, US combat units would search out and destroy enemy Main Force units and base areas. Next, ARVN troops would clear the area of Viet Cong guerrillas left after the large-scale search-and-destroy operations had ended. Finally, local South Vietnamese units—the Regional Forces (RFs) and Popular Forces (PFs)—would secure the area by providing a permanent defense against future attacks.

Although his plan was designed in part to protect the population of the countryside, Westmoreland's primary goal was the attrition of the enemy's Main Force units. Once that was achieved, reasoned the general, the

Communists would have no choice but to sue for peace. "We'll just go on bleeding them until Hanoi wakes up to the fact that they have bled their country to the point of national disaster for generations."

Westmoreland's strategy of attrition relied on a steadily increasing pool of US manpower, on the application of American technology to the task of locating the enemy, and on the ready availability of American firepower to destroy him—artillery, naval gunfire, helicopter gunships, fixed-wing attack aircraft, and awesome B-52 bombers from air bases in Guam and Thailand. So confident was he in the impact of such weapons that even before he had significant numbers of combat troops at hand, the American commander took the offensive.

Members of Bravo Company, 4th Battalion, 12th Infantry, 199th Infantry Brigade carry a wounded soldier from the field during a battle in the Lhu Duc district.

Westmoreland's willingness to send his green troops against the Viet Cong was also a reflection of the deteriorating position of the South Vietnamese army in the early summer of 1965. Anxious to strike back before ARVN collapsed entirely, the MACV commander urged Washington to abandon the defensive enclaves to which US forces had been deployed. On June 26, Westmoreland was given permission to commit US combat troops at his discretion. Within twenty-four hours, the 173rd Airborne Brigade began a search-and-destroy operation into War Zone D northeast of Saigon.

The first major American ground combat action of the war proved anticlimactic, the paratroopers encountering only scattered resistance during their four days in the field. But the die had been cast. Eight weeks later, when elements of the 1st and 3rd Marine Divisions cornered an entire VC regiment fifteen kilometers south of Chu Lai, the Americans dealt the enemy a stunning blow. A multipronged land, air, and sea assault, Operation Starlite caught the VC completely by surprise. From their entrenched positions, the Communists fought back furiously, but could not contend with the Americans' mobility and firepower. Using helicopter-borne troops to block avenues of escape, Marine infantrymen supported by tanks and amphibious tractors trapped the enemy regiment against the sea, where it was torn to pieces by Marine air and naval gunfire. In less than a week of fighting, the VC lost nearly seven hundred men. Their extensive tunnel and cave complexes, laboriously carved out over many years, were destroyed.

As the year wore on and US troop strength grew, the intensity of combat increased. American units penetrated Viet Cong base areas near Saigon, swept the Central Highlands around Kontum, and grappled with guerrillas in the villages along the central coast. But even as US soldiers and Marines poured into South Vietnam, the Communists more than matched the American buildup. By November, total VC/NVA strength was estimated at 140,000 men. Early that month, troops of the 1st Cavalry Division (Airmobile) met North Vietnamese regulars in a bloody battle that demonstrated both the advantages and limitations of the American way of war in Vietnam.

A Viet Cong prisoner captured during Operation Double Eagle twenty miles south of Quang Ngai is led to a prisoner collection area by a US Marine. Prisoners were tied and blindfolded to prevent escape attempts.

The 1st Cavalry Division (Airmobile)—or 1st Air Cav, as the troopers preferred—represented a new concept in warfare: air mobility. Its roots stretching back to the old horse cavalry of the Civil War, the new "First Team" was initiated in 1963 as part of President Kennedy's insistence on a more flexible military machine. The 1st Air Cav had staged only two full-scale maneuvers with its new helicopters before it became the first full division sent to Vietnam. When Communist troops attacked the Special Forces camp at Plei Me on October 19, elements of the division's 1st Brigade helped lift the siege. In the process, they discovered that two full NVA regiments were roaming the frontier area. That knowledge only whetted the appetite of the 1st Air Cav's commander, Gen. Harry W. O. Kinnard. Eager to try out his UH-1 Hueys over the trackless mountain jungle of the western highlands, Kinnard sought permission to go after the enemy. On October 27, Westmoreland gave Kinnard the order to "find, fix, and destroy" every enemy soldier between Plei Me and the Cambodian border.

Employing the new technique of aerial reconnaissance by fire, Kinnard's helicopter pilots began sighting an increasing number of North Vietnamese soldiers in the Ia Drang Valley. After several small engagements during the first weeks of the operation, Col. Harry G. Moore's 1st Battalion, 7th Cavalry set down at Landing Zone (LZ) X-Ray on the morning of November 14, virtually on top of two full NVA regiments. Pinned down by rocket and grenade fire, attacked on several sides by enemy infantry, Moore called in air and artillery strikes within 150 meters of the battalion's perimeter. By nightfall, reinforcements from the 2nd Battalion had arrived at the LZ, but the morning of the 15th brought renewed assaults that were only beaten off in fierce hand-to-hand fighting. When the NVA soldiers finally retreated the next day, they left behind 834 confirmed dead plus an estimated several hundred more KIA from artillery and air strikes, including several by B-52 Stratofortresses, the first time in the war the giant bombers were used for tactical support.

The 2nd Battalion moved out on foot on November 17 heading for LZ Albany ten kilometers away. Discovered en route, the troopers marched straight into an ambush.

Within a few minutes, NVA fire had decimated two companies, some of the terrorized green troops shooting wildly into their own ranks. Slowly, the surviving Americans fell back into a coherent perimeter. Helicopter gunships raked the enemy positions, followed by Air Force fighter-bombers discharging loads of napalm that seared the jungle in orange sheets of jellied fire. Even with the aerial support, enemy fire remained too intense to land reinforcements or evacuate wounded. By the next morning, the NVA had fled. Counting the more than four hundred enemy bodies littering the battleground, General Kinnard declared that the 2nd Battalion had "won the day." But the price of victory had been steep. Of the original five hundred men who had set out from LZ X-Ray, 150 had been killed and another 250 wounded.

Above: US Marines, grouped in fours and fives in outboard motorboats, approach the beach during an amphibious assault in the Rung Sat Zone, thirty-five miles from Saigon. Infested with Viet Cong, Rung Sat was the target of Operation Jackstay, which involved 1,200 Marines.

Left: During the second phase of Operation Thayer, the 1st Cav undertakes Operation Irving twenty-five miles north of Qui Nhon. Their mission was to clear a mountain range where an estimated two battalions of North Vietnam regulars were thought to be planning an attack on Hammond airstrip.

Opposite page, top: In Long Khanh Province, Spc. Ruediger Richter and Sgt. Daniel E. Spencer stand by their fallen comrade as they await a helicopter that will evacuate their fellow soldier from the jungle-covered hills.

Opposite page, bottom: A Marine Corps flame thrower tank in action.

After the battles at LZs X-Ray and Albany, the NVA staged one more attack against an artillery firebase, then withdrew across the border into Cambodia. During the month-long campaign, the 1st Air Cav had moved entire battalions by air, dropped artillery batteries into the middle of the jungle sixty-seven times, and ferried 7,500 tons of supplies to the men in the field. Even more important, in the course of some fifty thousand individual flights during the operation, only fifty-nine helicopters were hit by enemy fire, four were shot down, and but a single aircraft was lost. The concept of air mobility had been fully vindicated.

It was a sobering defeat for the Communists, who left 1,500 dead scattered on the battlefield and may have lost as many as two thousand more to air and artillery fire. But the Communists had also gained important information from the battle of the Ia Drang Valley. They discovered that they could neutralize the worst of American firepower by fighting at close range, and they learned not to reveal their positions by firing at low-flying reconnaissance helicopters. Moreover, the extent of their losses convinced the North Vietnamese to adopt a more cautious approach that kept the initiative in their hands and made US casualties their primary objective. By the end of 1965, Hanoi had adopted its own strategy of attrition, confident that eventually the bill of war would be greater than the Americans were willing to pay.

The idea that the Communists could outlast the United States was one General Westmoreland was determined to resist. Yet as the new year began, the American commander faced some serious problems. Despite the rapid deployment of US troops, the president's decision not to call up the reserves created a manpower crisis that delayed the dispatch of critically needed logistical units, sent infantry platoons into the field with as few as half their authorized complement of men, and threatened to neutralize the promise of air mobility because of an acute shortage of helicopter pilots. Westmoreland also had to contend with the inexperience of his young soldiers, who had to learn how to maneuver safely, react to ambush, and make use of the firepower at their command.

The most difficult problem for MACV, however, was the inability of the South Vietnamese army to provide security for the nation's twelve thousand hamlets. Although Westmoreland's strategy called for American troops to seek out and destroy the enemy's Main Force units in the sparsely inhabited border regions, most of his attention during the first half of the year was devoted to operations against the VC/NVA in the populated coastal lowlands and in the strategically vital region surrounding Saigon.

The task of guarding the capital fell in part to the 173rd Airborne Brigade and the 25th Infantry Division. During the first three months of the year, airborne elements repeatedly penetrated VC strongholds north and west of Saigon in operations such as Marauder, Crimp, and Mallet, provoking sharp firefights but no sustained contact. For the men of the 25th Division, now stationed at Cu Chi where they threatened a prime VC supply route to Cambodia, simply clearing the area immediately around their base camp proved an arduous process. Withstanding intense engagements against stubborn Viet Cong defenders, they captured large amounts of materiel, but only after deliberately working their way through enemy bunker and tunnel complexes.

The American unit most active in III Corps during the first half of the year was the 1st Infantry Division. Ranging north, east, and west of Saigon, elements of the division swept the Boi Loi Woods and the region around Long

Huey helicopters airlift members of the 2nd Battalion, 14th Infantry Regiment, from the Fihol Rubber Plantation to a new staging area during Operation Wahiawa, a search-and-destroy mission conducted by the 25th Infantry Division northeast of Cu Chi.

Thanh in February, then worked their way through the jungles of coastal Phuoc Tuy Province in April. That month, the division also sent two battalions north to Tay Ninh in Operation Birmingham, while other men of the "Big Red One" struggled through hip-deep mud in the mangrove swamps of the Rung Sat Special Zone southeast of the capital. After a fruitless sweep in May around Loc Ninh, division commander Maj. Gen. William E. DePuy pushed his men into War Zone C during June, where they met the 9th VC Division in Operation El Paso II. After several sharp encounters, the Americans drove the enemy into Cambodia, forestalling a threatened offensive against Saigon.

While the 1st Infantry Division struggled to keep the enemy at arm's length from the political center of South Vietnam, the 1st Cav brought its airmobile tactics out of the mountain jungles and onto the lowlands of Binh Dinh Province four hundred kilometers north. Beginning with Operation Masher/White Wing in January and continuing through the remainder of the year, the

Above: Staff Sergeant Joe Musial (left) of Delta Company, 1st Battalion, 8th Cavalry Regiment, 1st Cavalry Division, hears on the radio that the rest of his company is pinned down by withering fire from North Vietnamese soldiers on the Bong Son plain, February 14, 1967.

Left: Two battle-weary Leathernecks of the 26th Marine Regiment take cover in a rainstorm during Operation Bold Mariner. The cordon operation on the Batangan Peninsula in Quang Ngai Province was aimed at uncovering and destroying the Viet Cong and its political infrastructure in remote villages and hamlets.

Captain James P. Sheehan talks on the radio just before the final assault on Hill 881 N on April 30, 1967. The hill was one of several strategically important hills surrounding Khe Sahn. The Marines are from G (Golf) Company, 2nd Battalion, 3rd Marine Regiment, 3rd Marine Division.

1st Air Cav combed the Bong Son plain and the mountain valleys to the west, a Communist stronghold since World War II. Making effective use of their own helicopters and the added firepower of B-52s, Air Force fighter-bombers, and the guns of the 7th Fleet, the Cav decimated three enemy regiments, capturing numerous VC suspects and tons of war materiel.

Farther north, in Quang Ngai Province, the men of the 1st Marine Division pushed out from their Chu Lai enclave into the Viet Cong–dominated villages that surrounded them. Between February and early April, they battled the enemy and the monsoon rains in four separate excursions into the An Hoa basin. During Operation Utah, a joint effort with South Vietnamese forces, the Marines encountered NVA regulars for the first time. In three days of fierce battle, the heavily armed North Vietnamese regiment lost a third of its strength but inflicted more than five hundred casualties, including ninety-eight Marines killed in action. "They're not supermen," observed one survivor, "but they can fight."

It was a lesson that the rest of the Marines would learn in July when the 324B NVA Division crossed the DMZ and headed toward Quang Tri City with the apparent intention of annexing South Vietnam's northernmost provinces. Six Marine and five ARVN battalions struck back in Operation Hastings, the largest allied operation of the war to date. Establishing a forward base at Dong Ha, the Marines attacked north and west toward Cam Lo and "Helicopter Valley," where the 3rd Battalion of the 4th Marines endured a massed human-wave assault by one thousand NVA soldiers. Only after napalm strikes within fifty feet of their position were the Marines able to drive the attackers off. For the next three weeks, more than eight thousand Marines and three thousand South Vietnamese

As part of Operation Hastings, Marines of Hotel Company, 2nd Battalion, 4th Marine Regiment, take to the water as they move to join up with other elements of their battalion in Dong Ha.

soldiers fought a savage conventional battle against as many as twelve thousand enemy troops. By August 3, when Hastings came to an end, the North Vietnamese had been sent reeling back across the DMZ with more than eight hundred dead.

When the NVA resumed the attack several weeks later, the Marines met them again in Operation Prairie, employing helicopter assaults, massed artillery fire, naval gunfire, air support, and tanks in a series of costly assaults against enemy strongpoints. The operation, which continued into January 1967, netted more than one thousand enemy KIA. But the defense of the northern border cost the Marines as well. Despite lavish use of supporting arms, the fighting since July had claimed 365 Marine lives, with another 1,662 wounded. Forced to counter this new threat, the Marine command shifted 3rd Division headquarters plus two regiments and most of a Marine helicopter group to Quang Tri in October, leaving a severely stretched 1st Marine Division with responsibility for the three southern provinces of I Corps.

The fighting in the north was a sign of things to come, as was Operation Attleboro, a massive search-and-destroy sweep through the heart of the enemy's War Zone C. The initial penetration was made in September by the newly arrived 196th Light Infantry Brigade. For several weeks, contact with the enemy was sporadic, but by mid-October the 196th was beginning to uncover considerable quantities of rice and documents. When the brigade moved closer to the Cambodian border during the first days of November, it ran smack into the 9th VC Division, returning to the site of its June battles with the 1st Infantry Division.

While the outnumbered men of the 196th, plus reinforcements from the 25th Infantry Division, fought for their survival in the tangled jungle west of the Michelin rubber plantation, MACV hurled the 1st Infantry Division, the 173rd Airborne Battalion, and a brigade each from the 4th and 25th Infantry Divisions into the battle. The concentrated force of more than twenty-two thousand American troops, backed by B-52 strikes and more than ten thousand rounds of artillery, drove the twice-beaten enemy soldiers back into Cambodia. They left 1,100 dead and tons of supplies behind.

Less pleasing to MACV were the nearly one thousand American casualties, including 155 KIA, and the temporary disablement of the 196th, whose novice troops had been severely shaken by their rough initiation to combat. But Attleboro's resounding success convinced the American command that

US Air Force Capt. John R. Vydareny vaccinates a Vietnamese woman against plague during a medical civic action program (MEDCAP) visit to the village of Phu Gia in South Vietnam.

Private First Class Alan Wondra conducts a class in English at a Vietnamese school in Cat Lai during a civic action program of the 199th Infantry Brigade.

multidivisional search-and-destroy operations against Communist base areas and supply routes would bring the enemy to battle and destroy him. Much of 1967 would be spent testing that belief.

By the time Operation Attleboro came to an end, the military dimension of the Vietnamese conflict overshadowed all other aspects of US involvement in that troubled country. But alongside the cries of battle were the voices of other Americans—men and women, military and civilian, private and official, in Washington and Vietnam—who attempted in the midst of war to continue the job of nation-building that had first brought the United States to Vietnam.

To fight what Johnson called "the other war," the two nations devised an ambitious Rural Development (RD) Program featuring teams of young Vietnamese trained in propaganda and social services who would go out into the villages to build popular support for the government. Unfortunately, Saigon's interest in the program turned out to be largely rhetorical. Poorly trained and ill-supported, the RD cadres accomplished little.

Far more successful were the thousands of individual Americans working in the Vietnamese countryside: from employees of

A Marine officer radios in a situation report after fierce fighting for Hill 881 N.

the United States Agency for International Development (USAID), who sponsored programs in land reform, local government, and public health, to workers with the Christian and Missionary Alliance, who provided food, clothing, and medicine as well as spiritual comfort to the war-torn villages where they labored; from agents with the United States Information Service (USIS), who showed films on sanitation and democracy to rural peasants, to the young men and women of the private International Voluntary Service, who operated schools, experimented with new crops, and conducted family-planning clinics. Some of the most meaningful work was undertaken by American servicemen. Both under the official auspices of MACV's Civic Action Program and on their own initiative, US soldiers and Marines dug wells, built bridges, stocked pig farms, distributed food and clothing, dispensed medicine, and trained local volunteers in rudimentary healthcare techniques.

Unfortunately, by the end of 1966, the constantly growing armed conflict threatened to overwhelm everything the United States was trying to achieve for South Vietnam: democracy, development, independence. At the same time, the war rained down destruction on North Vietnam, eroded the prestige of the United States around the world, and jeopardized Johnson's Great Society. Yet neither side was ready for peace, except on its own terms.

North Vietnam, which refused to negotiate at all until the bombing stopped, insisted that the United States remove its troops from South Vietnam, withdraw support from the existing Saigon regime, recognize the National Liberation Front (NLF) as a legitimate partner in a coalition government, and accept the eventual unification of North and South as mandated by the Geneva agreements. But the Johnson administration would not stop the bombing until Hanoi ceased its support of the southern insurgency, and the US refused to accept any South Vietnamese government in which the Viet Cong played a role, implicitly denying the possibility of unification.

Neither Washington nor Hanoi was ready to concede defeat or compromise on the central issue that divided them—the political future of South Vietnam.

Hanoi's attempt to crush the ARVN had been thwarted, and US troop strength in Vietnam now totaled 385,000, and Westmoreland was even now drafting requests for more troops that would raise the level to 542,000. The buildup had enabled American forces to take the offensive in 1966 and make the first serious forays into major Communist base areas. Thanks to their superior mobility and firepower, American troops had yet to suffer a significant defeat, yet Washington's swift victory had been denied, and the gains made had not come cheaply. During the year, US forces had suffered more than thirty-five thousand casualties, including 5,008 dead.

By the end of 1966, it was becoming apparent that the real war was just beginning. If Johnson persisted because he thought the US would win, the North Vietnamese persisted because they believed they couldn't lose.

A Marine runs for cover while under fire on the top of Hill 881 N on April 30, 1967.

Prairie

During the first days of July 1966, the 324B NVA Division crossed the DMZ into Quang Tri Province. Within three weeks, eight thousand Marines drove the invaders back into North Vietnam after some of the toughest fighting of the war. Yet even then, US intelligence was reporting evidence of a new Communist incursion. To meet this threat, the Marine command launched Operation Prairie. The American plan of attack was to go after the enemy and go after him hard. Five-man Stingray reconnaissance teams would be inserted near the border to explore suspected enemy avenues of approach for signs of reinfiltration. Once contact was made, the recon teams would call in artillery from Cam Lo or helicopter gunships and strike aircraft from Da Nang. Meanwhile, Marine infantry units would wait nearby to relieve, reinforce, or exploit offensive opportunities.

Starting in early August, the 2nd Battalion clashed with North Vietnamese units over twenty square miles of mountain jungle. At the beginning of September, the area of operations shifted into the Con Thien region. The Marine command decided to meet the new threat with an amphibious assault from the coast. Called Deck House IV, the maneuver was carried out by the 1st Battalion, 26th Marines in its capacity as 7th Fleet Special Landing Force. Initial sea and helicopter assaults on September 15 met little resistance, but within hours the 1/26 was heavily engaged. For ten days, the battalion doggedly swept the Cua Viet River Valley, killing 254 NVA while suffering 203 casualties of its own, before driving the enemy back across the border.

Even as the North Vietnamese retreated from the coastal plain, they were trading savage blows with the 4th Marines for control of key infiltration routes through the mountain valleys north of the Rockpile. The battle centered on the Nui Cay Tre ridge line where the enemy had built his most elaborate fortifications, and in particular on two hills rising 400 and 480 meters out of the dense jungle. The first attempt to take the ridge was made by the 1/4 Marines, who battered enemy entrenchments on the southern slope for two and a half days with nothing to show for their efforts but nine dead men. When it became clear that attacking the ridge from the south was futile, Lt. Col. William J. Masterpool's 3rd Battalion was ordered to mount an assault from the east and turn the enemy's flank.

On the morning of September 22, helicopters carried the battalion into the jungle three miles from the ridge line. At first, the battalion had more trouble with the dense vegetation than it did with the NVA. For three days, the Marines struggled in the tangled green darkness, sometimes halting entirely until bombs or napalm blasted a path through the jungle. What they saw as they approached Hill 400 did not improve morale, either. Recalled one officer, there were "more and more enemy positions, including enough huts in the ravines to harbor a regiment, and piles and piles of ammunition."

Led by Kilo and Lima Companies, the 3rd Battalion began moving uphill on August 26 against determined resistance. "The NVA was damn clever," recounted Capt. Roger Ryman. "Invariably they'd pick just the right piece of terrain, where it was so narrow that we couldn't maneuver on the flanks, and they'd dig in and wait for us in the bottleneck." For two days, the Marines slowly gained ground behind periodic artillery barrages. Then, on

Opposite page: Heavily laden Marines patrol near the DMZ during Operation Prairie. Their objective was to seek out and destroy invading enemy units from NVA Division 324B.

the morning of the 28th, the NVA counterattacked. Without warning, dozens of grenades bounced down the hill into the Marine lines ahead of screaming North Vietnamese infantrymen. A platoon sergeant from Kilo Company remembered the battle: "The stuff was so thick you couldn't tell who was firing, Charlie or us. They had everything—mortars, mines, and heavy weapons—and they had ladders in the trees for spotters to climb up and direct fire." After an hour of fighting, the enemy backed off. By the end of the day, the Marines controlled Hill 400 and prepared to advance to their final objective, Hill 484.

With Mike Company in advance, the battalion spent five days covering the three kilometers separating the two hills, then launched an all-out assault on October 4 into the teeth of the NVA defenses. The attack stalled under a hail of automatic-weapons fire, and the steepness of the terrain made it impossible to call in artillery without risking the Marines themselves. Unable to drive the North Vietnamese from their fortifications, the infantry pulled back while Marine air and artillery pounded the enemy positions.

At 10:00 the next morning, Mike Company tried again, this time using direct fire from tanks on

An assault by the 3rd Battalion, 4th Marines, on the NVA holding Hill 484.

prearranged concentration points. By noon, the 2nd Platoon gained the summit. The fighting raged for another hour and a half before the NVA broke contact, leaving behind ten bodies and a score of bloody trails leading into the thick jungle. The long battle was finally over, but the hard-won victory was not soon forgotten. Hereafter, Nui Cay Tre would be known as Mutter's Ridge, after the radio call sign of the 3rd Battalion.

At its height, Operation Prairie involved eight Marine infantry battalions supported by artillery units, Navy gunships, and Marine tactical aircraft. The fighting killed nearly 1,400 NVA soldiers, the largest number of enemy casualties in a single Marine operation to that date, and seriously degraded the 324B Division. Yet the operation had also cost the Marines—more than two hundred dead and more than 1,200 wounded. And if the enemy was badly hurt, he was far from beaten. Driven back

Marines take a break and share a meal of C-rations during Operation Prairie.

across the DMZ for the second time in six months by the overwhelming weight of American men and machines, the enemy had again retreated to safe havens over the border to repair his losses and prepare for a fresh assault. One thing was for sure, concluded a senior Marine commander at year's end, "they haven't quit."

Masher/White Wing

When Maj. Gen. Harry W. O. Kinnard brought 1st Cav to An Khe in September 1965, his mission was clear: to stop the enemy from driving to the coast and cutting South Vietnam in two. Within weeks of their arrival in-country, Kinnard's men rose to that challenge in a series of violent battles along the Cambodian border. The bloody Ia Drang campaign of November 1965 blunted the Communist offensive in the Central Highlands and validated the concept of air mobility in land warfare. Heartened by the division's success, Kinnard immediately shifted his attention to another Communist stronghold, the northeastern corner of Binh Dinh Province.

The intended area of operations ranged from rice fields and tree lines along the thickly populated coastal plain to steep, bamboo-forested slopes and rugged mountain valleys farther inland. Designated by the Saigon government a "national priority area," the region was protected by the 22nd ARVN Division, which had more than it could handle trying to keep Highway 1 open and pacify villages dominated by the Communists for more than two decades.

Kinnard divided the target area into four sectors, then devised a plan of attack that made the most of the American advantages in firepower and mobility. Operating out of Bong Son, a small airstrip and Special Forces camp, the Air Cav would mount a series of fast-moving "hammer-and-anvil" operations in which some of the troopers flushed the enemy toward other friendly units waiting in blocking positions. The men on the ground would be supported by tactical air, gunships, and artillery batteries continuously moved forward by helicopter from one emplacement to another.

The American general dubbed his conception Operation Masher and selected the 1st Cav's 3rd Brigade to spearhead the attack. Normally consisting of the 1st and 2nd Battalions, 7th Cavalry, the brigade was now augmented by the 1st and 2nd Battalions, 12th Cavalry, the 1st Squadron, 9th Cavalry, and assorted artillery and aviation units. Directing the 5,700-man task force was 3rd Brigade commander Col. Harold G. "Hal" Moore, a tough, hard-driving officer who had recently received the Distinguished Service Cross for his actions during the Ia Drang campaign.

The first days of the operation were bedeviled by bad weather and bad luck. Moving out from An Khe toward forward staging areas on January 25, a C-123 carrying forty-two cavalrymen crashed into a fog-shrouded mountain, killing everyone on board. When the 3rd Brigade launched its initial assault into the Bong Son plain three days later, rain and low ceilings restricted helicopter flights and virtually eliminated tactical air support. These problems had little effect on the 1st Battalion, which encountered only mild enemy resistance. For the 2nd Battalion, however, D-day almost turned into disaster when Charlie Company dropped right on top of an NVA battalion at a village called Phung Du.

Enemy fire ripped through their helicopters before they ever touched down, scattering the Americans across a kilometer of rice fields. When the men tried to regroup, NVA machine guns and mortar fire methodically cut them down. Attempting to come to the rescue, Alpha Company ran into heavy resistance just south of the village, only barely making it into a nearby cemetery, where the troopers found what shelter they could behind waist-high mounds that marked the grave sites. During the afternoon, helicopters repeatedly attempted to land reinforcements but could not penetrate the intense enemy fire. By the end of the day, the 2nd Battalion was divided, pinned down, and cut off.

Under the cover of darkness and a heavy rain, the Americans managed to consolidate their positions and tend their wounded. Shortly after daybreak, the clouds began to lift, allowing A-1 Skyraiders and B-57 Canberra bombers to pummel enemy positions with napalm and high explosives. In midmorning, two companies from the 2nd Battalion, 12th Cavalry arrived on the scene accompanied by a furious Colonel Moore. "The old man was not pleased," remembered Sgt. Maj. Basil Plumley. "We moved around and talked to the men. The biggest thing they needed was leadership and guidance to move them out of there." Moore provided both, ordering preparatory artillery strikes and tear-gas barrages, then directing an assault by the 2/12 against the enemy fortifications. Once the village had been cleared, Masher began to move forward as planned.

During the first few days of February, the remaining North Vietnamese units slipped through the American net and withdrew to the west, their escape aided by bad weather that hampered US reconnaissance flights. As contact with the enemy decreased, the cavalrymen returned to their forward bases and the first phase of Operation Masher came to a close. Despite the early reverses, the results of a week's worth of fighting were impressive: an estimated 1,358 enemy dead, at a cost of 119 American lives, including those killed in the C-123 crash. US intelligence estimated that two battalions of the NVA 22nd Regiment had been put out of action, a "loss of equipment, personnel, and prestige," stated the division report, that "will be difficult to overcome."

A look of intensity rests on the face of a soldier from the 1st Cav as he fires his M60 machine gun during a firefight in the Central Lowlands of Vietnam.

Under NVA fire, Staff Sgt. Joe Musial crawls to the aid of a mortally wounded member of his squad, February 14, 1967.

Even as Phase I concluded, men and supplies were being readied for an immediate resumption of activity, and the name of the operation was changed to White Wing, reflecting Washington's desire to avoid overly aggressive connotations in its ongoing battle for public opinion back home. Delayed for what turned out to be three crucial days by more bad weather, the assault into the rugged mountain valley commenced on February 7, when four cavalry battalions were lifted by helicopter onto high ground, then swept down the mountain slopes to the valley floor. The Americans expected fierce resistance to their penetration of the Communist base area, and US troopers did find an elaborate system of fortifications and booby traps. But their tardy arrival had given the enemy time to escape. After three days of fruitless searching, disappointed division commanders closed out Phase II and turned their attention to the southwest sector of the operational area.

The third phase of Masher/White Wing was directed toward another mountain valley called Kim Son, also known as the Eagle's Claw because of its distinctive shape. Reversing the tactics used in Phase II, Colonel Moore put the 3rd Brigade and its supporting artillery down at the bottom of the valley, then sent patrols into subsidiary canyons to flush out the Viet Cong. After subduing a VC company, the 2/7 Cavalry began scouring the valley floor. The troopers discovered a Viet Cong hospital, a Communist weapons factory, and, most important, documents pinpointing a VC Main Force battalion in nearby Son Long Valley.

More successful than anyone had anticipated, the two-week Phase III campaign claimed in all more than seven hundred enemy KIA, plus a substantial quantity of arms, ammunition, and materiel.

Masher/White Wing was formally closed down on March 6. The operation had been an outstanding military success, proving again the effectiveness of air mobility and demonstrating anew the might of American firepower. During forty-one days of fighting against the NVA 3rd Division, the cavalrymen had slashed their way through four Communist base areas, killing 1,342 enemy soldiers, capturing 633, and detaining 1,087 VC suspects. Kinnard, who judged the division's performance "at least 50 percent better" than the thirty-eight-day campaign in the Ia Drang, claimed the 1st Cav had driven Communist military forces from the coastal plain, rendered five of the enemy's nine battalions unfit for combat, and freed 140,000 Vietnamese "from VC domination."

The violence the Americans visited upon the enemy, however, also proved devastating to the people who lived in the Bong Son district. The lavish use of firepower—more than 140,000 rounds of artillery alone during the six-week operation—ravaged the villages in which the Communists entrenched themselves and drove more than sixteen thousand civilians from their homes.

Nor were refugees the only problem. Smashing the enemy's military units was one thing; breaking up his political apparatus was quite another. Unless there was continuity between the military and pacification efforts, unless the Communist infrastructure was rooted out of the villages once the enemy's base areas had been cleared, his military forces were sure to return. But the South Vietnamese authorities were not prepared to carry out the security and pacification programs necessary to take advantage of the 1st Cav's battlefield victories. As a result, enemy soldiers began filtering back into the region less than a week after the end of Masher/White Wing, prompting new operations with names like Thayer and Irving and Crazy Horse and Davy Crockett.

But the results were always the same. Over the course of the war, the men of the 1st Cav would return to the area again and again as they struggled in vain to transfer control of Binh Dinh Province from the Communists to the Saigon government. In the process, they would learn to their bitter dismay what American arms and ingenuity could accomplish in Vietnam, and what they could not.

Opposite page: Marine Gunnery Sergeant Jeremiah Purdie (center), struggles for balance moments after an exploding shell from an NVA attack has wounded his commanding officer, Capt. James Carroll, and another man at Mutter's Ridge, October 5, 1966, during Operation Prairie.

Ignoring his own wounds, Gunnery Sergeant Purdie tries to aid Captain Carroll, who lies mortally wounded after the NVA attack.

CHAPTER THREE

STALEMATE

"The guerrilla swims in the sea of the people."

Attributed to Mao Zedong

"All who served the revolution have plowed the sea."

Attributed to Simon Bolivar

General Westmoreland must have acknowledged at times, if only to himself, the truth of Mao's oft-quoted aphorism, just as he must have felt empathy with The Liberator's frustration at trying to wrangle nineteenth-century Latin America's diverse and squabbling nations into a cohesive whole. While Westmoreland may have seen himself as a liberator, keeping South Vietnam free from communism, he would have had to admit that even he could not tell friend from foe in the sea of the Vietnamese population. The US forces were virtually invincible in battle—they won almost every fight, thanks to overwhelming superiority in firepower—but once the mighty war machine had plowed through an area, the conquered ground was abandoned and the sea closed in again. Nothing better illustrates this than Operation Cedar Falls.

A Marine stands watch in an observation tower as Lieutenant Commander McElroy, chaplain of the 3rd Battalion, 26th Marines, holds mass on Hill 950.

Bamboo huts go up in flames during an effort by US Army infantrymen to completely level the Viet Cong stronghold of Ben Suc during Operation Cedar Falls. Vietnamese had earlier been evacuated from the village area.

By the beginning of 1967, Westmoreland had at his disposal substantial South Vietnamese assets, including eleven Army divisions, two independent regiments, a Marine brigade, ten armored cavalry groups, twenty Ranger battalions, six artillery battalions, and a host of territorial and police units scattered about the country. In addition, the American commander could call upon the services of two Korean infantry divisions, a Korean Marine brigade, and a combined Australian–New Zealand task force.

Westmoreland's plans for the new year, however, depended chiefly on the hundreds of thousands of US soldiers and Marines who now called South Vietnam their temporary home. Organized into seven infantry divisions, two paratrooper brigades, two light infantry brigades, one armored cavalry regiment, and a reinforced Special Forces group, it was these men who would bear the primary responsibility for meeting the enemy's Main Force units in battle and defeating him. And it was from the big US bases and strongpoints that Westmoreland initiated Phase II of his strategy of attrition—moving out from the populated areas into the enemy's sanctuaries where the Communist Main Force units could be located and destroyed. The American command launched a series of multibattalion thrusts against Communist base areas and supply corridors. These huge search-and-destroy operations utilized superior American firepower and technology to reap a punishing harvest of enemy dead. But they also left behind a growing toll of American casualties while steadily drawing more and more US forces farther and farther from South Vietnam's cities and villages.*

Phase II began with Operation Cedar Falls, a massive search-and-destroy sweep against a longtime Communist stronghold northwest of Saigon known as the Iron Triangle. During the second week of January 1967, elements of the 1st, 25th, and 9th Infantry Divisions, the 196th Infantry Brigade, the 173rd Airborne Brigade, and the 11th Armored Cavalry Regiment—in all, some sixteen thousand American soldiers—joined an equal number of ARVN troops in the operation, named for the hometown of a 1st Division soldier, Robert J. Hibbs, who had been killed in 1966 and awarded the Medal of Honor. Preceded by B-52 strikes and twenty thousand airdropped leaflets warning inhabitants to leave the area, twenty battalions crashed into the sixty-square-mile triangle on January 8 in search of the 9th VC Division. By the end of the first day, the Americans had cordoned off the fortified village of Ben Suc, removed six thousand villagers to refugee camps, bulldozed the town's dwellings, and destroyed an elaborate network of tunnels and supply caches that honeycombed the ground beneath the surface.

Over the next eighteen days, American and South Vietnamese soldiers evacuated the region's four main villages as air strikes, artillery, and giant Rome plows demolished the surrounding jungle. Meanwhile, six- to ten-man teams of "tunnel rats" crawled through nearly twelve miles of underground corridors unearthing tons of supplies and thousands of enemy documents. By the time the operation ended, the Viet Cong had suffered the discovery and seizure of a key headquarters complex, the destruction of twenty years' worth of tunnels and fortifications, and the loss of nearly eight hundred men. After thirty thousand US and ARVN troops had spent three weeks blasting their way through the Iron Triangle, 1st Division commander Maj. Gen. William DePuy called the destruction of the Communist stronghold "a blow from which the VC in this area may never recover." But the elaborate operation had not been able to trap the main body of enemy soldiers, who filtered through allied lines toward the Cambodian border, and scarcely two weeks later an American officer reconnoitering the area by helicopter reported that "the Iron Triangle was again literally crawling with what appeared to be Viet Cong riding bicycles or wandering around on foot."

Westmoreland's strategy for defeating the Communists required a military force large enough to protect the populated areas of South Vietnam and to take the war to the enemy in the remote jungles along the border.

---

*By New Year's Day, 1967, 8,694 American servicemen had been killed in Vietnam. That year would add 11,363 names to that list.

Despite the increasing tempo of fighting during 1966, the first eighteen months of active US involvement had been devoted primarily to building up that military machine. By the close of 1966, there were 385,000 US troops in Vietnam, a figure that continued to grow like Jack's beanstalk; by Christmas 1967 there would be 485,600.

That sounds like a lot of soldiers, but only 20 percent of these men comprised American combat units; most Americans who served in Vietnam were staff and support personnel. For every mud-coated soldier humping through the rain, rice paddies, and jungles, there were a half-dozen mail clerks, typists, maintenance men, air traffic controllers, briefing officers, military policemen, transport pilots, supply sergeants, nurses, chaplains, or truck drivers. And for all the newspaper photos of mortar-blasted fire support bases carved out of the jungle, most Americans who served in Vietnam spent their tours of duty at sprawling rear-echelon bases like Bien Hoa, Tan Son Nhut, Qui Nhon, Nha Trang, Phu Bai, Da Nang, or Cam Ranh Bay.

Aside from an occasional rocket attack and the threat of VC terrorism, life in the rear could be quite agreeable. Living accommodations were comfortable, if not luxurious. The menus at messes and snack bars featured steaks and ice cream, while nearby officers' and enlisted men's clubs served liquor and cold beer at rock-bottom prices. Off-duty soldiers could read a book in air-conditioned libraries, play volleyball, go water-skiing on the Saigon River, or catch their favorite television shows on the Armed Forces Television Network. GIs stationed at the larger US installations could choose from two or three different first-run films a week at base movie theaters or pick up anything from potato chips to portable stereos and custom-tailored Hong Kong suits at the local PX.

The stateside food and drink, the elaborate recreational facilities, and bountiful consumer goods were a deliberate effort by MACV to maintain morale. Coupled with tight restrictions that isolated most servicemen from the surrounding Vietnamese community, however, the material abundance had a disorienting effect on many soldiers, who found it difficult to reconcile their relatively plush existence with the death and destruction that surrounded them. Critics charged that the profusion of clubs, slot machines, steam baths, luxury purchases, and other "nonessentials" overtaxed the US logistical system and created endless opportunities for corruption. It also exacerbated the division between rear-echelon personnel and those assigned to combat units.

For the men who actually fought the war, "home" was apt to be a good deal less comfortable. It might be a huge, dusty compound like the 1st Cav's headquarters at An Khe, which lacked many of the amenities of Saigon but still boasted its own twenty-five-acre "entertainment area" complete with bars and brothels. Or it might be the much smaller and starker confines of a fire support base. There a soldier could still count on a hot meal, a drink—sometimes even a cold one—and a change of clothes, but little more than sandbags and dirt to protect him from either the weather or enemy sapper attacks.

Then there was R&R. After serving a minimum of three to six months in-country, every soldier who served in Vietnam, whether he was a grunt or a file clerk, was entitled to a week-long, some-expenses-paid vacation from the war: R&R, which stood for Rest & Recreation, or Rest & Recuperation, or another variation on the theme. The US military paid for the airfare to

A Marine with 3rd Battalion, 3rd Marines, writes home from his bunker near Quang Tri. Candles were much sought after to light the dark bunkers. This Marine poured mortar wax into an empty can of Carling Black Label beer to create a handy desk lamp.

Right: Actress Carroll Baker throws her arms open to the men of aircraft carrier USS *Ticonderoga* as the ship steams through the South China Sea. Baker was a member of the Bob Hope troupe that brought cheer to US servicemen in Vietnam.

Below: Actor John Wayne signs Pfc. Fonsell Wofford's helmet during his visit to the 3rd Battalion, 7th Marines, at Chu Lai.

Thousands of service personnel listen to Ann-Margret sing during a show in Da Nang.

any of several approved destinations and a room at an approved hotel. Other expenses, which usually boiled down to food, drink, and sex, were the responsibility of the soldier. For an infantry soldier fighting day after day in the swamps, jungles, and hills of Vietnam, to be suddenly plucked from the field by chopper and within twenty-four hours find yourself in a Bangkok bar with a cold beer in your hand and a girl by your side was like taking the express elevator to heaven. Getting on the return flight was the hard part.

Other destination choices included Hawaii, Hong Kong, Sydney, and Tokyo. Most of the married men went to Hawaii to spend a week with their wives.

Some soldiers were also allowed to take in-country R&R. An in-country R&R was not a guaranteed perk. It was bonus handed out by commanders for outstanding performance, and did not count against regular R&R leave. Soldiers were billeted at an R&R center where they checked their weapons and then headed for the beaches and bars. For the Marines, the in-country R&R center was the beach at Da Nang; for the Army, it was the southern port city of Vung Tau, which in times past had been a favorite getaway spot for French colonials and the Saigon elite. During the war, the town was full of bars and steam-bath/massage-parlor operations. After a three-day R&R, the soldier returned to his unit somewhat refreshed and, if he had been careful, with a clean bill of health.

Above: Following a hard day during Operation Yellowstone, a few members of Alpha Company, 3rd Battalion, 22nd Infantry (Mechanized), 25th Infantry Division, gather around a guitar player and sing a few songs.

Right: Corporal Bob MacDonald, a rifleman with Headquarters, 9th Marine Regiment, takes time out to relax in a cool stream with an easy chair and his favorite magazine.

Four weeks after Operation Cedar Falls had killed an estimated eight hundred soldiers of the 9th VC Division and pushed many more across the border to the security of Cambodia, Westmoreland took up the pursuit, sending twenty-two American battalions northwest of the Iron Triangle into War Zone C as part of Operation Junction City. Spearheaded by the 503rd Airborne Brigade, which on February 22 conducted the first US combat parachute assault since the Korean War, Junction City was a classic "cordon and sweep" maneuver designed to trap the Viet Cong division with speed and numbers, then hammer it to pieces with overwhelming firepower.

An infantryman is lowered by members of a recon platoon during Operation Oregon, a search-and-destroy mission conducted by the 1st Reconnaissance Squadron, 9th Cavalry, 1st Cav three kilometers west of Duc Pho, Quang Ngai Province.

The paratroopers formed the eastern side of an enormous horseshoe. To the west were the 196th Light Infantry Brigade and the 3rd Brigade of the 4th Infantry Division. To the north were eight battalions of the 1st Infantry Division, carried into battle by some 250 helicopters in one of the largest air assaults in the history of Army aviation. As soon as the blocking forces were in place, units of the 25th Infantry Division and the 11th Armored Cavalry swept north through the thickly wooded terrain while Rome plows and heavy bulldozers stripped away great chunks of jungle to deprive the Communists of concealment. When the advancing troops collided with enemy concentrations, the Americans called in prodigious quantities of artillery and air power, including airdropped cluster bombs (CBUs) that ripped through the tangled foliage with devastating results.

The large size of the operational zone, the ruggedness of the terrain, and the noise generated by large, mechanized American units made it almost impossible to surprise the enemy, most of whom scattered west across the Cambodian border. The high point of the allied effort in III Corps during 1967, Junction City demonstrated MACV's ability to swiftly penetrate heretofore-inviolable enemy sanctuaries in force, but the massive shock power of the multidivisional operation had largely spent itself in futile pursuit of an elusive quarry at a cost—$25 million, 282 Americans killed, 1,576 wounded—that some thought was well out of proportion to the results.

An air drop of supplies during Junction City, a successful but costly operation for allied forces.

Two hundred miles north, in the western reaches of the Central Highlands, the US 4th Infantry Division, operating out of its base camp near Pleiku, fought a different kind of border campaign in 1967. Between January and April, in a series of engagements known as Operation Sam Houston, the division devoted its attention to the area west of the Nam Sathay River in Kontum Province. At first, the infantrymen encountered only light resistance as they systematically uncovered and destroyed enemy tunnels and fortifications. But in mid-February, the North Vietnamese began to strike back. Shadowed by NVA reconnaissance teams and trail watchers, harassed by daytime snipers and nighttime mortar attacks, the GIs endured a growing number of vicious ambushes that sapped both their numbers and their morale. The North Vietnamese learned to position themselves so close to the Americans that effective supporting fire was impossible. Counterattacks typically resulted in heavy casualties from carefully prepared enemy flanking positions. And although such firefights could last well into the night, by daylight the enemy had invariably disappeared, taking his dead and wounded with him.

For all its difficulties and dangers, however, the contest against the NVA in the western highlands could not compare in scope or savagery to the continuing battles waged by the US Marines along the shattered hills of the DMZ. By the end of 1966, the 3rd Marine Division had established a series of combat bases strung out between Route 9 and the DMZ. From these isolated strongpoints bristling with artillery and barbed wire, the Marines fought a succession of costly battles during 1967, as heavily armed Communist regulars tested the Americans in their own bloody war of attrition.

Heavy fighting broke out on February 27 when a Marine reconnaissance patrol intercepted an entire NVA regiment near Cam Lo, precipitating a series of ambushes against a hastily dispatched relief force that left one Marine battalion commander and dozens of his men dead. The same pattern was repeated on a much larger scale in April at Khe Sanh when a squad from Bravo Company, 9th Marines, ran into advance elements of the 325C NVA Division. As reinforcements poured into the small western outpost over the next three days, it quickly became apparent that the enemy was heavily entrenched in the hills surrounding the base. It took twelve days of continuous battle, a relentless bombardment by Marine artillery, helicopter gunships, attack aircraft, and nearly six hundred American casualties to drive the North Vietnamese back across the DMZ.

The Marines immediately sought to press their hard-won advantage with Operation Hickory. Launched on May 18, this multibattalion strike marked the first time that US forces had penetrated the demilitarized zone. The complex scheme of maneuvers utilized the full range of Marine combat assets, including helicopter gunships, fighter-bombers, and amphibious landing craft. Backed by a cascade of supporting arms, the Americans smashed through heavily fortified NVA bunker complexes all the way to the Ben Hai River, then wheeled south to sweep up the remnants of enemy units scattered by the lightning assault.

The first battle of Khe Sanh had cost the North Vietnamese an estimated one thousand KIA; Hickory, at least as many. But neither defeat had any appreciable effect on Hanoi. With the luxury of rear bases in Laos and North Vietnam secure from US attack, battered enemy units simply regrouped, refitted, and returned to battle. By midsummer, the NVA was threatening US

Private First Class David S. Whitman with a company of the 3rd Marine Division that fought its way up a mountain near the Laos border.

US Marines carry a fallen comrade in a makeshift litter along a trail to a landing zone. The Marine was killed during Operation Baxter, October 21, 1967.

defenses in the eastern part of the demilitarized zone where the Marines labored to construct the first stage of a massive anti-infiltration barrier. Dubbed "McNamara's Line" after its chief proponent, Secretary of Defense Robert McNamara, this combination of mines, electronic sensors, guard towers, and physical obstacles was an attempt to accomplish by other means what the bombing of North Vietnam had failed to do. Of dubious value and inordinate expense, the grandiose project did not survive the year. Nonetheless, the barrier and its initial terminus—the combat base at Con Thien—became the focal point of NVA artillery, rocket, and ground attacks.

Attempting to relieve the steadily growing pressure on Con Thien, three Marine battalions fought a furious battle with the 90th NVA Regiment in early July. Against waves of North Vietnamese infantry backed by intense enemy artillery fire, the Americans directed a thunderous bombardment of air, artillery, and naval gunfire that claimed more than 1,300 enemy lives but did nothing to stop the steady encirclement of the besieged combat base.

Throughout August and September, the two sides engaged in a fearful contest of supporting arms that drove Con Thien's defenders burrowing into the ground for protection and left the tortured landscape littered with the bodies of hundreds of North Vietnamese soldiers. Only under the devastating impact of nearly eight hundred B-52 bombing runs did the enemy finally retreat in early October.

Driven back along the northern frontier, the Communists struck farther south, attacking an ARVN outpost in Phuoc Long Province on October 27 and the Cambodian border town of Loc Ninh two days later. Both assaults were thrown back with heavy enemy casualties. Then on November 3, a defector revealed that the NVA 1st Division, after months of elaborate preparation, was poised to attack the highlands town of Dak To. Seizing the opportunity to engage the enemy in force, the American command deployed all sixteen battalions of the 4th Infantry Division, the entire 173rd Airborne Brigade, a brigade from the 1st Air Cavalry, and six ARVN battalions into the narrow valleys and onto the precipitous, jungle-canopied ridges that surrounded the remote district capital.

As allied units probed south from Dak To during the first two weeks of November, they clashed repeatedly with well-armed NVA regulars. From the labyrinth of tunnels and camouflaged fortifications they had laboriously carved out of the steep hillsides, the Communists took a steady toll of American lives during these encounters, including a Veterans Day ambush that left 20 dead, 154 wounded, and 2 missing from a 200-man airborne task force. Four days later, a North Vietnamese mortar attack on the Dak To airfield destroyed two C-130 transports and blew up an ammunition dump in an explosion that sent an enormous fireball shooting thousands of feet into the night sky.

American soldiers take cover during the bombing of an ammunition dump in Dak To.

Top: Air operations from both the land and sea were carried out around the clock. Between 1965 and 1975, more than 3,300 fixed-wing aircraft, such as the A-7 pictured, and more than 5,400 helicopters were lost to hostile action and accidents.

Above: Navy aircraft carriers stationed off the coast of North Vietnam flew many of their missions under the cover of darkness. More than 530 aircraft were lost in combat and 329 more to operational causes, resulting in the deaths of 377 naval aviators; 179 more were taken as prisoners of war.

The blazing airfield proved the high-water mark of the Communist attempt to take Dak To. By the middle of the month, the weight of men and machines that MACV had hurled into battle began to show, pushing enemy units southwest toward their Cambodian sanctuaries. As they retreated, the North Vietnamese fought tenacious rear-guard actions, forcing the Americans to literally obliterate whole hilltops with supporting fire before units on the ground could claw their way forward in vicious hand-to-hand engagements. During the course of the operation, US forces fired 151,000 rounds of artillery, flew 2,096 tactical air sorties, and mounted 257 B-52 bombing strikes against enemy positions. Finally, after a savage five-day battle for Hill 875 in which 158 Americans and at least twice as many NVA were killed, North Vietnamese resistance came to an end.

As the battered 1st NVA Division limped into Cambodia, the American command celebrated the tremendous effort that had transported sixteen thousand allied troops into some of the most hostile territory in South Vietnam, maintained an astonishing level of logistical and fire support, and driven one of the enemy's best divisions from the field with losses estimated as high as 1,600 killed in action.

Air Power

The bulk of enemy casualties at Dak To, as they had been in every other major battle during the year, were the result of air strikes. The expansion of American ground forces during the previous two years had been more than matched by the increase of US air assets in Southeast Asia. By the end of 1967, the Air Force had more than sixty thousand personnel organized into one air command wing, nine tactical fighter wings, three strategic bombardment wings, and one air commando/special operations wing, plus communications groups, tactical control groups, and a welter of subsidiary units operating out of sixteen major air bases in South Vietnam, Thailand, and Guam. Alongside the Air Force were the seventy to one hundred carrier-based US Navy aircraft flying from Yankee Station some one hundred miles off the northern coast of South Vietnam and the six air groups—representing approximately five hundred helicopter and fixed-wing aircraft—of the 1st Marine Air Wing scattered throughout I Corps.

The aircraft used to wage the in-country war over South Vietnam included B-57 Canberra light bombers, F-100 Super Sabres for close air support, supersonic F-4 Phantoms, and prop-driven A-1 Skyraiders.

Above North Vietnam and Laos, the Air Force relied heavily on the F-105 Thunderchief, while Navy pilots flew the F-8 Crusader, the A-6A Intruder—the first all-weather attack aircraft—and later the A-7 Corsair. Utilized extensively for close air support and interdiction over South Vietnam and Laos but not yet subjected to North Vietnam's main air defense system were the giant B-52 Stratofortresses based in Thailand and Guam.

American warplanes were far outnumbered, however, by the thousands of observation, reconnaissance, cargo, tanker, transport, and command aircraft that daily filled the skies over Southeast Asia, not to mention helicopters of every kind and description flying cargo, troop transport, gunship, rescue, and medevac missions around the clock. By 1967, this aerial armada was responsible for more than fifty-three thousand air traffic "movements"—takeoffs, landings, and major flight pattern changes—in South Vietnam alone every single day.

Along with this growing aerial armada came mounting pressure on President Johnson to employ it without restraint against the enemy's heartland. The North Vietnamese weakened the hand of those in Washington who argued for caution when they took advantage of a February 1967 bombing pause to resupply their forces in South Vietnam at an unprecedented rate. Just as important, the steady increase in the number of US casualties had begun to undermine public confidence in Johnson's handling of the war. Most troublesome to him, however, were congressional hawks led by Mississippi senator John C. Stennis whose August hearings into the conduct of the air war sharply challenged White House control over the air campaign. The result was a continuing escalation of the bombing throughout Indochina.

In July, the president added forty new transportation and military installations to the Rolling Thunder target list, including the crucial Paul Doumer Bridge on the outskirts of Hanoi, which Air Force fighter-bombers hit for the first time on August 2. That same month, strikes were made against previously prohibited regions within the city limits of Hanoi and along the buffer zone near the Chinese border. During the remainder of the year, American pilots were let loose on virtually every military, industrial, and transportation target recommended by the Stennis committee.

By December 1967, the United States had dropped a total of 864,000 tons of bombs on the North Vietnamese—70 percent more than had been dropped in the entire Pacific Theater during World War II. The bombing had inflicted an estimated $300 million in damage on North Vietnam, seriously disrupted its agricultural production, and crippled its fragile industrial base. Although civilian casualties had generally been kept low, some cities were severely damaged; others were almost entirely destroyed.

The actual dollar cost of the air war to the United States, however, was far greater—some $900 million in lost aircraft alone, not to mention enormous operating and munitions expenditures. Had the bombing been successful, such deficit spending might have been accepted with equanimity. But the hard fact was that the air campaign against North Vietnam had failed utterly to meet its original objectives.

The United States constructed its military strategy in Southeast Asia around the assumption that air power would so devastate the North Vietnamese economy, so dramatically impede the flow of men and materiel south, and so discourage the people of North Vietnam that Hanoi would have no choice but to sue for peace. Yet, after an aerial onslaught unparalleled in history, the North Vietnamese were no closer to giving up than they had been at the beginning of 1965. Despite the destruction, the economy functioned. Despite the shortages and dislocations, there was no evidence of a significant loss of morale. And despite everything that American air power could do to stop it, the infiltration of men and supplies to the southern battlefields during 1967 was nearly three times greater than it had been before the bombing began.

The reasons for these failures included the limitations on air power posed by Vietnam's monsoon climate, triple-canopy jungle, and mountainous terrain—and the ingenuity and resourcefulness of the North Vietnamese. By evacuating civilians from the cities, dispersing industries, scattering petroleum and other types of storage facilities across the countryside, and cleverly camouflaging those targets that could not be moved, they were able to minimize the damage done by the American air raids. By raising an army of civilian workers armed with picks and shovels, they were

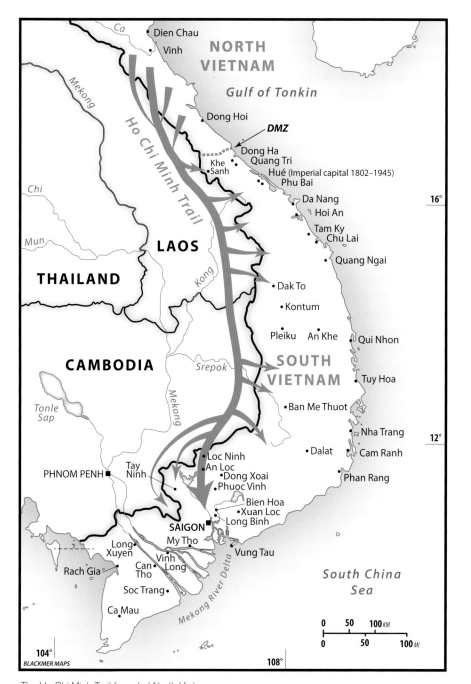

The Ho Chi Minh Trail funneled North Vietnamese troops, weapons, ammunition, and food from North Vietnam through the "neutral" nations of Laos and Cambodia into South Vietnam. Supplies were carried on the backs of soldiers and on bicycles, ox carts, and trucks rolling under a thick canopy of foliage. The trail remained in operation throughout the war despite years of deadly and destructive US bombing and defoliation.

able to effect repairs with remarkable speed and keep vital roadways open. And by creating one of the most sophisticated air defense systems in the world, they were able to make the United States pay a heavy price for its air offensive.

In the end, however, North Vietnamese survival rested on the material aid and technical assistance they received from their Communist allies, especially the Soviet Union and China. Hanoi's leaders took full advantage of the Sino-Soviet rivalry, skillfully playing one superpower against the other in their quest for increased aid. The success of their efforts was measured in the vast quantities of rice, small arms, ammunition, vehicles, fighter planes, surface-to-air missiles (SAMs), and tanks that their allies supplied. This cumulative contribution, estimated to be in excess of $2 billion from 1965 to 1968, more than made up for all the damage inflicted by the bombing.

To McNamara, the figures called for a reassessment of strategy. Convinced that the North Vietnamese would not give in "no matter how much bombing we do," McNamara proposed an unconditional bombing halt in hopes of appeasing antiwar critics within the United States and prodding Hanoi toward negotiations. He also urged the president to revise American ground strategy and place a ceiling on American troop levels. Although he did not put it in so many words, by the middle of 1967, the man who had once been a major proponent of escalation no longer had any hope of victory. For if air power had not brought the Communists to their knees, neither had General Westmoreland's strategy of attrition. The commitment of nearly half a million troops had saved South Vietnam from defeat and taken a heavy toll of enemy casualties. But the primary goal of grinding down the enemy until he hollered "uncle" was not happening. Despite official estimates of as many as 220,000 enemy soldiers killed since the deployment of US combat forces, overall Communist strength in South Vietnam stood at approximately 350,000 troops, compared to some two hundred thousand in June 1965.

In trying to account for this state of affairs, some questioned the accuracy of MACV's enemy casualty figures. There was little doubt that the confusions of battle, the difficulty of distinguishing Viet Cong guerrillas from ordinary peasants, command pressure, and the ambitions of junior officers all inflated the notoriously unreliable "body count"—by at least 30 percent, according to one Defense Department analysis. Far more important, however, Westmoreland's strategy ignored the fact that some two hundred thousand North Vietnamese reached draft age each year, a manpower pool far in excess of the number of enemy KIA, even when estimated by the most optimistic methods. Moreover, the Communists had time and terrain on their side. By fighting only when and where they chose, the Viet Cong and North Vietnamese were largely able to control how many casualties they suffered. When losses became too high, they simply scattered into the jungle or crossed the border into sanctuaries immune from US attack.

In short, Westmoreland's vaunted "cross-over point"—when enemy casualty rates would exceed the number of soldiers the Communists could replace through recruitment or infiltration—was never reached. Meanwhile, US casualty rates steadily increased, averaging 816 killed in action per month during the first half of 1967, compared to 477 per month during 1966. Along with swelling draft calls, the mounting American death toll further eroded domestic support for the war. On the other hand, Communist morale remained intact despite formidable losses and staggering hardships, thanks to an effective system of internal discipline and a firm conviction that they were defending their country against foreign invaders.

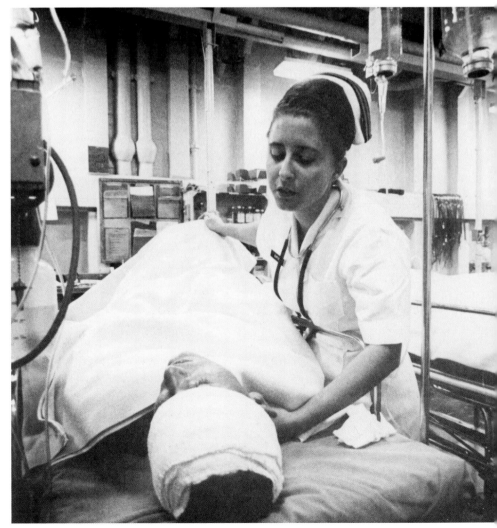

A nurse tends to a patient just out of surgery in the intensive care ward of the hospital ship USS *Repose*, steaming off the coast of Vietnam just south of the 17th parallel.

Neither the Americans nor their own political leaders had been able to inspire the same spirit of resistance among the people of South Vietnam. Much of the blame for this lay with the Saigon government, whose corrupt agents were more intent upon lining their own pockets than improving the living standards of the South Vietnamese people. Some of the onus rested on the ARVN, which ceded de facto control of whole provinces to the Viet Cong while alienating the rural population with its ineffectiveness and, often, its arrogance and brutality. But an important measure of responsibility also belonged to the US military command. The massive search-and-destroy operations that occupied so much of MACV's time and resources diverted attention from the social and political roots of the insurgency. They also wreaked havoc among the civilian population of the countryside.

Since it was common practice for the Viet Cong to fire on American troops from within villages, the Americans' reliance on firepower contributed to a

soaring rate of damage and death among the civilian population of the countryside. The widespread use of "free fire zones" and "harassment and interdiction" fire as a means of controlling enemy movements only made matters worse. So did the calculated attempt to discourage villagers from aiding the VC by burning their homes and evacuating them to crude refugee camps that eventually housed more than 20 percent of South Vietnam's population.

The results, observed one official pacification report, were highly counterproductive: "It becomes relatively easy for the VC to replace losses from a population resentful and disgruntled at the destruction of their lives and property and therefore hostile to the GVN [Government of Vietnam] and its allies." Informed at a press briefing that US forces had moved into one rural district behind 365 tactical air strikes, thirty B-52 sorties, and a barrage of more than a million artillery shells, an American correspondent had a similar reaction. "It appears you [have] leveled virtually every village and hamlet, killed or driven more than fifty thousand peasants off the land with your firepower. My question is, how do you intend to go about winning the hearts and minds of these people?" "I'm afraid you'll have to take that up with Civic Affairs, sir," replied the briefing officer, "but, jeez, it's a real good question."

Medical evacuation patients on the deck of the amphibious assault ship USS *Tripoli* await transfer to the 22nd Casualty Station in Da Nang, from which they will be sent to the US. Wounded Marines who could not be returned to duty or who required more than six days of hospital care were removed from the *Tripoli* and returned to the US.

What the United States had achieved in Vietnam after nearly three years of war was stalemate, but stalemate at a much higher level of commitment. In the air and on the ground, American forces were scoring ever-greater victories. But the war was not being won. It was not being won because it was being fought largely on the enemy's terms. By devoting US military assets to the pursuit of enemy Main Force units in remote war zones and base areas, the American command was losing men and machines with no commensurate increase in security for the bulk of the South Vietnamese population. Although most of the giant operations were "successful" in capturing Communist supplies and temporarily clearing enemy units from the area, once the Americans left in search of new targets, the Communists returned.

The border battles of 1967 exacerbated the security problem, stretched American forces to the limit, and enabled the Communists to regain the military initiative. With major US units lured into large frontier engagements, prophesied North Vietnam's General Giap, strongholds along the coast such as Da Nang and Chu Lai would become "isolated islands in the open sea of the people's war." The heavy cost in casualties was one Giap was more than willing to pay as long as sufficient replacements were available and substantial losses could also be inflicted on his adversary. As one authority on North Vietnamese strategy pointed out, it was not by battles won or lost but "by the traffic in homebound American coffins that Giap measures his success."

In that regard, the North Vietnamese general was most astute, for by the end of 1967 the war had produced sharp divisions among the American people. Believing that the strategy of attrition was bearing fruit, military leaders and congressional hawks pushed the president to remove remaining restrictions on the bombing, increase American troop strength by as many as two hundred thousand men, and permit Westmoreland to take the war to the enemy in Laos and Cambodia. At the same time, the growing antiwar movement castigated the government for its involvement in Southeast Asia, demanding that the administration end the bombing of North Vietnam and cease propping up the Saigon regime.

Meanwhile, opinion polls charted a steady decline in public support for the war and an equally steady rise in the number of Americans who disapproved of the way the president was handling the situation in Vietnam. What the polls revealed more than anything else was a profound confusion and uncertainty about the war. "I want to get out," explained one housewife, "but I don't want to give up."

President Johnson might well have said the very same thing. Discouraged by the lack of progress in Vietnam, yet reluctant to expand the war any further—sharing some of McNamara's reservations about the likelihood of military victory, yet unwilling to concede defeat—he once more sought a middle ground. To appease the hawks, he enlarged the Rolling Thunder target list, but he gave Westmoreland only a quarter of the two hundred thousand additional men the general sought. To keep his options open he placed no ceiling on American troop levels, but he began to consider ways of transferring greater responsibility for the ground war to the South Vietnamese. If he was not prepared to go further, Johnson surely was not ready to retreat. The American commitment to Vietnam would continue.

A US Navy river patrol boat crewman is vigilant at a .50-caliber machine gun during the boat's day-long patrol on the Go Cong River.

President Lyndon Johnson addresses US troops during a visit to Cam Ranh Bay. Also on stage are Rear Adm. Kenneth Veth (second from left), commander of US naval forces in Vietnam; Gen. William Westmoreland (second from right, in hat); and Ellsworth Bunker, US ambassador to South Vietnam (at right, in suit).

Having made his decision to stay the course, Johnson mounted a frenzied public relations campaign during the last month of the year, dispatching government "truth teams" around the country and recalling General Westmoreland to Washington to reassure the nation with an optimistic speech before Congress. "We are not going to yield," declared the president. "We are not going to shimmy. We are going to wind up with a peace with honor which all Americans seek." Yet, even as he spoke, Communist troops in unprecedented numbers were marshalling their forces all across South Vietnam. The stunning blow they were about to deliver would take the true measure of American determination.

Focus: Con Thien

Nothing better symbolized the stalemate reached by the end of 1967 than the struggle over Con Thien near the DMZ and the battle for Hill 875 in the Central Highlands. Both were long and hard fought, with each side taking heavy casualties. And both seemed, at least to the American troops who fought them, exercises in futility.

It was known to local missionaries as the Hill of Angels, but to the Marines who occupied it, it was a little piece of hell. Just two miles from the DMZ, Con Thien was a barren, bulldozed plateau of red dirt 160 meters high. The cramped outpost, barely big enough to hold an understrength battalion, was ringed by barbed wire, studded with artillery revetments, and crisscrossed with trenches and sandbag-covered bunkers. To the east stretched the Trace, the six-hundred-meter-wide firebreak the Marines had cleared for the McNamara Line. Equally important, the hilltop strongpoint overlooked one of the principal enemy routes into South Vietnam as well as the

General Westmoreland (right) confers with President Johnson during his visit to Cam Ranh Bay.

A Viet Cong prisoner awaits interrogation at the A-109 Special Forces Detachment in Thuong Duc, twenty-five kilometers west of Da Nang.

Pictured is the Recon team, Bravo Company, 3rd Reconnaissance, at Logistics Support Area, Khe Sanh Combat Base.

Vietnam was the scene of countless acts of bravery. For their intrepidity in the face of battle and valor in Vietnam "above and beyond the call of duty," 256 Americans (as of this writing) have received their country's highest award, the Medal of Honor. One of them was Sammy L. Davis, a twenty-one-year-old private first class in November 1967, when his 9th Infantry Division base came under attack in the Mekong Delta.

C Battery, 2nd Battalion, 4th Artillery, was a terrific, hard-working unit. We did our jobs very, very well. In fact, our call sign was "Automatic Five-Niner," which was a statement in itself because we were able to put out so many more rounds than the average artillery crew. The reason was that the unit had trained together and was used to working together as a crew. I was one of the first replacements to join it, and I learned how to work with them.

On the night of November 17, we were at Forward Base Cudgel, right on the Mekong River, south of My Tho. Just before dark, the major came to the camp in his helicopter and said, "The probability of you guys getting mortared tonight is very good."

At 2:00 on the button we heard the first enemy mortar slide down the tube. They were very close. Usually if a mortar attack lasts more than five minutes, it's a really long one. So when this one lasted half an hour, we knew something big was coming. And sure enough, at 2:30 we could hear the NVA starting to yell and run fast toward us. They were coming en masse from immediately across the river and from my right. We had four guns, each covering a different direction, and the majority of the NVA were coming from my direction.

We jumped up from our foxholes, dropped the tube on the 105mm gun for direct fire, loaded up a beehive, and started firing. I was the assistant gunner of our crew, the one firing the piece. When I pulled the lanyard on the third round, the NVA fired a rocket-propelled grenade right at our muzzle blast. It hit the shield that I was hiding behind and the shield kind of exploded. I got thousands of little bitty pieces of steel in my right side and was knocked unconscious, lying half in and half out of my foxhole. The other guys just gathered up the guys they thought were alive and would make it and fell back to the next piece. That's why my guys left me. They thought I was dead.

Our guys fired beehive to keep the NVA off the gun, and when they fired the round, some of the darts hit me and woke me up. I had a tremendous buzzing in my head, and it took a long time for me to get it together. After maybe a few minutes I realized what was happening and what I had to do. I picked up my M16 and fired it until it quit. Then I fired the M60 machine gun in my foxhole until it quit. Then I didn't have anything else to fire, and they just kept coming. The only alternative was to get hold of the 105 and see if I could get it fired up. So that's what I did.

My head was still ringing, but I fired quite a few rounds. The NVA were still on the other side of the river, about twenty-five to thirty meters away. I guess if I hadn't fired that gun we would have been overrun from that side. The grenade had hit the recoil mechanism on the howitzer, so when I fired it, the gun went crazy. It just rolled over onto me and broke some vertebrae in my back. If it hadn't been for the soft mud, it probably would have killed me. Every time I fired it, it just kept jumping back and back. It ended up in a little creek eight feet away. I had to load the last round underwater, but it went off.

After I finished with the gun I saw one of our guys lying wounded across the river. I knew I was hurting bad and couldn't get to him by myself, so I took an air mattress and made it across that way. On the other side, I reached the wounded guy and found two more with him. One was shot in the back, another in the head, and the third in the foot. I threw the guy who had been shot in the head over my back, and the two other guys leaned on each shoulder. We all kind of leaned on each other and helped each other back toward the river. Some NVA ran right past us; I don't think they thought there would be anybody on their side of the river.

I took the guy who was wounded the worst across first. Our guys saw me swimming across the river, so they helped me get him up on the bank. Then I went across and got the other two guys. I spent the rest of the time just tending to business, taking care of some of the guys who had been wounded. By that time the NVA had been pretty well whipped.

I had more problems when I was medevaced the next day. One of the beehive darts had penetrated my kidney and I got a kidney infection, then my whole body just kind of deteriorated. I had a 106-degree temperature for more than a week. I had lost a lot of blood anyway, and the fever dehydrated me to the point where my blood had almost turned to buttermilk. They would give me a transfusion, and within twenty-four hours my body would just suck all the moisture back out. They gave up on me and put me out in the hallway to die. Then one of the guys I swam across the river for told them to take blood out of his arm for me. He lay down in the hallway beside me. They hooked us up, and I lived.

I don't think that a person can be honest and say, "I only took care of myself in Vietnam." No one who served there could escape or endure the terror, the heat, or the tremendous physical demands made by the war simply by applying himself to the task. Most of what carried us through the experience came out of the sense that everyone needed everyone else, that if you helped me today, I would help you tomorrow. We would both help a third the next day. I would never have made it to that riverbank if it had not been for the efforts of the other men, and if the other men came away from the riverbank because of what I did there, then it simply was my turn. We all looked out for each other.

Sergeant Sammy L. Davis (third from left) receives the Medal of Honor from President Lyndon Johnson on November 19, 1968, along with four fellow recipients: in front of Johnson, Capt. Angelo Liteky; from left, Spc. Gary Wetzel, Spc. Dwight Johnson, and Capt. James Taylor.

vast US logistics complex at Dong Ha ten miles away. If the enemy ever occupied Con Thien, observed Col. Richard B. Smith, commander of the 9th Marines, "he would be looking down our throats."

The men of the 1st Battalion, 9th Marines who garrisoned the outpost suffered from blazing heat and choking dust, from snipers and threats of ground attack. But what made duty at Con Thien a special misery was the rain of artillery from NVA batteries tucked away in the northern hills of the DMZ. The Communist guns were not only well camouflaged, but also sheltered in caves and other protected positions. Rolled out to fire, then rolled back again, the guns were frequently shifted to prevent US spotters from fixing their locations for Air Force bombers. Although the Americans retaliated with artillery and air strikes of their own, they were not able to stop the hundreds of shells that each day took a steady toll on Con Thien's defenders.

The heaviest fighting took place outside the wire, however, as other Marine battalions clashed with enemy units trying to draw a noose around Con Thien. On July 2, a North Vietnamese ambush killed or wounded nearly 275 men from a single US company. During the fighting, the NVA fired more than one thousand artillery and mortar rounds at Con Thien and Gio Linh, while American air and artillery punished the North Vietnamese with more than one hundred tons of napalm and high explosives. The ambush set off a week of violent encounters climaxing on July 6, when American units, backed by tanks, naval gunfire, artillery,

Marines of the 9th Regiment, 3rd Division, take cover during an NVA rocket and artillery attack against the outpost at Con Thien in late 1967.

Two Marines sleep in the rain and cold in a trench line at Con Thien.

attack aircraft, and helicopter gunships, fought off a ferocious nighttime Communist ground attack. The battle left behind a scene of indescribable carnage, with some eight hundred enemy bodies and tons of demolished equipment scattered over the smoking, blasted landscape. By the time the NVA had retreated across the DMZ in mid-month, nearly 1,300 enemy soldiers had been killed and at least one first-line North Vietnamese regiment virtually destroyed.

Yet their horrendous casualties seemed to have little effect on the North Vietnamese. In late August, the enemy returned to the attack, and by early September, when the 3rd Battalion, 9th Marines took over from the 1/9, ground assaults had erupted south of the base. On September 10, the 3/26 Marines engaged an entire NVA regiment four miles from Con Thien, which itself was hit three days later.

Meanwhile, the Marines were experiencing one of the heaviest shellings of the war. Over one six-day period, Con Thien endured twenty-four separate bombardments, during which a total of more than three thousand rounds of artillery, rockets, and mortars crashed into the beleaguered garrison. On September 25 alone, more than 1,200 rounds fell within the perimeter. Under that thunderous cascade of shells, the Marines tried to pick out the sounds that could mean the difference between life and death—the "whump" of mortars that gave a man five to ten seconds to seek cover, the whine of artillery shells that could be heard three seconds before impact, and the terrible whisper of enemy rockets that gave no more than a second's warning. But the combined volume of fire from US and enemy guns left many temporarily deaf, so that even when the shelling stopped, the men had to shout to make themselves heard.

Adding to their misery was the northeast monsoon that arrived a month early in September, flooding trench lines, collapsing bunkers, and washing out land lines of communication. The rain turned the laterite soil into a muddy quagmire that absorbed some of the shrapnel from high-explosive artillery shells but made it difficult to run for cover and eventually concealed so many dud rounds that Con Thien became a minefield of unexploded ordnance. At night, fog shrouded the base, creating an even greater sense of isolation and magnifying every sound into an enemy attack. When it was not raining it was drizzling, the perpetual moisture producing skin rashes so painful that a mere touch was agony, and feet so sodden that skin a pale shade of green sloughed off in long strips.

They called themselves "the walking dead," the men of Con Thien—living in dank, filthy bunkers they shared with rats, eating only one or two C-rations a day to save space on resupply choppers for ammo and replacement troops, carrying wounded men through a sea of mud, and all the while listening for the constant cry of "Incoming!" In addition to the random pattern of deadly barrages that made superstition a way of life, there were also recoilless-rifle fire and rocket-propelled grenade (RPG) sniping to contend with, full-scale attacks that sent the adrenaline surging, and small probes along the wire that stretched a man's nerves to the breaking point. Shell shock, relatively unheard of elsewhere in Vietnam, was not unusual at Con Thien, nor was a growing anger and confusion among the Marines about their predicament.

They were frustrated with having to sit and take it, and bitter about being asked to die for "a shit-hole place," as one of them put it, whose value did not seem to measure up to that of the men beside them who were being wounded and crippled and killed. Despite the hazards of the journey, reporters and cameramen, including the great war photographer David Douglas Duncan, came to record what was happening at Con Thien. Some of them, too, questioned the wisdom of holding the isolated base, portraying a grim siege they likened to the French disaster at Dien Bien Phu. Westmoreland scoffed at their warnings. Happy to have the North Vietnamese stand and fight, he sent four Marine battalions circling the combat base to keep enemy units at arm's length and hammered at the NVA with "one of the greatest concentrations of firepower in the history of the Vietnam War."

It was called Operation Neutralize, a forty-nine-day campaign involving the entire spectrum of US supporting arms—strike aircraft, strategic bombers, offshore naval guns, and heavy artillery—along with forward air control pilots who pinpointed targets for aerial strikes and special long-range reconnaissance patrols that infiltrated the demilitarized

A Marine chaplain gives last rites for a dying trooper near Con Thien on July 4, 1967. A Communist trap built around the bodies of American dead cost the Marines twenty-one killed and forty wounded.

zone to assess bomb damage and locate additional targets. The concentrated, seven-week assault pummeled an area the size of Manhattan with nearly twenty thousand rounds from land artillery and naval gunfire and more than forty thousand tons of bombs. Together, US Air Force, Navy, and Marine pilots flew 5,200 sorties during the siege, including 820 B-52 Arc Light missions. Like a terrible plow, the torrent of firepower furrowed the earth for mile upon mile, saturating NVA troop sites, demolishing more than two hundred enemy gun positions, and leaving the land a desolate moonscape of water-filled craters devoid of life.

The fearful onslaught finally broke the back of the North Vietnamese offensive. Although willing to accept more than two thousand dead and many times that number wounded, NVA units were never able to concentrate sufficient forces for an all-out attack. Toward the end of September, enemy shelling began to taper off, and on October 4, MACV headquarters announced that the siege of Con Thien was over. As North Vietnamese troops staggered back across the DMZ, the 1/9 Marines relieved the battered 3rd Battalion. But the combat base itself remained— a grim, depressing place of danger and misery. From that there was no escape, not at Con Thien or anywhere along South Vietnam's northern frontier in the third year of a war whose end was nowhere in sight.

Focus: Hill 875

By the time of the "border battles" in late 1967, of which Con Thien was the first, the war had become a bloody contest of regular armies and conventional arms. Nowhere was this more evident than at Dak To, where beginning in early November, sixteen thousand allied troops took on the 1st NVA Division in the steep jungle wilderness of western Kontum Province.

For two weeks, American and Communist units fought a series of costly engagements until the incessant pounding of US air and artillery drove the North Vietnamese from the battlefield. Pursued by elements of the 4th Infantry Division and the 173rd Airborne Brigade, the Communists withdrew southwest toward their Cambodian sanctuaries. Left behind to guard their retreat was the 174th NVA Regiment. On November 18, a Special Forces mobile reaction company ran into the heavily entrenched enemy on Hill 875, ten miles from 173rd field headquarters at Ben Het. The next day, brigade commander Gen. Leo H. Schweiter ordered the 2nd Battalion, 503rd Infantry to take the hill. What followed was one of the most savage battles of the Vietnam War.

Covered with closely spaced trees, dense brush, and bamboo thickets, Hill 875 rose gradually from the surrounding jungle toward two ridge lines that leveled off at the top into a broad "saddle." The enemy had turned the hill into a fortress, lacing the slopes with bunkers and trenches linked by tunnels and well-constructed trails cut into the sides of the hill. The elaborate fortifications spiraling downward from the summit were camouflaged with natural vegetation that had grown up in the several months since they had been built and protected from air and artillery bombardment by up to twelve feet of overhead cover. The slit gun ports of the underground bunkers commanded excellent fields of fire, while the interconnecting tunnels enabled the enemy to shift troops rapidly from one bunker to the next without exposing them to danger. Six days earlier, men of the 2nd Battalion, 503rd Infantry had been badly mauled trying to take out a pair of NVA bunkers on another nearby hill. As the GIs checked their weapons in the early morning mist, they had few illusions about what lay ahead.

At 9:43 a.m., after preparatory artillery and air strikes, Charlie and Delta Companies started up the northern slope. At the base of the hill, Alpha Company began cutting a landing zone out of the thick jungle. The men of the lead companies advanced slowly over the tangled trees and splintered bamboo left by the bombing until they neared the crest of the first ridge. Suddenly, the NVA opened up with automatic weapons from a concealed bunker only five meters from the point squad. Two men fell within seconds. The rest of the squad dropped their packs and spread out behind fallen logs. As the Americans came forward, the enemy added recoilless-rifle fire and grenades to the withering barrage, then B40 rockets launched from farther up the hill. When the firing eased momentarily, the paratroopers resumed their advance, tossing grenades into the bunker as they passed. But no sooner had it stopped than the shooting resumed—both from above and from the bunker where those killed by the grenades had been replaced by other NVA soldiers scrambling through hidden tunnels. Artillery and tactical air tried to take the pressure off by pounding enemy positions above the line of advance. But the men on the ground were being hit by machine guns, mortars, and sniper fire. Then NVA attackers, helmets camouflaged, faces painted black, rifles wrapped in burlap, rushed the Americans from every direction. "Jesus, they were all over the place," remembered one GI. "The noncoms kept shouting, 'Get up the hill, get up the goddamn hill!' But we couldn't." With the assault bogged down and casualties mounting, Charlie Company commander Capt. Harold Kaufman ordered the men to pull back. The headlong withdrawal was so precipitous that Kaufman had to fire his pistol in the air to forestall a rout. Their panic averted, the paratroopers established a perimeter within a few meters of where the battle had begun, then dug in furiously with anything that came to hand.

At the bottom of the hill, meanwhile, a squad from Alpha Company was just collecting some power saws and other equipment dropped by helicopter when North Vietnamese soldiers tore through the clearing. A brief firefight drove the squad up the hill toward Alpha Company's main position, the GIs dropping fragmentation grenades back down the trail in a futile attempt to slow the enemy assault. As they reached the rest of the company, mortar shells erupted around the Americans followed by waves of screaming NVA infantrymen. Defense lines disintegrated under the impact of the mass attack, which also killed Capt. Michael Kiley and five other members of the Alpha Company command group. After fifteen minutes of vicious hand-to-hand combat, platoon Sgt. Jack Siggers collected what remained of the company and staggered up the hill toward Charlie and Delta Companies, whose men compounded the carnage by firing on the retreating men until cries of "Friendly! Friendly!" enabled the survivors to gain the perimeter.

Together, the Americans temporarily halted the main NVA assault. The battalion was now surrounded by up to three hundred North Vietnamese soldiers, who continued to attack the paratroopers with mortars, automatic weapons, and B40 rockets. One soldier had his M60 machine gun blown out of his hand. Nearby, a wounded sergeant was dragged to a tree for cover by a medic who himself was shot through the head. Despite the sergeant's shouted warnings, a lieutenant tried three times to reach him, suffering a new wound with each attempt. The sergeant finally died, still pleading with the officer not to try to rescue him.

Supplies of water and ammunition dwindled steadily during the afternoon, but relief helicopters were driven off by heavy enemy fire that brought down six of the choppers. Just before dusk, helicopter crews dodging snipers in trees dropped

Members of the 4th Battalion, 173rd Airborne Brigade, are pinned down in a bomb crater on the side of Hill 875 by mortar fire during the assault on the hill.

two pallets of ammunition inside the American perimeter. The beleaguered paratroopers reloaded their weapons, but few believed they would make it through the night.

What hopes they had rested largely with air support. As darkness fell, F-100s, propeller-driven A-1 Skyraiders, and helicopter gunships bombarded enemy positions within fifty meters of US lines. One fighter-bomber, screaming toward the enemy at 300 miles an hour, dropped a five hundred-pound bomb short of the target. The high-explosive canister fell on the battalion command post and aid station, killing forty-two men and wounding forty-five more in a gigantic concussion that sent human limbs, bloody bandages, and pieces of charred uniforms hurtling through the night. "Heaps of dead after that bomb," recalled a stunned defender. "You didn't know where to go, you didn't know where to hide. You slept with the corpses."

With most of the battalion's company commanders dead or wounded, junior officers and NCOs took charge of the situation, which continued to deteriorate. After the mistaken bombing, US artillery rounds started to hit the men until a platoon sergeant crawling frantically from one shattered radio to another finally raised the fire direction center and adjusted the errant guns. As the ninety-degree daytime temperature fell toward fifty, the troopers cursed the warm clothing left in rucksacks scattered across the battlefield. Soldiers seeking protection from man and nature by burrowing into the earth found their task complicated by discarded ammo boxes, splintered weapons, and worse. Said one survivor, "Every time you tried to dig, you put your shovel in somebody."

All during the hours of darkness, AC-47 gunships flew over the hill, illuminating the eerie scene with brilliant flares. But nothing could abate the terror of that night: sporadic mortar and recoilless-rifle fire ripping across the perimeter, wounded men begging for water that did not exist, GIs hollering in frustration and rage at enemy soldiers who taunted them with threats of destruction. Meanwhile, at the bottom of the hill, reinforcements checked their weapons and filled their packs with extra ammunition as they prepared to relieve their fellow paratroopers.

On the morning of November 20, Lt. Col. James H. Johnson's 4th Battalion, 503rd Infantry moved up the hill through a litter of smashed vegetation, abandoned gear, and lifeless bodies. Climbing cautiously, the battalion spent all day negotiating the seven thousand yards to the 2nd Battalion. Along the way, they passed so many dead Americans that they began to wonder whether anyone was left alive to save. In fact, the situation at the perimeter remained precarious. As the Associated Press's Peter Arnett reported from the hill, "Some of the wounded cracked under the strain. 'It's a goddamn shame that they haven't gotten us out of here,' gasped one paratroop sergeant with tears in his eyes early afternoon Tuesday [the 21st]. He had been lying on the hill for fifty hours with a painful groin wound. All around him lay scores of other wounded. You could see who had lain there the longest. Blood had clotted their bandages, they had ceased moaning, their eyes were glazed." Enemy snipers firing automatic weapons from treetops continued to drive off relief helicopters. Just before dark, one medevac chopper managed to land and carry out five critically wounded men, but dozens more were left to suffer through another night. As the clatter of helicopter blades faded in the early evening darkness, the 4th Battalion's Bravo Company finally reached the men of the 2nd, who cried openly at the sight of their rescuers. By 10:00 p.m., the remainder of the 4th Battalion had arrived at the US perimeter.

Early the next morning, the North Vietnamese renewed their furious attack, pounding the Americans with 82mm mortars throughout the day. Peter Arnett wrote that "the foxholes got deeper as the day wore on. Foxhole after foxhole took hits. A dog handler and his German shepherd died together. Men who were joking with you and offering cigarettes would be writhing on the ground wounded and pleading for water minutes later. There was no water for them or anyone else."

That day, however, the paratroopers cut a hillside landing zone out of the bullet-scarred trees surrounding their position. Helicopters were finally able to bring in desperately needed food and water and evacuate the 2nd Battalion's wounded. The dead would remain on the hill for another day. While these tasks were going

A member of the 173rd Airborne Brigade crouches beside the body of a fallen comrade and equipment left by wounded at the height of the battle on Hill 875. US Army paratroopers then began a final assault up the bloody slopes of the hill.

The tumult of the battle over, Sgt. John G. Sheehan, radio still switched on and pressed to his ear, takes a well-earned rest atop Hill 875 following its capture by elements of the 173rd Airborne Brigade. Conquest of the hill ended five days of some of the bitterest fighting of the war.

on halfway up the north slope, the top of the hill was being pounded with every supporting arm II Corps could muster. For seven hours, air strikes and artillery battered the summit with more than fifteen thousand pounds of napalm and high explosives. At 3:00 in the afternoon, behind a last-minute wall of artillery, the 4th Battalion resumed the assault.

Armed with flame throwers, shoulder-fired antitank rockets, and 81mm mortars, the troopers had moved out through a ravine and started uphill when a mortar barrage crashed down on the head of the column, killing or wounding dozens of men. While medics tended the casualties, the battalion grimly pushed forward. Crawling up the steep slope, the soldiers found themselves under intense fire from mutually supporting bunkers. Not until they managed to pull themselves within a few meters of the concealed fortifications, however, could they locate the bunkers by the muzzle smoke of enemy rifles. Their ranks had been steadily thinned by NVA machine-gun fire and grenades during the climb. Now, when they finally found the enemy entrenchments, their weapons proved useless.

Part of the problem was that none of the men had been trained to use flame throwers. More to the point was the care the North Vietnamese had devoted to their fortifications. Mortar shells failed to penetrate the thick dirt covering that protected the bunkers, while rockets required a direct hit into narrow bunker firing holes. Even when marksmen occasionally managed to do so, the results were not always satisfactory. One group of troopers fired a dozen rockets directly into a bunker port-hole, only to be met with grenades and machine-gun fire from enemy soldiers who had taken refuge in a connecting tunnel during the barrage. Some platoon commanders tried sending individuals with satchel charges or napalm and grenades against the bunkers, but the intensity of fire made it difficult to get close enough.

Making matters worse, the NVA began firing rockets of their own that bounced down the slope and exploded among the fallen logs and mounds of dirt that sheltered the paratroopers. As the advance began to falter, enemy infantrymen using prepared avenues of entry and withdrawal from the battlefield attacked the battalion's flanks and rear, isolating small units and wiping them out one by one as they had done to the 2nd Battalion two days earlier. By sheer determination, the Americans captured a pair of trench lines within 250 feet of the summit, but the gains could not be consolidated, and the assault ground to a halt. After dark, the battered troopers gathered their casualties and pulled back to the original perimeter, more than half their number killed or wounded.

Since the beginning of the battle on November 19, Maj. Gen. William R. Peers, commander of the 4th Infantry Division, had promised reporters at his headquarters that Hill 875 would soon be in US hands. Now, after two attempts to do so had failed, Peers vowed to end North Vietnamese resistance once and for all. All day and into the night of November 22, American aircraft blasted Hill 875 with tons of bombs, napalm, and rockets in a thunderous effort to soften up the enemy before a final assault by the airborne troopers. Simultaneously, Peers placed the fresh 1st Battalion, 12th Infantry in a supporting position south of the hill. By 11:00 a.m. on November 23, Thanksgiving Day, everything was ready.

Led by Bravo Company, the 4th Battalion scrambled back up the hill behind a shield of 81mm mortars. Although they encountered some sniper fire as they clambered over the horrific landscape left by five days of fighting, there was little resistance. Twenty-two minutes later, shouting "Geronimo!" and "Airborne!" the troopers scaled the ravaged summit. But their cries echoed hollowly in the smoke that still swirled around the bomb craters and clung to the charred tree stumps. Sometime during the previous night, the NVA had slipped away, taking most of their dead along with their weapons. All that remained of the enemy presence atop the hill were a few blackened bodies and the NVA's trenchworks and bunkers. To cover their retreat, the Communists harassed the paratroopers arriving on the summit with mortar fire from a nearby ridge-top, but their fire soon ended. Said 1st Lt. Alfred Lindseth of Bravo Company, 4th Battalion, "It was a happy day when we found they had left the hill."

After all the sweat and all the blood, there would be no final battle. The weary GIs simply sat down in the dust and surveyed what remained of the enemy fortifications. Later that afternoon, helicopters carried in a Thanksgiving dinner of hot sliced turkey, cranberry sauce, and potatoes.

The battle of Hill 875 was the climax of the Dak To campaign. During the remainder of November, enemy resistance in the area disappeared as the 1st NVA Division withdrew into Cambodia. The battle had cost the North Vietnamese an estimated 325 dead and sufficiently damaged the 174th NVA Regiment to keep it out of action during the next phase of the Communist winter-spring offensive. General Westmoreland lauded the paratroopers for their part in denying the enemy the spectacular victory he sought, and the 173rd received a Presidential Unit Citation for what it had accomplished on Hill 875.

But the men of the 2nd and 4th Battalions, 503rd Infantry had paid a stiff price for their heroism: 158 dead and 402 wounded—nearly 15 percent of the brigade's strength. "With victories like this," wondered a US correspondent watching the wounded disembarking from helicopters, "who needs defeats?" If that question was being asked more and more as 1967 came to a close, it was not a question for soldiers to answer. While journalists and politicians debated the course of the war, the men of the 173rd held a service for the dead, laying out the boots of their fallen comrades in simple tribute to those who had perished in a terrible battle on a nameless hill in the middle of a jungle half a world from home.

Paratroopers of the 173rd Airborne Brigade honor their comrades killed on Hill 875 by laying out their boots at their base camp near the airstrip at Dak To. Survivors spoke of Maj. Charles Watters, a chaplain, and Pfc. Carlos Lozada, who would both earn a posthumous Medal of Honor for their actions in the battle.

CHAPTER FOUR

1968: A HINGE
of HISTORY

"Khe Sanh will stand in history, I am convinced, as a classic example of how to defeat a numerically superior besieging force by coordinated application of firepower. . . . Khe Sanh was one of the most damaging, one-sided defeats among many that the North Vietnamese incurred, and the myth of General Giap's military genius was discredited."

—General William C. Westmoreland

"Dienbienphu, Dienbienphu, look, it's not always true that history repeats itself. Khe Sanh didn't try to be, nor could it have been, a Dienbienphu. Khe Sanh wasn't that important to us. Or it was only to the extent that it was important to the Americans—in fact, at Khe Sanh their prestige was at stake.

Because just look at the usual paradox that you will always find with the Americans: as long as they stayed in Khe Sanh to defend their prestige, they said Khe Sanh was important; when they abandoned Khe Sanh, they said Khe Sanh had never been important.

Besides, don't you think we won at Khe Sanh? I say yes."

—General Vo Nguyen Giap

"I don't want any damn Dinbinfoo."

—President Lyndon B. Johnson

In November 1967, General Westmoreland boldly stated to the National Press Club in Washington, D.C., that, as of the end of 1967, the Communists were "unable to mount a major offensive. . . . I am absolutely certain that whereas in 1965 the enemy was winning, today he is certainly losing. . . . We have reached an important point when the end begins to come into view."

A Viet Cong rocket explodes into Da Nang Air Base in the early morning hours of January 30, 1968.

There would not be the end that Westmoreland had envisioned, and his overconfidence was later seen as an example of the military's lack of candor with the American public about the conduct of the war. The year to come would prove to be one of the most extraordinary years in American history, a year that would alter not only the course of the war but of the nation. Journalism historian Chris Daly calls 1968 "A Hinge in History." (see sidebar, page 132).

Westmoreland's overarching strategy of attrition—killing so many enemy soldiers and destroying so much of North Vietnam's infrastructure that the Communists would lose the will, the manpower, and the resources to continue the war—was partially mirrored by North Vietnam's minister of defense, Vo Nguyen Giap, who was generally considered to be the architect of the Communist war effort. It was Giap who had engineered the Viet Minh triumph at Dien Bien Phu in 1954, and in 1968 he was hoping for another victory, this time over the US. His attrition strategy encompassed the American home front. He felt that as American losses in Vietnam mounted, even though his own losses were far greater, the war would become so politically unpopular in the US that the American government would essentially sue for peace and accept a negotiated settlement.

Giap was a survivor, and his survival depended as least in part to his long partnership with Ho Chi Minh. When, in 1967, hardliners in the North Vietnamese Politburo purged hundreds of moderates from the party, including much of Giap's staff, Giap was forced to go along with a plan that was not of his making. Giap had been a proponent of the long view, waging a protracted guerrilla-based struggle. The hardliners felt the time had come for a Main Force general offensive that would deal the Americans a decisive, crushing blow.

At the end of January, the ARVN forces were at less than full strength, as many soldiers spent the Tet holiday with their families. The NVA strategists believed that by catching the ARVN at a weak moment, while attacking population centers and pinning down US reaction forces, they would force the ARVN to collapse. When that happened, they calculated, the South Vietnamese population would rise up and join the Communists to oust the corrupt Saigon regime and force the American military to withdraw.

The plan hatched in Hanoi would be known as the Tet Offensive, a coordinated assault on the major cities and US bases in South Vietnam that would catch the military off-guard. News of the Communist offensive stunned Americans at home, who saw images on television and in newspapers of Viet Cong inside the grounds of the American Embassy in Saigon. Also in 1968, the US military engaged in big battles that often baffled the American public—ugly, bloody battles for remote hilltops that were no sooner conquered, at the cost of many American lives, than they were abandoned. Perhaps the battle that confused and disturbed the public more than any other was the fight for Khe Sanh, the remote Marine Corps combat base that General Westmoreland and President Johnson vowed would be held "at all costs."

Khe Sanh

The combat base near the South Vietnamese village of Khe Sanh, in northwest Quang Tri Province, had humble origins that did not foreshadow its future importance in the war, in the news headlines, or in the minds of Gen. William Westmoreland and President Lyndon Johnson. An old

French fortification outside the village was taken over in 1962 by US Army Green Berets, who were recruiting ethnic Montagnards, the "mountain people," to fight against the Viet Cong.

The base was manned by Vietnamese irregular troops, part of the Civilian Irregular Defense Group formed by the Special Forces. Khe Sanh's geographical position made it an ideal observation post, as it straddled Route 9, the northernmost east-west road in South Vietnam, just below the DMZ and only eleven miles from the border with Laos. When Westmoreland assumed command of MACV in June 1964, he was intrigued by Khe Sanh's potential usefulness. He saw the base as a barrier to NVA infiltration, an air reconnaissance outpost, and a launching pad for clandestine cross-border operations into Laos or infantry operations to sever the Ho Chi Minh Trail, the multitrack network of roads and footpaths through Laos and Cambodia that the North Vietnamese used to supply their forces in the south. Khe Sanh also guarded the western end of the DMZ. In November 1964, the Green Berets, perhaps recalling the lessons of Dien Bien Phu, moved their camp to higher ground, to the Xom Cham Plateau; that camp would become Khe Sanh Combat Base in 1967, when the Marines assumed control and established a "permanent" base. By then, the Special Forces troops had moved their base to Lang Vei, a few miles closer to the Laotian border.

The more Westmoreland thought about Khe Sanh, the larger it grew in importance in the general's mind. He began planning for an invasion of Laos, and he told the Marine commander, Lt. Gen. Lewis Walt, that Khe Sanh was essential to his strategy. Walt was unconvinced and argued for a strategy of pacification rather than hot pursuit, but Westmoreland overruled him. The deputy commander of the 3rd Marine Division, Brig. Gen. Lowell English, was even more blunt than Walt had been. English thought it was ludicrous to attach so much importance to the defense of Khe Sanh: "When you're at Khe Sanh, you're not really anywhere. You could lose it and you really haven't lost a damn thing." So vulnerable was Khe Sanh, in fact, that the Marines initially balked at the idea of defending the site. Former JCS chairman Gen. Maxwell Taylor, President Johnson's chief military advisor, believed that the base was simply too isolated to be adequately defended, and urged Johnson to consider ordering a withdrawal.

In early 1967, the North Vietnamese began laying plans to attack Khe Sanh, and the NVA took up positions on the hills near the combat base, which lay within easy striking distance of NVA base areas across the Laotian border and inside the DMZ. Moreover, it was surrounded by dense forests and fog-shrouded valleys that made it difficult for the defenders to detect the presence of even large numbers of troops. From their hilltop bunkers and gun emplacements, the North Vietnamese gunners could rain artillery and mortars on the Marines, who were thus forced into a series of hill fights to drive off the NVA. Two battalions of Marines, the 2nd and 3rd Battalions of the 3rd Marine Regiment, were brought in to push the NVA off Hills 861, 881 North, and 881 South (hills were named for their elevations), which they accomplished at a price: 155 Marines killed, 425 wounded. After the hill fights, Khe Sanh was relatively quiet—but it had also become isolated, cut off from overland resupply following the ambush of a convoy that was headed for Khe Sanh on Route 9. After that failed attempt, Khe Sanh was accessible only by air.

Essay by Christopher B. Daly

As 1968 began, the Beatles' song from the year before was still playing on record players and radios:

 ₀I read the news today, oh boy . . .

And what a flashing kaleidoscope of news it was. By turns amazing, shocking, depressing, inspiring, and enraging, the news in 1968 seemed to have entered some uncharted realm. Things started normally enough. Americans woke on the first day of the year to read a UPI story reporting that the Census Bureau put the US population at just over 200 million. During the first few days of January, they could also read about the exploits of the dashing O. J. Simpson, who rushed USC to victory in the Rose Bowl over Indiana. *Newsweek* reported that its own poll showed Republicans favoring Richard Nixon over his GOP rivals at the start of that presidential election year. Gary, Indiana, got a new "Negro" mayor, Richard Hatcher, whose first act was to appoint a white chief of police and order him to crack down on crime.

Then there was the news from Vietnam, all of it bad.

According to a Saigon newspaper, American psy-ops forces were blanketing Vietnam with propaganda leaflets. The only problem: Six years into the war, Americans still had not learned to speak the language. The level of Vietnamese used in the leaflets ranged from "consistently awful" to "unintelligible."

From Hanoi came an AP report that North Vietnam had shot down 1,063 American warplanes in the previous year. Trying to sum up the overall situation in a front-page piece on January 1, *Times* correspondent Johnny Apple wrote:

SAIGON, South Vietnam, Dec. 31—American officials at almost all levels, both in Saigon and in the provinces, say they are under steadily increasing pressure from Washington to produce convincing evidence of progress, especially by the South Vietnamese . . .

So many portents and signals, and so much noise, too. During the first week of 1968, readers could also find an AP story under the headline, DUTY LIFTED ON BAGPIPES.

Yes, President Johnson had signed a bill lifting the 15 percent tax, but only after having certified that there "is no known commercial production of bagpipes in the United States." (Who knew?)

The *Times* reported that cigarette sales were up 7.5 percent, to 46.6 billion smokes, and the paper documented the new year's social news, noting that twenty-nine debutantes had been "presented" at the Waldorf Astoria. The *Times* also took note of the fashion trend of the era, the miniskirt, and asked the classic question during periods when the hemline is up: "Will It Go Down?" The paper waffled and said only that the issue was a "cliff-hanger" heading into 1968.

The cover of the Beatles' *Sgt. Pepper's Lonely Hearts Club Band* album, released in 1967. Among the notable figures featured in the design, which won a Grammy Award for best album cover, are Mae West, Fred Astaire, Bob Dylan, Aldous Huxley, Marilyn Monroe, Oscar Wilde, and Karl Marx—and, of course, the Beatles.

Readers would have also found the following item in the *Times* on the first day of the year, a sort of all-purpose headline that the newspaper could have kept on file for use throughout the year, TOP OFFICIALS FRET OVER NATION'S ILLS.

There was plenty to fret about: the problems of crime, housing, violence, race, and war were not getting any better.

Then, on January 30, South Vietnam erupted in flames as the Communists launched the Tet Offensive.

As the year continued, the headlines from the home front kept growing larger and larger. At the end of February, the Kerner Commission weighed in on the previous year's urban riots. "Our nation is moving toward two societies, one black, one white—separate and unequal," the report warned, adding that the news media were part of the problem because "the media report and write from the standpoint of a white man's world." And, incidentally, the report pointed out that it was high time the news media hired some black reporters. Within weeks, more shocks: The US abandoned the gold standard in March.

In April, the news was suddenly wall-to-wall. In the estimation of the *Times* managing editor, Arthur Gelb, the first week of April 1968 was "the most crowded week of news since World War II." It actually began on March 31. The president requested airtime on

A photograph of Earth taken by astronaut William Anders in 1968 during the Apollo 8 mission.

year before in San Francisco by a Berkeley dropout named Jann Wenner, but in 1968 it really began to take off, gaining national circulation. *Rolling Stone* had caught the wave of hip culture, youth culture, and rock 'n roll. It was not the first "alternative" paper, and it was far from the only one; it was not even the only one covering the music scene, but *Rolling Stone* was one of a kind.

Out with the old.

Christopher Daly is a journalism professor at Boston University's College of Communication, and is the author of Covering America: A Narrative History of a Nation's Journalism (*University of Massachusetts Press, 2012*).

The cover of the first issue of *Rolling Stone*, founded in 1967 by Jann Wenner and music critic Ralph Gleason. The magazine reviewed popular music and featured political reporting by "gonzo journalist" Hunter S. Thompson.

These two cultures began to gawk at one another, even as they drifted further and further apart.

One place to find the new culture was in music. Suddenly, the radio mattered, more than ever. New songs by Dylan or the Beatles were stunning, stopping people in their tracks. Pop music was not just silly love songs anymore. Now, it could be about anything; it could be plasticine porters with looking-glass ties, or an opera about a blind boy who's a wizard at pinball, or about the dark side of the moon. Bob Dylan sang,

> Johnny's in the basement,
> Mixin' up the medicine,
> I'm on the pavement,
> Thinking 'bout the government . . .

(Who's Johnny? What's the government up to? Who knows? Who cares? The thing was to open your mind, to seek, and to question everything. Music led the way.)

In 1968, this music got a major new partner, in the form of a new magazine called *Rolling Stone*. It had been founded the

By late 1967, the NVA had moved one, two, or three divisions into the Khe Sanh area, boxing the base in from the northwest, southwest, and east. (No one seemed to know for sure how many NVA troops were actually there—relatively few bodies were found, adding to the "riddle" of Khe Sanh.) The NVA dug in, establishing well-protected artillery, rocket, and mortar positions. The six thousand Marines at the base were surrounded by about twenty thousand NVA troops, according to some estimates.

But Westmoreland felt he had the enemy right where he wanted him. The NVA had massed its forces for a set-piece battle, exactly what Westmoreland had hoped for. He knew that if the NVA stood and fought, they would be decimated by the vastly superior firepower and air power of the US.

On the eve of what was to become known as the Tet Offensive, American commanders did not know exactly what was about to happen, but they knew the broad outlines, as revealed in captured documents—and they mostly ignored the evidence they had collected.

Navy Corpsman David Lewis Boucher and Marine Staff Sgt. Ruben Santos treat Pvt. William Vizzerra near the crest of Hill 881 N during fighting between the Marines and NVA regulars on April 30, 1967.

At 10:30 p.m. on January 2, 1968, the bark of a sentry dog at Khe Sanh Combat Base in northwestern Quang Tri Province alerted US Marine lookouts to the presence of someone just outside the defensive wire. Peering through their night-vision Starlight scopes, the Marines could see six men, all dressed in American uniforms, nonchalantly walking along. Since no friendly patrols were reported in the area, a squad led by 2nd Lt. Nile B. Buffington was sent to investigate. As he approached the perimeter, Buffington called out to the men to identify themselves. There was no reply. The lieutenant repeated the challenge. At that point one of the strangers made a quick movement, as if reaching for a weapon or grenade. The Marines opened fire. Five of the intruders fell dead, while the sixth escaped into the darkness carrying what was believed to be a case of maps. Intelligence later identified three of those killed as the commander, operations officer, and communications officer of a North Vietnamese regiment.

When news of the incident reached MACV headquarters in Saigon, General Westmoreland was not surprised. In recent weeks, the pace of NVA infiltration into northern I Corps had increased dramatically, particularly in the vicinity of Khe Sanh. American intelligence analysts believed that one, perhaps two full North Vietnamese divisions had moved into the area, while elements of two other divisions had been sighted inside the DMZ within striking distance of the base. Convinced that the enemy intended to "restage Dien Bien Phu," where Ho Chi Minh's Viet Minh had decisively beaten the French fourteen years before, Westmoreland had ordered the Marines to reinforce Khe Sanh in mid-December. Now, faced with fresh evidence of the enemy's presence, the American commander decided to meet the Communist challenge head-on.

To bolster allied manpower in the north, Westmoreland shifted more than half of his maneuver battalions to I Corps, beginning with the redeployment of the 1st Air Cav on January 9. He also dispatched two more battalions of Marines to Khe Sanh, along with a battalion of South Vietnamese Rangers. In the meantime, MACV officials began laying plans for the most concentrated application of aerial firepower in the history of warfare. Called Niagara, a name chosen "to evoke the image of cascading bombs and shells," the operation called for the use of some three thousand strike aircraft to pound suspected enemy positions around the clock, as well as three thousand helicopters and cargo planes to keep the base resupplied.

In Washington, President Johnson closely monitored the impending confrontation with growing unease. As the prospect of a major attack grew more imminent, the president repeatedly questioned his advisors about the wisdom of holding the base and ultimately took the unprecedented step of requiring a written endorsement of General Westmoreland's decision from each member of the Joint Chiefs of Staff.

The high-level debate over the investment of Khe Sanh was still going on when, on the afternoon of January 20, a North Vietnamese officer holding a white flag suddenly materialized at the eastern end of the combat base. He identified himself as 1st Lt. La Thanh Tonc, and told Marine interrogators that he wanted to defect. He then proceeded to provide a wealth of information about the enemy's intentions that confirmed what the Americans already suspected. According to Tonc, the 325C NVA Division and the 304th NVA Division, an elite home-guard unit from Hanoi, were preparing to

An eruption of smoke and dust obscures part of the beleaguered Marine combat base at Khe Sanh during a North Vietnamese rocket attack.

overrun Khe Sanh, then sweep eastward across Quang Tri and Thua Thien Provinces toward Hue. The campaign was to begin that very night with attacks on the main base and two outlying hills occupied by the Marines.

Though Tonc was suspected of being a plant, as he seemed to know more "than would be expected of an officer in his position," Marine Gen. Rathvon McClure Tompkins decided that "we had nothing to lose and stood to gain a great deal" by acting on the intelligence. As a result, when the North Vietnamese assaulted Hill 861 at half past midnight on January 21, the Marines were waiting for them. After turning back the NVA's initial charge, the men of Kilo Company, 3rd Battalion, 26th Marines counterattacked down the hill and overran the enemy in savage hand-to-hand combat. No sooner had the fighting subsided than a heavy barrage of artillery and rocket fire slammed into the main base, blasting holes in the airstrip, destroying several helicopters, and detonating some 1,500 tons of stored ammunition. The Marines scrambled for cover, expecting a mass assault. It never came. For reasons that would become clear only later, the NVA had decided not to exploit their advantage, at least for the moment. The siege of Khe Sanh had begun.

Despite all the measures and countermeasures that Westmoreland took to protect Khe Sanh, the six thousand Marines stationed there knew that they alone would bear the brunt of a full-scale enemy assault. Every day they had to endure the shocks of fifty, or two hundred, or five hundred incoming rounds, a form of random terror that one Marine compared to "sitting in an electric chair and waiting for someone to pull the switch." Every day they reinforced their positions—digging their holes a little deeper, filling a few more sandbags to add to their bunkers. And every day they stared into the opaque gray mist surrounding their base and wondered, "Are they coming tonight?"

Right: A Marine of the 3rd Marine Division takes cover in his foxhole at Khe Sanh during a North Vietnamese rocket attack.

Bottom: A C-123 lands at Khe Sanh with fresh troops and supplies. The enemy attacked with mortars, but the aircraft was not hit and completed a perfect landing and takeoff.

Tensions ran especially high following the outbreak of the countrywide Tet Offensive on the nights of January 30 and 31, but aside from an NVA ground assault on one of the outlying hills on the night of February 5, Khe Sanh remained quiet in the immediate aftermath of Tet.

The next moment of crisis came on the night of February 7, when the North Vietnamese attacked a camp at Lang Vei manned by US Special Forces and locally recruited recruited CIDG soldiers seven miles southwest of Khe Sanh. Striking from three directions behind Soviet-made PT76 tanks, a battalion-size force of NVA sappers and infantrymen, some armed with flame throwers, smashed through the perimeter and quickly overran the fortified compound. By morning, two hundred of the five hundred CIDG troops at Lang Vei were dead or missing, along with ten of the twenty-four Americans, while the camp itself had been reduced to bleak, smoldering ruins.

The fall of Lang Vei had a profound psychological impact on the Marines at Khe Sanh, stirring their most deep-seated fear. Despite recent reports that the enemy was moving armored vehicles into the area, no one knew—perhaps because no one wanted to believe—that the NVA had tanks. Now, observed journalist Michael Herr, who was present at the time, "[H]ow could you look out of your perimeter at night without hearing the treads coming?"

The ebb and flow of anxiety and adrenaline took a toll on the Marines, many of whom developed that blank look in the eyes known as the "ten-thousand-yard stare." To relieve the stress and fatigue, they did what combat troops often do: They played cards and exchanged news from home, sang songs, and listened to music. They accumulated omens of good fortune and displayed them prominently—a lucky playing card stuck in a helmet band, a soldier's cross, or even a peace symbol chained around the neck.

To counter the obvious fact that Khe Sanh was under siege, the Marine commander, Col. David E. Lownds, continued to send patrols outside the perimeter, where they were routinely ambushed by the entrenched NVA troops. "They would go out on patrol, to do what, I don't know, and they were promptly slaughtered," recalled medical Corpsman Richard Heath. But Colonel Lownds's superiors felt the Marines' defensive posture at Khe Sanh was contrary to the heritage and spirit of the Corps, so patrols continued.

As Communist forces laid siege to Khe Sanh, comparisons were made to the French defeat at Dien Bien Phu fourteen years earlier. Would Khe Sanh be America's Dien Bien Phu? President Johnson became obsessed with Khe Sanh to the point of visiting the White House Situation Room in his bathrobe in the small hours of the night to study a sand-table scale model of the base and the surrounding terrain.

By mid-February, as the Tet Offensive ran out of steam, fighting in and around Khe Sanh also abated, and there were no major NVA ground attacks, though regular artillery shelling continued. At the end of the month, however, a Marine patrol discovered a maze of enemy trench lines, some more than a mile long, leading toward the combat base. Westmoreland ordered B-52 strikes just outside the perimeter, but the NVA kept digging. Some trenches ran to within one hundred yards of the base perimeter and ended in a T, an indication that assault ramps were about to be used for an all-out ground assault. A date freighted with ominous significance was approaching: March 13, the day the Viet Minh had begun their final assault

President Lyndon Johnson studies a relief map of the Khe Sanh area. Left to right: Press Secretary George Christian, Johnson, Gen. Robert Ginsburg, and National Security Advisor Walt Rostow.

on Dien Bien Phu. The Marines braced for an attack. None came. By the end of March, the Marine patrols were finding that many of the trenches had been long abandoned.

Tet

While Westmoreland and the president focused their attention on the showdown in northern I Corps, some American military officials were becoming equally concerned about the pattern of Communist activity elsewhere in South Vietnam. In Saigon, II Field Force commander Lt. Gen. Frederick C. Weyand was troubled by reports that several Main Force Viet Cong units had left their jungle base camps and moved closer to the capital. Uncertain what to make of it but assuming the worst, Weyand convinced Westmoreland in early January to pull fifteen American battalions back from border assignments to the outskirts of Saigon. US and ARVN forces, meanwhile, uncovered a series of enemy orders calling for attacks on other population centers. On January 4, soldiers of the 4th Infantry Division captured Operation Order No. 1, calling for an assault on the provincial capital of Pleiku. On January 20, the 23rd ARVN Division discovered similar plans for an attack on Ban Me Thuot, capital of Darlac

Province. A week later, South Vietnamese military security agents in Qui Nhon broke into a meeting of Viet Cong cadres and seized two prerecorded tapes declaring the "liberation" of the port town and calling on the local population to rise up against the GVN.

Aside from the redeployment recommended by General Weyand, however, the American command paid little heed to the accumulated evidence that had fallen into its hands. Believing the enemy incapable of mounting serious attacks on the cities, most US intelligence specialists dismissed the captured orders as empty boasts designed to lift flagging Communist troop morale. Westmoreland was convinced that the enemy's main objective was Khe Sanh, and that any attacks in the south would be an attempt to divert attention and resources from the battlefield to the north.

The plan that defied the credulity of the Americans was hatched in Hanoi in the spring of 1967, the product of a major strategic reappraisal by the North Vietnamese leadership. Under pressure from the southern Communists to accelerate the timetable for "liberation," yet unable to break the military stalemate brought on by the introduction of US troops, the Politburo decided to inaugurate the third and final stage of the revolutionary struggle—the General Offensive, General Uprising—with a wave of simultaneous attacks on virtually every population center in South Vietnam. By taking the war to the cities, the Communist leaders hoped to achieve several purposes at once. At the very least, they would shatter any illusions of American invulnerability, as well as the sense of security felt by hundreds of thousands of refugees who had fled from the war in the countryside. At best, they would break the back of ARVN, instigate a popular overthrow of the GVN, and force the Americans to accept a negotiated settlement.

Responsibility for planning the campaign was placed in the reluctant hands of Gen. Vo Nguyen Giap. He had personally opposed the idea of launching a general offensive, considering it too premature, too risky, and potentially too costly, but his authority had been diminished; his philosophy of slowly and steadily punishing the enemy—known as the Chinese approach—had been muscled out by hardliners who took what was called the Soviet approach, striking hard and fast with everything you've got. Giap dutifully carried out the Politburo's will. During the fall of 1967, in an effort to lure the Americans away from the cities and screen the infiltration of fresh troops and supplies from the North, he initiated a series of major confrontations along the South Vietnamese frontier—at Con Thien along the DMZ, at Dak To in the Central Highlands, at Loc Ninh in the Fishhook region along the Cambodian border, and finally at Khe Sanh.

In each case, the Americans responded as Giap presumed they would, diverting large numbers of troops to the remote battle zones in the hope of dealing the Communists a crushing blow.

In January 1968, Viet Cong guerrillas began infiltrating the cities disguised as civilians or ARVN soldiers returning home for the upcoming Tet (Lunar New Year) holiday. Weapons and munitions were also smuggled in, concealed in false-bottom trucks or vegetable carts and then buried at predetermined sites. Preparations intensified during the last week of the month as unit commanders learned for the first time what their missions would be. Finally, on January 29, the eve of Tet, came the order to attack. Broadcast by Radio Hanoi, it took the form of a poetic exhortation written by Ho Chi Minh to mark the advent of the Year of the Monkey:

This Spring far outshines the previous springs.
Of victories throughout the land come happy tidings.
Forward!
Total Victory will be ours.

During the next twenty-four hours, more than seventy thousand soldiers of the People's Liberation Army—the Viet Cong—backed by regular units of the North Vietnamese Army, launched attacks on thirty-six of forty-four provincial capitals, five of six major cities, sixty-four district towns, and fifty hamlets across the length and breadth of South Vietnam. The coastal town of Nha Trang, headquarters of the US First Field Force, was the first to be hit, shortly after midnight on January 30. Assaults on other towns within the II Corps area—Ban Me Thuot, Kontum, Hoi An, Qui Nhon, and Pleiku—followed in rapid succession. The next night, the Communists expanded the scope of the offensive, penetrating in strength into Quang Tri City, Tam Ky, and Hue in I Corps, Tuy Hoa and Phan Thiet in II Corps, the Capital Military District of Saigon, and every provincial and district capital in the Mekong Delta.

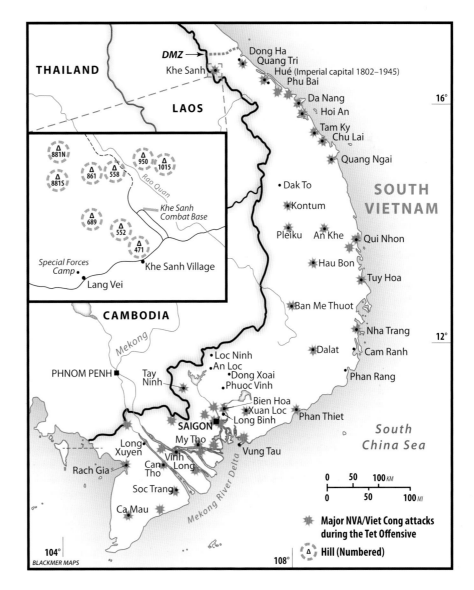

In the months before the Tet Offensive, NVA and VC forces launched numerous attacks on South Vietnam's western border, drawing allied forces away from Saigon and the other population centers that would be targeted by the Tet attacks, shown here. On January 21, 1968, the NVA began a brutal seventy-seven-day siege of the Marine combat base at Khe Sanh, which was seen by Gen. William Westmoreland as worth defending "at all costs." But when the siege ended, the Marines dismantled the base and abandoned it.

Not surprisingly, the Communists directed their heaviest blow against Saigon and its densely populated environs, hurling thirty-five battalions into the battle under the command of North Vietnamese Gen. Tran Van Do. Assigned the task of paralyzing the "nerve centers" of the allied war effort, the highly trained men and women of the Viet Cong C-10 Sapper Battalion spearheaded the assault with a series of daring raids on the presidential palace, the ARVN Joint General Staff headquarters, the national radio station, and, most memorably if not most successfully, the United States Embassy compound. A nineteen-man sapper squad occupied part of the embassy grounds for six hours that night while a small contingent of Marine guards held the consulate building, until an assault force of US paratroopers relieved them and killed or captured the sappers. Some four to five thousand Viet Cong local troops struck other key targets simultaneously, including the Tan Son Nhut airfield, while small squads of armed political cadres fanned out into the city's residential districts and exhorted the Saigonese to rise up against "the dictatorial Thieu-Ky regime." Outside the capital, NVA and VC Main Force units tried to pin down allied reaction forces by assaulting the US military bases at Bien Hoa, Lai Khe, and Cu Chi.

Opposite page: A large section of rubble is all that remains in this one-block-square area of Saigon on February 5, 1968, after fierce Tet Offensive fighting. Rockets and grenades, combined with fires, laid waste to the area. Quang Pagoda, location of Viet Cong headquarters during the fighting, is at the top of the photo.

One of the few survivors from the Communist sapper team that penetrated the US Embassy compound in Saigon is led away by military police.

A Vietnamese man carries his wounded wife out of a threatened area in Saigon in May 1968. Day-long fighting in the area erupted at dawn with a daring Viet Cong attack on a police station. As they did during the Tet Offensive, residents abandoned their homes and escaped to safer parts of the city.

Elsewhere, the enemy's plan of attack was much the same, and so were the results. Although caught by surprise, South Vietnamese and American forces reacted swiftly, using their superior mobility and firepower to maximum advantage and with devastating effect. Poor timing and faulty execution also undermined the Communists' efforts, as did the unwillingness of most civilians to take up arms in support of their would-be "liberators." Only in a dozen places, such as the populous district of Cholon in Saigon, did the invaders manage to hold on for more than a few days, and even then only at staggeringly high cost. US estimates of Communist casualties during the Tet campaign ranged as high as forty thousand killed, the vast majority of whom came from the ranks of Viet Cong Main Force units. The NLF political infrastructure also suffered crippling losses, as many previously unidentified local cadres exposed themselves in an attempt to foment a general uprising.

The exception to the pattern was the brutal battle of Hue. After storming the city and seizing the imperial Citadel on the night of January 31, 7,500 NVA regulars held out for more than three weeks in the face of an increasingly furious counterattack. While the fighting raged, the Communists set up their own "revolutionary government" and began rounding up alleged "collaborators," more than two thousand of whom were summarily executed. By the time the ordeal came to an end, much of the once beautiful city had been reduced to ruins, "its streets choked with rubble and rotting bodies."

Years later, a number of high-ranking Communist officials candidly admitted their disappointment at the outcome of the Tet Offensive. General Do put it succinctly: "In all honesty," he told an American interviewer in 1982, "we didn't achieve our main objective, which was to spur uprisings throughout the South."

Yet if the Communists failed to achieve their ultimate objectives, they succeeded nonetheless in altering irrevocably the course of the Vietnam War. The unprecedented magnitude and intensity of the offensive stunned the South Vietnamese and sent shock waves across the United States. Though initial news reports tended to exaggerate the enemy's military successes, the sense of pervasive confusion that they conveyed was not far off the mark. Having been repeatedly assured in recent months that the allies were making "steady progress," that "the light at the end of the tunnel" had at last come into view, many Americans shared the reaction of venerable television newsman Walter Cronkite. "What the hell is going on here?" Cronkite reportedly exclaimed soon after the fighting erupted. "I thought we were winning the war!"

General Westmoreland's attempts to downplay the significance of the attacks, including his claim that they were "diversionary" from the fight over Khe Sanh, did little to lessen the widening credibility gap between official pronouncements and popular perceptions. Dramatic film footage of the bloody fighting in Saigon and Hue, the stark photograph of the South Vietnamese police chief, General Loan, executing a Viet Cong prisoner at point-blank range, the offhand remark of an Army major at Ben Tre that "it became necessary to destroy the town to save it"—all seemed to confirm the growing conviction, as the editors of the *Cleveland Press* put it, "that something enormous has gone wrong [that] cannot be shrugged off with the kind of flimsy explanations given so far."

Characteristically, President Johnson's initial public response to the mounting chorus of criticism was to hang tough. At a White House press conference on February 2, he described the offensive as a "complete failure." "We have known for some time that this offensive was planned by the enemy," the president declared. "The ability to do what they have done has been anticipated, prepared for, and met." For all his apparent confidence, however, Johnson was deeply troubled by the unexpected turn of events. Although Westmoreland continued to assure him that the situation was "well in hand," the president still feared the possibility of a major military setback at Khe Sanh. Insisting that the combat base must be held and that Westmoreland be given whatever reinforcements he needed, Johnson told his senior advisors to "review all options," including an extension of enlistments, a call-up of the reserves, a troop increase in Vietnam, even a declaration of war.

To the chairman of the Joint Chiefs of Staff, Gen. Earle Wheeler, the president's new mood of urgency offered an opportunity to resolve fundamental issues that had been deferred too long. Since 1965, Wheeler and the other Joint Chiefs had urged Johnson to mobilize the reserves, not only to meet the demands of the escalating Vietnam War effort but to ensure that the nation continued to meet its other global military commitments. But LBJ, remembering the public outcry that greeted President Kennedy's reserve call-up during the 1961 Berlin crisis, had repeatedly vetoed the idea. Now, in the wake of Tet, it suddenly seemed that the president might at last accede to a full mobilization, provided that Wheeler played his cards right.

Walter Cronkite and a CBS News camera crew use a jeep for a dolly during an interview with the commanding officer of the 1st Battalion, 1st Marines, during the battle of Hue.

By 1968, CBS News anchorman Walter Cronkite was known as "the most trusted man in America." Cronkite had covered World War II as a United Press International reporter, and was one of a handful of newsmen who flew on bombing missions over Germany. He covered the famous Battle of the Bulge in late 1944, and reported on the Nuremberg war crimes trials after the war. In 1950, Edward R. Murrow recruited him for CBS Radio, and in 1962 Cronkite took over the CBS Evening News anchor desk. On November 22, 1963, choking up and near tears, he delivered the news of President Kennedy's death to a stunned nation.

When the Tet Offensive erupted, Cronkite proposed that he go to Vietnam to see for himself what was happening. Worried about compromising his neutrality as a reporter and the reputation of CBS News, he and CBS News President Richard Salant had discussed the proposed trip and concluded, he later wrote, that "this was too parochial a consideration in regard to an issue as large as any that had faced our nation—in fact, one that threatened to split the nation. It was agreed that I should go to Vietnam, do my best to get the answers, and broadcast my conclusions."

Cronkite met with soldiers, other reporters, military officers, and Gen. Creighton Abrams, who would in a few months succeed Westmoreland as MACV commander. According to Cronkite's producer, Ernest Leiser, who traveled to Vietnam with him, Abrams told Cronkite that the US could not win "this goddamned war" and

should find a way out. Back in New York, on February 27, Cronkite, long a supporter of the war, stepped out of his role as an objective reporter and told an estimated audience of nine million Americans, "To say that we are mired in stalemate seems the only realistic, yet unsatisfactory, conclusion," and "it is increasingly clear to this reporter that the only rational way out then will be to negotiate, not as victors, but as an honorable people who had lived up to their pledge to defend democracy, and did the best they could."

Lyndon Johnson did not see the broadcast. He was in Texas at a birthday party for Governor John Connally. Longtime CBS News correspondent Bob Schieffer claimed that he was told by Johnson aide George Christian that Johnson watched a recording of Cronkite's editorial the next day and said, "If I've lost Cronkite, I've lost middle America." In a 1979 interview, Christian said he had no recollection of what Johnson had said. Speechwriter Bill Moyers has also been cited as the source, but Moyers told journalism historian Christopher Daly, "I wasn't even there!"

Whether or not Johnson actually uttered the quote, on March 31 the president shocked the nation with a televised announcement of his own: "I shall not seek, and I will not accept, the nomination of my party for another term as your president," adding, "America stands ready tonight to seek an honorable peace."

South Vietnamese Gen. Nguyen Ngoc Loan, chief of the national police, fires his pistol into the head of a suspected Viet Cong officer on a Saigon street February 1, 1968, early in the Tet Offensive.

Wheeler flew to Saigon on February 23 to confer with Westmoreland. During his two-day visit, Wheeler intimated that the president at last seemed ready to relax long-standing constraints on ground operations in Laos and Cambodia. The two generals then discussed the forces that would be required to carry out such operations, as well as to replenish the strategic reserve if a major troop increase were approved. In the end, they settled on a figure of 206,000 men.

When Wheeler returned to Washington to lobby for the gigantic troop increase, however, he described the Tet Offensive as "a very near thing . . . that has by no means run its course," he told Johnson that "MACV will be hard pressed" to meet the continuing threat in northern I Corps and to restore security in the cities. "We must be prepared to accept some reverses," Wheeler concluded, unless the troop increase was approved. Left unspoken, but nonetheless clear, was that any sizable deployment would require a mobilization of the reserves.

For President Johnson, Wheeler's somber report posed an agonizing dilemma. Acceptance of the general's recommendations meant putting the nation on a virtual war footing in an election year amid growing criticism of his management of the conflict. Yet to deny the troop request was to invite an indefinite continuation of the war and perhaps even to risk military defeat. Unable to reach a decision without a full-scale review of the options, Johnson turned the matter over to an "intensive working group" headed by his longtime friend and newly appointed secretary of defense, Clark Clifford. "Give me the lesser of evils," the president told Clifford. "Give me your recommendations."

Clifford demanded that the JCS provide precise information on how the additional troops might be used and instructed officials at the Defense, State, and Treasury Departments to study the implications of the troop request and review possible alternatives.

Seizing the opportunity to express views that had long been ignored or suppressed, senior civilians at the Pentagon responded with a thoroughgoing indictment of the prevailing policy. "Our strategy of attrition has not worked," reported systems analyst Alain Enthoven, challenging the argument that a large troop increase could shorten the war. Other Defense Department officials said the escalation would also "entail substantial costs," including higher American casualties, new taxes, possibly even a wage-price freeze, thus risking "a domestic crisis of unprecedented proportions."

In the end, the report that Clifford submitted to the president on March 4 contained few specific recommendations. "Big questions remained," recalled William Bundy, assistant secretary of state for Far Eastern affairs. "There were stop signs—caution signs—all over the draft. Anybody could see that . . . no president would decide on the basis of these recommendations."

Though the findings of the Clifford task force effectively killed any chance of a major troop increase, news of the proposed escalation soon filtered back to the press, eventually producing a front-page story in the March 10 edition of the *New York Times*. WESTMORELAND REQUESTS 206,000 MORE MEN, the three-column headline blared, STIRRING DEBATE IN ADMINISTRATION. For the Johnson administration, the leak could hardly have come at a worse time. In recent weeks, public opinion had begun to shift decisively against the president, as hawks and doves alike registered their dissatisfaction with prevailing Vietnam policy. A series of opinion surveys taken in late February 1968, for example, revealed that only 26 percent of the American people approved of the president's handling of the war and that a near majority considered US involvement in the conflict a "mistake." Perhaps more significant, many of the more influential members of the national news media had withdrawn their support. On February 23, the prestigious *Wall Street Journal* ran an editorial declaring that "the American people should be getting ready to accept, if they haven't already, the prospect that the whole Vietnam effort may be doomed."

The expansion of antiwar sentiment was also evident on Capitol Hill, where, in mid-March, 139 members of the House of Representatives cosponsored a resolution calling for a full review of American policy in Southeast Asia.

The most dramatic indication of the president's growing political vulnerability, however, came on March 12, when Sen. Eugene McCarthy of Minnesota came within three hundred votes of defeating Johnson in the New Hampshire primary election. An avowed peace candidate, McCarthy had been given little chance of mounting a serious challenge to Johnson when he announced his candidacy for the Democratic nomination the preceding December. But after Tet, the senator's quixotic crusade had steadily gained momentum, in part due to the efforts of several thousand student volunteers.

The president barely had time to absorb the shock of McCarthy's stunning showing when, on March 16, Sen. Robert Kennedy of New York announced that he, too, would run against Johnson on a platform of opposition to the war. Johnson well knew that with his name and his powerful party connections, Kennedy made a far more formidable opponent than the scholarly maverick McCarthy.

Instinctively, if imprudently, Johnson decided to fight back by taking his case to the country and demanding "a total national effort to win the war." "We must meet our commitments in the world and in Vietnam," he told a business group in Chicago on March 17. "We shall and we are going to win the war!"

When the public response to Johnson's speeches proved overwhelmingly negative, the president's advisors became deeply worried. Pointing out that "McCarthy and Kennedy are the candidates of peace and the president is the war candidate," campaign strategist James L. Rowe Jr., strongly urged Johnson to "do something exciting and dramatic to recapture the peace issue" before the April 2 Wisconsin primary. "Hardly anyone today is interested in winning the war," Rowe asserted in a blunt memorandum. "Everyone wants to get out, and the only question is how." The message sank in. The next morning, Johnson telephoned Defense Secretary Clifford and said: "I've got to get me a peace proposal."

On March 20 and again on March 22, Johnson conferred with his senior advisors about a possible new peace initiative. While most agreed that the president should propose to limit in some way the bombing of North Vietnam, fundamental differences of opinion over the purpose of such a gesture undermined any firm consensus. Convinced that the North Vietnamese would reject the offer, Rusk and National Security Advisor Walt Rostow hoped to placate public opinion long enough to allow for US participation in the war to continue. In Clark Clifford's view, however, the task was not simply to stabilize the home front but to find a way out of the "hopeless bog" in which the United States had become mired. He therefore argued that a partial bombing halt should be implemented as the first in a series of concrete "de-escalatory steps" leading to a negotiated settlement and total American withdrawal.

Though for the moment the president made no decision about the bombing halt proposal, the deliberations persuaded him that any further expansion of the US war effort was no longer an option. At the March 22 meeting, he formally rejected the Wheeler-Westmoreland troop request, instead approving only a modest deployment of 13,500 support troops to augment the emergency reinforcements dispatched in March. He also informed his advisors that he had decided to recall Westmoreland from South Vietnam to assume the position of Army chief of staff. Whether the move had been

Secretary of State Dean Rusk, President Lyndon Johnson, and Secretary of Defense Robert McNamara (left to right) hold a Cabinet Room meeting.

planned long in advance, as the general himself later claimed, or rather resulted from Westmoreland's failure to anticipate the Tet Offensive, is not clear. It seemed nevertheless to signify that the Johnson administration had decided upon a change of course.

Clifford, however, was still not convinced that Johnson fully appreciated the need to take bold and decisive action toward an acceptable peace. Concluding that the president required "some stiff medicine to bring home to [him] what was happening in the country," he proposed that the president reconvene a group of elder statesmen—the so-called wise men—who had endorsed his Vietnam policy in April 1965 and again in November 1967. The group, numbering fourteen, included many of the more prominent members of the post-World War II American foreign policy establishment, including former Secretary of State Dean Acheson, George Ball, McGeorge Bundy, Arthur Goldberg, Henry Cabot Lodge, Cyrus Vance, and Generals Omar Bradley, Matthew Ridgway, and Maxwell Taylor.

Before meeting with the president, the wise men assembled on the evening of March 25 for a series of briefings from officials of the State Department, the CIA, and the JCS. Many of those present were shaken by what they learned. Asked how long it would take to win the war at the

In the early morning hours of January 31, 1968, the Viet Cong attacked the US Embassy in Saigon. As American military commanders and the news media waited in uncertainty, nineteen enemy sappers roamed the courtyard of the embassy complex and tried, unsuccessfully, to penetrate the embassy building. More than any other incident of the Tet Offensive, the attack suggested to the American people, who awoke that morning to screaming headlines announcing the embassy raid, that the US was far from victory. The sole American defending the front lobby was twenty-year-old Sgt. Ronald W. Harper of the Marine Security Guards.

As usual, there were two guards scheduled to work in the embassy building that night—myself and Cpl. George Zachuranic—in addition to the two Army MPs who were always at the gate. But that night the command said it was going to start putting extra men on posts because something might be going on. No one took it seriously because we'd had these alerts before, on and off.

Zach was posted in the lobby, and I was the "roving guard," so I went upstairs and talked to the third man on that night, Sgt. Rudy Soto. At about 2:30 a.m. I went next door to the consulate compound, on the other side of an eight-foot wall from the embassy. I was talking to the two guards over there at about 2:45 when I heard a big explosion. Sappers had blown out part of the front wall of the embassy complex.

My first thought was that I had the master key to the embassy, that Zach was new and might not know which key to use to lock the door. So I left the consulate, went through the gate, and scooted to the back door of the embassy lobby. On the way I ran right past a Vietnamese guy just wandering around by the consulate in shock. He wasn't one of the local guards, because they weren't working there that night. I didn't realize until later that he was actually one of the Viet Cong.

As I got to the back door, I looked over at the side gate for the MPs. The Viet Cong had shot heavy machine-gun fire at those guys, and they were apparently down already. All I could see was a cloud of dust, flying dirt, and no people. I ran into the lobby and Zach was on the phone, apparently calling for help. So I ran out to the front door, got the old Vietnamese guard, and pulled the big teak doors shut.

I pushed the old man into an office and ran to lock the rear doors, too. I still didn't know what was going on. All I knew was that there was machine-gun fire, crap was flying all over the place, and there were flashes outside. As I was running to the armory, right near the desk where Zach was standing, an antitank rocket came through the side windows at the front door and hit the wall near us, knocking me on my rear end and blowing Zach's eardrums out and hitting him with shrapnel. It exploded in the wall right over my head, ripping apart the seal of the United States.

When I got up, there were dust and smoke all over the place. Zach was moaning and groaning and couldn't hear me. I dragged him into the armory and bandaged his head to stop the bleeding, but he was in shock and kept making noise. I said, "Zach, be quiet!" because I knew someone was outside. But I didn't know if we were being attacked by one person or ten people.

There was enemy fire inside and outside the lobby all night. The bullets ricocheted off the granite walls and occasionally it got heavy. The lobby was always lit so anyone outside could see me when I moved around, but I couldn't see them. I could even hear them chattering outside. But still no one came in.

It was little things that night, stupid little things that happened that probably saved everyone. I found out later that Rudy was on the roof. He fired down and probably killed one of them and slowed them down. The embassy was supposed to be completely dark, but there were a few lights left on upstairs. So after Rudy fired, the Viet Cong started shooting into those offices, thinking more people were up there guarding the place than there actually were. They could have walked in and taken us, but they thought we were a lot more heavily manned and armed. These things slowed them down long enough for us to get help.

I felt better when it got light at about 5:30 or 6:00. I could see outside, but there wasn't anything happening. Finally at about 8:00 a platoon from the 101st Airborne came down into the lobby from the roof and some others broke through the front gate in a jeep. But there was no one left to shoot—all of the enemy had been killed.

For his actions during the attack on the embassy, Sergeant Harper was later awarded the Bronze Star. He was honorably discharged from the Marines in 1969.

current level of commitment, Deputy Assistant Secretary of State Philip Habib replied: "Maybe five years, maybe ten." A dramatic exchange between US ambassador to the United Nations Arthur Goldberg and Gen. William DePuy proved equally unsettling. After DePuy asserted that the enemy had lost more than eighty thousand troops since the beginning of the year, Goldberg inquired about the number of wounded. DePuy responded that standard military estimates were based on a ratio of three to one. Then Goldberg asked, "How many effectives do you think they have operating in the field?" DePuy cited the official MACV estimate of 230,000. "Well, General," Goldberg said, "I am not a great mathematician, but with 80,000 killed and with a wounded ratio of three to one, or 240,000, for a total of 320,000, who the hell are we fighting?"

The following day, the group met with Johnson and rendered their verdict. "The majority feeling," said Bundy, "is that we can no longer do the job we set out to do in the time we have left and we must begin to move to disengage."

Johnson listened impassively as each man expressed his views. In the end, however, he knew that he had no choice but to accept their collective judgment.

Five days later, on the evening of March 31, Lyndon Johnson addressed the nation. He announced in the televised speech that the bombing of North Vietnam would henceforth be limited to the area just north of the

Opposite page: An American tank leads the way down Route 9 toward Khe Sanh, part of the joint US and South Vietnamese task force sent to relieve the Marines as part of Operation Pegasus in early April 1968.

Private First Class Juan Fordona, a 1st Cav trooper, shakes hands with Marine Cpl. James Hellebuick over barbed wire at the perimeter of the Marine base at Khe Sanh in early April 1968. The meeting marked the first overland linkup between troops of the 1st Cav and the encircled Marine garrison at Khe Sanh.

demilitarized zone and held out the possibility of a "complete bombing halt" if the North Vietnamese responded favorably. He characterized the unilateral move as "the first in what I hope will be a series of steps toward peace" and made it clear that the United States was prepared to begin talks at any time and any place. When he reached the end of his speech, Johnson paused briefly before reading words that he had appended at the last moment, announcing he would not run for another term.

On April 1, 1968, the day after President Johnson spoke to the nation, a combined US-ARVN task force totaling some thirty thousand troops set out along Route 9 in Quang Tri Province to relieve the Marine garrison at Khe Sanh. In a spectacular display of air mobility, soldiers of the US 1st Air Cav spearheaded the drive, leapfrogging ahead of a seemingly endless column of tanks, trucks, and troops on foot. Meeting with only token resistance along the way, the first wave of cavalrymen finally linked up with the Marines outside the base on the morning of April 8. The seventy-seven-day siege of Khe Sanh was over.

Two months later, the Marines began to dismantle the base. They blew up their bunkers and carried off the remaining ammo and supplies. When

journalists began to inquire why the "western anchor" of the allies' northern defense line had suddenly become expendable, they were told that the NVA had changed their tactics, that they had carved new infiltration routes, and that a fixed base in the corner of Quang Tri Province was no longer necessary. "We don't want any more Khe Sanhs," said one Marine junior officer. "To defeat an enemy, you've got to keep moving." On July 9, after a siege of five months and eighteen days, after 274 Marines had been killed and 2,541 wounded, after one hundred thousand tons of bombs had been dropped on enemy positions around Khe Sanh, the Marines abandoned the base. The same day, the flag of the National Liberation Front was raised over the Khe Sanh airfield.

Focus: The Battle for Hue

Like most of the larger cities of South Vietnam, Hue, the former seat of the Nguyen emperors, had been spared from extensive damage in the first few years of the war. Hue was the South Vietnamese social and religious center and a virtual oasis from war. Some called the beautiful city "a lotus in a sea of fire."

But Hue's calm had been shattered in the early morning hours of January 31, 1968, the second day of Tet, when Communist 122mm rockets screamed through the low fog and exploded in the center of the ancient Citadel, a fortress on the north bank of the Perfume River surrounded by a moat and zigzag stone walls. Almost simultaneously, soldiers of the 800th and 802nd Battalions of the 6th NVA Regiment stormed through the lightly defended western gates of the Citadel and made for the headquarters of the ARVN 1st Division in the northeast corner of the fortress. Attacks on Da Nang and cities in II Corps the night before had put some of them on guard, and Brig. Gen. Ngo Quang Truong, commander of the ARVN 1st Division in Hue, had placed men on alert that night. Thus, when the 800th Battalion arrived at the Tay Loc airfield in the middle of the Citadel, they were met by the elite ARVN Black Panther Company and forced to turn south into the residential sections of the Citadel. The 802nd initially penetrated the ARVN compound, but was also driven back by the Black Panthers.

Elsewhere in the city, though, defense was scattered, and waves of enemy troops continued to fan out into the streets. As daylight broke and the chilly fog lifted, the gold-starred, red-and-blue flag of the NLF flew over the old emperor's palace. Hue was in Communist hands. The only significant pockets of resistance were the ARVN and MACV compounds, where the besieged occupants could only wait for reinforcements as they watched the NVA and VC dig in.

For General Westmoreland and the American and South Vietnamese command, the loss of Hue would have meant disaster. "Taking it," the American general wrote later, "would have a profound psychological impact on the Vietnamese in both the North and South, and in the process, the North Vietnamese might seize the two north provinces as bargaining points in any negotiations." For all its strategic significance, however, the initial efforts to retake Hue were unsuccessful. The Marine command at Phu Bai, eight miles to the south, believed that the attacking force was small and dispatched a single company to Hue. Along the way, the unit, Alpha Company, 1st Battalion, 1st Marines, met up with four American tanks and headed up Highway 1. A sudden barrage of intense fire from one of the two NVA battalions blocking the approaches to the city pinned down the Marines, and the call went out for reinforcements. A second company arrived, and the combined American force broke through to MACV headquarters, but only after taking forty casualties, including ten dead. The fight for Hue would demand more manpower, and over the next three days, three more companies, three command groups, and a tank platoon—about a thousand Marines in all—arrived to join in the fight. After a failed American attempt to cross the river, it was decided that the Marines would concentrate on the south side of the river, while ARVN forces worked to dislodge the NVA and VC from the Citadel.

The South Vietnamese had a more difficult task. General Truong had been able to pull back his troops to consolidate defense of the ARVN compound, but enemy control over the two square miles inside the Citadel was strong. NVA troops and supplies continued to flow into the old fortress through the well-defended west gates; over the next week, ten battalions totaling more than a division would be committed to the battle for Hue. The twenty-foot-thick, thirty-foot-high walls, built to defend the old emperors from ancient enemies, now provided the modern-day attackers a virtually impregnable fortress.

For several days, Marines surrounded and stormed buildings, supported by fire from tanks, recoilless rifles, and machine guns. Howitzers fired huge shells at enemy positions, while fighter-bombers dropped 500- and 750-pound bombs and Navy ships off the coast hurled shells several miles from five-, six-, and eight-inch guns. Beautiful pagodas, modest stucco houses, and sprawling French villas all crumbled under the rain of firepower as Americans, enemy troops, and civilians scurried to safety or became casualties.

During the battle for Hue, US troops move through an area scarred from heavy artillery fire.

Despite the best efforts of the Americans to clear the south bank of the Perfume, the well-entrenched and well-supplied enemy held on. The NVA contested each step the Marines took and often carried the day. By the end of the first week, it was estimated that the Americans had not yet taken half of the south bank of the Perfume, while incurring 250 casualties. In the damp weather, the stench from the dead soldiers and civilians became unbearable, and the almost constant cloudiness lent a funereal dankness to the city.

By February 10, the area on the south bank of the Perfume River was finally declared secure, and most of the fighting there abated, though there were still occasional mortar explosions and sniper attacks on Marine patrols. Exhausted and chilled, the Americans looked through the fog and smoke at their next objective: the Citadel.

On the north side of the Perfume, the 1st ARVN Division had not been able to match the apparent success of its American allies. The South Vietnamese had been able to regain some territory around their base, but the NVA still held 60 percent of the Citadel, including the southern sector of the fortress. The North Vietnamese established their command post in the middle of this territory, in the Imperial Palace.

US Marines huddle around a field radio behind the Citadel in Hue, waiting for their next command. An American plane passes overhead. Marines moved back from the Citadel to allow allied dive bombers to pound the twelve-foot-thick walls of the stronghold, where Communists had been entrenched for almost three weeks.

In the heart of the city, the Communists tightened their grip. NLF cadres quickly established a revolutionary government, headed by a Hue University professor and the principal of a local girls' high school. A former police chief became the new mayor. In the streets, soldiers and sympathizers hoisted banners denouncing the South Vietnamese and Americans and exhorting the people to join them.

The Communists also employed more heavy-handed methods to try to control the population. It was later estimated that approximately three thousand people were systematically executed by the Communists during their occupation of Hue. Many were found months after the battle for Hue in shallow, mass graves; others were never recovered and were presumed dead. Later, American and South Vietnamese authorities would point to the massacre of these civilians as evidence of the ruthlessness of the North Vietnamese and Viet Cong and a ghastly hint of the massacre that would ensue if they won the war.

While the Communists rounded up their enemies, the Americans on the south bank of the Perfume prepared to cross the river to the walls of the Citadel. On the evening of February 11, the men, tanks, and Ontos armored vehicles of the 1st

Marine Lance Corporal Gene Davis, a sniper with Delta Company, 1st Battalion, 5th Marines, takes aim during operations to retake Hue during the Tet Offensive, February 22, 1968.

Private First Class D. A. Cruz of Hotel Company, 2nd Battalion, 5th Marines, is treated for wounds by Navy Corpsman D. R. Howe during fighting in Hue, February 6, 1968.

Battalion, 5th Marines crossed the Perfume. In their first assault on the south wall the next day, the battalion suffered fifteen men killed and forty wounded. The fighting at the ramparts promised to be even bloodier than the clashes on the south bank of the Perfume.

In the first week, it was estimated that the Marines took one casualty for every meter of ground gained. The scores of wounded were carried out on top of tanks or on the backs of fellow Marines. Those who had been spared physical injury began to show the strain, bursting into tears or simply staring blankly into the distance, victims of a form of shell shock.

On February 16, an NVA radio transmission from inside the Citadel was intercepted, disclosing that the enemy commander had been killed and that his successor had asked permission to withdraw. The request was denied by NVA superiors, but it was evidence that enemy morale was dissipating.

The end of the three-week battle proved to be anticlimactic. NVA resistance inside the Citadel crumbled, and Vietnamese marines and the ARVN 1st Division pushed the remaining enemy up against the south fortress wall where they were scattered or destroyed. In the early morning hours of February 24, the 2nd Battalion, 3rd Regiment of the ARVN 1st Division arrived at the main flagpole at the Imperial Palace, where they tore down the NLF banner and replaced it with the South Vietnamese flag. The next day, ARVN Rangers stormed the Imperial Palace, only to find it empty. The enemy had fled in the night.

The battle for Hue was over, but it was unclear who had emerged the real victor. For their part, the American and South Vietnamese commands pointed to the favorable casualty figures as an indicator of their success. Enemy losses were estimated at more than 5,000 killed and 89 captured. American losses totaled 216 killed and 1,364 seriously wounded, and ARVN figures were 384 KIA and 1,830 wounded.

But while the Americans and South Vietnamese regained the city, the jarring fact was that the Communists had been able to seize and hold it for three weeks;

Marines advance up the outer wall of the Citadel.

An exhausted Marine rests on his M50, a light antitank vehicle known as the Ontos, during the fighting in Hue, February 23, 1968.

in fact, North Vietnamese commanders claimed later, the original plan had been to hold it for just seven days. In its length and severity, the occupation contributed to the devastating psychological impact of Tet upon the Americans and South Vietnamese, setting in motion events that ultimately proved more advantageous to the Communists than a military victory would have.

Whatever standards of victory were applied, the definite losers were the people of Hue. What had been "a lotus in a sea of fire" had been engulfed in a storm of death.

The Vietnam War has been called the "helicopter war," and the signature helicopter of the war was the UH-1 Iroquois, a utility craft built by Bell and more commonly known as the Huey. The Vietnam Helicopter Pilots Association calculates that of the twelve thousand helicopters that flew in Vietnam, 7,013 were Hueys, and they logged a collective 7.5 million flight hours. There were two basic configurations: "slicks," which carried troops into and out of battle, and gunships, heavily armed for combat support. Richard Melis flew both slicks and gunships as a US Army warrant officer based in the Mekong Delta at Vinh Long with the 7th Regiment, 1st Cavalry.

US Army Warrant Officer Richard Melis (in helicopter) and crew chief in Vinh Long, 1968.

The Warrant Officer Candidate/flight school at Fort Rucker, Alabama, was tough. Fewer than half of the people who started the program when I did were standing beside me when I was sworn in as a Warrant Officer aviator. After six months at Fort Knox, Kentucky, learning new aircraft and tactics, I left for Vietnam, arriving just in time for the 1968 Tet Offensive; our first job was to retake Vinh Long airfield from the VC.

Airlifting soldiers to block or attack the enemy was what the tadpole-shaped Huey was made for. The earliest version of these aircraft, the "A" model, had seats for a pilot and a co-pilot, and seven passengers. This model could actually fly very well with this many people aboard—if they were all skinny teenagers, with no seat armor, body armor, weapons, ammunition, equipment, food, or water. The tactical maneuverability of the 1-A was wonderful; the engine power needed to accomplish the missions, not so much.

So a new engine was designed into the "B" model, so that the helicopter could actually fly with soldiers and their equipment. Then the aircraft designers stretched the Huey airframe, providing a place for the crew chiefs and door gunners to sit with their M60 machine guns and ammunition and freeing up the main cabin area for the transport of troops and supplies, and called it the UH-1D. Then came the UH-1H, just like the "D" model but with a more powerful engine. This was the model I was flying in the 7/1 Cavalry in 1968. I loved this machine.

The UH designation stands for "Utility Helicopter," and this aircraft was very utilitarian. For a machine that was fifty feet long and weighed almost five tons, it was agile, sensitive to control inputs from the pilots. You didn't move the controls to get a response so much as you just thought about which direction you wanted to go, and it happened. If on final approach the crew chief called out "Slide three right, stump under the skid!" the pilot on the controls made it happen—instantly.

The Huey was a flying truck, and we operated them like they were pickup trucks—open to our passengers and cargo. We re-moved the doors because when you are dropping off or picking up

soldiers in the heat of battle, there just isn't time for opening and closing doors, and the door gunners needed to have the doors open (off) in order to operate their M60 machine guns.

"Wounded twenty yards right." And the helicopter that had just dropped off troops on the forward edge of battle was now an air ambulance picking up wounded from where they had fallen. I was an ugly air ambulance. It didn't have stretchers, clean sheets or IV bags operated by medics, but it could carry the wounded quickly to a field hospital and many lives that might have been lost were saved. It wasn't pretty. It just worked really well.

I flew the Huey "C" model gunship during the second half of my tour. It carried a pair of M60 machine guns on flexible mounts that could be controlled and fired from the cockpit, and bundles of rocket tubes on each side. The C-1 had a door gunner and a crew chief in the back, each with a machine gun. It was a very good aircraft for helicopter assault missions and armed reconnaissance missions not just because it could better tolerate being in a dive and carry lots of weapons, but because it operated with a crew of four. Four sets of eyes to see to the sides, below, and even behind the helicopter when the gunners leaned out.

In June 1968, I was tasked to pick up a Special Forces team from somewhere near the Cambodian border. I was not a Warrant Officer who was easy to supervise, but I had been identified as a pilot with decent skills, excellent night vision, irrepressible enthusiasm, and irrational self-confidence—as was confirmed by my being

My crew and I were to fly a Huey slick late at night, all alone — no wingman, no gunship support, no Command and Control ship in the distance behind us. We were to set the cockpit lights absolutely no brighter than was essential to fly the aircraft, and have no exterior lights at any time during the mission. We were to fly as low as we safely could above the trees to the intersection of two canals that we were to find by starlight alone, then turn to a specified heading, begin to slow down, and listen for instructions over a secure FM radio channel.

We found the intersection. I turned the nose to the specified heading. A quiet voice came into my headset.

"I have you silhouetted against the stars," the voice whispered, with no formalities. "Turn ten degrees right and slow down. Begin descent. When you see the Zippo lighter come on under the poncho tent pointed at you, come forward until you blow the light out, the grass is soft there, bottom the collective to land hard, count to one and then pull full power climbing to the stars. We will be aboard."

"Is the LZ cold?" I asked.

"Oh yeah. Cold."

"Then why are you whispering?" I asked.

"Laryngitis," he said softly.

I did what he told me to do. I felt the aircraft rock with the weight of the team leaping aboard the same second that I felt the skids thump onto the ground. His laryngitis cured, the man I had been whispering to yelled, "Go! Go! Go!"

Even with full power, it takes a few seconds to get an aircraft that big and that loaded well up above the trees. During those few seconds, all hell broke loose. There were so many tracers flying around us, and flashes from the RPGs exploding where we had just been, that it was easy to read the torque meter and the tachometer for the climb over the trees ahead. Once we were beyond the trees and the shooting stopped, the Special Forces fellow put on the headset the crew chief had handed him and profusely thanked us for doing such a good job.

"I thought you said the LZ was cold!" I said.

"It was until you showed up," he replied.

Army Hueys navigate through dense fog and smoke in the Vietnam highlands as they fly to a mountaintop landing zone to medevac wounded soldiers to Da Nang

CHAPTER FIVE

THE HOME FRONT

During John F. Kennedy's presidency, Vietnam was flying below the radar of most Americans, although by the time of his assassination he had boosted the number of military advisors in Vietnam from fewer than a thousand to more than sixteen thousand; a monk had self-immolated in Saigon protesting the treatment of Buddhists by the regime of the Catholic Ngo Dinh Diem; and President Diem himself had been overthrown and killed in a military coup aided and abetted by the American CIA. The Malcolm Browne photograph of the burning monk was given worldwide circulation, and the coup against Diem likewise made headlines in most of the world's newspapers.

Military police keep back protesters during a sit-in outside the Pentagon on October 21, 1967.

As 1964 began, with Lyndon Johnson in the White House, undercurrents of discontent began to rumble across America. In May, the socialist Progressive Labor Movement organized the first significant street demonstration against the Vietnam War; hundreds of students and organizers marched from Times Square to the United Nations headquarters in New York City. A few days later, a dozen young men in New York burned their draft cards. Largely ignored by the public because of its socialist roots, the early antiwar movement would spread to college campuses the following year and eventually to mainstream America. In August, the Gulf of Tonkin incident—in which the US military and the Johnson administration alleged that North Vietnamese gunboats attacked a US Navy destroyer off the coast of North Vietnam on August 2 and again on August 4—led to the congressional resolution of the same name, intensified bombing of North Vietnam, and a sudden growth of antiwar sentiment.*

Trying to manage the increasingly vexatious conflict in Southeast Asia was not Johnson's only concern. Chief among the unfinished business of Kennedy's abbreviated presidency was the civil rights bill that he had sent to Congress in June 1963. Despite opposition by a number of Southern members, the bill was brought to the House floor in October and was passed and sent to the Senate.

In Lyndon Johnson's first address to a joint session of Congress, less than a week after Kennedy's assassination, Johnson said, "No memorial oration or eulogy could more eloquently honor President Kennedy's memory than the earliest possible passage of the civil rights bill for which he fought so long." Johnson, a Southerner, had committed himself to the most far-reaching civil rights legislation since Reconstruction. His fellow Southern Democrats in the Senate were no less committed to killing the bill.

A slightly weakened compromise bill was brought to the Senate floor, where a Southern bloc of eighteen senators filibustered against it for fifty-seven days, until Majority Whip Hubert Humphrey rounded up enough votes to end the filibuster and bring the bill to a vote. It passed 73–27, cleared a House-Senate conference committee, and was approved by both House and Senate. On July 2, forty-eight hours before the nation's birthday celebration, President Johnson signed the Civil Rights Act of 1964 into law.

(Most historians agree that Kennedy, the elite Yankee, probably could not have gotten the Civil Rights Act, or the Voting Rights Act, through Congress. It required the consummate political skills, and the Southern heritage, of LBJ to reach the goals that Kennedy had set.)

The act drove five Southern Democrat states into the arms of the more conservative Republican Party in the November election, but neither the political defections nor the threat of a wider war in Vietnam, precipitated by the Gulf of Tonkin incident, prevented Johnson from being elected to his own full term as president by a landslide in November. In what could be seen as a classic irony, Johnson campaigned as the antiwar candidate against the strident hawkishness of his Republican opponent, Sen. Barry Goldwater of Arizona. The famous—or infamous—television campaign ad known as the "Daisy Girl"

---

*The alleged August 4 attack, the veracity of which was dubious at best even then, was completely denied by North Vietnam's wartime military leader, Vo Nguyen Giap, in a 1995 meeting with former US Defense Secretary Robert McNamara. "What happened on August 4?" McNamara asked. "Absolutely nothing," Giap replied.

President Lyndon Johnson moves to shake hands with Dr. Martin Luther King Jr. while others look on at the signing of the Voting Rights Act in 1965.

ad suggested that if elected, Goldwater would somehow bring on a nuclear holocaust.

As the ad begins, the viewers see a little girl standing in a field, counting as she plucks petals from a daisy. The girl's counting is replaced by the ominous sound of a missile launch countdown, and at zero the screen lights up with a nuclear explosion and a mushroom cloud. The voice of Lyndon Johnson intones, *These are the stakes! To make a world in which all of God's children can live, or to go into the dark. We must either love each other, or we must die.* It aired only one time, during NBC's Movie of the Week on September 7, 1964, but it caused an immediate storm of protest whose impact reverberated throughout the nation on election Tuesday. Johnson and his running mate, Sen. Hubert Humphrey of Minnesota, captured 60 percent of the popular vote and 90 percent of the Electoral College votes, at the time the most lopsided electoral victory in the history of the presidency.

But during the next four years, dramatic events in Vietnam and at home would discourage Johnson from seeking a second term and would produce another chance at the White House for Richard Nixon.

"President Johnson's decision to sacrifice himself on the altar of peace and national unity is an act of statesmanship which entitles him to the American people's deepest respect and sympathy." So wrote the editors of the *Los Angeles Times*, voicing a view shared by many in the immediate aftermath of Johnson's historic speech of March 31, 1968. Praise of the president's actions was even more widespread after Hanoi announced on April 3 that it would accept the American offer to begin preliminary peace talks. Infused with fresh hope that the Vietnam War might at last be brought to an end, a mood of near exhilaration temporarily gripped the American people. In New York, throngs of well-wishers cheered the president during a visit for the investiture of Archbishop Terence Cardinal Cooke, while on Wall Street the stock market recorded its greatest single-day gain to that date.

For Lyndon Johnson, there must have been more than a touch of irony in that transitory moment of renewed popularity. Barely three years had passed since he stood at the apex of power and prestige, after his stunning electoral victory. With the Democratic Party in firm control of both houses of Congress and the economy booming, his dream of creating the Great Society on the foundations of Kennedy's New Frontier had seemed well within reach. During his State of the Union address on January 4, 1965, the House chamber had thundered with applause as Johnson laid out his agenda for the future: to extend federal aid to education and medical aid to the elderly, to eradicate poverty and refurbish the cities, and to cut excise taxes and ensure equal rights for all. "This, then, is the State of the Union," the president had concluded, "free, growing, restless, and full of hope."

Only one major problem confronted Johnson as he set out to transform his social vision into reality: the war in that "damn little piss-ant country," as he privately referred to Vietnam. Despite the commitment of more than twenty-two thousand American military advisors, the might of some twelve thousand American bombing missions, and the influx of thousands of tons of American war materiel, the struggle against the Communists in Southeast Asia was going badly. Even more disquieting from Johnson's point of view, it was becoming a political liability. Public opinion polls taken at the end of 1964 revealed that fully 50 percent of the public was dissatisfied with the administration's handling of the war, though the same surveys also indicated sharp disagreement over what course the president should follow. During the election campaign, Johnson himself had seemed undecided, promising not to widen the war or "send American boys to do what Asian boys ought to do for themselves," while at the same time vowing never "to yield to Communist aggression."

By early 1965, however, it had become clear that the time for such ambivalence had passed. With the threat of a decisive Communist victory in South Vietnam growing more imminent with each passing day, Johnson would have to make "harder choices," special assistant McGeorge Bundy advised him. He would have to choose between "escalation and withdrawal," between using "our military power to force a change in Communist policy" and applying "all our resources along a track of negotiation, aimed at salvaging what little can be preserved." Fearful that he would be vilified by the Republican right if he "lost" South Vietnam to the Communists and confident that the nation would tolerate the war as long as its costs remained relatively modest, Johnson opted to raise the American stakes in Southeast Asia by stepping up the bombing of North Vietnam and sending US combat troops to the South. In so doing, he set in motion forces that would divide the nation, shatter his plans for the Great Society, and ultimately deprive him of the presidency itself.

From the outset, there had been dissenting voices. Eminent journalist Walter Lippmann—who had helped popularize the term "cold war," feuded with Johnson and repeatedly warned that there could be "no military solution" to the Vietnam conflict—was one. (Lippmann had a mixed record as a prophet; he insisted in 1959 that Cuba had "no real prospect of becoming a Soviet satellite state.") Senators Wayne Morse of Oregon and Ernest Gruening of Alaska, the only members of Congress to vote against the 1964 Gulf of Tonkin Resolution, were others. When the Marines went ashore at Da Nang in the spring of 1965, however, public opposition to the deepening American involvement in Vietnam rapidly expanded and intensified.

University students were among the first to register their protest. Beginning in late March at the University of Michigan, activists at more than a hundred colleges and universities boycotted classes and staged a series of "teach-ins" to discuss the war and its implications. Others, seeking to express their dissent more directly, left their campuses to participate in the mass antiwar rallies that took place in New York on April 15 and in Washington, D.C., two days later. In Berkeley, California, the newly formed Vietnam Day Committee organized similar demonstrations during the spring and later attempted to block troop trains heading into the Oakland Army Terminal, the point of departure for many Vietnam-bound GIs.

Antiwar demonstrators gather in front of the Lincoln Memorial in Washington, D.C., on October 21, 1967. Behind them is the Washington Monument, and in the distance, the Capitol Building.

Swelling the ranks of the student protesters were many clergymen, educators, and civil rights leaders, as well as members of such liberal, middle-class organizations as the Committee for a Sane Nuclear Policy (SANE) and the American Friends Service Committee. A product of the earlier "ban the bomb" movement, SANE mounted the largest single antiwar protest of the year when it attracted thirty thousand marchers to Washington, D.C., on November 27. Led by pediatrician Dr. Benjamin Spock, socialist Norman Thomas, and Coretta Scott King, the wife of Dr. Martin Luther King Jr., the demonstrators carried placards demanding an end to US bombing in Vietnam and a supervised cease-fire.

In 1966, the antiwar movement continued to gain momentum, as more and more ordinary citizens began to question the American commitment to South Vietnam. In late January, a group of one hundred Veterans and Reservists to End the War in Vietnam picketed the White House to protest the resumption of US air strikes over North Vietnam after a thirty-seven-day bombing pause. Several days later, five thousand American scientists, seventeen of them former Nobel Prize winners, petitioned the president to review US chemical and biological warfare in Southeast Asia.

Serious doubts about the war also began to surface in Congress, prompting the Senate Armed Services Committee to initiate in early February 1966 an "investigation" of the administration's Vietnam policy. Under the chairmanship of Sen. J. William Fulbright, the distinguished Arkansas Democrat, the committee set out to find answers to basic questions surrounding military strategy, troop deployments, bombing policy, and peace negotiations.

Opposite page, top: During an anti-Vietnam demonstration in Washington, D.C., US Marshals bodily remove a protester amid the outbreak of violence at the Pentagon.

Opposite page, bottom: Martin Luther King Jr. addresses a large peace demonstration against the Vietnam War at the United Nations Plaza in New York City, April 15, 1967.

Jeffrey Hahn grew up a Christian Scientist in a politically conservative family that voted for Barry Goldwater in 1964. By then, Jeff had graduated from Newton (Mass.) High School and enrolled in the University of Pennsylvania. He was very clear on his life goals—he wanted to become a university professor. Sometime after the 1964 election, which Lyndon Johnson won by a landslide, Hahn began dating a Quaker girl who took him to a civil rights rally at the Convention Center in Philadelphia. It was the first time in his life he had sung "We Shall Overcome."

As a student, Hahn read US senator J. William Fulbright's 1966 book, *The Arrogance of Power,* which disputed the justification of the Vietnam War. A Southern Democrat and segregationist, Fulbright nonetheless supported the creation of the United Nations and opposed McCarthyism, and started the foundation that bears his name, which offers fellowships to a wide variety of scholars. Hahn also read journalist Bernard Fall's book on Vietnam, *Hell in a Very Small Place: The Battle of Dien Bien Phu.* He was seeing the grim images—and the body bags—being sent back from Vietnam. By the time he enrolled as a graduate student in Russian studies at Duke University in the fall of 1966, he had turned 180 degrees from his parents' political leanings and was ready to rebel against the war.

The final straw for Hahn was the death of his high school friend Danny Kent, who had enlisted for Officer Candidate School and been killed in Vietnam.

"It had become clear to me that the Vietnam War was costing the US lives and money and no one had offered a good reason for being there," Hahn said, "except that it was anticommunism." Hahn had studied the containment theory of diplomat/historian George F. Kennan, who advocated building a strong circle of allies around the Soviet Union to contain its expansion rather than confront it militarily. "The containment theory should not have been applied to the Far East," Hahn believes, "because the Soviets were already 'contained' by China." Far from being a monolithic Communist bloc, as many in the US believed, the USSR and China had been divided by the famous Sino-Soviet Split, which became public

knowledge in 1961 when China denounced Soviet communism as "revisionist."

"By the mid-1960s, US policymakers should have known that the Soviets and the Chinese had more differences in national security interests than points of ideological commonality," said Hahn. They should have also seen that Ho Chi Minh, who had sought the help of every US president since Woodrow Wilson to win Vietnam's independence, was much more of a nationalist than a Communist. "If we had really wanted to stop communism in Southeast Asia," Hahn said, "we would have let Ho Chi Minh win."

By 1967, Hahn was following Minnesota Democratic senator Eugene "Clean Gene" McCarthy, who announced in November that he would run for president on an antiwar platform. Then came 1968. First, the assassination of Martin Luther King. Then in March, McCarthy stunned President Johnson by nearly upsetting the incumbent president in the New Hampshire primary, demonstrating how divided Democrats were over the war. By the end of the month, Johnson had taken himself out of the race. Then came the murder of Robert F. Kennedy, the tumultuous Democratic National Convention in Chicago, and the election of Richard Nixon.

The antiwar movement at Duke was small in 1967, but it grew as the war escalated, and when Nixon sent US troops into Cambodia in 1970, the movement exploded on campuses all over America. At Kent State in Ohio, four students were shot to death by National Guard troops. At Duke, the outspoken Jeff Hahn became the leader of the university's protest movement. He led door-to-door canvassing in Durham to get signatures on a petition in support of the McGovern-Hatfield amendment, which would have required the US to end all combat operations in Vietnam by the end of the year. He convinced the university president, Terry Sanford, the former governor of North Carolina, later a US senator) to help him recruit one hundred prominent North Carolinians to lobby the US Congress. They chartered a plane, flew to Washington, D.C., and knocked on the doors of the North Carolina congressional delegation, with special attention given to the state's senators, Sam Ervin and B. Everett Jordan, asking for support of McGovern-Hatfield (which ultimately was defeated in the Senate). "Pretty heady stuff for a young grad student," Hahn said.

Hahn himself was not drafted. He was awarded a National Defense Education Act Fellowship, aimed at creating a corps of highly trained specialists in areas thought useful to the national defense—in Hahn's case, this was Soviet communism. "Many of my college peers went to grad school to avoid the draft," Hahn said. "I went to grad school because I knew exactly what I wanted to do with my life, and that was to become a professor of Russian studies. The deferment was incidental for me."

Hahn taught Russian studies at Villanova University for thirty-seven years before retiring in 2008. Looking back on his years as a protester, Hahn said he is "terribly proud" of what he did.

Duke University president Terry Sanford addresses student and faculty demonstrators supporting the Vietnam Moratorium, May 6, 1970.

A longtime friend and legislative ally of Johnson, Fulbright had been instrumental in steering through Congress the August 1964 Southeast Asia (Tonkin Gulf) Resolution, empowering the president "to take all necessary steps, including the use of armed force," to defend the freedom of South Vietnam. Like many of his colleagues, however, Fulbright had become increasingly irritated by Johnson's highhanded use of that authority to escalate the war without consulting the legislative branch. Although Secretary of Defense McNamara and JCS chairman General Wheeler refused to testify before the committee, Fulbright pressed on with the inquiry, calling on a parade of high-ranking government officials to defend the administration's position.

In the end, the month-long hearings failed to produce any concrete results, since few congressmen were prepared to challenge the president directly or to cut off funds for the war. Nevertheless, by providing an open forum for a debate over American policy objectives in Vietnam, the nationally televised proceedings made dissent more respectable, thus paving the way for a herd of nearly fifty "peace candidates" in the November 1966 congressional elections. Though all were defeated, some drew significant support, including Robert Scheer, the editor of the radical journal *Ramparts*, who received 45 percent of the Democratic primary vote in California's 7th District. Moreover, as journalist Andrew Kopkind observed in the *New Republic*, opponents of the war could find a "measure of hope" in the election of a "minibloc" of dovish Republicans, including Sens. Mark Hatfield of Oregon, Charles Percy of Illinois, and Edward Brooke of Massachusetts.

In the meantime, mass demonstrations against the war continued to proliferate, culminating in the largest antiwar rally in US history—a march by three hundred thousand Americans in New York City on April 15, 1967. Six months later, on October 21, a much smaller but equally determined group of protesters gathered in front of the Lincoln Memorial in Washington, D.C., to hear speakers condemn the war amid signs demanding that President Johnson "Bring Home the GIs Now!" As the last speeches came to an end, an estimated thirty thousand demonstrators linked arms, crossed the Arlington Memorial Bridge, and marched on the Pentagon. Met by a line of military police as the protesters approached the main entrance to what they called "the center of the American war machine," several hundred of them attempted to break through and race up the steps. The troops responded with tear gas and truncheons, inflicting dozens of injuries as they drove the surging crowd back. After a second charge met with the same result, the demonstrators fell back and held a nightlong candlelight vigil. By the time the protest came to an end the following afternoon, seven hundred people had been arrested and twice that number reported as casualties.

Although the motives of the protesters varied, from the ideological radicalism of the student "New Left" to the religious pacifism of the Quakers, the principal target of much early antiwar dissent was the same. As monthly draft calls shot up to meet the demands of the expanding US war effort—from 13,700 in April 1965 to nearly thirty thousand in August 1967—protest against administration policy increasingly took the form of protest against the Selective Service System. In addition to counseling potential inductees to resist conscription, antiwar activists picketed local draft boards, staged "sit-ins" at military induction centers, and publicly burned their own draft cards. Congress swiftly retaliated by stiffening the penalties for such acts and extending the range of punishable offenses. But even the vigorous enforcement of the new laws could not curtail the steady growth of the antidraft movement.

For all the publicity they generated, however, those who actively resisted the draft remained a small, if vocal, minority. Faced with the prospect of conscription, most draft-age males either accepted their lot or found other ways to avoid military service. Many took advantage of the long-standing system of exemptions and deferments instituted by the SSS to "channel" the nation's youth in "socially desirable" ways.

Local draft boards could, for example, craft their own definitions and grant exemptions for "family hardship" or "critical occupational skills" and to issue deferments to ministers, farmers, and college students "making satisfactory progress toward a degree." Other young men took their cases to court, drawing on the expertise of a growing number of draft-law specialists to establish their credentials as conscientious objectors or to challenge the procedures employed by their local boards. Still others contrived to fail their pre-induction physical exams by artificially elevating their blood pressure, aggravating old sports injuries, or simulating more serious disorders.

Though the military did its best to discriminate between legitimate and illegitimate cases, in the end, more than one-quarter of all prospective conscripts were disqualified from military service for medical reasons. Each year, another third obtained exemptions or deferments, while 5 percent avoided serving in Vietnam by enlisting in the National Guard or the reserves, as relatively few guardsmen or reservists were called up to active duty in Vietnam (*relatively* few: nearly six thousand reservists and 101 guardsmen were killed in Vietnam). Since the classification system by design allowed the better educated and better off to not serve, those actually inducted into the military tended to come from working-class families earning less than $10,000 a year. Inductees typically lived in cities or small towns rather than suburbs and had no education beyond high school. According to one 1968 study, a high school dropout from a low-income family faced a 70 percent chance of serving in Vietnam, whereas the corresponding odds for a college graduate were only 42 percent. Once in Vietnam, moreover, draftees were more likely to be assigned to combat roles than those who enlisted voluntarily, and consequently they suffered a higher casualty rate. Of the total number of US forces that served in Vietnam, one-quarter were draftees. They accounted for 30.4 percent of all combat deaths.

The social imbalances of the Vietnam War military became even more glaring following the introduction of Project 100,000 in 1966. Heralded as a Great Society program designed to "rehabilitate the subterranean poor," especially young African Americans, the project quickly evolved into a vehicle for funneling underprivileged and unemployed youths from the streets of America to the battlefields of Indochina. By lowering the minimum intellectual and physical standards for induction, recruiters eventually brought more than 350,000 men into the military under the program. Of that total, 41 percent were black, and 40 percent served in the infantry. A Pentagon study later determined that the "attrition-by-death" rate of Project 100,000 soldiers was nearly twice as high as that of Vietnam-era veterans as a whole. Overall, however, the number of black soldiers who died in Vietnam amounted to 12.5 percent of the total, while draft-age black men comprised 13.5 percent of the total of draft-age males in the US. (Not all the black soldiers in the American military were draftees, and nearly a third of the enlistees chose to serve in one of the combat arms—infantry, armor, or artillery.)

Rather than answer the call to arms, thousands of American men refused to go to war. Some fled the country to avoid the draft or even went to prison for violating Selective Service laws. More than 170,000 won the classification of Conscientious Objector (CO) after showing their moral opposition to service. One of the COs was James Quay of Pennsylvania. His wrote this essay in 1987.

I was supposed to register at my local Selective Service board when I turned eighteen—September 26, 1964—but I forgot. Didn't go for three weeks. It was no big deal. I never considered not registering, and they didn't think my being late meant anything. That wouldn't be true later.

In my junior year in high school, I applied to become a candidate to the US Military Academy and took and passed all the necessary tests. I changed my mind before the selection was made, because the only degree offered at West Point was a bachelor's in science and I didn't want to limit my options. I already had an inkling that West Point might be confining in other ways, but I don't remember having any moral objection to entering the military. As it was, I never had to decide: my congressman named me only first alternate.

What turned a candidate to West Point in 1963 into a conscientious objector by 1967? My growing awareness during those years of the enormous destruction being visited upon the people of North and South Vietnam by the American military. I knew there was plenty of suffering caused by "the other side," but because of the massive technological resources America alone possessed, the US had the capacity to inflict horrific damage far beyond anything available to its enemies in Vietnam. Regardless of whether Vietnam was two countries or one, or whether Ho Chi Minh was a Communist aggressor or a popular nationalist, I came to feel that the destruction America was causing was incompatible with any proper American objective in Vietnam. During the Tet Offensive, an American artillery officer said of the village of Ben Tre, "It became necessary to destroy the town in order to save it." That phrase crystallized what I felt about the war. If we were killing Vietnamese and destroying Vietnam in the name of freedom, who and what would be left to be free?

My very first demonstration could not have been more American. In May 1967, an official from the South Vietnamese embassy came to speak at a hall at Lafayette College, where I was a junior. A dozen people I knew stood in front with signs that read "Stop the Bombing." I was not one of them. For this, they were surrounded by hundreds of fraternity boys and subjected to hours of water-and-ink bombs and verbal abuse. The campus police were strangely absent. A rally was organized to support the right of free speech; my first antiwar demonstration was really for the First Amendment.

Fortunately for me and for all antiwar protesters, this country has a long tradition of resistance to authority. The tradition of conscientious objection is even older, arriving with the first Quakers in 1635. James Madison, one of the architects of the US Constitution, proposed making objection to war a constitutional right. Conscientious objection is as American as cherry pie. You see how fortunate I was. I could oppose American policy in Vietnam secure in the knowledge that I was upholding the finest American ideals. It was not I who was betraying America, it was Lyndon Johnson and his government.

My claim to conscientious-objector status was not based on traditional religious beliefs. In fact, I was interviewed earlier by my college's alumni magazine as an example of an agnostic. Until 1965, you could be released from military service only if you could demonstrate that your opposition to participation in war was by reason of "religious training or belief." But in 1965, the Supreme Court had ruled that a person could not be denied CO status simply because he did not belong to an orthodox religious sect. It was enough, the high court ruled, if the belief that prompted your decision occupied the same place in your life that the belief in a traditional deity occupied in the life of a believer.

I knew I objected to the war in Vietnam. What I had to discover was the ultimate source of that objection and describe it for myself and for the five ordinary Americans who comprised draft board number 90 in Allentown, Pennsylvania, in the space provided on Special Form 150. The first question on that form was, "Do you believe in a Supreme Being?" There were two boxes: YES/NO. I checked YES. Second item: "Describe the nature of your belief which is the basis of your claim and state whether or not your belief in a Supreme Being involves duties which to you are superior to those arising from any human relation." Here is part of what I wrote:

> Because I believe that from man all awareness and order come, because I believe that each man is a divine being striving to become more divine, and because I believe that divinity manifests itself only through the love and justice of human relationships, I believe that human relationships are the highest relationships. Therefore there are no duties which to me are superior to those arising from human relations.

I made a point to get letters of support not only from people who agreed with my position but from those who disagreed as well, including the dean and the president of my college, who surely didn't appreciate the trouble I was causing them but who could confirm that I was sincere. I filed for conscientious-objector status on the first day of spring, 1968. I did not know what I would do if the draft board refused my claim. I did know I would not enter the military. I felt I was prepared to go to prison rather than flee to Canada, but, fortunately, I never had to find out. On June 14, Flag Day, my draft board informed me that I had been classified I-O, a conscientious objector.

Three days later, I began working for the New York City Department of Social Services, where a conscientious objector I knew was performing his alternative service, and I was given a caseload of families in central Harlem. My draft board informed me

that they did not expect to receive a call for draftees until t[...] which meant I could sit it out and possibly not be called. In [...] I volunteered for two years' alternative service. When I was [...] for a physical examination in September, I informed my draft [...] I would not appear, which meant I would be passed autom[...] ly. All around me, young men were going to war or to priso[...] I did not want to avoid service. I remember telling people [...] time that twenty years into the future, if my children asked [...] had done during the Vietnam War, I did not want to tell the[...] I had gotten out on a technicality. It is now twenty years [...] and my son knows that his father is one of 170,000 who [...] granted CO status during the Vietnam War and one of nin[...] thousand who completed the two years of alternative servi[...]

The *Lafayette* newspaper reports on antiwar protests at Lafayette College in May 1967, when antiwar protester Jim Quay attended the school. Protesters were subjected to water bombs and other abuse by their fellow students. Quay was a conscientious objector to the Vietnam War, one of many who perfo[...]

The racial inequities of the draft explain in part why antiwar sentiment consistently ran higher among African Americans than among whites. Already engaged in a domestic struggle to end legal discrimination in the South and de facto segregation in the North, the leaders of the civil rights movement had refrained from challenging US foreign policy goals throughout the late 1950s and early 1960s. But as the Vietnam War began to take a toll on black youth, as well as on the antipoverty programs of Johnson's Great Society, many came to regard the conflict as an obstacle to further social progress. The more radical activists, like Black Power advocate Stokely Carmichael of the Student Nonviolent Coordinating Committee (SNCC) and Huey Newton of the Black Panther Party, were in the forefront of the opposition by early 1966.

By early 1967, even the moderate leaders of the civil rights movement had turned against the war. "A time comes when silence is betrayed," proclaimed Dr. Martin Luther King Jr., in a sermon at Riverside Church in New York City on April 4, 1967. "That time has come for us in relation to Vietnam." Reminding his audience that only a few years before, the Johnson administration had declared a "war on poverty" at home, King traced the course of his own disillusionment with the undeclared war in Vietnam. "I watched the program broken and eviscerated as if it were some idle plaything of a society gone mad on war," King asserted, "and I knew that I could never again raise my voice against the violence of the oppressed in the ghettos without having first spoken clearly to the greatest purveyor of violence in the world today— my own government."

King's claim that the rising costs of the war had compromised the dream of the Great Society was not without foundation. Despite President Johnson's belief that the nation was "rich enough and strong enough" to fight a two-front war—against poverty at home and communism abroad—by early 1967, the American economy was beginning to show signs of strain. Faced with the threat of runaway inflation, which had been triggered by the sharp and unanticipated increase in military expenditures over the previous eighteen months, Johnson was forced to choose between raising taxes and cutting domestic spending. Politically unpalatable as both alternatives were, in August 1967 the president put before Congress a request for a 10 percent income-tax surcharge. By that point, however, dissatisfaction with Johnson's social reform agenda had become so widespread that congressional conservatives were in a position to demand a quid pro quo. If the president wanted a tax hike, they insisted, he would first have to make deep cuts in social spending. Although Johnson ultimately agreed, by then even the combination of increased federal revenues and decreased expenditures could not cool down the overheated US economy.

Opposition to the administration's domestic policies had, in fact, mounted steadily since 1965. Troubled by the recurrent outbreak of urban riots, the growth of black radicalism, and the perceived excesses of some federal antipoverty programs, many white Americans had become convinced that the government was moving too far, too fast in its efforts to remedy long-standing social problems. The so-called white backlash was especially pronounced among blue-collar workers, many of whom came to see themselves as victims of a system that had someone else's interests at heart. Forced to endure the dislocations of a rapidly changing society—

Opposite page: Pro-war activists stage a demonstration on the streets of New York City in early April 1967.

crime, inflation, rising taxes, and disintegrating neighborhoods—they fought back by resisting desegregation of their schools and communities and by withdrawing their support from liberal politicians whose social programs rarely addressed their own needs.

More complicated were the attitudes of working-class whites toward the war in Vietnam. On one hand, blue-collar workers were among the more visible and vocal supporters of the war effort, as evidenced by the seventy thousand longshoremen, carpenters, seamen, and mechanics who marched down Fifth Avenue in New York City in May 1967. Carrying banners reading "Down with the Reds," "God Bless Us Patriots," and "Support Our Boys," they denounced the antiwar protesters and called upon the government to "escalate, not capitulate." On the other hand, they were well aware that their own sons were bearing a disproportionate burden of the fighting and dying in Southeast Asia. Though they deeply resented those who avoided the draft and they regarded much antiwar protest as treasonous, as time went on and casualties multiplied, many working-class parents came to share the dissenters' view that the war was a mistake. Unlike the organized peace movement, however, their opposition was not so much ideological or moral as pragmatic, based on the conviction that the price they were paying was simply too high. As one Long Island construction worker put it after watching the funeral procession of a local boy killed in Vietnam: "The whole damn country of South Vietnam is not worth the life of one American boy, no matter what the hell our politicians tell us. I'm damn sick and tired of watching these funerals go by."

The pattern of gradual disillusionment with the war was also evident in the popular press. Like most Americans, the journalists who covered the war initially backed the US commitment to Vietnam, believing that it was in the nation's interest to "contain" the spread of communism in Southeast Asia. As UPI correspondent Neil Sheehan later recalled, when he first arrived in Saigon in 1962, he was convinced that the US was helping the South Vietnamese "to build a viable and independent nation-state and defeat a Communist insurgency that would subject them to a dour tyranny."

According to the correspondents themselves, the American government was largely responsible for undermining faith in the war effort. In their zeal to put the best face on all political and military developments, US officials in Washington and Saigon repeatedly provided information that was at odds with the reporters' own observations or with intelligence gleaned from other sources. Early on, for example, correspondents were told that American forces were only "advising" the South Vietnamese, even though the reporters saw them fighting and dying. Similarly, battles in which ARVN forces were routed by the Viet Cong were described as victories in official briefings. "No responsible US official in Saigon ever told a newsman a really big falsehood," recalled John Mecklin, chief of the US Information Service. "Instead there were endless little falsehoods."

As a result, a "credibility gap" soon emerged between the US government and the Saigon press corps. That gap would widen over time. The skepticism of the correspondents manifested itself in increasingly critical accounts of the war effort that often directly contradicted what the Johnson administration was saying back in Washington. In many instances, however, their negative accounts were either buried on the back pages or revised by editors who preferred to rely on official Pentagon assessments, frequently expressed in the hard, quantitative language of enemy body counts, kill ratios, weapons captured, and hamlets pacified. "We were largely at the mercy of the administration then," said Peter Lisagor, then Washington bureau chief of the *Chicago Daily News*. "There was a tendency to believe them more because they were supposed to have the facts, and we were inclined to accept an official's word on something as cosmic as war."

Eventually, however, the flood of pessimistic dispatches from the war zone became too overwhelming to ignore. Though few correspondents went so far as to challenge the legitimacy of the US presence in Vietnam, by the summer of 1967 many had come to the conclusion that the war was not being fought effectively, that the pacification program was failing, and that South Vietnam was still far from becoming a viable nation-state. "Everyone thought I was against the war," recalled Charles Mohr, who resigned his post as *Time*'s Saigon correspondent after his managing editor ordered him to rewrite a story that claimed the war was being lost. "I just thought it wasn't working. I didn't come to think of it as immoral until the very end."

Troubled by the growing perception that the war was a "stalemate," the Johnson administration launched an all-out public relations campaign in the fall of 1967 "to get the message out" that "we are winning." Under the direction of National Security Advisor Walt W. Rostow, who was also chief of the White House Psychological Strategy Committee, government officials inundated the major news media with an endless stream of charts, graphs, statistics, and previously classified documents showing "steady progress" on every front in the struggle against the Vietnamese Communists. Vice President Hubert H. Humphrey, Secretary of Defense Robert McNamara, and Secretary of State Dean Rusk offered equally optimistic appraisals in televised appearances on weekly news shows as well as in private chats with favored reporters. The campaign reached its high point in mid-November, when the president summoned Gen. William Westmoreland, ambassador Ellsworth Bunker, and pacification chief Robert W. Komer from Saigon to confirm the administration's assessment. "I am absolutely certain that whereas in 1965 the enemy was winning, today he is certainly losing," Westmoreland asserted in an address before the National Press Club on November 21. "We have reached an important point when the end begins to come into view."

As Johnson had hoped, the administration's "success offensive" brought to a halt the steady erosion of popular support for the war. Opinion polls conducted toward the end of the year showed a 7 percent increase in approval of the president's handling of the war since the preceding August. Even more striking was the shift in the public's perception of US "progress" in Vietnam. Between July and December 1967, the percentage of people who thought the US was "losing ground" or "standing still" plummeted, while those who thought that the Americans were "making progress" rose from 34 percent to more than 50 percent.

Then came Tet in 1968. With the outbreak of the Communists' cataclysmic, countrywide offensive in late January 1968, public confidence in the American war effort suffered a grievous and ultimately fatal blow. Confronted with evidence of the enemy's capacity to mount coordinated, surprise attacks on a massive scale, many Americans found it difficult to believe the administration's claims that the US was "winning" the war. Nor could they place much faith in General Westmoreland's sanguine prediction that "the end" had "come into view." By mid-February, two weeks after the offensive began, popular disapproval of the president's Vietnam policy had reached an all-time high of 50 percent; by the end of the month the figure was 58 percent. More telling still, only one out of three Americans now thought that the United States was "making progress" in Vietnam, and one in four believed that the allies were "losing ground."

The judgments rendered by the nation's leading news organizations reinforced the verdict reflected by the polls. "After three years of gradual escalation, President Johnson's strategy for Vietnam has run into a dead end," wrote the editors of *Newsweek*, expressing a view held by many Americans in the wake of the Tet Offensive. Not only had the US military buildup in Vietnam failed to quell the Communist insurgency, but the government of South Vietnam remained a "political morass," riddled with corruption and unable to earn the allegiance of its own people. What was required was "the courage to face the truth"—that "the war cannot be won by military means without tearing apart the whole fabric of national life and international relations."

Although President Johnson initially resisted the press's assessment, in the end he had no choice but to accept it. Having lost the trust of his "fellow Americans," as he always called them, he knew that he could no longer govern effectively. Not only had a majority of the public repudiated his Vietnam policies, but by mid-March 1968 Johnson could not even count on the continuing support of his own political party. Sen. Eugene McCarthy's startling showing in the New Hampshire primary and Sen. Robert Kennedy's subsequent entrance into the presidential race made it clear that Johnson faced a bitter fight for the Democratic nomination. By announcing on March 31 his intention to relinquish the presidency, Johnson hoped at once to salvage a measure of his own personal authority and to restore a semblance of unity to a nation increasingly divided against itself.

Yet such was not to be. On April 4, 1968, the day after the North Vietnamese rekindled hopes for peace by accepting Johnson's offer to begin negotiations, Dr. Martin Luther King Jr. was killed by an assassin's bullet in Memphis, Tennessee. For thirteen years, the charismatic leader of the black civil rights movement, winner of the Nobel Peace Prize, eloquent speaker, and moral teacher had stood as a symbol of nonviolent social reform. Now, with tragic irony, his murder by white ex-convict James Earl Ray became the occasion for the most widespread racial violence in the nation's history. Within minutes after learning of King's death, crowds of angry African Americans began roaming the streets of many major cities, breaking windows, looting stores, and setting fire to white-owned businesses. Black colleges seethed with rage while urban high schools across the country closed down in the face of violent racial confrontations. In Baltimore, Detroit, and four Southern cities, overwhelmed local officials were forced to request the assistance of the National Guard, while in Chicago regular Army troops had to be called in after entire blocks of the West Side ghetto went up in flames. All told, 169 cities reported incidents of racial violence in the wake of the King assassination, resulting in some $130 million in property damage, nearly 24,000 arrests, and 43 deaths, 36 of them black.

King's death was not the only reason for violence that spring. Three weeks later, on April 23, a coalition of radical white and black students at Columbia University in New York City seized a number of administration buildings, signaling the advent of a new phase in the politics of student protest. At issue were the university's decision to construct a new gymnasium in Morningside Park, a city-owned plot of land in the adjacent Harlem neighborhood, and its affiliation with the Institute for Defense Analysis (IDA), a multimillion-dollar consortium founded in 1955 to test weapons and military strategy. Led by members of the local chapter of the Students for a Democratic Society (SDS) and in loose alliance with the Students' Afro-American Society (SAS), the protesters demanded that the administration abandon its allegedly racist "land-grab" policies and end its "complicity" in the Vietnam War. When university officials failed to comply, the students moved in and occupied Low Library, the main administration offices at Hamilton Hall, and several other campus buildings. After a week of inconclusive negotiations, punctuated by a series of violent clashes between allies and opponents of the occupiers, on April 29 President Grayson Kirk called in the New York City police to clear the buildings. Crashing through a set of makeshift barricades, the police stormed Low Library, bludgeoned the students with fists and nightsticks, and then dragged them downstairs to waiting paddy wagons. A second occupation several weeks later produced even bloodier results, as students and police engaged in what amounted to hand-to-hand combat throughout the campus.

By the time it ended in late May 1968, the rebellion at Columbia had resulted in nearly 900 arrests, 180 injuries (34 to police), and the suspension of 73 students. It had also spawned similar demonstrations at hundreds of other campuses, including forty major confrontations, and provoked a torrent of criticism against the new politics of "direct action." While President Johnson condemned the Columbia militants as "young totalitarians," the editors of *Fortune* warned its readers that the new generation of student activists sought to instigate a revolution—"not a protest . . . but an honest-to-God revolution." Mark Rudd, the leader of the Columbia SDS "action faction," could only agree. "Liberal solutions . . . are not allowed anymore," he declared. "We are out for social and political revolution, nothing less."

Yet if militant African Americans and student radicals had abandoned their faith in peaceful political change, the vast majority of Americans were still committed to working within the system. For those seeking to bring the Vietnam War to an end, President Johnson's unexpected withdrawal from the presidential race had opened a new range of possibilities. Suddenly it seemed that what had not been gained through protest in the

Columbia University protest leader Mark Rudd speaks to students occupying Fayerweather Hall.

New York City police move in to break up the
Columbia University protests on April 30, 1968.

streets might be achieved through the ballot, particularly after Senator
McCarthy followed his astonishing performance in New Hampshire with
a decisive victory in the April 2 Wisconsin primary.

But the other Democratic antiwar candidate, Robert F. Kennedy, was to
steal the thunder from McCarthy's single-issue candidacy. Although his
tardy entrance into the race had produced charges of opportunism, not even
his enemies within the party could deny that he was a political force to be
reckoned with. In part because of his name, in part because of his gift for stirring oratory, and in part because of his capacity to reach the disaffected and
the dispossessed, Kennedy had an appeal that extended far beyond that of any
other national political figure. His campaign entourage included members of
the Eastern establishment who had served under his brother as well as former members of the SDS. He enjoyed strong support among urban African
Americans and also, remarkably, among working-class whites. And he promised not only to end the war in Vietnam, but to heal the wounds that the war
had inflicted on the American nation.

Recognizing that he would have to "win through the people," Kennedy
launched his campaign with an exhausting whirlwind tour of sixteen states
in twenty-one days. Everywhere he went, the people responded, wrote one
reporter, with "an intensity and scope that was awesome and frightening"—

clutching at his coat sleeves as he moved through ghetto neighborhoods, chanting his name as he delivered his impassioned indictments of the Johnson administration's policies. The results at the polls were equally dramatic: victory in Indiana on May 7; victory in Nebraska on May 14. Then, after losing the Oregon primary to Senator McCarthy by six percentage points on May 28, Kennedy moved on to California. With its large bloc of delegates and "winner take all" rules, the June 4 California primary loomed as the crucial test of who would challenge the Johnson-Humphrey forces at the Democratic convention in August.

Kennedy won. In his victory statement at the Ambassador Hotel in Los Angeles, the New York senator told cheering campaign workers that their success had proved that "the violence, the disenchantments with our society, the divisions . . . between blacks and whites, between the poor and the affluent, or between age groups or on the war in Vietnam" could be overcome. Then, as he left the dais to hold a press conference in another part of the building, Sirhan Bishara Sirhan, a Palestinian Arab angered over Kennedy's support for Israel, suddenly raised a revolver and fired one shot into the senator's head and two more shots into his chest. Sirhan kept firing, wounding five other people, as members of Kennedy's entourage struggled to wrest the

Senator Robert Kennedy and his wife, Ethel, address constituents and the press at the Ambassador Hotel after his California primary victory, moments before his assassination.

.22-caliber pistol from his grip. Kennedy clung to life through many hours of desperate efforts by skilled doctors to save him, but was finally pronounced dead at 1:44 a.m. on June 6, nearly twenty-six hours after the shooting.

His candidacy had for a time brought together many of the disparate elements of a perilously fragmented nation. An assassin's bullet had destroyed the hope for national reconciliation shared by Kennedy's followers. One of them, speechwriter Jack Newfield, formerly a member of SDS, put it this way: "We had already glimpsed the most compassionate leaders our nation could produce, and they had all been assassinated. And from this time forward, things would get worse. Our best political leaders were part of memory now, not hope." Although it is impossible to know what might have happened had Kennedy lived, it is certain that the nation's divisions deepened after his death. Later that summer, the Democratic Convention in Chicago was to dramatize just how divided America had already become.

Senator Robert Kennedy lies semiconscious in his own blood after being shot in the head and chest while busboy Juan Romero tries to comfort him.

Focus: Chicago

In the words of the presidential candidate nominated at the 1968 Democratic Convention, "Chicago was a catastrophe. My wife and I went home heartbroken, battered, and beaten. I told her I felt just like we had been in a shipwreck." While its participants knew the convention would be a struggle, none could predict just how disastrous it would be for the Democratic Party and, indeed, for the nation.

Robert Kennedy's death had all but assured that the nomination would go to Vice President Humphrey, but his accession to the party's leadership would not be unopposed. In the weeks that followed the assassination, Sen. Eugene McCarthy's campaign gained fresh momentum, propelling him to victory in the June 18 New York primary and bringing a substantial influx of much-needed money. A small boomlet of support also began to gather around Sen. George McGovern of South Dakota, after family members and aides of Robert Kennedy gave him their endorsement. There was even talk in some party circles of a possible convention draft for Sen. Edward Kennedy of Massachusetts, Bobby's younger brother.

Nor were the politicians the only ones planning to exert their influence on the proceedings of the convention. Under the leadership of the National Mobilization Committee to End the War, a number of antiwar groups were hoping to rally as

Delegates at the 1968 Democratic National Convention in Chicago.

many as half a million protesters in Chicago while the delegates met. Members of the outlandish Youth International Party, or Yippies, also planned to be in attendance and hold their own mock convention, culminating in the nomination of "Pigasus," a live pig, as their party standard bearer. Far more serious were the intentions and objectives of the Reverend Ralph Abernathy, the man who had succeeded Dr. Martin Luther King Jr. as head of the Southern Christian Leadership Conference. Determined to remind the Democratic Party of the broken promise of the Great Society, Abernathy had decided to bring a group of poverty-stricken Americans to the doors of the convention hall as part of his recently launched Poor People's Campaign.

Fearing the worst, Mayor Richard Daley of Chicago prepared for the onslaught by placing the entire metropolitan police force of twelve thousand on weeklong, twelve-hour shifts. More than five thousand Illinois National Guardsmen were also deployed to the city, while an additional 7,500 regular Army troops were placed on twenty-four-hour alert. The convention site itself was especially well fortified, its main entrance barricaded with barbed wire and chain-link fencing and its approaches guarded by some two thousand police.

As it turned out, Daley's well-publicized security measures, together with his refusal to grant marching permits, dissuaded large numbers of would-be demonstrators from going to Chicago. The ten thousand youthful protesters who did eventually arrive, however, were among the more committed apostles of the antiwar movement. Though most had no intention of provoking violence, some clearly expected a confrontation. "To remain passive in the face of escalating police brutality is foolish and degrading," one young activist told a reporter. "We're going to march and they're going to stop us," said another. "How can you avoid violence?"

And violence there was. On Sunday, August 25, the eve of the convention, and again the next night, riot police moved in with nightsticks and tear gas to disperse demonstrators who had encamped in Lincoln Park in defiance of an 11:00 p.m. curfew. The protesters then moved on to Grant Park, where they began laying plans to march on the amphitheater. As darkness fell on Wednesday evening, August 28, a crowd of at least five thousand gathered in the park across from the Conrad Hilton Hotel on Michigan Avenue, the city's central thoroughfare. There they remained until some caught sight of Reverend Abernathy and his supporters from the Poor People's Campaign, the only group that had been granted a legal permit to march. Beckoned by shouts of "Join us!" several thousand antiwar protesters surged forward, crossed a small bridge to Michigan Avenue, and fell in behind Abernathy's motley train.

Inside the convention hall, meanwhile, a bitter battle over the Vietnam plank of the Democratic Party platform was coming to a head. Although by that point Senator McCarthy had all but conceded the nomination to Humphrey, a large bloc of antiwar delegates from New York, California, Wisconsin, and several other states were determined to put their stamp on the party's official policy. Based on a minority report hammered out at the platform committee hearings the previous week, the dissidents' position called for "an unconditional end to all bombing of North Vietnam," the mutual withdrawal of all US and North Vietnamese forces from South Vietnam, and a "political reconciliation" between the Saigon government and the Viet Cong leading to a coalition government. By contrast, the majority plank recommended a gradual reduction of the US troop presence "as the South Vietnamese are able to take over larger responsibilities" and a cessation of bombing only "when the action would not endanger US lives." As speaker after speaker rose to defend his respective position, the debate turned increasingly acrimonious. Even before the final tally was read—1,567 in favor of the majority plank, 1,041 for the minority—the New York delegation began singing "We Shall Overcome," while spectators in the gallery chanted "Stop the War! Stop the War!"

As a result of the fight over the Vietnam plank, the nomination balloting was delayed until late in the evening. It was nearly 11:00 p.m., in fact, when Mayor Joseph Alioto of San Francisco stood before the convention to nominate Hubert Humphrey as the Democratic presidential candidate. Barely had Alioto begun to speak when CBS anchorman Walter Cronkite received news of a bloody clash between police and demonstrators outside the convention hall. "There has been a display of naked violence in the streets of Chicago," Cronkite declared, as he interrupted the convention proceedings to show a tape of events that had actually taken place more than two hours before. Ordered to halt and disperse the demonstrators who had set out from Grant Park, a phalanx of helmeted riot police had intercepted the marchers at the corner of Michigan Avenue and Balbo shortly before 8:00. When the protesters refused to move, the police first made a series of peaceful arrests, then charged into the crowd with their nightsticks flailing. While some of the demonstrators fought back, many fell limp and began screaming, "The whole world is watching! The whole world is watching!"

An unidentified bystander points accusingly at Illinois National Guardsmen as they stand guard at Grant Park early on August 28, 1968, following a large-scale confrontation with protestors. Seven hundred troops were ordered into the park, across the street from Democratic National Convention headquarters at the Conrad Hilton Hotel.

As scenes of the violence appeared on television sets throughout the convention hall, the nominating process was soon overwhelmed by a series of angry denunciations of Mayor Daley and the Chicago police. The crescendo of criticism reached its peak when Sen. Abraham Ribicoff of Connecticut rose to deplore the "Gestapo tactics in the streets of Chicago," a choice of words that brought a stream of obscenities from the mayor himself. "How hard it is to accept the truth," Ribicoff replied, staring down at Daley from the podium. "How hard it is."

The formal balloting that followed proved anticlimactic, as Humphrey outdistanced his only serious challenger, Senator McCarthy, by more than one thousand votes. For Humphrey, the nomination was a bitter prize indeed. The tumultuous Chicago convention had left the party he proposed to lead deeply, perhaps hopelessly divided, with only eight weeks to go before the general election. To defeat his formidable Republican challenger, Richard Nixon, who held a fifteen-percentage-point lead in the polls, he would have to use that time to bring the Democrats back together. In the process, he would also have to convince the electorate that he could restore unity to America by bringing peace to Vietnam.

Chicago police (at center), backed up by the National Guard (in foreground), move against a large group of demonstrators on August 28, 1968, in a view from the Conrad Hilton Hotel, headquarters of the Democratic National Convention.

CHAPTER SIX

NIXON'S WAR

Richard Milhous Nixon—who had lost the 1960 presidential race to John F. Kennedy, who had lost the 1962 California governor's race, and who had stormed off the political stage with the bitter words "you won't have Nixon to kick around anymore, because, gentlemen, this is my last press conference"—was back. He began his 1968 campaign for the presidency with a promise to "end the war and win the peace," intimating that he had a "secret plan." He sailed through the primaries and won the Republican nomination with ease. Now, in the early fall of 1968, Nixon at last seemed poised to capture the prize that had so narrowly eluded him eight years before.

President Richard Nixon shakes hands with members of the armed forces in Vietnam, July 30, 1969.

President Nixon gives his trademark "victory" sign while in Philadelphia during his successful presidential campaign.

As it became clear later, Nixon didn't really have a plan to end the war, secret or otherwise. Meanwhile, Lyndon Johnson, who had taken himself out of contention for the presidency, was working on an actual plan that he hoped to unveil just before Election Day and boost Democratic nominee Hubert Humphrey's bid for the presidency. In peace talks in Paris, Johnson's chief negotiator, W. Averell Harriman, had worked out a secret "understanding" with the North Vietnamese that called for a series of concrete, de-escalatory steps by both sides. As the presidential campaign was heating up, the Paris talks were drawing closer to an agreement that could be publicly announced.

In the aftermath of the tumultuous Chicago convention, the Democratic Party was in shambles and Humphrey's campaign was foundering. Humphrey had been abandoned by liberals and Southern Democrats, and a sizable segment of the white working class had defected to the camp of populist third-party candidate George Wallace, the once and future Alabama governor, who said that he would end the Vietnam War within ninety days or immediately withdraw US forces. On the campaign trail, Humphrey was met by hecklers who greeted him with catcalls of "Fascist," "Warmonger," and "Dump the Hump." Democratic state and local party leaders, wrote veteran political journalist Theodore White, "fled him as if he were the bearer of contagion." In September, Humphrey trailed Nixon in the polls by fifteen points.

Humphrey wanted to flee, too—from the stigma of President Johnson's discredited Vietnam policy. To distance himself from Johnson, on September 30, he unveiled a three-point peace initiative of his own, calling for a US bombing halt, a turnover of the fighting to the South Vietnamese, and the withdrawal of all "foreign forces" from South Vietnam under UN supervision. Though the proposal differed only slightly from the administration's official position, it convinced many disaffected Democrats that the vice president was not simply "Johnson's boy." In the days that followed, money poured into the campaign treasury, volunteers joined up in droves, and the labor unions redoubled their efforts to bring the rank and file back to the fold. Humphrey's attacks on George Wallace as a racist, and Wallace's choice of Gen. Curtis LeMay as his running mate, knocked Wallace down in the polls, to Humphrey's gain. (LeMay's suggestion of possibly using nuclear weapons in Vietnam reminded voters of the 1964 Johnson-Goldwater race and the "Daisy Girl" ad.) By the middle of October, Nixon's lead in the polls had fallen from fifteen points to twelve; a week later it was down to eight.

Although Humphrey's sudden resurgence gave Nixon cause for concern, it did not induce him to panic. As in the past, the Republican challenger refused to be pinned down on his own secret plan to end the war, preferring instead to address the issue only in vague, general terms. He also opposed an unconditional US bombing halt and warned of the dangers of "precipitate withdrawal." To justify his evasiveness, Nixon claimed that he did not want to undermine the Johnson administration's negotiations with Hanoi, even though part of his campaign strategy was a clandestine effort to do just that. Henry Kissinger, who was to become Nixon's national security advisor and secretary of state, flew to Paris to try to learn from the North Vietnamese delegation what Johnson was planning. Nixon also engaged Chinese-born Anna Chennault, the widow of famous World War II aviator Claire Chennault, who had led the Flying Tigers and the Chinese air force against Japan, to be a secret intermediary to the Saigon government. Kissinger claimed that he learned in Paris that President Johnson was going to spring an "October surprise" just before the election, an announcement of a peace deal with Hanoi. (Historian Robert Dallek later wrote that Kissinger simply made the educated guess of an "astute analyst.") Chennault's communication with the Saigon government, meanwhile, was being secretly monitored by the National Security Agency. When Chennault indicated to the South Vietnamese ambassador that the Thieu government should not take part in Johnson's plan because Nixon would offer a better deal after the election, Johnson was enraged and privately called Nixon's actions "treason," as White House tapes revealed years later. But neither Johnson nor Humphrey went public with the information, something Humphrey regretted after the votes were counted.

The main elements of Johnson's announcement were in place by mid-October, and the prospects of a breakthrough in Paris seemed brighter than ever before. Under the terms of the informal agreement, the US offered to stop its bombing unilaterally in exchange for a cessation of rocket and mortar attacks on South Vietnamese cities and a limitation of NVA infiltration across the DMZ. More substantive peace talks would follow, based on a subtle "our side, your side" formula that would permit the inclusion of both the South Vietnamese government and the NLF without requiring the formal recognition of either party.

Ever skeptical of Hanoi's intentions, President Johnson initially opposed Harriman's ingeniously devised proposal. But after General Abrams convinced him that a bombing halt would not jeopardize US troops in the field, he reluctantly gave his assent. "I don't want to have it said of me that one man died tomorrow who could have been saved by this plan," the president told his advisors. "I don't think it will happen, but there is a chance. We'll try it."

No sooner had the president reached that decision, however, than the South Vietnamese balked. Declaring that his government was not a "car that can be hitched to a locomotive and taken anywhere the locomotive wants to go," South Vietnamese President Nguyen Van Thieu flatly refused to join in any negotiations that included the Viet Cong. As a result, when Johnson announced the new peace initiative on the night of October 31, he could only say that the South Vietnamese were "free to participate" in the expanded talks scheduled to follow.

Despite Thieu's intransigence, news of the bombing halt provided an immediate boost to the Humphrey campaign. Opinion surveys taken in the wake of the president's speech revealed that Nixon's lead had dwindled to an insignificant two percentage points with only a few days to go before the general election. Just when it seemed that Humphrey might overtake his Republican rival, however, President Thieu intensified his protests, accusing the Johnson administration of "betrayal of an ally" and vowing to boycott the Paris talks until Hanoi agreed to negotiate directly with Saigon. On Tuesday, November 5, as hopes of an imminent peace settlement faded, seventy-three million Americans went to the polls and elected Richard Nixon the thirty-seventh president of the United States. The margin of victory—511,944 votes out of those cast, or 0.7 percent of the total electorate—hardly amounted to a mandate. Nevertheless, the new

An ammunition dump explodes at Ben Het, near the Laotian border, as NVA troops batter the base with artillery during a month-long siege.

The Special Forces commander at Ben Het waits out the NVA barrage at the camp.

president-elect fully understood the task that lay before him. To avoid the fate of his predecessor, he would have to fulfill the promise that launched his election campaign. He would have "to end the war and win the peace," and he would have to do it in a way acceptable to a nation increasingly at war with itself.

As many of his critics had suspected all along, Nixon in fact had no "secret plan" to end the war, though he did have a number of strong ideas and impulses that informed his approach to the problem. Perhaps first and foremost, he had been deeply influenced by President Eisenhower's quick resolution of the Korean conflict. Soon after taking office in 1953, "Eisenhower let the word go out diplomatically to the Chinese and the North Koreans that we would not tolerate this continual war of attrition," the former vice president recalled, "and within a matter of months, they negotiated." Nixon believed that he could exploit his own reputation as a hardline anti-Communist to similar advantage. "I call it the Madman Theory," he explained to one of his advisors. "We'll just let the word slip to [the North Vietnamese] that, 'For God's sake, you know Nixon is obsessed about Communists. We can't restrain him when he's angry—and he has his hand on the nuclear button.'"

Nixon also thought he could cajole the Soviet Union and perhaps even China into serving US interests. Relying on a concept he called "linkage," he planned to use the lure of arms control and expanded trade to win Soviet cooperation in moving the North Vietnamese toward a peaceful settlement of the war. In the case of China, he speculated that the offer of a rapprochement with the United States might induce Mao Zedong to put increased pressure on Hanoi.

Even though Nixon regarded himself as an expert in the field of foreign affairs, he still needed someone capable of translating his grand geopolitical designs into reality. The man he selected, national security advisor

Henry Kissinger, was in some respects an unlikely choice. A senior professor of government at Harvard University, a frequent contributor to the Council on Foreign Relations, and a former advisor to New York governor Nelson Rockefeller, the erudite Kissinger seemed to personify the Eastern liberal establishment that Nixon had battled throughout his political life. Yet for all their differences in background and temperament, the German-born academician and the Middle-American politician also had much in common. Both believed that the conduct of foreign policy ought to be centrally directed and tightly controlled, bold in conception but pragmatic in execution. Both shared a contempt for career diplomats and bureaucrats as well as a penchant for secrecy and intrigue. And both were fascinated by, if not wholly obsessed with, the uses of power.

Kissinger wasted no time. Shortly after noon on inauguration day, January 20, 1969, he ordered his staff to canvass American officials in Washington and Saigon for their appraisals of the situation in Vietnam. Senior military officials tended to be more optimistic about current and future prospects, while civilian analysts were "decidedly more skeptical," Kissinger informed the president.

Neither group foresaw a rapid conclusion to the war, however. The "bulls" estimated that it would take at least eight years, the "bears" more than thirteen years, for the GVN to gain sufficient popular support to crush the Viet Cong insurgency.

The findings reaffirmed Kissinger's conviction that the US would have to negotiate its way out of the war. The only question was how. Like Nixon, Kissinger believed that the war had to be ended honorably for the sake of America's global prestige. But while Nixon envisioned a durable peace agreement that would preserve a non-Communist regime in South Vietnam, Kissinger was far less concerned about the ultimate fate of America's ally. For Kissinger, a settlement that gave South Vietnam a "reasonable" chance to survive would suffice, as long as the United States was perceived to have lived up to its commitment.

Though Nixon and Kissinger were confident that they could succeed where their predecessors had failed, their initial negotiating position was essentially the same as that of the Johnson administration. Employing a two-tiered approach, they sought to reach agreement with Hanoi on the mutual withdrawal of all "external" forces, leaving it to the GVN and the NLF to resolve their own "internal" political dispute. As in the past, however, the North Vietnamese resisted any attempt to separate military and political issues, while the South Vietnamese remained adamantly opposed to talks with the NLF.

To a large extent, the stalemate in negotiations was a direct reflection of the continuing stalemate on the battlefield. Having already committed themselves to a strategy of "fighting while negotiating," the North Vietnamese lacked any incentive to make concessions as long as they retained the capacity to wage war effectively. As if to underscore that point, on February 23, Communist forces throughout South Vietnam launched their 1969 post–Tet Offensive, a coordinated series of attacks directed primarily against allied logistical and support installations. But, unlike in the 1968 offensive, only in a few places were the Communists able to mount large-scale ground assaults, and nowhere did they succeed in penetrating the cities.

Nevertheless, the timing of the attacks, according to Kissinger, "humiliated the new president." Already frustrated by Hanoi's intransigence at the negotiating table, an enraged Nixon decided "to do something [the Communists] will understand." Against the advice of Kissinger, who worried about the long-range diplomatic consequences of any impulsive action, but with the full endorsement of the JCS, on March 16 Nixon ordered the bombing of North Vietnamese base camps in Cambodia. He assumed, correctly as it turned out, that the North Vietnamese would not protest any such raids, since their objection would indirectly confirm the long-denied presence of NVA troops inside Cambodia. But the president thought that disclosure of the bombing might have severe repercussions at home and abroad. Accordingly, elaborate precautions were taken to shroud the operation in near total secrecy. Not only were the details withheld from most government officials, including the secretary and chief of staff of the Air Force, but an intricate dual reporting system was introduced at the Pentagon to divert information on the air strikes from normal channels. Under the code name Menu, the air strikes began the following day, March 18, unbeknown to the American people. Though originally intended to be of short duration, the operation continued for the next fourteen months. All told, 3,630 B-52 Arc Light missions were flown, dropping more than one hundred thousand tons of bombs on Cambodian territory.

Sergeant Don Fredericks of the 9th Infantry Division turns in his field equipment during processing-out procedures at the 9th Division base camp at Dong Tam. The division was among the first units withdrawn from Vietnam under President Nixon's "Vietnamization" policy.

Nixon had good reason to be concerned about the public's reaction to his policies. Though opinion polls taken in the early spring of 1969 suggested that most Americans had adopted a wait-and-see attitude toward the new president's handling of the war, Nixon knew that criticism would mount quickly if he failed to make progress toward peace. He therefore decided to make public the proposals he had already communicated privately to Hanoi. In a major address to the nation on May 14, he set forth an eight-point plan calling for a cease-fire, a pullout of all American and North Vietnamese troops over a one-year period, and an exchange of prisoners of war. At the urging of Secretary of Defense Melvin Laird, a staunch advocate of "Vietnamization"—that is, turning the fighting over to the South Vietnamese—Nixon also initiated planning for a phased withdrawal of US combat forces. In June, after conferring with President Thieu on Midway Island, he announced the immediate redeployment of the first increment of twenty-five thousand US troops.

Neither the peace initiative of May 14 nor the prospect of GIs coming home, however, was enough to curb growing opposition to Nixon's Vietnam policy. After the North Vietnamese publicly denounced the president's latest offer as a "farce," indicating they were prepared to sit in Paris "until the chairs rot," it became clear that there would be no diplomatic breakthrough in the near future. And, while most Americans favored a shift of the burden of fighting to the South Vietnamese, the absence of any set timetable diminished the appeal of Nixon's phased withdrawal plan. By midsummer, congressional doves were calling for a total US troop pullout by the end of 1970, while hawks rallied behind Georgia senator Richard Russell's demand for a "meaningful move" against North Vietnam. More ominous still, from Nixon's point of view, the organized peace movement, dormant since the previous fall, began stirring again with plans for large demonstrations in the fall.

In July, in response to the mounting chorus of criticism, Nixon hastily adopted a new "go for broke" strategy designed, as he put it, "to end the war one way or the other, either by negotiated agreement or by force." Through

With President Nguyen Van Thieu at his side, President Richard Nixon reports on his talks with the South Vietnamese leader on Midway Island, June 8, 1969.

Right: A wounded Marine is helped to an evacuation point during Operation Dewey Canyon, northwest of the A Shau Valley, January 13, 1969.

Bottom: Soldiers carry a wounded comrade through a swampy area.

French intermediaries, he sent a personal message to Ho Chi Minh, expressing his sincere desire for a "just peace" but also threatening to resort "to measures of great consequence and force" if the Paris negotiations did not move forward by November 1—the first anniversary of President Johnson's bombing halt. To underscore the gravity of the message, Kissinger met again with Soviet ambassador Dobrynin, warning him that "as far as Vietnam is concerned, the train has just left the station and is now heading down the track."

Nixon's ultimatum drew a "cold rebuff" from the ailing Ho Chi Minh, whose written reply reached Washington only a few days before his death on September 2.

Hanoi's continuing intransigence infuriated Nixon, who now had to decide whether to carry out his threat to escalate the war or fall back entirely on the Vietnamization plan he had inherited from the Johnson administration. Kissinger, convinced that "a fourth-rate power like North Vietnam" had to have "a breaking point," urged Nixon to inflict a "savage, punishing blow" on North Vietnam. Defense Secretary Laird and Secretary of State William Rogers vehemently opposed Kissinger's recommendation, imploring the president not to take any action that would incite further domestic protest.

Nixon reluctantly shelved the Kissinger plan, at least for the time being. At the time, Nixon's approval rating in the polls stood at an extraordinary 71 percent, largely as a result of his September announcement of a second troop withdrawal as well as a reduction in draft calls. Yet despite considerable public support, he had not been able to stop the spread of antiwar sentiment among the more vocal and influential elements of the population—labor leaders, educators, press commentators, clergy, and even corporate executives.

The extent to which antiwar protest had become respectable was demonstrated dramatically on October 15,

when hundreds of thousands of middle-class Americans heeded the call of the organized peace movement to observe a national "Moratorium Day." Across the nation, church bells tolled in remembrance of the American war dead, the names of those killed were read at candlelight services, and peaceful marchers sang the antiwar chant "Give Peace a Chance." Outside the United States, moratorium demonstrations were held in London, Paris, Copenhagen, Tokyo, and Sydney, while in Vietnam some American servicemen joined in the observance by wearing black armbands on patrol.

Though he feigned indifference, the president was deeply angered and alarmed by the mass protests. Not only did such demonstrations encourage North Vietnamese intractability, but, perhaps more important in his view, they also threatened to undermine his own credibility. As a result, when antiwar leaders announced plans to hold a second moratorium on November 15, Nixon went on the counterattack. In a shrewdly crafted address to the nation on November 3, he staunchly defended the American commitment to Saigon, warning that an abrupt pullout would lead to a "bloodbath" in Vietnam and a loss of faith abroad in American leadership. He then proceeded to lay out his Vietnamization plan in some detail, saying that it promised to reduce American casualties and bring the war to an end regardless of what the North Vietnamese did. Finally, against the advice of his entire cabinet, the president attacked the antiwar protesters as "irresponsible" and accused them of sabotaging his quest for an honorable peace. Appealing to what he called "the great silent majority," he asked for "united" support and concluded with a melodramatic admonition: "North Vietnam cannot defeat or humiliate the United States. Only Americans can do that."

Much to Nixon's delight, the response to his "silent majority" speech was overwhelmingly positive, once again boosting his standing in the polls and bringing a bipartisan vote of confidence from Congress. "We've got those liberal bastards on the run now," the president told his aides, "and we're going to keep them on the run."

Yet if the president and his men succeeded for the moment in putting their critics on the defensive, they soon learned that they could not silence them. The November 15 moratorium drew even more participants than the October demonstrations, as more than a quarter-million protesters converged on Washington, D.C., alone. Carrying placards bearing the names of US war dead and describing themselves as the "Silent Majority for Peace," they served notice to the Nixon administration that there would be no lasting peace in America until there was peace in Vietnam.

Thus, as the year drew to a close, the American president was rapidly running out of options. But by early 1970, as Nixon entered his second year in office, it looked as though Vietnamization might actually work. Supplied with huge quantities of the latest American weaponry and expanded to a force level of more than one million men, ARVN had already become one of the largest, best-equipped armies in the world. Many of its units had shown, moreover, that they could fight aggressively and effectively when well led, and in some cases they had even improved their performance after supporting US forces were withdrawn.

Equally encouraging, allied efforts to extend government control over the countryside were at last beginning to bear fruit. In accordance with the "one war" strategy adopted by General Abrams in 1969, American

Opposite page: A Marine of I (India) Company, 3rd Battalion, 1st Marine Regiment, keeps a watchful eye as his platoon crosses an open area during a patrol eight miles south of Da Nang.

Private First Class William R. Kryscnski of Bravo Company, 4th Battalion, 31st Infantry Regiment, 196th Light Infantry Brigade, Americal Division, hurls a grenade at an enemy position during a firefight in the Hiep Duc Valley, the site of some of the fiercest fighting between American forces and the NVA. In the background are Charles Kiewell (left) and Steve Lannert (right).

and South Vietnamese forces had shifted their emphasis from large-scale search-and-destroy missions to smaller "clearing" operations designed to protect the rural population. Under the new pacification-oriented plan, elected village councils were entrusted with responsibility for local security, territorial defense forces were given formal training and equipped with M16s, and a variety of "civic action" programs were reintroduced to promote economic development. In conjunction with these self-help measures, the CIA's controversial Phoenix Program succeeded in inflicting severe damage to the Viet Cong. According to US Embassy figures, in 1969 alone, nearly twenty thousand VC cadres were "neutralized" through arrest or assassination under the auspices of Phoenix, sharply reducing the enemy's ability to tax and recruit.

Yet for all the new gains that had been made, many of the same old problems persisted. Despite its increased size and modern look, ARVN still suffered from a shortage of competent officers and NCOs, an abundance of corruption at almost every level, and a seemingly unshakable reliance on American advice and firepower. Despite improved security and increased democracy in the villages, signs of genuine enthusiasm for the Thieu government were still scarce. And despite the inroads of Phoenix, the Viet Cong infrastructure remained intact, its relative inactivity in large part reflecting Hanoi's decision to wait until the Americans left for good.

In the opinion of many senior US officials, what the South Vietnamese needed, above all, was more time. General Abrams, for one, strongly believed that the American pullout was proceeding too quickly, and he therefore urged the president to defer plans for another major troop withdrawal. But Nixon, under unrelenting domestic pressure to "bring the boys home," overruled his commander. Hoping to "drop a bombshell on the gathering spring storm of antiwar protest," as he put it, in late April, Nixon announced that 150,000 more troops would be redeployed from Vietnam by the end of 1970. At the same time, however, he acceded to the military's long-standing request that allied ground forces be allowed to attack North Vietnamese sanctuaries inside Cambodia.

Nixon's decision to authorize a cross-border invasion seems to have been motivated by a variety of considerations. To begin with, he accepted the judgment of Abrams and other high-ranking military officials that such a move would relieve pressure on US forces guarding Saigon and buy valuable

Frank Eates comforts Pfc. James Doughty, who was hit during intense fighting in the Hiep Duc Valley. Doughty succumbed to his wounds moments later.

Senior writer Nick Mills describes an attack he endured as officer in charge of a photo team in Vietnam and the toll it took on a photographer in his command.

By the time Richard Nixon was sworn in as the thirty-seventh president of the United States, I had been sent to Qui Nhon, on South Vietnam's central coast, to establish a new detachment of the 221st Signal Company (Pictorial). The 221st was the manpower company for the Southeast Asia Pictorial Center (SEAPC) and worked directly under the Department of the Army. The mission was to "film and photograph US Army operations in Southeast Asia." Because we worked in small teams and each team was led by an officer, the 221st had probably more lieutenants than any company in the Army—I count sixteen in one group photo. We carried DA press cards, and had the freedom to link up with any unit in the field and hitch rides on whatever transport was available.

The approach of the Tet holiday in 1969 had everyone on high alert, thinking that the Communists might try to repeat the attacks of 1968, though we had been told that the enemy had been decimated in that offensive. I was sent with two of my photographers, Howard Nuernberger and Dwight Carter, to Chu Lai, in southern I Corps, a Marine Corps base about sixty miles south of Da Nang where the Army's 23rd Infantry (Americal) Division was also based. We found bunk space—I moved in with an OCS classmate, Lt. Gerry Cronlund—and waited for something to happen.

Tet, the lunar new year, was observed on February 16 in 1969. The date came and went, and all was quiet. We were getting bored in Chu Lai. Then in the early morning hours of February 22, the big base lit up with incoming mortars and rockets, and small arms fire erupted on the perimeter as the enemy tried to break through. The action continued into the daylight hours, but by 9:00 the attack was over. Most of the Communist fire had been directed at the airfield, but all things considered, the damage was not great and the airfield was operational. I managed to call my CO in Long Binh, which had also been attacked, and was told to bring my team back to headquarters. We got out on a C-130 the next day.

The big Long Binh base, home of the US Army–Vietnam (USARV) headquarters and around fifty thousand logistics and support troops, had been hit, and the perimeter briefly breached. The war rarely came to Long Binh, so there were a lot of shaken rear-area personnel in the mess halls the next morning. On the 26th, the enemy offensive continued. A combined NVA–Viet Cong force tried to attack the nearby Bien Hoa Air Base but had been trapped in a village by American and ARVN forces. My CO, Major Carson, told me to take my team over there to photograph the action. Carter, Nuernberger, and another

An NVA soldier surrenders to ARVN troops during a battle for the village near Bien Hoa Air Base.

photographer, David Russell, went with me in a company jeep. As we approached the village, I fell in behind a column of tanks that were maneuvering to skirt the village and cut off the route of escape. I heard odd pinging sounds up ahead, then realized it was the sound of small-arms fire hitting the tank in front of me. I made a U-turn as an enemy RPG that had been aimed at my jeep exploded in the ditch just ahead of us. We joined an American advisor who was directing an ARVN Ranger force as they tried to penetrate the village where the enemy were dug in, and we advanced on foot behind a small group of APCs until driven back by heavy fire from the village.

Helicopter gunships strafed the village, which was quickly being reduced to rubble by the fighting, but the enemy kept on popping up and shooting back.

In the afternoon, more teams from SEAPC joined my team, recording the battle on mopic and still cameras. In midafternoon, the ARVN Rangers began a determined assault on the village. Carter, Nuernberger, and I advanced with different elements of the assault force. An American photographer—not one of ours—was killed and Carter helped bring his body to the rear. Suddenly the enemy launched a counterattack. I was pinned down in a building, flat on the floor as machine-gun and AK-47 fire rattled close by, punctuated by the louder booms of exploding RPGs. The ARVN pulled back in a hurry, carrying their dead and wounded, and I ran with them, crossing a flat open area and finally reaching the safety of a cluster of buildings where I found a group of SEAPC photographers huddled around a badly wounded man. I looked but could not identify him. His face was blackened and bloody, his uniform shredded, and most of his right arm was missing; a jagged white bone stuck out of the mangled flesh just below the shoulder. I asked who it was.

"Nuernberger," was the reply.

Howard Nuernberger was a tall, quiet kid from Pennsylvania, and a terrific photographer. We had been together in Chu Lai when the offensive started a few nights before. He had been hit by an RPG as he stood in a doorway when the enemy counterattacked.

An RTO was trying to call for a dust-off chopper but was being told there were none available. I kept yelling at the RTO, but there was nothing he could do—the dust-offs were very busy that day. I spotted a number of ARVN ambulances a hundred yards away, so I've got Howard onto a litter, carried him to an ambulance and tried to load him on board—but the Vietnamese driver said no, he would not take the wounded American. Like hell. I stuck the muzzle of my M16 in his face and said he would take Howard or I would shoot him and take his ambulance. The driver then decided he would take Howard, and I told Carter to ride with him and use his weapon if necessary. Howard was taken to the 21st Evac Hospital at Long Binh, a fifteen-minute drive, and rushed into surgery.

Late that afternoon, when the fighting was over, I went to the 21st Evac and asked a nurse about Howard. She went into the OR, and in a minute a surgeon in scrubs charged out of the OR, straight at me, peeling off his bloody latex gloves. It was Howard's blood.

"Are you that man's commanding officer?" he shouted.

"Yes," I said. "How is he?"

"How *is* he? What the hell do you mean, how *is* he? He's lost an arm, that's how he is," the surgeon roared. He was so angry he was sputtering, screaming at me. I thought he might hit me.

"Can you justify that, lieutenant? Can you justify that? Losing an arm to take a goddamn picture?"

I was too stunned to answer. The surgeon finally stomped off. Howard was wheeled out of the OR. The stump of his arm was now encased in clean white bandages. I stayed with him for a while and then drove back to SEAPC, where I vented my own anger.

It did not occur to me until much later—maybe the surgeon had not understood that we were combat photographers, not sightseeing tourists. Taking pictures was our job, as justifiable—or not—as anyone's in Vietnam.

Howard Nuernberger went home to recuperate, and when he left the Army he landed a job with Pittsburgh Plate Glass as a corporate photographer.

Lieutenant Nick Mills of the 221st Signal Company (Pictorial) takes cover during a battle for the village near Bien Hoa Air Base.

In the wake of the Tet Offensive, American and South Vietnamese units struggled to regain and control areas that had been contested or even lost in the attack. Particularly important was the populated countryside between Saigon and the Cambodian border, where North Vietnamese and Viet Cong units attacked US and ARVN forces, then slipped to the sanctuary of Cambodia. One of the members of a combined US-ARVN reconnaissance team in this area was Al Santoli, a sergeant with the 25th Infantry Division from March 1968 to March 1969.

In my time in Vietnam, I came to understand that there were actually two wars going on simultaneously, each as important as the other. The first was the conventional war against regular North Vietnamese units; the second was for the support of the population, winning the "hearts and minds" of the people. It was in this second aspect of the conflict that I had my most valuable experience in Vietnam, one that gave me a unique view of the war and of human nature. From October 1968 to February 1969, I served in a Combined Reconnaissance and Intelligence Platoon (CRIP) with twenty Americans and twenty South Vietnamese and lived along the North Vietnamese invasion route to the capital, independent of American forces.

Our platoon, far removed from American fire support bases, had to rely on the loyalty of the black-pajama-clad villagers, who were as fearful and suspicious of us as we were of them. Although the twenty GIs in our platoon had only limited knowledge of the Vietnamese language and culture, we had no choice but to learn to coexist with villagers in an area notorious for Viet Cong activity.

Our objective was to monitor NVA troop movement out of Cambodia. If we could locate them in the forests of Tay Ninh and pinpoint their bases for air strikes, countless South Vietnamese and American lives would be saved. Communist strategy during and after the Tet Offensive was to turn populated areas into battlefields. They wanted American firepower to "destroy villages in order to save them" and to create unintentional civilian casualties. Such destruction would cause bitter feelings toward American and South Vietnamese soldiers and produce news photos and television images that horrified the international community.

It was hard for a regular infantry soldier to understand the pressure the people here lived under. Their silence and lack of cooperation earned them the label "VC" or "VC sympathizer," but silence was their only hope for survival. After a few months of living among them, we came to understand that they had no interest in politics, taxes, or armies. They wished only to continue their ancestral heritage and work their land in peace. I think they came to understand that we were risking our lives for them to have the peace they desperately hoped for. We awkwardly tried to understand their ways, ate their food, and attended local ceremonies. An unusual bond developed between us. We became friends. And in a contested area, friendship can have a heavy price.

COSVN did not take kindly to our success and was always seeking to destroy us. We learned that whenever we left a campsite, VC agents would come in to search through garbage and to plant booby traps, expecting us to return. We began surprising them by leaving behind an ambush team of three to six of our people, who turned the tables on the saboteurs.

We rarely camped near any particular location for more than one or two nights. Once, we got a little complacent or tired, though, and stayed almost a week near one village. Every morning a little girl would ride by us on her bicycle, giving us a warm grin. One morning, an explosion rocked our camp. We ran to the road and found a huge mine crater and a crumpled bicycle blown fifty meters away. The little girl was gone. Her parents were walking circles around the crater, weeping and searching. We tried to find the child, but all that remained of her was a handful of pieces of flesh. The mother used chopsticks to place them tenderly in a plastic bag. The bomb had been meant for us.

By living with the people and sharing their fears, I realized that no matter how valiantly American soldiers performed in combat, the key to winning the population's support was respect for their traditions. Through our Vietnamese platoon members, we had prolonged discussions with villagers. Discreetly, they confided their distrust and fear of the Viet Cong and North Vietnamese soldiers who took both their rice and their sons, but a very effective VC shadow presence made them reluctant to cooperate with the South Vietnamese government.

Through my relationship with these proud people, I learned that regardless of our many differences, we had a lot in common. With the passive support of the villagers, we were able to beat the VC and North Vietnamese on their own turf, and we helped deny them the ability to launch surprise attacks on outposts or towns. At the same time, we gained respect and understanding for the people we were protecting.

time for Vietnamization. In addition, he had not yet abandoned his conviction that he could bludgeon the North Vietnamese into a compromise settlement through a dramatic show of force. An unexpected thrust into theoretically neutral Cambodia would prove once again that he was willing to take more extreme measures than had President Johnson, compelling Hanoi to decide "whether they want to take us on all over again." Finally, the recent overthrow of Cambodia's neutralist leader, Prince Norodom Sihanouk, by the pro-American Lon Nol provided a previously lacking rationale for widening the war. By mid-April, Cambodia was in a state of near anarchy. North Vietnamese and Khmer Rouge forces were pushing the Cambodian army back into the interior, and Lon Nol, with American encouragement, was openly calling for outside help. "We need a bold move . . . to show that we stand with Lon Nol," Nixon informed Kissinger on April 26. Even though he might fall anyway, "we must do something symbolic" for the only Cambodian leader in the last twenty-five years "with the guts to take a pro-Western and pro-American stand."

The president revealed his decision on the evening of April 30, 1970, in a televised speech that was, in Kissinger's words, "vintage Nixon." Rather than soft-selling his action simply as a matter of "good tactics," as the military had recommended, he attempted to justify the Cambodian "incursion" in hyperbolic, even global terms. The North Vietnamese, he contended, were preparing "to launch massive attacks on our forces and those of the South Vietnamese" from their sanctuaries in Cambodia. Hanoi was testing the "will and character" of the United States in an effort to expose "the world's most powerful nation" as a "pitiful, helpless giant." Failure to respond to the enemy's "direct challenge" would only encourage "the forces of totalitarianism and anarchy [to] threaten free nations and free institutions throughout the world." Spurning "all political considerations," Nixon declared, he had decided to follow his conscience rather than be "a two-term president at the cost of seeing America . . . accept the first defeat in its sound 190-years' history."

Even as Nixon spoke, South Vietnamese forces were already operating inside the Parrot's Beak, a narrow protrusion of Cambodian territory northwest of Saigon, having first crossed the border on April 29. Two days later, on the morning of May 1, a combined US-ARVN force of fifteen thousand men plunged into the Fishhook region farther north. Moving behind a shield of heavy artillery fire and air strikes, columns of tanks and armored personnel carriers of the 11th Armored Cavalry Regiment led the way, followed by troop-laden helicopters of the 1st Air Cav. Though the invading troops expected to meet with heavy resistance, it soon became apparent that the North Vietnamese had fled in advance, leaving behind vast storehouses of weapons, ammunition, and other war materiel. The allied command had also hoped to discover COSVN (Central Office for South Vietnam), the alleged headquarters for all Communist forces operating in the South. Instead they found only "a scattering of empty huts" that bore little resemblance to the miniature Pentagon they had imagined. The Americans nevertheless pronounced the operation a success, since the destruction of the enemy's base camps relieved any immediate threat to the heavily populated Saigon–Bien Hoa corridor.

If the military benefits of the Cambodian invasion fell short of Nixon's hopes, the domestic reaction to it exceeded his worst expectations. As prominent media commentators lashed out at the president, university campuses

Above: Mary Ann Vecchio screams as she kneels over the body of fellow student Jeffrey Miller during an antiwar demonstration at Kent State University, May 4, 1970. Four students were killed when Ohio National Guard troops fired at some six hundred demonstrators.

Left: A large crowd of students demonstrate outside the White House against the violence used to break up a war protest at Kent State University.

across the country erupted in protest, in some instances with tragic results. On May 4, thirteen Kent State students were shot, four of them fatally, by Ohio National Guardsmen sent in to maintain "law and order." Several days later, two more students were killed at Jackson State College in Mississippi during an angry confrontation with local police. By the end of the first week in May, hundreds of thousands of students and faculty had gone on strike to protest the shootings, prompting more than four hundred colleges and universities to shut down entirely.

The expansion of the war into Cambodia also provoked an angry response from Congress. In the first direct challenge to presidential authority since the beginning of the war, the Senate voted overwhelmingly in June to rescind the Gulf of Tonkin Resolution of 1964. Senators John Sherman Cooper of Kentucky and Frank Church of Idaho drafted a resolution setting a June 30 deadline for the termination of all US military operations in Cambodia, while Sens. George McGovern of South Dakota and Mark Hatfield of Oregon co-sponsored an even more restrictive proposal requiring a total US pullout from Vietnam by the end of 1971.

Characteristically, Nixon immediately launched a counterattack. The time had come to stop "screwing around" with his congressional opponents, he told his staff. "Don't worry about divisiveness. Having drawn the sword, don't take it out—stick it in hard. Hit 'em in the gut." Warning that if "Congress undertakes to restrict me, Congress will have to assume the consequences," he blamed his adversaries for undermining US credibility and prolonging the war. He also ordered the formation of a special covert team to monitor his domestic critics and verify suspected links between radical groups in the US and foreign governments. The project represented one of the most serious abuses of presidential authority in US history and would later come under investigation during the 1973 Watergate hearings.

In the end, neither the Cooper-Church amendment nor the more extreme McGovern-Hatfield proposal won the approval of Congress, in part because most legislators were still unwilling to accept responsibility for the war and in part because Nixon stole the opposition's thunder by removing all US troops from Cambodia before June 30. Yet if the president had survived the latest crisis with his authority intact, his options for future action were more restricted than ever. The Cambodian venture may have bought time for Vietnamization, but it had neither seriously diminished Hanoi's capacity to make war nor broken the deadlock in negotiations. It had also provoked the most violent outburst of antiwar protest since the war began, intensifying pressure to speed up the pace of the American withdrawal and imposing clear limits on the future use of US combat troops. A year and a half after Richard Nixon assumed the presidency, the war that he had pledged to end was still going on, and the peace that he promised to win was still not in sight.

Focus: Cambodian Incursion

From the outset of the Vietnam War, the Communists enjoyed one enormous advantage over their American adversaries: the network of secure bases and staging areas just beyond the boundaries of South Vietnam. American intelligence eventually located fourteen major enemy bases inside Cambodia, some only thirty-five miles from Saigon. MACV repeatedly sought permission to launch operations against these sanctuaries; President Johnson, who wanted to contain the ground war and feared the political repercussions of violating the territory of "neutral"

Men of the 3rd Battalion, 23rd Infantry, 25th Infantry Division, take up positions outside the village of Ph Tasuos, just south of the Fishhook, five kilometers inside Cambodia, in early May, 1970.

Opposite page: A soldier stands with arms raised near purple smoke, guiding a group of Hueys as they approach a landing zone in Cambodia, 1970.

states, just as regularly refused. Johnson's prohibitions frustrated American troops who believed that if they were allowed to pursue the North Vietnamese across the frontier, they could hurt the enemy where he lived. Fifteen months after he came to office, Richard Nixon gave them the chance.

On May 1, 1970, following a predawn air and artillery bombardment, tanks and armored personnel carriers (APCs) of the 11th Armored Cavalry Regiment churned across the border into the Fishhook, a narrow swath of land jutting into Binh Long Province. Overhead, wave after wave of CH-47 Chinook helicopters carried troopers from the 1st Air Cav into landing zones blasted out of the jungle by gigantic fifteen-thousand-pound bombs. "This Cambodian operation is pure blitzkrieg," one senior US officer told a reporter, "like something from a World War II Panzer division's book of tactics."

While 1st Cav troopers consolidated their positions and fanned out in search of the enemy, the 11th Cavalry brushed through scattered RPG fire along the frontier, then rolled north across flat, open terrain. Late in the afternoon, the tanks collided with an entrenched North Vietnamese battalion. The ensuing fight "looked like the Fourth of July," recalled 11th Cav commander Brig. Gen. Donn Starry. For sixty minutes the Americans blasted enemy bunkers from the ground with tank-mounted cannon fire and pounded them from the sky with tactical air strikes. When the stubborn defenders were finally driven from their fortifications, fifty-two NVA dead lay sprawled across the smoking battlefield.

US soldiers of the 11th Armored Cavalry Regiment, among the first to enter Cambodia in April and May, celebrate as they return to South Vietnam in late June 1970, riding a tank past a bullet-riddled sign at the border north of Katum.

By and large, however, the Americans encountered only scattered resistance. Well aware of the armored might being readied across the border, most enemy units had chosen discretion over valor and withdrawn to the west ahead of the American advance.

Most, but not all. On May 4, the 11th Cavalry was ordered to proceed to the town of Snuol, a strategically located supply depot still occupied by a large enemy force. The hundred-tank column raced north along Highway 7 at speeds of up to sixty-five miles per hour, throwing armored-vehicle-launched bridges (AVLBs) across three rivers and reaching the outskirts of Snuol by the afternoon of the 5th. Immediately, the tanks formed up and stormed the town's airstrip, using canisters filled with thousands of steel pellets to silence enemy positions. Once the airstrip was secured, the tanks advanced toward the central marketplace where they were met by concentrated rocket and automatic-weapons fire.

For the rest of the day and through the night, Air Force fighter-bombers screamed through the sky, plastering the town with napalm and high explosives. Periodically, the tanks returned to the task, firing volley after volley of cannon fire into the crumbling, burning buildings, while helicopter gunships rocketed pockets of enemy resistance and mortars crashed into the rubble. When the 11th Cavalry entered the city on the morning of May 6, there was nothing left but ruins. The NVA had fled during the night. The only bodies were those of four civilians. "We didn't want to blow this town away," said one senior officer, "but we had no choice." American troops coined a new word after the battle—to "snuol," meaning to obliterate.

Yet the fighting of the first few days only cleared the way for what turned out to be the real work of the operation. Hoping to bag enemy troops, the Americans found themselves instead the heir to the enemy's treasure, for the fleeing NVA had left behind a staggering quantity of equipment and supplies.

One of the most remarkable finds was "The City," a two-square-mile complex buried deep in the jungle south of Snuol complete with street signs, barracks, mess halls, classrooms, firing range, lumberyard, recreation hall, swimming pool, and pig farm. Inside the four hundred huts, storage sheds, and bunkers linked by three-foot-deep trenches and miles of tunnels, the troopers found sixty thousand pounds of rice, sixteen thousand pounds of corn, fifty-eight thousand pounds of plastic explosives, 1.5 million rounds of ammunition, three hundred trucks, more than two hundred crew-served weapons, and enough small arms for fifty-five battalions. Two days later and forty kilometers northeast, 1st Air Cav soldiers discovered another NVA installation that the troopers dubbed Rock Island East after the Rock Island Arsenal in Illinois. The Cambodian version, the largest cache of enemy materiel ever captured during the war, contained in all some 329 tons of munitions.

Responding to a storm of domestic protest, President Nixon announced that the incursion would penetrate no deeper than thirty-four kilometers and conclude by June 30. Although US gunships, fighter-bombers, and B-52s continued to pummel suspected enemy positions and special land-clearing units slashed through the dense forest with giant Rome plows, American ground troops had to content themselves with the backbreaking work of emptying the enemy sanctuaries. Engineers built roads to haul out as much as possible, and smaller caches were simply put to the torch. But supplies continued to be discovered faster than they could be destroyed.

In mid-May, the Communists launched scattered assaults on American firebases in what appeared to be the prelude to a concerted counterattack. But the arrival of the monsoon rains in early June brought fighting on both sides to a halt. On June 28, two days before the president's deadline, the last American tanks rumbled back across the border while US air and artillery hammered what was left of the enemy sanctuaries with a farewell bombardment.

When they first learned they would be going into Cambodia, many GIs had reacted with pleasure. As one helicopter pilot put it, "We had lost many men in combat assaults near the Cambodia border while the gooks would go back into Cambodia, sit there, and laugh at us, so we were all together for going in."

In American terms, they largely got what they wanted. The incursion dealt the enemy a significant setback, killing an estimated 4,776 men, destroying nearly twelve thousand bunkers, and capturing enough rice to feed every Communist unit in South Vietnam for four months, enough ammunition for ten months, and enough individual weapons to equip seventy-four battalions. The resulting decline in enemy activity sharply reduced US casualties during the remainder of the year. That enemy Main Force units had largely escaped intact, that much of the supplies would be replaced within a few months, and that the boundaries of the war had been irreversibly widened were facts the South Vietnamese and Cambodians would ultimately have to face. US ground troops had delivered their last major blow of the war.

CHAPTER SEVEN

THE LONG GOODBYE

The election of Richard Nixon, with his promises of a "secret plan" to end the war—promises that were met with skepticism by many Americans—marked the beginning of the end of America's involvement in Vietnam. But the end—Nixon's "peace with honor"—would not be reached for another four years, until Nixon had conducted massive secret bombing campaigns against the NVA supply lines and troop movements in Cambodia and Laos, and another twenty thousand Americans, one hundred thousand South Vietnamese troops, a half-million NVA, and as many as two million Vietnamese, Laotian, and Cambodian civilians had died. Although US troop strength would reach its peak during Nixon's first year as president, the newly arriving troops, already in the pipeline when Nixon took office, heard the word *Vietnamization,* which Nixon had adopted from the plan that Lyndon Johnson had announced in 1968. It is not clear whether Nixon still felt the war was winnable, but in the aftermath of the Cambodian incursion there was no longer any talk of victory. On April 30, 1969, there were more than 540,000 U.S military personnel in South Vietnam, but nearly one hundred thousand fewer by the end of the year. By the end of 1971, only 184,000 remained. American combat deaths fell from the high of 16,589 in 1968 to 11,614 in 1969, and would drop to 6,083 in 1970 and 2,357 in 1971.

US armored units move back into a combat base recently turned over to Vietnamese forces. In Washington, the US Senate, in a second rebuff of Presisdent Nixon's Vietnam policies, voted for a total US withdrawal from Indochina by spring 1972.

Vietnamese girls present gifts to members of the 3rd Battalion, 60th Infantry, 2nd Brigade, 9th Infantry Division during a farewell ceremony at Tan Son Nhut Air Base.

One by one, American units assembled their men for stand-down ceremonies replete with speeches and ritual flag lowerings, withdrew from outlying bases into coastal enclaves or populated areas, and prepared to return home. The 9th Infantry Division and 3rd Marine Division, which had left Vietnam in the last months of 1969, were soon followed home by the 1st Infantry Division, which left in April 1970, and in October by the 199th Infantry Brigade. During December, the bulk of the 4th and 25th Infantry Divisions headed home. April 1971 witnessed the departure of the 1st Marine Division, 1st Cavalry Division, and 11th Armored Cavalry Regiment, followed in August by the 1st Brigade of the 5th Infantry Division. One month later, the 173rd Airborne Brigade quit Vietnam after six long years of service, followed in November by two brigades of the 23rd Infantry Division. By the middle of 1971, the ARVN had taken over nearly 250 American bases and other installations.

As more and more American soldiers left Vietnam, those who remained found their role increasingly limited to protective security and static defense. Since Gen. Creighton Abrams succeeded William Westmoreland as MACV chief in June 1968, US forces had steadily abandoned multibattalion forays into remote frontier regions. Some units continued to mount sweep operations and mobile reconnaissance efforts. By the end of 1970, though, most of the Americans' time was devoted to shielding the lowland population from attack through constant patrolling and the destruction of Communist supply caches, without which the enemy could not sustain offensive operations. The shift away from the earlier large search-and-destroy operations, and General Abrams's insistence that the enemy be fought on his own terms, made the war more than ever a contest in which platoons, even squads, became major actors in the military drama.

The change placed enormous responsibility on the shoulders of inexperienced junior officers and NCOs, whose jobs were made more difficult by serious manpower shortages that regularly sent companies and platoons into the field at half-strength or less. Moreover, those troops who were available exhibited little of the discipline or enthusiasm of the men who served before them. If some commanders were still able to inspire troops to effective, aggressive action, many others were less interested in hunting the enemy or capturing a tactical objective than in seeing to it that their men returned home safely.

In any case, the enemy was making himself very difficult to find. The staggering losses suffered by the Communists during the Tet Offensive of 1968 and the yearlong American counterattack that followed forced Hanoi to break up most of its Main Force and local units and curtail conventional attacks in favor of guerrilla activities that maintained military pressure without risking large additional casualties. Meanwhile, the Politburo rebuilt its forces in preparation for the day when the Americans left South Vietnam.

The Cambodian incursion and the overthrow of the Sihanouk government by pro-American general Lon Nol in the spring of 1970 made the Communist task much more difficult. Not only did these events set back Hanoi's schedule, they also forced the redeployment of four divisions from Vietnam and the border sanctuaries to protect vital North Vietnamese lines of supply in the eastern half of Cambodia. Those enemy units that remained in South Vietnam continued to harass allied installations with mortar and rocket attacks and occasionally marshaled sufficient forces to mount ground assaults against US fire support bases. By and large, however, the Communists avoided battle. "Things were so quiet during the final four months of 1970," recalled one Army intelligence officer, "we were almost tripping over each other in an effort to find something to do."

The relative calm was shattered at the end of January 1971 when an American task force composed of artillery, airborne, engineer, armored cavalry, infantry, and aviation units—ten thousand troops, two thousand fixed-wing aircraft, and six hundred helicopters—launched Operation

US and ARVN soldiers salute the colors during a ceremony in which members of the 2nd Brigade, 9th Infantry Division, turn over their base camp to the 7th ARVN Division, July 3, 1969.

Dewey Canyon II to clear Route 9 and reopen Khe Sanh Combat Base in preparation for a major ARVN penetration of Laos, code-named Operation Lam Son 719. Once the South Vietnamese crossed the border on February 8, American pilots played a crucial air support and logistics role in the subsequent fighting. Battling ferocious antiaircraft fire, US Army aviators flew some one hundred thousand helicopter sorties during a seven-week operation that ultimately cost the Americans more than 1,400 casualties, including 253 killed and missing, plus the loss of more than a hundred aircraft.

During the remainder of the year, American aircraft continued to pound the Ho Chi Minh Trail and provide support to government forces in Laos and Cambodia, while a renewed air campaign against North Vietnam struck military targets in the demilitarized zone and the Hanoi-Haiphong area. On the ground in South Vietnam, however, there was little action. US troops near Saigon fought occasional sharp encounters against enemy bunker complexes, and the 23rd Infantry (Americal) Division's 11th Infantry Brigade spent weeks in futile pursuit of the Viet Cong province headquarters in Quang Ngai. When 101st Airborne troopers completed the construction of three firebases in coastal Thua Thien Province and wrapped up Operation Jefferson Glenn on October 8, they brought to an end the last major American ground combat operation of the war.

Most of the American troops remaining in Vietnam during 1971 spent their time guarding military bases, urban areas, and highways, or sweeping back and forth across the so-called rocket belts that encircled major cities and critical installations. It could be a dangerous assignment, for the Viet Cong laced their launching sites with booby traps. Indeed, these brutal devices were taking a far heavier toll on GIs than was enemy fire. Meanwhile, the Communists avoided direct contact except where lax security left strategically placed US installations vulnerable to attack.

Such was the case at Fire Support Base Mary Ann, a 23rd Infantry Division outpost in the western highlands of Quang Tin Province manned by a battalion of the 196th Infantry Brigade. In the early morning hours of March 28, a company of NVA sappers cut through the unguarded perimeter and swarmed over Mary Ann behind a barrage of 82mm mortar rounds. In no more than half an hour they were gone, having killed or wounded half of the firebase's 250 defenders, including most of the officers, at a cost of only ten of their own dead. The disaster prompted a full-scale investigation that culminated in disciplinary action against six officers, among them the division and assistant division commanders, but did little to arrest the steady deterioration that bedeviled American forces as they waited to disengage from a war they no longer wanted to fight.

The sharp decline in the number of encounters with the enemy from mid-1970 on meant a similar decline in the number of US casualties. Yet, the period of withdrawal was in some ways far more damaging to American military forces in Vietnam than the years of heaviest combat.

The defensive posture mandated by Washington left most soldiers with little sense of mission other than personal survival. This situation might have been controlled had the Army's officer corps maintained the high standards of professionalism with which it entered the war. Unfortunately, by 1970 the cumulative impact of college deferments, declining ROTC enrollments, careerism within the military, and the Johnson administration's decision not to call up the reserves had degraded the overall quality and competence of

Marines of 3/3/Mike manage to find some levity at their desolate post near the DMZ.

the junior officers sent to Vietnam. Coupled with an uncertain schedule of unit withdrawals and the news of mounting antiwar protests back home, these conditions provoked within the disengagement forces an epidemic of "short-timer's fever" that corroded morale and seriously threatened discipline both on and off the battlefield.

The contagion manifested itself in growing tension between draftees and "lifers," the career officers and NCOs still intent on fighting the war in earnest. It could be seen in the "search-and-evade" maneuvers that supplanted the aggressive tactics of earlier years. It was visible in the fake patrols that some platoons substituted for the real thing when they thought their assigned patrol sector was too hot for comfort, as well as in acts of disobedience, insubordination, and outright mutiny under fire. More disturbing even than such combat refusals, however, was the mounting incidence of attacks by enlisted men on unpopular officers and noncoms. The number of these so-called "fraggings" more than doubled between 1969 and 1970, spurred on by bounties as high as $10,000 offered by disgruntled troops for the assassination of "overaggressive" commanders.

A significant portion of fragging incidents took place in the rear, where racial tensions suppressed during combat added fuel to the fires of resentment. In the early years of the conflict, 1961–1966, black soldiers comprised around 10 percent of the armed forces but suffered almost 20 percent of the combat deaths in Vietnam. Black soldiers often comprised more than half the manpower of frontline infantry units and suffered battle casualties at rates well out of proportion to their numbers in Vietnam. Dr. Martin Luther

US soldiers outside a command post in Hue, 1968.

In the jungle battlefields of South Vietnam, this soldier came across a message written on a tombstone-like marking. The writing, addressed to black US soldiers, is an example of the propaganda promoted by the Viet Cong.

King Jr. led the criticism of the military's use of African American soldiers, calling it "a white man's war, a black man's fight." Political pressure from King and others led commanders in Vietnam to try to reduce the casualty rate of black soldiers, and by the end of the war the overall combat death rate for African American troops had dropped to around 12 percent, equaling their representation in the military.

In the rear, black soldiers were far more likely than whites to be assigned to low-skilled specialties. This apparent discrimination was more the result of socioeconomic factors than institutional racism, but there was no denying the hostility that black soldiers frequently encountered from some white officers and enlisted men. Energized by the civil rights revolution within the United States, many black soldiers demanded changes, adopting a militant stance that increasingly echoed Black Power advocates back home. The military instituted a number of measures to reduce friction, but it could not forestall ugly eruptions of racial violence.

Racial prejudice also contributed to a rising tide of violence by US troops against those whom they had come so far to help. Barriers of language and custom had long obstructed relations between American soldiers and the Vietnamese. During the early years of the war, mutual antipathies had been largely held in check. But the slow redeployment of US troops provoked noisy anti-American demonstrations and a dramatic increase in American criminal offenses against Vietnamese civilians.

These ranged from shooting water buffaloes for sport to running cyclists off the road, from throwing C-ration cans at Vietnamese children to using peasants for target practice. As large numbers of US troops withdrew into heavily populated rear areas, public drunkenness, disorderly conduct, and theft became more common. In the countryside, a deadly combination of too much frustration and too little discipline led to a substantial increase in formal allegations of war crimes, including manslaughter, rape, murder, and mutilation. The massacre by men of the US Americal Division of more than 450 Vietnamese villagers at My Lai in March 1968 (but not discovered by the American public until more than a year later) was unprecedented in the numbers involved and the extent of command breakdown. But atrocities were committed by American troops and in greater numbers as the war went on.

Certain expressions used by US troops reflected their indifference to the suffering they caused the Vietnamese people. Incidents of what's now called "collateral damage"—civilian casualties—were treated with a shrug and a "Sorry 'bout that," which later morphed into the more fatalistic, I-don't-give-a-damn "There it is."

While some US servicemen reacted to the difficulties of the withdrawal years with aggressive behavior against one another or the Vietnamese, others simply tried to escape, a few through desertion, a great many more through drugs. Marijuana was the most frequently used substance, but heroin, opium, cocaine, and amphetamines were all readily available at rock-bottom

In the relaxed atmosphere of their living quarters—equipped with a stereo and poster-lined walls—GIs pass around a "smoke" (marijuana) in the midst of a joint US–South Vietnam antidrug crackdown.

prices. As was the case with racial unrest, drug use skyrocketed after 1968. One Defense Department survey in 1971 found that almost 50 percent of American troops in Vietnam were either occasional or habitual users of marijuana. Despite twenty thousand arrests by the military during 1969 and 1970, the number of marijuana and heroin users within the armed forces continued to increase, as did a host of drug-related crimes, from petty theft to murder. And though most drug use took place in rear areas, tales of combat troops smoking pot before going out on patrol were too numerous to discount entirely.

So serious was the crisis of discipline that afflicted the disengaging forces that some feared catastrophe. "By every conceivable indicator," wrote one retired Marine officer and military analyst in June 1971, "our Army that now remains in Vietnam is in a state approaching collapse, with individual units avoiding or having refused combat, murdering their officers and noncommissioned officers, drug-ridden, and dispirited where not near mutinous." Although that sweeping indictment was overdrawn, there was no doubt in the minds of most professional military men that the health and effectiveness of the US Army required that the war be turned over to the Vietnamese as swiftly as possible.

That job was entrusted to Gen. Creighton Abrams, who had been appointed by Johnson to succeed General Westmoreland in 1968. Abrams helped his South Vietnamese counterparts build up their forces and expand their training programs. To improve combat leadership, MACV designed programs for commissioning experienced NCOs. To provide the necessary firepower and mobility, the US command funneled the latest American equipment into South Vietnamese hands. And to ensure they knew how to use the new hardware, Abrams sent the ARVN on combined operations with American units.

By 1971, these efforts had resulted in a South Vietnamese army of more than one million soldiers, each one armed with an M16 rifle. The ARVN also boasted twelve thousand M60 machine guns, forty thousand M79 grenade launchers, two thousand heavy mortars and howitzers, and an armada of new ships, airplanes, helicopters, tanks, and armored personnel carriers.

The new men and new weapons, however, could not themselves correct such fundamental problems as uninspired troops, staggering rates of desertion, lack of trained personnel to maintain the sophisticated equipment supplied by the US, severe shortages of experienced junior officers, corruption and incompetence among the senior officer corps, heavy dependence on the US logistics system, and a continuing overreliance on American artillery and air support. These weaknesses had been to some extent obscured by the successful combined operation into

Guns ready, ARVN soldiers peer into the entrance of a bunker. The incursion in Laos turned up arms and supplies found in bunkers along the Ho Chi Minh Trail. North Vietnamese used the bunkers as storage depots and protective cover.

Cambodia and the relatively low level of fighting during the remainder of 1970. But when Vietnamization was put to the test with a preemptive strike into the Laotian panhandle at the beginning of 1971, the results were disastrous.

In conception, the Laotian incursion was similar to the foray into Cambodia nine months earlier. The purpose of the operation, Lam Son 719, was to capture NVA equipment and supplies, cut infiltration routes, and generally create as much havoc for the enemy as possible while US aviation and artillery assets still remained for support. Beyond these specific objectives, Lam Son was an opportunity to demonstrate that Vietnamization was working, to show the Communists that the South Vietnamese armed forces had come of age. Although US aircraft and pilots would be employed, no American ground troops or advisors would accompany the ARVN beyond the border.

The sixteen thousand-man South Vietnamese task force crossed into Laos on February 8 against minimal resistance. While troops from the ARVN Airborne Division, 1st Infantry Division and a Ranger group established bases to the north and south of Route 9, the 1st Armored Brigade advanced along the highway hampered only by rain and mud. At the end of the third day, the main South Vietnamese thrust was only twenty miles from Tchepone, a main hub of the Ho Chi Minh Trail. Beginning on February 12, however, the outlying firebases began to come under heavy attack from tank-supported NVA infantry. American gunships and supply helicopters flew through withering antiaircraft fire in support of the beleaguered defenders, but by March 1 the entire northern flank was collapsing under the weight of three enemy divisions.

While the NVA rushed more and more troops into battle, the armored column stalled along Route 9 waiting for orders from higher command. On March 6, behind B-52 raids that reduced the Laotian town to rubble, helicopter-borne ARVN troops seized Tchepone but almost immediately began a general withdrawal toward the South Vietnamese border. Pursued by enemy forces now totaling thirty-four thousand men, the withdrawal quickly became a disorganized retreat and finally disintegrated into a total rout as panicked soldiers abandoned equipment and fought each other to reach evacuation helicopters. Despite thousands of sorties by American fighter-bombers and B-52s, some units were almost entirely annihilated. Thousands more South Vietnamese soldiers were saved only by American helicopter crews who braved intense fire to rescue them.

Although many South Vietnamese troops performed well in individual battles during the course of the operation, President Thieu's announcement that Lam Son 719 was "the biggest victory ever" struck many in Vietnam and the United States as ludicrous. The ARVN had destroyed several enemy stockpiles and to some extent interrupted the Communist logistical build-up. But the delay at best amounted to no more than a few months. Against this had to be placed the nine thousand South Vietnamese soldiers killed, wounded, or captured—nearly half of the twenty thousand-man force ultimately committed to the invasion.

Plagued by faulty planning and poor leadership at every command level, the elite troops of the ARVN had taken a terrible beating. Were it not for US air support, the outcome could well have been catastrophic. As the last American ground combat units prepared to leave the country and

the Communists resumed their preparations for a new offensive, it appeared that American air power might be the only sure defense that South Vietnam still possessed. One year later, that weapon would again be called upon to prevent disaster.

On March 30, 1972, two months after the departure of the last major American ground contingent, forty thousand North Vietnamese troops backed by tanks and mobile armor units smashed across the DMZ heading for the provincial capital of Quang Tri City. Within two weeks, the NVA had opened two more fronts in a stunning Easter offensive that everywhere sent ARVN units reeling backward in disarray. By mid-April, all that stood between the Communists and victory were pockets of South Vietnamese resistance and a greatly diminished American military presence.

Unwilling to delay the withdrawal of the remaining US ground troops, President Nixon instead pledged air and naval support to halt the enemy advance. The promise of help was more difficult to keep than ever before. Compelled to draw down their numbers over the previous twelve months, the Air Force had fewer than ninety combat aircraft left in South Vietnam at the time of the Communist assault; the Navy had only two carriers with 170 airplanes on station in the Gulf of Tonkin. Even with the addition of Air Force B-52s and F-4 Phantoms diverted to Da Nang and Bien Hoa from Thailand, neither the American nor the South Vietnamese air force had enough firepower to stabilize the disintegrating ARVN lines. Within six weeks, however, the call for reinforcements brought US strength in Southeast Asia up to twenty American cruisers and destroyers, a half-dozen aircraft carriers, seventy thousand Air Force personnel, and nearly a thousand US warplanes.

American pilots found the skies over South Vietnam far more dangerous than ever, thanks to new Communist air defenses, including large-caliber guns, surface-to-air missile (SAM) sites, and the small, shoulder-fired SA-7 SAMs that were particularly deadly to helicopters. But they also discovered a heavily mechanized North Vietnamese Army highly vulnerable to air attack. At Quang Tri, An Loc, and Kontum, American B-52s, fighter-bombers, and AC-47 gunships blasted enemy concentrations and cut enemy supply lines while American transports delivered thousands of tons of equipment to battered South Vietnamese defenders. By the end of June, the aerial onslaught had stalled the Communist offensive amid the smoking wreckage of thousands of North Vietnamese tanks, trucks, and self-propelled artillery pieces.

Long before that—less than sixty hours after the start of the invasion—American aircraft were hitting Communist staging areas north of the DMZ. Then on May 8, as soldiers and refugees fled from Quang Tri City under a merciless Communist artillery barrage, President Nixon authorized the resumption of full-scale bombing against North Vietnam. The operation was code-named Linebacker. It would be different from previous air assaults against the North in three key ways: the employment of new weapons, the inclusion of new targets, and the absence of tight civilian oversight.

Because Washington felt it could now discount the prospect of Chinese or Soviet intervention, Nixon left target selection and tactical control in the hands of his field commanders, providing them with a long-awaited flexibility they utilized to the fullest. Beginning on May 10, Linebacker missions struck fuel dumps, warehouses, railroad marshaling yards, rolling stock, trucks, petroleum pipelines, and power plants all across North Vietnam—from SAM sites along the DMZ to MiG air bases within ten miles of the center of Hanoi to railroad bridges near the Chinese border. The president also gave Navy leaders something they had long sought—permission to mine North Vietnam's harbors and blockade the coast. Using airdropped magnetic-acoustic mines, the Navy seeded coastal approaches and major river estuaries so effectively that no ship of any size either entered or left a North Vietnamese port for the rest of the war.

The air raids were enormously successful, thanks to a new family of laser-guided and electro-optically guided "smart" bombs that offered unprecedented accuracy, and to such improved electronic counter-measures equipment as radar-detection and jamming devices. These technological developments made it possible to destroy more targets with fewer sorties and less bomb tonnage, and at a lower rate of aircraft losses, than had been experienced during the earlier Rolling Thunder campaign. In fact, the damage inflicted by American bombers from April to October 1972 exceeded all that had been accomplished between 1965 and 1968: North Vietnam's transportation system was crippled, the shipment of goods through Haiphong and other ports virtually eliminated, and the flow of war materiel to southern battlefields cut by as much as 50 percent.

Henry Kissinger (left), President Nixon's national security advisor, and North Vietnam's Le Duc Tho (right) engage in animated conversation in the garden of a Gif-sur-Yvette villa November 23, 1972, during a round of private talks on Vietnam peace negotiations.

The massive damage and staggering casualties endured by Vietnamese on both sides during the summer of 1972 marked a new level of violence in what already had been a costly war. But the bloodletting finally prodded negotiators six thousand miles away toward an agreement that would bring the fighting to at least a temporary halt.

By the summer of 1972, Washington's desire for detente with China and the Soviet Union gave both sides reason for compromise. Hanoi's fears of diplomatic isolation, the fearful pounding North Vietnam had undergone from the latest round of US bombing, and the prospect of complete American withdrawal inclined the Communist leadership to take what they could get at the negotiating table and wait for the Americans to leave. Eager to remove the chief obstacle to his larger foreign policy designs and anxious to put Vietnam behind him before the upcoming presidential election, Nixon was willing to meet them halfway.

Even before the talks resumed, National Security Advisor Henry Kissinger gave Hanoi private assurances that the United States was willing to permit North Vietnamese troops to remain in the South after a cease-fire. Now Kissinger hedged Washington's commitment to Thieu by accepting an electoral commission—made up of neutralists, Viet Cong, and members of the Saigon government—that would supervise a political settlement for South Vietnam. In return, the North dropped its insistence upon the departure of Thieu as a precondition for any cease-fire so long as the National Liberation Front was granted political status in the South.

On this basis, negotiations between Kissinger and North Vietnam's Le Duc Tho moved into high gear. By early October, a provisional cease-fire agreement had been reached. The tentative accord provided for the simultaneous withdrawal of US troops and the return of American POWs, followed by a political settlement worked out through a tripartite National Council of Reconciliation and Concord. Infiltration of new NVA troops into the South would end, and Washington would extend postwar economic assistance to help North Vietnam rebuild its economic infrastructure. On October 22, President Nixon suspended all bombing north of the twentieth parallel. Four days later, Henry Kissinger announced that "peace was at hand."

In fact, the painfully garnered accord was in grave jeopardy. Thieu, who had not been consulted during the negotiations, demanded wholesale changes that Hanoi would never accept. When the talks resumed in early November, the US, at Thieu's insistence, proposed sixty-nine amendments to the agreement. The North Vietnamese responded with dozens of demands of their own. After weeks of increasingly heated exchanges, the two sides broke off talks on December 13. Caught between a truculent ally and a stubborn adversary, Richard Nixon determined to teach both a lesson.

To the South Vietnamese, the president extended weapons, promises, and threats. First, he authorized the immediate delivery of more than $1 billion in military equipment and supplies, including enough aircraft to make South Vietnam's air force the fourth largest in the world. At the same time,

Above An Loc, an O-2 spotter plane piloted by a forward air controller dives to mark targets for US fighter-bombers trying to loosen the NVA's hold on the city.

Nixon gave Saigon "absolute assurances" that should North Vietnam violate any peace agreement signed with the United States, he would order "swift and severe retaliatory action." But the president also warned Thieu that if the Saigon government did not accept the cease-fire terms ultimately worked out between Washington and Hanoi, South Vietnam would be on its own.

Meanwhile, Nixon sent a different kind of ultimatum to the Communists, demanding that Hanoi return to the bargaining table within seventy-two hours. When no reply was forthcoming, the president summoned Adm. Thomas Moorer, the chairman of the Joint Chiefs of Staff, and told him to prepare a massive air attack against the North Vietnamese heartland. "I don't want any more of this crap about the fact that we couldn't hit this target or that one," Nixon told the admiral. "This is your chance to use military power to win this war. And if you don't, I'll hold you responsible." The resulting operation, called Linebacker II, was the most concentrated air offensive of the war.

On the night of December 18, 1972, 129 B-52 Stratofortresses took off from Andersen Air Force Base on Guam in the largest heavy bomber operation mounted by the United States Air Force since World War II. Their targets were heavily defended MiG airfields around Hanoi. As the first wave approached the North Vietnamese capital, salvos of SA-2 surface-to-air missiles lit up the sky around them. So thickly did they fly among the American planes, said one pilot, that he could have read by the light of the rocket engines as the missiles rushed past. In all, the enemy fired more than two hundred SAMs at the B-52s that night, forcing one aircraft back to base, damaging two more, and bringing down three of the giant bombers. But the rest of the heavily loaded aircraft hit their targets and returned safely to Guam.

Linebacker II continued day and night for almost two weeks, interrupted only by a thirty-six-hour Christmas truce. Day after day the giant bombers took to the North Vietnamese skies supported by hundreds of fighters, fighter-bombers, tankers, radar-jamming EA-6s, F-105 Wild Weasels crammed with electronic countermeasures equipment, F-4 Phantoms laying down corridors of chaff to confuse enemy radar, and the newly deployed, supersonic F-111s that the North Vietnamese called "whispering death." During twelve days of intensive bombing, the American planes flew nearly two thousand sorties and delivered thirty-five thousand tons of bombs against transportation terminals, rail yards, warehouses, military barracks, oil and gas tank farms, factories, airfields, and power plants in the Hanoi-Haiphong corridor.

The scope of the air campaign and the concentration on targets in heavily populated areas led critics to charge Nixon with indiscriminate destruction and even genocide. To the contrary, most of the bombing was conducted with extraordinary precision, thanks to advanced onboard radar systems and laser-guided bombs. Some "spillage" from the target areas did result in residential damage and civilian deaths. The most notable case was the destruction of the Bach Mai Hospital outside a military airstrip in Hanoi. Accusations of terror bombing or deliberate attacks on civilian targets, however, were totally unfounded. Indeed, the number of civilian deaths—approximately 1,400 by Hanoi's own count, some of whom were killed by North Vietnamese missiles falling back to earth—was remarkably low considering the weight of bombs dropped

North Vietnamese doctors and nurses carry medical supplies out of the destroyed Bach Mai Hospital, bombed by US B-52 air raids on December 19, 1972.

and the experience of comparable bombing operations during World War II.

On December 26, Hanoi signaled to Washington its willingness to talk once the bombing stopped. Four days later, Linebacker II came to an end. By then, the Americans had exhausted their targets, and the North Vietnamese had run out of missiles.

The final American blow of a long and terrible war, Linebacker II cut North Vietnamese rail lines at more than five hundred points, demolished nearly four hundred pieces of rolling stock, heavily damaged ten airfields, shattered Hanoi's air defenses, and left some 1,600 separate military structures in ruins. In two short weeks, 25 percent of North Vietnam's petroleum reserves and 80 percent of its electrical generating capacity had been destroyed. The United States had by no means escaped unscathed from battle, losing twenty-six aircraft, among them fifteen B-52s, along with ninety-three pilots and crew members, including thirty-three taken prisoner by the North Vietnamese.

When peace talks resumed in Paris on January 8, 1973, both sides sought a quick settlement. The leaders of North Vietnam were not willing to endure more punishment to no purpose. Richard Nixon was not prepared to wait until after his inauguration to a second term or risk the loss of military aid for South Vietnam threatened by the new, dovish Congress. After six days of marathon negotiations, an agreement was reached that scarcely differed from what had been drafted in October, meaning that Nixon's brutal Christmas bombing campaign, Linebacker II, had produced no effect on the final accord. As one of Kissinger's aides wryly put it, "We bombed the North Vietnamese into accepting our concessions." The United States would complete the withdrawal of its forces from South Vietnam, the POWs would come home, the Thieu government would be left intact. At the same time, North Vietnamese troops would remain in the South, and the PRG (Provisional Revolutionary Government, the government of the National

Liberation Front) would be provided status as a legal organization. The military cease-fire would be administered by an International Commission of Control and Supervision (ICCS) composed of representatives from Poland, Hungary, Canada, and Indonesia. The ultimate political future of South Vietnam—the central issue over which the war had been fought—was to be resolved later by the amorphous reconciliation council.

Thieu, for one, was not reconciled. But, threatened with the loss of US aid, he decided he could not allow himself the luxury of resisting any further. On January 21, he grudgingly acceded to the treaty after receiving assurances of continued American assistance. Two days later, Henry Kissinger and Le Duc Tho initialed the "Paris Agreement Ending the War and Restoring Peace in Vietnam." With the formal signing of the document at the Hotel Majestic on January 27, 1973, America's longest war was officially over.

The peace agreement did not bring an immediate end to American military involvement in the region. B-52 strikes continued over Laos and Cambodia, where the Vietnam cease-fire had no effect whatsoever. Not until Congress cut off all funds for American military operations in Indochina, mandating an August 15 end to the air raids, did the last US military forces leave Southeast Asia.

For most Americans, however, the war ended on the gray tarmac of Hanoi's Gia Lam Airport, where on February 12 the first 116 US prisoners of war crossed an imaginary line to freedom. Once in American hands, the former captives were taken to Clark Air Force Base in the Philippines for medical examinations before flying home to families some had not seen for as long as eight and a half years. Minor problems and delays disturbed the repatriation process, but on March 29, 1973, the last prisoners were freed. At the same time, the final contingent of American combat troops withdrew from South Vietnam. With their departure, the American war in Vietnam came at last to an end.

Henry Kissinger (background left) and Le Duc Tho (seated foreground) sit across from each other as they initial the Vietnam peace agreement in Paris, January 24, 1973. The men were awarded the 1973 Nobel Peace Prize for their efforts in officially bringing an end to the Vietnam War.

Fleeing refugees pass a South Vietnamese military personnel carrier, heading north in an effort to stop a Communist breakthrough at the DMZ during the Easter Offensive.

During more than a decade of political and military involvement, the United States spent almost $200 billion to fight the war and improve the lives of the people of South Vietnam. Over that period, more than 3 million American men and women served in Southeast Asia. Of those, nearly 304,000 were wounded and fifty-seven thousand killed in action. More than one hundred Americans died in captivity during the course of the war, with 1,284 still listed as missing in action when the last POWs returned home. Whether this long and costly commitment had been worth the price was a question that still lay in the balance in the spring of 1973. But the Americans would no longer have a hand in the answer. The future of Vietnam was now something the Vietnamese alone would decide.

Easter Offensive

Noon, March 30, 1972. With a sharp crack and a thunderous explosion, a high-velocity 130mm howitzer shell crashed into the Ai Tu Combat Base just north of Quang Tri City. The first round was followed by a barrage of long-range

Communist artillery shells that blanketed the thirty-kilometer-long South Vietnamese defensive line below the DMZ. Behind the lethal rain of fire, three North Vietnamese divisions—some thirty thousand troops supported by more than two hundred Soviet T54 tanks—poured across the border.

The Easter offensive had begun. Before it was over, North Vietnam would commit two hundred thousand men in fourteen divisions to the greatest military operation since the Chinese crossed the Yalu River into Korea twenty-one years earlier. With American combat troops almost completely withdrawn from the South, the Communists discarded a strategy of protracted war in hopes of crushing the South Vietnamese army and forcing a negotiated settlement on their own terms. They learned to their regret that the ARVN would fight back and that Washington was not yet prepared to abandon South Vietnam to defeat. During the first weeks of the invasion, however, Hanoi had reason to celebrate.

The green recruits of the 3rd ARVN Division, deployed along the northern frontier precisely because no one expected an overt breach of the DMZ, buckled under the pressure of the mechanized enemy columns and raced for the protection of the Cua Viet River. At Dong Ha, South Vietnamese marines held off the invaders long enough for a pair of US Army advisors to blow up a crucial bridge along Highway 1. But farther west near Camp Carroll, enemy tanks rumbled across the Cam Lo Bridge when the 56th ARVN Regiment surrendered en masse.

As northern soldiers raced through the gap in the South Vietnamese lines, ARVN troops abandoned their fortifications and fled south through Quang Tri City, where they were joined by thousands of frightened refugees. Crammed together along Highway 1, the mass of soldiers, trucks, and civilians proved an irresistible target for Communist gunners who lashed the confused column with 130mm fire. Those troops who survived the carnage finally established a new defensive line south of the My Chanh River. Behind them lay twenty kilometers of smashed bodies, broken vehicles, and smoking debris.

While ARVN units in the northern part of the country reeled under the shock of the invasion, North Vietnamese troops opened two more fronts in their far-flung offensive. On April 5, the 5th NVA/VC Division, supported by tanks and armored personnel carriers, rolled out of its Cambodia base area, and after a two-day battle, seized the ARVN outpost at Loc Ninh. Any defenders not dead or captured had fled south toward An Loc, the political and commercial center of Binh Long Province, only ninety kilometers from Saigon. Fearing its loss would open the way for a drive on the nation's capital, President Thieu dispatched the 5th ARVN Division and ordered the city "held at all costs." Even as South Vietnamese troops moved into position, however, the Communist forces that overran Loc Ninh were joined by two more NVA divisions moving out of Cambodia. Together they surrounded An Loc, blocking further overland reinforcements, and began shelling the city with artillery captured during the 1971 ARVN invasion of Laos.

Opposite page: Just south of An Loc, encircled by Communist forces as they opened another front in their offensive, the ARVN ammunition dump at Lai Khe explodes after being hit by an enemy round.

US Army Cobra gunships and US Air Force and Navy fighter-bombers pounded enemy positions. But North Vietnamese soldiers, backed by artillery, tanks, and armored personnel carriers, ground forward relentlessly, smashing into the city, seizing the airfield, and reducing the South Vietnamese perimeter to a square kilometer. On April 20, the senior US adviser on the scene reported a desperate situation: "Supplies minimal, casualties continue to mount, medical supplies low. Wounded a major problem, mass burials for military and civilian, morale at low ebb." Most discouraging of all, "In spite of incurring heavy losses from US air strikes, the enemy continues to persist."

With An Loc invested, three more Communist divisions struck the Central Highlands town of Dak To on April 12, opening the third phase of the North Vietnamese offensive. After capturing the high ground to the west, enemy units overran the military camps of Tan Canh and Dak To II. An armored column from Ben Het attempting to come to the rescue drove straight into an ambush and disintegrated under concentrated enemy fire that included Russian AT-3 radio-controlled Sagger antitank rockets. Scattered into small groups, the surviving ARVN soldiers limped down Highway 14 toward Kontum—only twenty-five miles away and now completely defenseless.

A North Vietnamese mobile anti-aircraft gun destroyed by a five-hundred-pound aerial bomb during the siege of An Loc.

Inexplicably, the NVA waited three weeks to attack the province capital. "It was the dumbest possible thing they could have done," said US Army Col. Joseph Pizzi, "and I'm very grateful they did because there was nobody to stop them except a few people like me with pistols." Given the reprieve, the ARVN command moved the 23rd Division and several Ranger groups into the city, where they raced to construct trenches, dugouts, and other fortifications before the enemy's inevitable arrival. On May 16, when the Communists finally swung down Highway 14, they attacked right into the teeth of the ARVN defenses.

The tank-supported assault made an ideal target for B-52 bombers, which pounded the enemy column without mercy. For ten days, the NVA attempted without success to smash through the ARVN lines, absorbing horrific casualties with each new assault. Then, in the early morning hours of May 27, Communist forces located a gap in the South Vietnamese defenses. Advancing behind a spearhead of armor, three enemy regiments fought their way into Kontum, when out of the smoke hanging over the city flew two US helicopters carrying experimental airborne TOW missiles. By day's end, the "tube-launched, optically tracked, wire-guided" rockets had destroyed ten enemy tanks. When the North Vietnamese attempted to withdraw, they were blasted by fighter-bombers and B-52s. Their fuel running out, their losses reaching critical proportions, the NVA had no option but to retreat.

Everywhere across the country, the lethal impact of American air power, the mistakes of Communist commanders, and the stubborn courage of South Vietnamese soldiers were having the same effect. Nowhere was this more true than at An Loc, where government troops held out for ninety-five days under constant shelling and ground attacks. By the middle of June, the enemy's offensive potential had been exhausted. Communist artillery bombardments continued to make life difficult at Kontum and An Loc, but decimated NVA armor and infantry units had already begun to withdraw toward the sanctuary of their bases in Cambodia and Laos. The North Vietnamese invasion had reached its high-water mark. Now it was Saigon's turn.

The loss of Quang Tri Province and the near collapse of the 3rd ARVN Division had precipitated a change in personnel and approach on the northern front. Taking over command of I Corps on May 3, Lt. Gen. Ngo Quang Truong wasted no time in proving his reputation as South Vietnam's best general officer. To restore discipline, Truong issued orders for the execution of deserters and looters. To regain the initiative, he sent South Vietnamese marines on raids behind NVA lines. And to recapture the territory lost in April, Truong gathered new troops and supplies for a major counteroffensive. By the last week of June, he was ready.

Marked by boldness and audacity unusual for South Vietnamese operations, Truong's attack began with diversionary feints west of Hue and north of the Cua Viet River. With the Communists preoccupied by these simultaneous assaults, the ARVN Airborne Division quietly crossed the My Chanh on the night of June 27 and fell upon unsuspecting North Vietnamese troops along the north side of the river. The stunned enemy soldiers tried to withdraw to new positions, only to discover four ARVN and Marine battalions blocking their path. Within hours, the NVA defensive line had completely unraveled, as Communist officers accustomed to a primitive supply system and light arms struggled to protect the vulnerable logistical network of their new mechanized army. By the end of the first week of July, the South Vietnamese counterattack had rolled the NVA all the way back to the outskirts of Quang Tri City.

During the two months since they occupied it, the Communists had laced the city and its suburbs with a formidable network of bunkers, strongpoints, trenches, and observation posts. Any assault would have to cross pre-targeted fields of artillery, mortar, and machine-gun fire. Even when these obstacles would be overcome, Truong's men would face enemy troops barricaded behind the thick stone walls of Quang Tri's central citadel, a miniature version of the fortress at Hue that the NVA had held for more than a month during the 1968 Tet Offensive. Moreover, since the North Vietnamese still controlled two sides of the city, they were able to funnel supplies and reinforcements to defend their captured prize.

Truong gave the job of regaining Quang Tri to the Airborne Division. The paratroopers advanced one house at a time, enduring a continuous barrage of 130mm howitzer fire until they clawed their way to within one hundred meters of the citadel. After US aircraft carrying laser-guided bombs blasted a hole in the northeast wall, three airborne companies swarmed through the breach. Then, with victory at hand, an errant South Vietnamese air strike dropped three five hundred-pound bombs on the troopers, killing forty-five and wounding twenty. The dazed survivors stumbled back through the gap in the wall, their dead comrades in their arms.

The disaster stalled the counteroffensive for more than a month. During the interval, Truong replaced the battered Airborne Division with new units, realigned his own defenses, and finally asked for full US air support. On September 9, behind a cascade of explosives from American fighter-bombers and B-52s, five battalions of Marines began another assault. Finally, at noon on September 16, the bloodied victors raised the South Vietnamese flag over the walled fortress.

By then, observed Maj. John Howard, a US Army advisor who had survived An Loc and witnessed the costly northern counterattack, the opposing armies were like "two fighters in the fourteenth or fifteenth round; they could hardly do anything but hold on to each other." With the recapture of Quang Tri City, the Easter offensive came to an end, the existing battle lines transformed into de facto boundaries of occupation.

The offensive had killed thirty thousand ARVN soldiers, reduced three province capitals to rubble, and gained for Hanoi a narrow strip of land along the northern and western borders of South Vietnam. The new territory helped safeguard Communist base areas in Laos and Cambodia, simplified the task of supplying troops in the South, and permitted political cadres to renew organizational work among the rural farmers. The price for these modest gains was an estimated one hundred thousand North Vietnamese dead. The staggering casualty figures were due in part to the failure of the Communist military command to concentrate its forces, the inexperience of field officers in coordinating infantry and armor, and an overreliance on shock assaults into heavily defended positions—all valuable lessons the Communists would put to good use in the future.

For all the NVA mistakes and all the tenacity displayed by the ARVN, what ultimately saved South Vietnam in the spring and summer of 1972 was the devastating weight of American air power. If that could be removed, concluded Hanoi, nothing would stand in the way of victory but time. In the final analysis, that was the most important lesson of all.

Leo Thorsness as a POW (left) and being released from prison in Hanoi, March 1973 (right).

POW

During the course of the war, some seven hundred US military and civilian personnel were taken prisoner by the Communists. Among them were Army soldiers and Marines, development workers, and missionaries captured in South Vietnam. But the vast majority were Air Force and Navy pilots shot down over North Vietnam and Laos.

Wherever they were captured, most were sooner or later taken to

Major Norman McDaniel is greeted by the Gia Lam Airport returnee delegation upon his release from a POW camp, 1973.

one of a half-dozen prison camps scattered across North Vietnam. The most famous was Hoa Lo in downtown Hanoi, nicknamed the Hanoi Hilton. The POWs had names for the other camps, too—the Plantation, the Zoo, the Rockpile, Alcatraz—names that came closer to conveying what went on behind the prison wire. To the North Vietnamese, the POWs were not unfortunate victims of war but valuable pawns to be used without compunction for whatever advantage Hanoi could derive.

For much of the war, the conditions of captivity for US prisoners in Vietnam remained generally unknown to the American public. North Vietnam had ratified the Geneva convention regulating the treatment of POWs in 1957. But, since there was no formal declaration of war between the United States and the Democratic Republic of Vietnam, Hanoi maintained that captured Americans were not entitled to POW status. Nor would the North Vietnamese or Viet Cong allow representatives from the International Red Cross to visit the camps. The handful of Americans who escaped or were released from Communist captivity were constrained from public description of their treatment by fears of retaliation against the remaining POWs. What glimpses Americans did get of North Vietnamese prisons were carefully selected by the Communists themselves and scarcely conveyed the reality of the prisoners' existence.

On August 5, 1964, during American retaliatory raids on North Vietnam after the Gulf of Tonkin incident, an A-4 Skyhawk from the carrier USS Constellation *was shot down over Hon Gai, and its pilot, Lt. j.g. Everett Alvarez Jr., ejected into the water. He was the first pilot taken prisoner by North Vietnam. Alvarez would spend more than eight years in captivity, one of the longest terms as a prisoner of war in American history.*

As I floated in the water, all sorts of things ran through my mind. I thought, "My poor wife. What's she going to do! My poor mother. What's she going to do! How's she going to feel!" I also had visions of them capturing me, hanging me by my feet, and skinning me alive. I even remembered that I was going to miss roast beef night on the ship. All this went through my mind as I was trying to swim, dragging my seat pan. Finally, after about thirty minutes, I felt something graze my elbow. I looked behind me and saw a fishing boat with guns sticking over the side and smoke drifting from the barrels. They could have hit me if they wanted to—they were that close. I was captured.

I was taken to a nearby prison, then to a farmhouse. In the first couple of days they didn't try to harass or abuse me. I was sleeping most of the time because I was hurting. I got so stiff that I could hardly walk, and I had hurt my back during ejection. Years later, after I was released, the doctors found evidence of a hairline fracture from the ejection that had eventually healed.

"A week later, when they put me in a jeep to go somewhere, I thought I was going home. I mean, the United States was a world power. They were going to fix things up really fast. But then I saw a road sign that said "Hanoi" and we went into Hoa Lo Prison. I didn't think I was going to be there very long, until a week passed, and I thought, "Well, I guess I will."

I went through some interrogation, but nothing too difficult. I talked to them but didn't tell them anything. They thought I was showing a "good attitude." They wanted to know things like the layout of a carrier and how a plane took off, but I was telling them such things as how I was in charge of the popcorn machine on the ship and how I made popcorn. They quit after about six weeks.

They let me receive and write letters until the bombing started again, in February 1965. Then they came back with equipment from planes that were shot down that they wanted me to explain

In this still from a documentary film taken by a Japanese cameraman who was on the scene accidentally when this incident took place, a man identified as Lt. j.g. Everett Alvarez (left) is escorted by a North Vietnamese sailor.

to them. I refused to do that, so they said I had a bad attitude, cut off my mail, and stuck me in a very small cell. Then I found out they had captured a second American, Bob Shumaker. Then I thought, "Well, this is it. We're really in a war." Before that, I debated what my tactics should be and what I was expected to do. But after the bombing it was very clear: From now on we don't help our captors or answer questions.

From then on, I got very meager rations, which I wolfed down, and I lost quite a lot of weight. For a few years I was down by about 50 pounds, to between 100 and 105 pounds.

As more men came in, we worked to maintain communications. Messages were dropped at certain places, such as where you would clean out your latrine can. Words were scratched at the bottom of bowls. We also used a tap code and hand code, especially

Former POW Everett Alvarez speaks to the public and press greeting the planeload of former POWs returning home. Alvarez was released by the North Vietnamese in Hanoi on February 12, 1973.

for the men who didn't have roommates. We always managed to keep the lines open. That was very important. The senior officers were able to pass along orders to all the prisoners, and we sent all kinds of information back and forth, mostly just anecdotes and sea stories.

The North Vietnamese were always trying to use us for propaganda. They would show us movies of the antiwar movement in the United States, like Berkeley and the march on Washington, and ask us if we would also protest. "Hell no," we'd say. They got many of us to sign "confessions" stating that we were war criminals who had attacked innocent civilians and things like that, but we agreed only after days of torture. They'd tie your arms together at the shoulders and lift you off the ground or beat you with a rubber strip. That was tough. There was fear, and not only that, there was punishment. They were very brutal at times. There was no lying back. I mean, they actually killed guys. Others got sick from the diet or the treatment. In late 1969, the last time I was really physically abused, I got sick with jaundice and hepatitis.

From 1970 to 1973, we began to see a gradual improvement in our diet and treatment. By the summer of 1972, they were bringing in wagonloads of canned meat and canned fish, even bread, to fatten us up. We could get a lot more exercise and recreation. We got playing cards, packages, and letters from home, and got more up to date on what had happened in the years since we had been shot down. We were getting the royal treatment—I guess in preparation for eventual release.

During the whole time we never thought that our government would forget us or just drop us. When we were put together at the Hanoi Hilton in late 1970, we found out it was because there had been a raid by American forces on the Son Tay camp. That showed they hadn't forgotten and were still concerned. Then by the 1972 elections in the United States, we could tell that the Vietnamese were hurting. When the bombing started after the election, we were cheering for joy. We knew it wouldn't stop. The bombing got to the point where the Vietnamese wouldn't even bother to man their guns anymore. Those people were tired. We knew it was close to the end.

A few weeks later, in January 1973, they marched us all out into the yard and read us the peace agreement. We all just sat and listened. Nobody cheered. It was so long overdue. We just went back and finished our bridge games. It was sort of anticlimactic. I was emotionally drained by that time. I still wasn't sure that this was it, the end of the war.

But on February 12, Lincoln's birthday, the first group of forty prisoners, the ones there the longest, got on buses and went to the airport. We sat on the bus at the field, still wondering if it would fall through when, sure enough, an American C-141 landed. A colonel came up and said, "Just a few more minutes, guys, hang on." Then we just stepped over the line and into the hands of the Americans. It wasn't until we had taken off and the wheels were in the well that I felt elated and everyone went crazy.

Life has its way of taking its turns and, you know, I'm very lucky to be alive. We had to face each day one at a time. We had to be positive. We couldn't give up. We also learned the value of having each other. You gain individual strength through the chain; each link contributes to the strength of the chain, and through group unity each individual that I was there with gathered his own strength. We had won. We had maintained our strength.

As the war went on, support from back home also became more vigorous. Hoping to gain North Vietnamese cooperation and fearful of endangering the prisoners further, the Johnson administration refrained from publicizing abusive treatment of the POWs. Since this restraint produced nothing, President Nixon adopted a much tougher policy. Beginning in 1969, US officials made formal complaints to the United Nations while publicly pressing Hanoi to cease its brutality and exchange prisoners of war. Meanwhile, POW wives and other family members mobilized for action, dispatching representatives to demand information from the Communist delegation to the Paris peace talks and establishing the National League of Families of American Prisoners and Missing in Southeast Asia. The mounting pressure on Hanoi produced some improvement in living conditions at the prisons, including the initiation of limited mail privileges.

Ironically, the greatest change occurred as the result of a spectacularly unsuccessful rescue mission. On November 20, 1970, a select group of Air Force and Special Forces volunteers hit the Son Tay Prison twenty-three miles from Hanoi. Within minutes, the commandos knocked out the guard towers, broke into the cells, and escaped in their helicopters, leaving up to two hundred dead NVA behind. The Americans suffered only two minor injuries. The daring raid had gone like clockwork, with one single exception: The prisoners at Son Tay had been moved out four months earlier.

While recriminations flew thick and fast in Washington, the startled North Vietnamese evacuated all their outlying camps and brought the POWs into Hanoi. The consolidation had a profound impact on the prisoners' lives. Placed in large, open rooms housing twenty to fifty men each, the POWs were able to meet, talk, and organize as never before. Although senior officers remained in isolation, they were now able to exert more effective command and provide the

American servicemen, former POWs, cheer as their aircraft takes off from an airfield near Hanoi as part of Operation Homecoming.

Wives of Marines stationed at Camp Pendleton, California, wait at Miramar Naval Air Station for repatriated Marine POWs to arrive. During the war, twenty-six Marines were captured and held as prisoners of war.

younger men with much greater support. "The raid may have failed in its primary objectives," one POW later wrote, "but it boosted our morale sky-high!"

It would be two more years, however, before the American POWs again had cause for celebration. And once more it would be the result of dramatic US military action. On the night of December 18, 1972, in an attempt to force the North Vietnamese to complete negotiations on a peace agreement with the United States, President Nixon sent 126 B-52 bombers against Hanoi. Even as cracks appeared in the walls of their cells and dust swirled around them, the POWs rejoiced. Col. Jon A. Reynolds, a long-time prisoner, immediately noted the effect of the bombing raid on the prison guards. "There was no joking, no laughing, no acts of defiance or reprisal. They simply headed for their shelters and pulled the lids over their heads. For the first time, the United States meant business. We knew it, the guards knew it, and it seems clear that the leaders of North Vietnam knew it."

Within a month, Henry Kissinger and North Vietnam's Le Duc Tho had initialed a cease-fire agreement. The document provided for the repatriation of 591 American POWs in four increments over a period of sixty days, their release tied to the withdrawal of the remaining US combat forces in South Vietnam. On February 12, 1973, the first group of prisoners was brought to Hanoi's Gia Lam Airport and marched up to an imaginary line serving as a boundary between the US and North Vietnam. Waiting to receive them were American military personnel. As his name was called, each man walked across the line to freedom. Despite more problems and delays with subsequent releases, on March 29, only twenty-four hours behind schedule, the last of the 591 American POWs left Hanoi.

The Pentagon had been planning Operation Homecoming for years. As they were released, the former POWs were flown to Clark Air Force Base in the Philippines. Greeted by cheering crowds and specially selected escort officers, they were given medical examinations, outfitted with new uniforms, brought up to date on personal family news as well as recent world events, and provided with information on accrued salary, promotions, and decorations. In between, the men gobbled down hamburgers and banana splits and received gifts from schoolchildren at the base. Once certified fit to travel, each man was flown to the military hospital closest to his home and reunited with his family.

Although the military officially regarded the status of prisoners as neither honorable nor dishonorable but rather as an accident of war, the American people welcomed home the former POWs as heroes. In personal homecomings all across the United States, the men were surrounded by joyous neighbors, feted with parades and special ceremonies, and showered with gifts. In the months that followed, the former captives found that much had changed during their imprisonment, and not all of it would be easy to get used to. For some, the transition to "normal" life would be long and difficult. But to the American people, the return of the POWs marked, at last, more certainly than any other event, the end of the Vietnam War.

CHAPTER EIGHT

FALL of the SOUTH

The Vietnam War was over for America, but not for Vietnam. To the disappointment of many but the surprise of no one, the Paris Peace Accords did not bring peace to Vietnam. Even as the mutually proclaimed cease-fire went into effect at 8:00 a.m. on January 28, 1973, fighting between ARVN and Communist forces continued to rage across the length and breadth of South Vietnam. Hoping to gain control of as much territory as possible before the International Commission of Control and Supervision overseeing the cease-fire certified their claims, both sides took to the offensive in what came to be known as "the war of flags." In the days leading up to the cease-fire, South Vietnamese forces hastily established forward outposts and resettled refugees in Communist-dominated areas, while Communist cadres slipped into countless villages and hamlets to proclaim their "liberation." When counterattacks followed, both Hanoi and Saigon charged that their "legitimate" claims had been "violated" by the enemy.

An American Marine guard dislodges two Vietnamese men trying to climb over a barbed-wire wall into the American Embassy to escape advancing North Vietnamese troops on the last day of the US involvement in the Vietnam War, April 30, 1975.

Efforts to affix blame for the failure of the peace agreement proved pointless, since neither party had abandoned its long-range goals and each seemed willing to observe the accords only to the extent that suited its interests. For his part, President Thieu acted from the outset as if the accords did not exist. Still wedded to the "four nos" he had first proclaimed in 1969—no negotiating with the enemy, no Communist activity in South Vietnam, no surrender of territory, no coalition government—he systematically undercut any possibility of a political solution by denying any legitimacy whatsoever to the Provisional Revolutionary Government set up by the National Liberation Front by cracking down on all domestic political opponents and refusing to cooperate with the ICCS and Joint Military Commission. Nor did he make any effort to curtail offensive operations. Even though the GVN controlled approximately 80 percent of the land and 90 percent of the people at the time of the cease-fire, Thieu immediately ordered his military forces to attack NVA military bases and PRG-held villages in the delta, the coastal lowlands, and the environs of Saigon. As a result, during the first three months of "peace," ARVN lost more than six thousand men, among the highest quarterly totals of the war.

In adopting his belligerent stance, Thieu drew encouragement from the promises he had received of continuing US support. Though Henry Kissinger seemed to have sought nothing more than a "decent interval" between the signing of the Paris pact and a final settlement in Vietnam, Richard Nixon remained as determined as ever not to be the first American president to lose a war. In addition to supplying the South Vietnamese with vast stores of war materiel in the months preceding the cease-fire, Nixon secretly assured Thieu that the United States would continue to provide "full economic and military aid" and would "respond with full force" if the North Vietnamese violated the agreements. In an April 1973 meeting with Thieu at the Western White House in San Clemente, California, Nixon reiterated his pledge. "You can count on us," he told the Vietnamese leader.

For a variety of reasons, the Communists approached the "postwar war" much more cautiously than did their South Vietnamese adversaries. Still suffering the effects of the bloody campaigns of 1972, forced to accept cutbacks in Russian and Chinese aid, and eager to ensure the complete withdrawal of all US forces, the North Vietnamese leadership decided to avoid any major military action and focus its energies on economic reconstruction, military regrouping, and political organization. During the first year of the cease-fire, Communist military forces in the South were ordered to assume a primarily defensive posture while the PRC concentrated on consolidating the newly gained territories under its control. To assist in the creation of this Third Vietnam, as it came to be called, as many as five thousand political cadres headed south to establish local administrative offices, set up new schools, and organize collective farms among the peasantry.

Although the United States formally protested the continued infiltration of North Vietnamese troops into South Vietnam, President Nixon could do little to stop it. Already reeling from the political shock of the unfolding Watergate scandal, Nixon found his ability to take unilateral military action sharply limited by the assertive 93rd Congress. As soon as all American troops and POWs were safely home, liberal and conservative legislators alike moved swiftly to halt any further US military operations "in or over or from

Opposite page: The battle-scarred village of Sa Huynh on South Vietnam's central coast on February 28, 1973, where fighting destroyed many homes after the cease-fire began and touched off charges of violations between the Saigon government and the Viet Cong.

the shores of South Vietnam, Laos, or Cambodia." Several months later, in November 1973, Congress raised the "Indochina Prohibition" to the level of principle by passing the War Powers Act, which required the president to inform the legislative branch within forty-eight hours of the deployment of US troops abroad and obligated him to withdraw them within sixty days in the absence of explicit congressional approval.

Despite these clear signals of flagging American support, President Thieu refused to scale back either his political ambitions or his military offensives. After talks aimed at political settlement formally broke off in late 1973, South Vietnamese forces stepped up ground and air attacks on NVA base camps and launched a new series of land-grabbing operations in PRG strongholds along the eastern seaboard, in Tay Ninh Province north of Saigon, and in the Mekong Delta. "We will not allow the Communists to enjoy stable security in their staging areas from which they will harass us," Thieu told officers of the delta command in early January 1974, as he proclaimed the advent of the "Third Indochina War." Taken by surprise, the NVA and PRG suffered heavy losses during the early stages of the campaign. In the late spring, however, the Communists went on the counteroffensive and scored success after success, mauling ARVN units in the Iron Triangle, recapturing much of the territory they had lost, and seizing additional lands previously under the control of the GVN.

The willingness of the Communists to resume full-fledged, open warfare reflected a major shift in strategy. Yielding to the hawks within the Hanoi Politburo, notably NVA chief of staff Gen. Van Tien Dung, the Communist

Party central committee had passed a compromise resolution in October 1973 reaffirming the priority of reconstruction in the North but also authorizing a return to "revolutionary violence" in the South. Armed forces were henceforth to strike back at the GVN whenever possible and to initiate strategic raids that would bleed ARVN units, allow further expansion of NVA base areas and supply corridors, and undermine support for the Thieu regime. Rather than an all-out offensive, the new campaign would take the form of a "protracted and complex" struggle, General Dung observed, between "antinibbling forces and the nibblers."

For the Saigon government, the escalation of the fighting could hardly have come at a worse time. By mid-1974, the South Vietnamese economy was teetering on the brink of total collapse, partly as a result of the American withdrawal and partly as a result of President Thieu's aggressive policies. Loss of the $400 million that the United States annually spent in Vietnam, a cutback in American military aid from $2.3 billion in 1973 to about $1 billion in 1974, a series of poor rice harvests, and a sharp rise in worldwide oil prices had combined to produce massive unemployment, soaring inflation, and a marked increase in corruption at every level of society. The economic crisis had an especially profound impact on Saigon's one-million-man army, causing chronic shortages of vital military necessities, sapping morale, and promoting further corruption. The payment of bribes for air and artillery support became commonplace, and desertion reached epidemic proportions. Compounding the government's problems, the Buddhist opposition began agitating during the late summer for peace and accommodation with the PRG, while the Catholics—Thieu's principal base of support—launched a nationwide anticorruption campaign aimed at the president himself.

As the situation steadily deteriorated, officials at the US Defense Attache's Office (DAO) in Saigon pleaded with Washington to find some way to provide an additional $500 million in military aid. Secretary of State Kissinger echoed their entreaties, warning that the failure of the United States to uphold its "moral obligation" to the South Vietnamese would have "a corrosive effect on our interests beyond Indochina." But Congress, reflecting the mood of a war-weary nation, refused to be swayed. Faced with the threat of runaway inflation at home, angered by reports of rampant corruption in South Vietnam, and tired of underwriting what one legislator described as a "self-perpetuating dictatorship," many legislators agreed with Sen. Edward Kennedy that the time had come to terminate America's "endless support for an endless war." Some even believed that a reduction in aid would enhance the prospects for peace by forcing President Thieu to negotiate a political settlement of the conflict. As a result, in September 1974, Congress voted to cut military aid to South Vietnam for fiscal 1975 to $700 million, half of which would be consumed in shipping costs alone.

A month before, the Watergate scandal had finally ended in President Nixon's forced resignation. That and the vote reducing aid together had a devastating impact on the South Vietnamese, intensifying Thieu's political and economic problems and encouraging what one historian has called "a psychology of accommodation and retreat that sometimes approached despair." Unaccountably, however, neither Thieu nor the members of his Joint General Staff made any effort to adjust to their country's radically altered strategic situation. Though ARVN outposts continued to fall to the enemy with alarming regularity, no attempt was made to concentrate scattered South Vietnamese forces along more defensible lines. Nor were any contingency plans drawn up in anticipation of a major North Vietnamese offensive. "Our leaders continued to believe in US air intervention even after the US Congress had expressly forbidden it," one high-ranking ARVN general later wrote. "They deluded themselves into thinking that perhaps this simply meant that US intervention would take a longer time to come because of the complex procedures involved."

While the leaders of the GVN waited and hoped, their North Vietnamese counterparts carefully reassessed the shifting military balance in the South. At a joint meeting of the Politburo and the central military committee in early October 1974, the hawks once again pressed their case for all-out war, arguing that the growing vulnerability of ARVN availed "new opportunities" only waiting to be grasped. By that point, the North Vietnamese had already infiltrated ten full divisions into the South—some two hundred thousand troops—backed by seven hundred tanks and 450 long-range artillery pieces as well as twenty antiaircraft regiments armed with sophisticated SA-7 Strela surface-to-air missiles. Another seven reserve divisions had been mobilized in the North, several taking up positions just across the DMZ. Vast quantities of weapons, ammunition, and supplies had been stockpiled, new training and hospital facilities built, and the logistical network under construction since early 1973 all but completed. "It was a picture to be proud of," General Dung later recalled. "In that region of our Fatherland were more than twenty thousand kilometers of strategic roads running north and south, with campaign roads running east and west—strong ropes inching gradually, day by day, around the neck, arms, and legs of a demon, awaiting the order to jerk tight and bring the creature's life to an end."

Before that order could be given, however, the North Vietnamese first had to consider the likelihood of American intervention. Though even Dung agreed that caution was in order, the consensus of the conference was summed up by Le Duan, Communist Party first secretary-general. "Now that the United States has pulled out of the South," he declared, "it will be hard to jump back in. And no matter how they may intervene, they cannot rescue the Saigon administration from its disastrous collapse." What finally emerged from the October deliberations was a document known as the Resolution for 1975, a two-year plan to "liberate" the South not through negotiations but by force of arms. During the first year of the campaign, Communist forces would move out of their jungle base camps and systematically eliminate exposed ARVN outposts, further extend supply corridors, and force ARVN to retreat to urban areas. Large-scale attacks against the cities and major ARVN garrisons were to be launched in the following year, 1976, culminating in a "General Offensive, General Uprising" that would topple the Saigon regime or, at the very least, force acceptance of a coalition government.

As outlined by General Dung, the centerpiece of the 1975 offensive would be a thrust into the vast, lightly defended region that the Vietnamese called Tan Nguyen, known by the Americans as the Central Highlands. In early December, however, Dung was forced to modify his plans after Lt. Gen. Tran Van Tra, the commander of Communist forces in the lowlands–Mekong Delta region, and Pham Hung, the chief political officer of COSVN, the Central Office for South Vietnam, convinced the Politburo to begin the campaign with a major assault on Phuoc Long Province northeast of Saigon. Not only would the liberation of Phuoc Long make a mockery of Thieu's "no territorial concession" policy, the two men argued, it would also tie down ARVN's mobile reserves and thus prepare the way for a bold strike against the capital in 1976.

As it turned out, the attack on Phuoc Long proved even more successful than Tra had anticipated. Beginning on December 13, the 7th and newly formed 3rd NVA Divisions quickly captured a series of key outposts, surrounded the garrison town of Don Luan, and severed the main road leading through the province. During the next two weeks, the remaining ARVN garrisons were also cut off and the province capital of Phuoc Binh brought under siege. As the Communists bombarded the town with long-range 130mm artillery shells, two companies of highly trained Rangers were dispatched to bolster ARVN's defenses. But it was hardly enough. Outgunned and outnumbered nearly four to one, the defenders of Phuoc Binh finally succumbed on January 6, 1975.

Emboldened by the ease with which Phuoc Long had been liberated, the Hanoi Politburo immediately directed the NVA General Staff to revise its plans for Campaign 275, the previously planned drive into the Central Highlands. Scrapping the conservative objectives initially outlined by General Dung, which called for a series of attacks on exposed outposts, new orders were now drawn up for a surprise attack on Ban Me Thuot, capital of Darlac Province and headquarters of the 23rd ARVN Division. "Never have we had military and political conditions so perfect or a strategic advantage so great as we have now," Le Duan told Dung, as he dispatched the general south to take personal charge of the highlands offensive.

In Saigon, meanwhile, the South Vietnamese Joint General Staff scrambled to cope with the unfolding military crisis. Uncertain where the enemy might strike next and lacking the manpower to defend every front, the ARVN commanders began fleshing out plans to shorten their defense lines and at the same time reconstitute a national mobile reserve capable of rapid deployment. As in the past, however, President Thieu refused even to consider a strategic withdrawal since it violated his policy of "no retreat." Instead, he continued to cling to the hope that somehow, in some way, the Americans would eventually come to his rescue. His faith derived in part from the secret assurances given by the past president, in part from his calculation of US geopolitical interests, and in part from his ignorance of the American political system. In South Vietnam, Nguyen Van Thieu *was* the government; it seems he never comprehended that in the United States, the president was not.

When news of the fall of Phuoc Long reached Washington in early January 1975, Richard Nixon's successor, Gerald Ford, had been in office only five months. Already burdened by a host of domestic problems ranging from rising inflation and widespread unemployment to a CIA wiretapping scandal, and further preoccupied by the threat of renewed war between Egypt and Israel in the Middle East, he was hardly inclined to risk his political capital by taking forceful military action in Southeast Asia. Even if he had been willing to do so, the Indochina Prohibition of 1973 and the War Powers Act of 1974 sharply limited his options. As interpreted by Congress, Ford could not even send a US naval task force to the coast of Vietnam without legislative approval, much less unleash thundering fleets of B-52s. He therefore decided that the only alternative was to seek a supplemental appropriation of $300 million in military aid for South Vietnam and an additional $222 million for Cambodia, where Khmer Rouge forces were rapidly closing in on the capital city of Phnom Penh.

At Ford's urging, in late February a special congressional delegation traveled to South Vietnam and Cambodia for an on-the-spot appraisal of the deteriorating military situation. Though skeptical at the outset, all but one of the legislators—Congresswoman Bella Abzug of New York—returned to Washington on March 2 favoring some additional military and humanitarian aid to both countries. But their recommendations had little effect. Most members of Congress, and with them the majority of Americans, thought giving South Vietnam more aid would be throwing good money after bad.

While the president's supplemental-aid request languished on Capitol Hill, the North Vietnamese Army resumed the offensive. In accordance with the Politburo's latest directive, early on the morning of March 10, the 320th, 316th, and 10th NVA Divisions surged out of the jungle and attacked the ARVN garrison at Ban Me Thuot. Employing a tactic that General Dung called the "blossoming lotus," a single regiment of infantrymen and sappers spearheaded the assault, striking quickly at the government command centers inside the town and then turning outward, "like a flower bud slowly opening the petals." In the meantime, columns of tanks and armored personnel carriers closed in from the north and south behind a shield of long-range artillery, trapping the ARVN defenders between the claws of an ever-tightening pincer. Although the South Vietnamese troops fought bravely, at times savagely, to hold their ground, within two days only a few pockets of organized resistance remained. By March 15, the battle for the Darlac Province capital was over.

The fall of Ban Me Thuot finally convinced President Thieu that he would have to start trading land for time. In order to prevent the North Vietnamese from marching to the sea and cutting the country in two, he decided to withdraw his remaining highland forces from Kontum and Pleiku to the coastal town of Tuy Hoa and from there to mount a counterattack on Ban Me Thuot. Since the main road leading to the coast, Route 19, had already been cut by the NVA, retreating forces were to descend along interprovincial Route 7B, an old logging road that snaked its way from the outskirts of Pleiku through Phu Bon Province. Though the road had rarely been used in recent years and parts of it were known to be heavily mined, it had the advantage of passing through territory that the enemy had largely ignored in the past. With careful planning and any luck, the force would be gone before the North Vietnamese realized what was happening.

Once the order was given, II Corps commander Maj. Gen. Pham Van Phu immediately began planning the evacuation. Thinking only of speed, he decided that the withdrawal would begin within two days, on March 16, with the 20th Combat Engineer Group leading the way. As the engineers repaired the road, built fords, and replaced bridges—a process that, in Phu's estimation, would take no more than two days in total—infantry, armor, and medical units would follow. Crack South Vietnamese Ranger groups would act as a rear guard, while the Territorial Forces at Pleiku remained behind to screen the movement of the column.

A South Vietnamese soldier on crutches leads other refugees ahead of advancing Communist forces near Nha Trang, along the central coast, on March 21. The refugees had spent a week on the dirt trails from the highlands city of Ban Me Thuot after it fell to the North Vietnamese earlier in the month.

Desperate South Vietnamese cling to vehicles along Highway 1 as they flee North Vietnamese troops advancing to capture Saigon days before the fall of Saigon, which marked the end of the Vietnam War.

Even before the first convoy departed, however, serious problems arose. On March 15, Phu himself departed for Nha Trang, leaving contradictory orders as to who was in command and without alerting the Territorial Forces of their assigned role in the withdrawal. As a result, as soon as the regular units began moving out, many Regional Force and Popular Force troops gathered their families and joined the mass exodus. So did thousands of other civilians. As the military convoys headed south kicking up clouds of red dust, unbroken lines of refugees on foot paralleled the path of the army on each side of the road.

As the South Vietnamese had hoped, General Dung and his staff were initially fooled by ARVN's strategic retreat. But after receiving both Western news reports of civilians fleeing the highlands and radio intercepts of flights from Pleiku to the coast, the North Vietnamese general became convinced that the enemy was on the move. Seizing the opportunity to destroy a major ARVN command, Dung immediately ordered the 320th NVA Division to drive northeast, attack the flank of the column, and stall the retreat long enough to allow the 968th Regiment to close in from the rear. Other forces along the coast were to cut 7B in advance of the withdrawing South Vietnamese as they headed toward their refuge at Tuy Hoa.

Darkness was falling on the evening of March 18 when the lead elements of the NVA 320th caught up with the II Corps column at Cheo Reo (Hau Bon), where engineers had been frantically working for two days to construct a pontoon bridge across the Ea Pa River. Just as they completed their work, a shower of heavy artillery shells, mortar rounds, and rockets rained down on the throngs of soldiers and refugees who had converged on the riverbank, waiting to cross. At the same time, other Communist units began hitting the tail end of the column, which still stretched back to the outskirts of Pleiku.

Nevertheless, the next day the column pushed on, as helicopters darted in to evacuate the sick and wounded and Vietnam Air Force (VNAF) aircraft bombed the advancing NVA troops. The convoy continued to flow through Cheo Reo until March 21, when the North Vietnamese finally broke through the Ranger rear guard and seized the town. On orders from General Phu, the trapped Rangers abandoned their heavy weapons and fled into the jungle. Elsewhere along the column, panic dissolved into chaos as roving bands of leaderless soldiers fought with civilians over dwindling supplies of food and water. One priest later reported seeing people so weak and exhausted they could "barely climb onto helicopters" and children dying of starvation.

By the time the lead elements of what had come to be called the Convoy of Tears fought through the last NVA roadblocks and reached Tuy Hoa on March 25, the losses were staggering. Of an estimated 180,000 civilian refugees who began the journey, only one-third were accounted for. Of seven thousand Rangers, only nine hundred eventually made it to the newly established II Corps headquarters at Nha Trang, while about one-quarter of twenty thousand logistics and support troops completed the withdrawal. All told, JGS chairman Gen. Cao Van Vien later reported, "Seventy-five percent of II Corps combat strength, to include the 23rd Infantry Division as well as Ranger, armor artillery, engineer, and signal units, had been tragically expended."

The morale-shattering defeat in the Central Highlands was soon followed by an equally disastrous collapse of ARVN forces in the northern provinces. There, too, a decision to pull back to more defensible positions precipitated a mass panic among the civilian population after President Thieu ordered the redeployment of the elite ARVN Airborne Division to Saigon and the withdrawal of other units to enclaves along the coast. Further complicating matters, Thieu repeatedly failed to clarify his commands, at first indicating that the city of Hue should be abandoned and then demanding that it be held "at all costs." In the meantime, the NVA 324B and 325C Divisions rapidly closed on the retreating army, cut Route 1 to the north and south of Hue, and isolated the city from all overland access. Realizing that he could not possibly hold out against the enemy's superior force, I Corps commander General Truong ordered his troops on March 24 to head for the shore, where a flotilla of South Vietnamese naval vessels was to carry them south to Da Nang.

The hastily planned evacuation soon turned into a rout, as soldiers scrambled to locate their families and then dissolved into the civilian throngs streaming toward the coast. Behind them the NVA, with their own troops now entering Hue, trained their artillery guns on the ten-mile stretch of road leading to the port town of Tan My, the principal embarkation point, inflicting heavy casualties and feeding panic among those waiting to be evacuated. When the promised naval fleet at last appeared, a combination of low tides, rough seas, and increasingly accurate enemy shellfire prevented the ships from reaching the shore. Dozens of soldiers and civilian refugees drowned as they attempted to swim to the one hundred or so junks, river craft, and barges that the South Vietnamese navy had brought from Da Nang. In the end, most of one regiment of the 1st ARVN Division and a single boatload of South Vietnamese marines were successfully evacuated to Da Nang, along with 7,700 people on Vinh Loc Island. Thousands of others were left on the beach to await the arrival of the conquerors of Hue.

Although President Thieu still entertained hopes of holding the line at Da Nang, it soon became apparent that any attempt to resist the advancing North Vietnamese Army would be futile. As tens of thousands of terrified refugees poured into the city during the last days of March, doubling the population to some two million, any semblance of order or discipline evaporated. By March 27, crowds of Vietnamese occupied every inch of ground in the downtown area, bringing traffic to a virtual standstill. Along the streets, armed soldiers, no longer under any control, wandered aimlessly, while at the main airport, frenzied mobs converged on every aircraft shuttling in and out of the city.

Amid the mounting anarchy, South Vietnamese and American authorities frantically pressed ahead with plans to evacuate as many people as possible to Cam Ranh Bay and Saigon. Nonessential US consular personnel, senior GVN officials, and third-country nationals were among the first to leave,

Bodies of refugees trampled in the rush to escape lie on the Nha Trang dock on April 1, as a crowded barge headed for Saigon approaches.

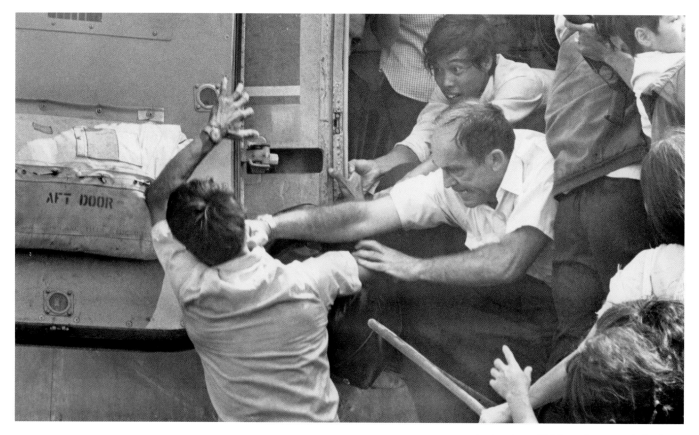

An American official punches a man in the face, trying to break him from the doorway of an airplane already overloaded with refugees seeking to flee Nha Trang.

flying out in aircraft provided by Air Vietnam, World Airways, Air America, and the Vietnamese air force. But as the backlog of passengers grew and the crowds at the airfield became increasingly unruly, the airlift had to be suspended and some other means of escape found. At the suggestion of an American DAO official, it was decided that a small fleet of tugs and barges assigned to move military supplies would instead be used to transport people. In the meantime, several large cargo ships were dispatched from Saigon to assist in the evacuation.

As rumors of the impending sealift spread through the city, thousands of civilians and renegade soldiers rushed the docks, overwhelmed a cordon of ARVN security guards, and tried to board the waiting boats and barges. Many civilians drowned or were trampled to death in the crush. Others were shot by South Vietnamese soldiers determined to make room for themselves. Still others waded into the sea, hoping to be picked up by one of the boats already making their way out to sea. "Vietnamese mothers saved their children by throwing them to British girls, Aussies—everybody grabbing babies," recalled one American.

The North Vietnamese 2nd Army Corps waited until Easter morning, March 30, before entering Da Nang. By that point, much of the madness that had gripped the city had already burnt itself out, even though only fifty thousand civilians and sixteen thousand soldiers had managed to escape. Resigned to their fate, those who remained offered no resistance as the Communists raised their flag over South Vietnam's second-largest city, where ten years before the first contingent of American combat troops had splashed ashore.

The following day, March 31, a flash telegram arrived at General Dung's command post near Ban Me Thuot, informing him that the Politburo had reached a "historic decision." Abandoning the two-year plan outlined the preceding fall, the North Vietnamese leadership had decided to seize the "once-in-a-thousand-years opportunity" that lay before them and "liberate Saigon before the rainy season." All available units were to be committed at once to the southern front, while Dung himself was to proceed to the regional military base camp at Loc Ninh. There he would be joined by COSVN political chief Pham Hung and Gen. Tran Van Tra to begin preparations for the "final decisive battle" of the Vietnam War.

Le Duc Tho joined Dung and his comrades in the South to apprise them in detail of the Politburo's latest resolutions and to monitor the final phase of what had been designated the Ho Chi Minh Campaign. Dung was to serve as supreme commander and Hung as chief political officer, with Generals Tra and Le Duc Anh, a northerner, their deputies. The offensive against Saigon was to be launched no later than the last week of April. "From then on," General Tra later wrote, "we were racing against the clock."

In the meantime, the North Vietnamese Army continued its seemingly inexorable southward advance. Along coastal Route 1 and the newly paved roads of the Central Highlands, long convoys of trucks, armored personnel carriers, tanks, and artillery pieces ran bumper to bumper, day and night, throughout the first week of April. As the NVA juggernaut rolled forward, the principal population centers of II Corps fell in rapid succession. On April 1, the coastal city of Nha Trang, the northernmost point on ARVN's latest defense line, fell without a fight after II Corps commander General Phu panicked and fled to Saigon. Two days later, the huge installation at Cam Ranh Bay was similarly abandoned as the 10th NVA Division closed in.

In Saigon, news of the latest territorial losses raised tensions to the brink of panic, sparking a run on the banks as well as widespread calls for President Thieu's resignation. In characteristic fashion, the South Vietnamese leader lashed back by censoring opposition newspapers, arresting alleged "plotters," and authorizing local police to "shoot and kill on the spot" anyone who violated a 9:00 p.m. curfew. Yet aside from promising to form a new "fighting cabinet," he made no effort to rally the nation behind him or to provide any real leadership to the government or armed forces. Plans to reorganize and re-equip the troops that had straggled back to the South were in disarray, while inside the GVN bureaucracy, one American reporter noted, "officials either stopped working altogether or kept mindlessly issuing instructions that could not be carried out."

"The president had all the power in his hands and could easily impose his policy," recalled Bui Diem, former South Vietnamese ambassador to the US, "but somehow there was no sense of purpose or direction among the high officials of the government," nor "strangely enough . . . any sense of urgency about the situation."

Convinced that an independent, if "truncated," South Vietnam might still be salvaged from the wreckage of the current military campaign, US ambassador Graham Martin and other American officials eventually persuaded Thieu to organize a new defense line centered around the garrison town of Xuan Loc, thirty-five miles northeast of the capital along strategically vital Route 1. At the same time, however, Martin authorized US defense

Many Vietnamese, *particularly those who* had served in the ARVN or the national police, were desperate to flee the NVA. Associated Press Bureau Chief George Esper, who was on the streets of Saigon as the NVA approached, watched ARVN soldiers as they "marched from their outposts and garrisons into Saigon to stack their weapons and surrender. . . . They were beaten men," he would write later in *The Eyewitness History of the Vietnam War*. As Esper watched, a police officer walked to a war memorial near the National Assembly building, saluted, and shot himself in the head.

Esper and several of his colleagues, refusing evacuation, witnessed the North Vietnamese Army tanks drive up to the presidential palace and knock down the huge iron gates. Later, some NVA officers came to the AP offices, where Esper served them "warm Cokes and cookies," he later recalled, and they showed Esper on their maps the long route they had taken to arrive in Saigon. Then they left, and Esper was allowed to remain in Saigon—by then Ho Chi Minh City—for a few more weeks before he was told he would have to leave. When, in 1993, the AP was allowed to open a new bureau in Vietnam, it was in Hanoi, and Esper, last man out of the Saigon Bureau, was sent to be the first chief of the Hanoi Bureau. He was joined by photographer Nick Ut, who had taken the iconic photo of Phan Thi Kim Phuc, the South Vietnamese girl who had been burned by napalm dropped by a South Vietnamese air force plane in 1972.

Crewmen of the amphibious cargo ship USS *Durham* take Vietnamese refugees aboard from the small boat they used to escape as the NVA approached. They will be transferred to the freighter SS *Transcolorado*, one of many civilian ships commissioned to carry refugees.

attaché Gen. Homer Smith to update contingency plans for a full-scale US evacuation in the event that ARVN failed to hold the line. Smith promptly ordered his staff to set up an evacuation processing center adjacent to Tan Son Nhut Air Base to draw up lists of nonessential US personnel and "high-risk" Vietnamese, and to identify and locate any other Americans still living in Saigon. Yet Ambassador Martin wanted to proceed slowly, since he feared that any visible sign of a US pullout might precipitate the same kind of mass panic that had engulfed Da Nang and Nha Trang. As a result, out of a total American population of more than six thousand, only 1,285 left the country during the first two weeks of April.

By that point, twelve Communist Main Force divisions were bearing down on the South Vietnamese capital from three directions—from the northwest in the area surrounding Tay Ninh, from the south along Route 4 leading from the delta, and from the east along Route 1. Only at Xuan Loc did General Dung's army meet with more than token resistance. There, the 18th ARVN Division dug in for what would prove to be a desperate last stand. Though heavily outnumbered and outgunned, the South Vietnamese troops launched counterattack after counterattack, stalling the North Vietnamese advance for nearly a week. Yet once fresh NVA forces began to arrive from the coast on April 15, it became clear that the defenders of Xuan Loc could not hold out for long. "It's like running a twenty-mile race with one contestant going the distance while the other runs a four-man relay," one Western military analyst lamented. "There's simply no way ARVN can win."

As the North Vietnamese Army tightened its noose around Saigon, Ambassador Martin came under increasing pressure to accelerate the pace of the US withdrawal. On April 19, two days after the Senate Armed Services Committee formally rejected President Ford's aid request, Adm. Noel Gayler, the US commander-in-chief, Pacific, was dispatched to inform Martin that Washington wanted the American presence reduced to no more than 1,100 as soon as possible. To facilitate the departure of Vietnamese nationals, US and GVN authorities agreed to relax their respective immigration and emigration rules, while Martin and Gayler devised a scheme that broadly expanded the definition of "dependent." In the days that followed, the number of evacuees leaving the Tan Son Nhut airfield on outbound C-130 and C-141 cargo planes grew dramatically from an average of two hundred to more than three thousand per day. In addition, DAO officials organized a series of ultrasecret "black flights" to ensure that especially "sensitive" Vietnamese, many of them former US intelligence operatives, could get out of the country without the knowledge of the GVN.

The American decision to begin a full-scale evacuation came as no surprise to President Thieu. Having finally realized that there would be no eleventh-hour US rescue, he knew that the end was drawing near. The government he ruled no longer supported him, his once loyal generals were threatening to depose him, and his army was collapsing on every front. On April 18, a group of leading political moderates and opposition figures had informed him that they would publicly demand his resignation in six days if he did not step down. Two days later, Ambassador Martin carried a similar message to Independence Palace. Emphasizing that he was speaking "only as an individual" and not as a representative of the US government, Martin told Thieu that "almost all of his generals" considered the military situation hopeless and that most Vietnamese believed his departure would facilitate a negotiated settlement with the Communists. Though Martin personally thought it would make little difference, many GVN officials "felt it might buy time, which was now the essential commodity for South Vietnam."

The next day, April 21, Thieu announced his resignation in a ninety-minute televised address to the National Assembly. Often rambling and at times choked with tears, the South Vietnamese leader devoted most of his speech to a bitter attack on the United States, recounting President Nixon's "solemn pledge" to "respond with full force . . . if North Vietnam renewed its aggression" and comparing the recent congressional aid debate to "fish market bargaining . . . over the bodies of our soldiers."

In the wake of Thieu's resignation, it was widely hoped that the aged and enfeebled Huong would immediately transfer power to a coalition government headed by self-styled "neutralist" Gen. Duong Van Minh, thus paving the way for a negotiated settlement. If there were ever a time when such a bargain might have been acceptable to the Communists, however, it had long since passed. By April 26, when Huong finally agreed to put the question of Minh's accession before the National Assembly, General Dung and his staff had already put the finishing touches on their plan for the last offensive of the Ho Chi Minh Campaign. The formal "resolution for attack" had been approved and signed. At precisely 5:00 p.m. on April 27, the "final decisive battle" of the Vietnam War—the "liberation" of Saigon—would begin.

The Fall of Saigon

During the predawn hours of April 27, 1975, four heavy rockets slammed into the South Vietnamese capital, signaling the onset of the Communists' final offensive. As fires from the blasts raged out of control, 130,000 NVA soldiers went on the attack, pressing in toward the capital on five fronts.

Though the South Vietnamese forces defending the city fought "stubbornly," NVA chief of staff General Dung later wrote, his own troops

Evacuees board an Air America helicopter in downtown Saigon on April 29, 1975. In the nineteen hours before the collapse of the capital, US helicopters evacuated more than seven thousand US personnel and select South Vietnamese citizens to ships of the Seventh Fleet waiting offshore.

"attacked like a hurricane" and made rapid progress. To the east, the 4th North Vietnamese Army Corps closed in on Bien Hoa Air Base behind a wall of long-range artillery fire, while the 2nd Army Corps cut off coastal Route 15 and surrounded the port town of Vung Tau. To the south, a combined VC/NVA tactical force pushed up from the delta and permanently severed Route 4 nineteen miles from the city's edge. And to the north and northwest, the 3rd Army Corps blocked Route 1 at several points between Saigon and Tay Ninh and encircled the 25th ARVN Division at Cu Chi.

As news of the latest Communist advances reached Washington, President Gerald Ford and his senior advisors quickly determined that the time had come for a total US pullout. While some administration officials advocated the immediate implementation of Option IV, a worst-case emergency plan to remove all remaining Americans by helicopter to an offshore US fleet, Ambassador Graham Martin assured the White House that such "extraordinary measures" were not yet required. Since no more than one thousand Americans remained in Saigon and the Tan Son Nhut airfield seemed in no imminent danger, Martin was confident that he "could get a maximum number of Vietnamese and Americans out by the thirtieth" by means of the ongoing fixed-wing airlift. Deferring to their "man on the scene," the president and his men agreed to delay. That day, more than 7,500 evacuees left Saigon on outbound cargo planes destined for the Philippines or Guam, the largest single daily exodus since the airlift began. Only 219 of those departing, however, were Americans.

Among the new leaders of the South Vietnamese government, the accelerated pace of the US withdrawal went virtually unnoticed. Throughout the afternoon and early evening of the 27th, the 125 members of the National Assembly engaged in a meaningless constitutional debate over the prospective transfer of power from President Tran Van Huong to Gen. Duong Van Minh. Not until 8:15 p.m. did the legislature finally agree to elevate Minh to the presidency to "carry out the mission of seeking ways and means to restore peace to South Vietnam." Minh, in turn, postponed his inauguration until the following evening so that he might have time to interview candidates for his new cabinet.

Loud thunderclaps mingled with the boom of distant artillery fire as Minh rose to deliver his acceptance speech at 5:30 p.m. on April 28. Still convinced that the Communists would negotiate with him, he called for an immediate cease-fire and a resumption of formal talks in accordance with the 1973 Paris agreement. Further pledging to free all political prisoners, lift restrictions on the press, and form a coalition government acceptable to all parties, Minh concluded with an appeal to those attempting to flee abroad to "remain here to join us and all those with good will to join in the building of a new South for our future generations."

As if to underscore the futility of Minh's eleventh-hour plea, no sooner had he finished his address than the Communists launched their first and only air strike of the war. Led by a former South Vietnamese pilot who had defected to the enemy earlier in the month, a group of five captured A-37 Dragonfly jets streaked over Tan Son Nhut Air Base and bombed a line of Vietnamese air force planes parked along the main runway. Though several aircraft were destroyed and others badly damaged, the runway itself did not come under attack until early the next morning, when an intense barrage of

Above: Vietnamese refugees cluster together aboard the USS *Hancock* after being relieved of their valuables and baggage. They were given numbered tags to help identify their belongings because of the language barrier that existed between them and the Marines during the evacuation of Saigon.

Below: A South Vietnamese helicopter pilot and his family, safely aboard the *Hancock*, are escorted by a Marine security guard to the refugee area during evacuation exercises.

130mm artillery shells crashed into the sprawling air base. Pandemonium broke out as ARVN soldiers swarmed onto the tarmac and VNAF pilots fired up their aircraft in a desperate attempt to get out of the country.

By mid-morning on April 29, it was clear that the fixed-wing airlift could no longer continue. Jettisoned fuel tanks, abandoned trucks, and other pieces of discarded equipment littered the runways, while rampaging Vietnamese troops still chased any aircraft that moved. Realizing he had no choice but to go to Option IV, Ambassador Martin telephoned the White House. At 10:51 a.m. Saigon time, President Ford gave the execute order for Operation Frequent Wind, code name for the emergency pull-out. A short time later, operators at the American radio station in Saigon began playing a tape of Bing Crosby's "White Christmas," a prearranged signal that the final evacuation had begun.

As conceived by US officials, the worst-case extraction plan called for all remaining Americans and certain select Vietnamese to be shuttled by bus to the DAO compound at Tan Son Nhut, where they would board huge CH-53 helicopters dispatched from the offshore US fleet. From the very outset, however, the operation ran into unanticipated delays, as large crowds of Saigonese converged on the designated assembly points throughout the city. "At every stop Vietnamese beat on the doors and windows pleading to be taken inside," recalled journalist Keyes Beech of the *Chicago Daily News.* "Every time we opened the door we had to beat and kick them back." Unable to bulldoze their way through the growing throngs, many drivers abandoned hope of reaching Tan Son Nhut and dropped off their passengers at the US Embassy compound. As a result, by the time the first wave of helicopters arrived at the airfield, between two thousand and three thousand people slated for evacuation were still inside the city.

Despite rapidly deteriorating weather conditions, the evacuation from the DAO compound proceeded like clockwork. Beginning at 3:00 in the afternoon, an average of thirty-six helicopters per hour landed at Tan Son Nhut, boarded up more than fifty passengers each, and whisked them away to the armada of ships anchored off the coast. By 8:00 p.m., more than six thousand people, five thousand of them Vietnamese, had been safely extracted. Only a Marine security force remained, plus an undetermined number of American and Vietnamese civilians still awaiting evacuation from the US Embassy.

With the operation now more than five hours old and visibility steadily diminishing in the deepening twilight, Secretary of Defense James Schlesinger strongly urged the president to suspend the operation until morning. But Ambassador Martin balked. Making it clear that he "damn well didn't want to spend another night here," he cabled the White House that "I need thirty CH-53s and I need them now." Secretary of State Kissinger then called and asked the ambassador how many people still remained in the compound. Unaware that the administration intended to use his estimate to calculate the number of helicopters required, Martin gave him a figure off the top of his head. "Seven hundred twenty-six," he said. As a result, when the last contingent of helicopters finally arrived to clear the embassy compound, more than four hundred people were left behind.

President Duong Van Minh went on national radio and called on his soldiers "to remain calm, to stop fighting, and to stay put." Throughout the

The 336th Aviation Company sprays a defoliation agent on a dense jungle area in the Mekong Delta. Many soldiers came home from Vietnam with various maladies resulting from exposure to these kinds of chemicals.

environs of Saigon, the last vestiges of resistance wilted and the Army of the Republic of Vietnam began to disappear as thousands of soldiers discarded their weapons and uniforms and awaited the arrival of their conquerors. At midday, a convoy of tanks and trucks rumbled down Hong Thap Tu Street and turned left onto Thong Nhut Boulevard to face the presidential palace. Without slowing down, the lead tank crashed through the high, steel front gate and coughed to a halt inside the spacious courtyard. Other tanks followed, forming a huge semicircle before the main entrance. As one of the crewmen raced up the steps and unfurled a huge gold-starred liberation flag, the ranking North Vietnamese officer entered the palace and confronted President Minh. "You have nothing to fear," the officer declared. "Between Vietnamese, there are no victors and no vanquished. Only the Americans have been beaten. If you are patriots, consider this a moment of joy. The war for our country is over."

Focus: Coming Home

With the fall of Saigon, the people of the United States began a headlong rush into the post-Vietnam era. Some Americans had not even waited that long. Five days before the last Marine helicopter lifted off the roof of the US Embassy, President Gerald Ford announced that the evacuation of Saigon "closes a chapter in the American experience." By and large, his countrymen seemed to agree. Wearied of the bitter conflict and appalled at its conclusion, the American people began a period of national denial. "Today, it is almost as though the war had never happened," wrote newspaper columnist Joseph Harsch in late 1975. "Americans have somehow blocked it out of their consciousness."

Ironically, many of those who served in Vietnam acquiesced in this conspiracy of silence—not out of shame, but out of bitter experience with the indifference and hostility of their countrymen. Unlike servicemen in World War II who came home with their units to formal ceremonies of welcome, most Vietnam veterans returned

Opposite page: North Vietnamese troops enter Saigon on tanks in a final act of the Vietnam War.

by themselves to the emptiness of an airport waiting lounge. Transported back to the United States with no time for readjustment, they were left to their own devices in a nation increasingly uncomfortable with their presence.

The veterans discovered that both ends of the political spectrum had rejected them. To those who backed the war, they were losers. To those who protested the war, they were either fools or criminals. "When I arrived in L.A., the first people I saw who were my own age gave me a look of such overwhelming contempt, I felt as if they had slapped me in the face," recalled a former 1st Cav platoon leader. Others recoiled from movies and television shows that depicted Vietnam veterans as psychotic killers or freaked-out drug abusers.

In fact, the vast majority of veterans readjusted well to civilian life. Some became successful businessmen, professional athletes, actors, and elected officials (including within a decade of the war's end two governors and three US senators). Most simply settled down like others of their generation. "We're just ordinary guys," said one veteran. "We live ordinary lives; we have wives and kids and ordinary jobs. We're OK. But you never hear about us. You only hear about the guys who are messed up." In a country unwilling to face its own responsibility for the past, the "taint" of Vietnam persisted. It became easier for some men to avoid the insults and disdain by simply hiding the fact that they had been in Vietnam. Said one New York City native, "When I go out for jobs, I don't put down that I was a vet. People think you're a time bomb or an addict."

Those fears, however compounded by guilt or ignorance, also reflected the very real problems of a minority of Vietnam veterans. In most cases, these afflictions tormented only the individual; occasionally, the pain and anger turned outward in violence toward others. Regardless, veterans initially found little help from the government in whose name they had served.

Nearly one hundred thousand Americans left Vietnam with acute physical disabilities, ranging from amputated limbs to shattered spines to blindness. Thousands more returned to the United States addicted to drugs or alcohol. A 1971 Harris survey indicated that 26 percent of Vietnam veterans took drugs, including at least 7 percent who were addicted to heroin or cocaine. Seven years later, the Veterans Administration reported that alcoholics or problem drinkers accounted for 31 percent of the VA hospital population.

Less well recognized was a collection of infirmities—chronic skin rashes, respiratory problems, impaired hearing and vision, violent headaches, loss of sex drive, and cancer—resulting from exposure to Agent Orange. Widely used in Vietnam to deny cover to the enemy and to clear friendly perimeters, the herbicide not only produced a multitude of problems for its original victims, but also was suspected of causing higher rates of stillbirths and birth defects among their children.

Even more insidious were the hidden, psychological wounds that some veterans suffered. These disorders took the form of extreme restlessness, depression, sleep disturbance, and paranoia. Such problems were particularly acute for combat veterans, many of whom wrestled for years to suppress a nameless anger they were barely able to contain. "No matter how much I was able to keep a lid on it," said one former infantryman, "I was always aware that just beneath the surface there was this rage, this tremendous, almost uncontrollable volatility that I somehow had to absorb." Others became victims of posttraumatic stress disorder (PTSD), in which the individual actually re-experience traumatic incidents—often as recurring nightmares, sometimes in the form of psychotic hallucinations.

The terror, guilt, and rage that frequently accompanied such episodes contributed to a higher suicide rate among veterans than for nonveterans of their generation.

Vietnam veteran James Burdge shows a rash on his arms that he claims was caused by exposure to Agent Orange. He said the rash covers 50 percent of his body. Chemical companies that made the herbicide and veterans who blame illnesses on exposure to it agreed to a $250 million settlement in court.

Nguyen Thi Ly and her mother, Le Thi Thu, are afflicted with diseases associated with Agent Orange, passed down from Le Thi Thu's father, who was a soldier in the Vietnam War. During the war, the US military sprayed some twelve million gallons of the chemical over Vietnam.

Psychological disorders and substance abuse also played a large role in the disturbing number of violent crimes committed by men who had experienced heavy combat and in occasional outbursts of unprovoked violence that claimed the lives of family members and total strangers.

Unfortunately, the Veterans Administration did not have the facilities, resources, or understanding to cope with the manifold problems encountered by Vietnam vets. In response to complaints that its hospitals and clinics were overcrowded, unsanitary, and understaffed, the VA blamed Congress for insufficient funds. But VA officials could not escape responsibility for a lack of communication with the veteran population and an unwillingness to confront the unconventional ailments of a new generation of servicemen. Despite additional funds, new programs, and a concerted effort to increase the number of Vietnam veterans employed by the agency, many vets complained that the bureaucracy remained unresponsive and insensitive. The VA refused to accept PTSD as a diagnosis meriting treatment until 1981 and continued to insist there was no proof that exposure to Agent Orange could cause serious illness or death.

Seemingly rejected by the larger society and unable to find the help they needed from the government, Vietnam veterans broke through their self-imposed isolation and banded together in their own defense. The first self-help efforts began in the mid-1970s with discussion groups and vocational training programs in California and a successful employment referral service in Detroit. Then, in 1978, a disabled ex-Marine named Robert Muller founded the Vietnam Veterans of America, the most visible of several national Vietnam veterans' organizations. The VVA initiated a vigorous lobbying campaign in Washington, finding an ally in President Jimmy Carter, who upgraded veterans' services across the board and appointed a former Vietnam combat officer, Max Cleland, as director of the Veterans Administration. The VVA went on to take up the cause of the MIAs, fight for official recognition of PTSD, support victims of Agent Orange, help form the Vietnam Veterans in Congress caucus, and shepherd two job-training acts through Capitol Hill. Perhaps the VVA's greatest accomplishment was Operation Outreach, a congressionally funded, independent counseling program for Vietnam veterans. By 1983, its 137 centers had assisted more than two hundred thousand veterans.

The legislation and the rehabilitation programs were all vitally necessary. But still lacking was any larger national recognition for the men and women who served in Vietnam and for the sacrifices of those who had not returned. Once again, the veterans had to look to themselves for the answer. In 1979, the same year that Robert Muller began the VVA, a former Army infantryman named Jan Scruggs started raising money to build a Vietnam Veterans Memorial in Washington, D.C. Over the next three years, Scruggs and many others labored to make his dream a reality. In the process, they ignited passions that had once divided the nation. But this time the storm acted as a catharsis: on Veterans Day, 1982, the dedication of the memorial became a celebration of national reconciliation. "We waited fifteen years to get here, man," said one former soldier, still wearing the patch of the 101st Airborne Division on his faded green fatigues. "But it's not too late. I'm just proud to be here. We made it. It's like coming home."

CHAPTER NINE

LOOKING BACK

Never has a war been looked back on by so many. More books have been written about the Vietnam War than any other American war—some thirty thousand and counting. Histories, novels, memoirs galore, and movies and television programs testify to how deeply Vietnam is embedded in the American soul and how it continues to inform and affect American foreign policy and military strategy. Yet the combined efforts of all the scholars and novelists and filmmakers have somehow fallen short of providing definitive answers to the most basic questions:

Was the war a victory? A loss? A draw?

Was the US right to be there?

Were our sacrifices worth the price?

The facts of the war are known, but are interpreted variously and debated endlessly. This book does not attempt to settle those debates, but to add new stories, new images, and new reflections on a defining era in the history of America.

Two Perspectives
Essay by Clark Dougan

A half-century after the first American combat troops landed at Da Nang, the Vietnam War still haunts the nation's collective memory. Its lessons, real and imagined, continue to shape US foreign policy as well as the military's strategy and tactics. The passions and divisions it spawned continue to infect our domestic politics and fuel our so-called culture wars. The longest US war when it ended, it cost more than $650 billion in today's dollars, nearly sixty thousand American lives, and more than two million Vietnamese lives. It left as many as three hundred thousand North Vietnamese and NLF soldiers missing in action, and resulted in the devastation of a beautiful country.

A double-amputee Vietnam veteran, giving only his first name, Morgan, is thanked for his service near the Vietnam Veterans Memorial on Veterans Day, 2013.

The question is, why? To what end? How do we explain this enormous investment of American resources in a tiny country on the edge of the Southeast Asian peninsula, thousands of miles from the US mainland—a country that posed no direct threat to our national security and that many Americans could not even locate on a map? It is not an easy question to answer. But with the benefit of hindsight, it is possible to reevaluate what happened from different perspectives.

President Harry Truman confers with Gen. Douglas MacArthur in 1950. Truman was accused of "losing China" and inviting Communist aggression in Korea in the wake of the Korean War, making it difficult for future US presidents to be seen as soft on communism and paving the way for US involvement in Vietnam.

From an American point of view, the Vietnam War is best understood within the broader context of the Cold War between the United States and the Soviet Union that emerged in the wake of World War II. As the USSR extended its reach into Eastern Europe by establishing Communist regimes in Poland, Hungary, Romania, Bulgaria, Czechoslovakia, and East Germany, the United States committed itself to containing Soviet influence behind what Winston Churchill called the "Iron Curtain." Following the Chinese Revolution in 1949, the policy of "containment" was expanded. With the threat now perceived to be not just the USSR but "World Communism," the logic of containment was applied to Asia as well as Europe. Though there were tensions even then between the Soviets and Mao Zedong, these differences seemed less important than the fact that they shared a common ideology that was opposed to the American way of life.

The outbreak of the Korean War a year after the fall of China reinforced US fears of Communist expansion in Asia. Occupied by the Japanese during

World War II, the peninsular nation of Korea had been divided after the war along the thirty-eighth parallel, with Soviet forces occupying the North and Americans the South. In 1948, the Soviets and Americans withdrew. Two years later, in June 1950, North Korean troops launched a massive invasion across the demarcation line and nearly succeeded in conquering the entire peninsula. Though stunned by the boldness of the attack, President Truman quickly ordered a counterattack, after securing a resolution from the newly formed United Nations sanctioning the American action.

By September, American-led allied forces had not only halted the North Koreans but driven them back beyond the thirty-eighth parallel. A month later, with North Korea on the brink of defeat, tens of thousands of Chinese troops came pouring across the Yalu River and sent the allies into retreat. In the months that followed, the war seesawed back and forth, eventually settling into a military stalemate. It finally ended in 1953 after Dwight Eisenhower was elected with a promise to end the conflict and, once in office, threatened to use nuclear weapons unless the North Koreans agreed to restore the previous dividing line between North and South.

The Korean War was the background for the domestic anti-Communist crusade that became known as McCarthyism. In addition to searching for Communist spies in the government, Republican conservatives in Congress assailed the Truman administration for "losing China" and inviting Communist aggression in Korea. By feeding fears that the US had become weak in the face of a growing international threat, such attacks made it a political liability for any president to be perceived as "soft on communism" or to be accused of having "lost" a nation to Communist revolutionaries. It was a lesson that would not be forgotten by future Democratic presidents John F. Kennedy and Lyndon Johnson as they weighed the American commitment to "save" the non-Communist government of South Vietnam.

From the perspective of the Vietnamese who opposed the Americans, however, the war that was fought at such enormous cost looked much different. For them, as for many other subject peoples who had for centuries lived under foreign domination, it was less a crusade on behalf of "World Communism" than a struggle to gain national independence. Between 1945 and 1975—the first three decades of what Americans think of as the Cold War era—more than 60 percent of the world's population freed themselves from colonial rule, from India and Pakistan in South Asia to most of the continent of Africa to much of Southeast Asia. Although some were able to win their independence nonviolently, many had to achieve their goal through force of arms.

Vietnam fell into the second category. Colonized by the French in the late nineteenth century and occupied by the Japanese during World War II, Vietnam had emerged from the war hoping to secure its independence. President Roosevelt was sympathetic, given the support that the Viet Minh provided the US in fighting the Japanese in Vietnam during World War II, but after his death and the war's end, the imperatives of the Cold War dictated US policy. With Western Europe's economy in ruins and Soviet-supported left-wing parties on the rise, the Truman administration was more concerned with shoring up the new government of Charles de Gaulle in France, and minimizing the influence of the French Communist Party, than supporting a small, relatively unknown nation in Asia. He therefore agreed to the reimposition of French rule in Indochina, as war-weary France sought to reclaim elements of its once proud empire. The Vietnamese responded by organizing a guerrilla army under the leadership of Ho Chi Minh, a Communist and ardent nationalist who had been a US ally during World War II, working with the American OSS in the fight against the Japanese.

History is filled with ironies, and the letters that Ho wrote to President Truman asking for assistance against the French—letters that received no response—offer another poignant example. It should be noted, however, that the US also ignored French pleas for help when the French Foreign Legion was being defeated at Dien Bien Phu in 1954; US policy at the time was to provide support for US allies in Europe to counter Soviet expansionism while not becoming involved with conflicts occurring in Asia.

Yet to imagine that either the coming or the outcome of the Vietnam War might have been different "if only" American leaders had been wiser and more farsighted would be a mistake. Even if Ho Chi Minh was first and foremost a nationalist, he was also a Communist, and in the context of the Cold War, it is hard to imagine the United States seeing him as anything other than a Communist. In the context of Vietnamese history, however, it is easy to understand why so many Vietnamese revered him as a patriot, the heir to all the other heroes celebrated in Vietnamese literature who had struggled against the Chinese for a thousand years before the French arrived.

In short, what the Americans call the Vietnam War and the Vietnamese call the American War was as much a clash of cultures and histories as armies and ideologies, framed by two different perspectives on a changing world.

Hanoi, 1997

In June 1997, former US secretary of defense Robert McNamara flew to Hanoi to discuss the lessons of the war with former North Vietnamese officials. Two years earlier, he had published his own book on that topic, *In Retrospect: The Tragedy and Lessons of Vietnam*, in which he conceded that "we were wrong, terribly wrong" to have fought the war and "owe it to future generations to explain why."

While the Vietnamese welcomed McNamara's "confession," in the United States his comments drew fire from hawks and doves alike. To conservatives, it represented an affront to American pride and patriotism and a betrayal of those who had served and died in the war. To opponents of the war, it was simply too little, too late—a view further reinforced by McNamara's admission that by late 1965, when fewer than two thousand Americans had been killed in Vietnam, he had already concluded that the war was militarily unwinnable.

But McNamara remained undaunted. In returning to Vietnam to meet with former North Vietnamese diplomats and generals, he sought to affirm his growing conviction that both sides "could have achieved our geopolitical objectives without that terrible loss of life," that there had been "missed opportunities" to stop the fighting during his tenure as defense secretary from 1961 to 1968. During four days of discussion, McNamara and his team—three other former US officials, two retired generals, and six historians—tried to identify the moments and circumstances in which a peaceful settlement might have been possible. McNamara wanted to know why Hanoi repeatedly rebuffed American efforts to open secret talks from 1965 to 1968, why the bombing of the North had not forced the leadership to

Former defense secretary Robert McNamara (left) chats with his onetime foe, Gen. Vo Nguyen Giap, in Hanoi in 1997.

capitulate, and above all, why they had been willing to suffer such heavy battlefield losses over so many years.

To McNamara's frustration, the Vietnamese provided few clear answers to the questions he raised, mainly because they considered them irrelevant. Not only had their strategy and tactics, diplomatic as well as military, proved successful, but their victory in the war had vindicated their understanding of its meaning and purpose. The "American War" had resulted in a reunified, independent Vietnam. Though the government was Communist, it did not become the pawn of Soviet and Chinese communism that Washington had feared. Nor had the "dominoes" of Thailand, Malaysia, Indonesia, and other Asian countries fallen to the Communists, as Dwight Eisenhower had predicted when he yielded the presidency to John F. Kennedy. It was the necessity of resisting the United States, the former North Vietnamese leaders explained, that drove them into a pragmatic reliance on Soviet and Chinese aid. And far from forming alliances with their Communist neighbors after the American War, the Vietnamese invaded Cambodia and expelled the Khmer Rouge while also clashing with Chinese forces along their northern border.

News organizations rarely published negative views of General Westmoreland, although reporters who covered the war generally held him in low esteem (as did some of the general's subordinates). ABC News reporter Don North's first encounter with Westmoreland was in August 1965 at a US Special Forces camp in Duc Co, near the Cambodian border, which had survived a weeklong assault by a large North Vietnamese force until South Vietnamese Airborne Rangers finally pushed them back into Cambodia. The US advisor to the ARVN troops was a young Army major named Norman Schwarzkopf, who would later command Coalition forces in Operation Desert Storm.

At dawn, Westmoreland, in his usual freshly starched fatigues and polished boots, arrived by helicopter at Duc Co to review the successful troops and be briefed on the battle. Westmoreland took Schwarzkopf aside to question him, as North rolled film. Schwarzkopf related this moment in his 2010 memoir, *It Doesn't Take a Hero*. Although Schwarzkopf never identified Westmoreland by name, North's photos provide the ID. Schwarzkopf wrote:

The General came over and recoiled because I hadn't had a change of clothes in a week and had been handling bodies and stank. The cameramen followed with microphones. "No, no," the General said. "Get the microphones out of here. I want to talk to this man."

I'm not sure what I expected him to say. Perhaps, good job, we're proud of you. Instead, there was an awkward silence and then he asked, "How's the chow been?"

The chow? For chrissakes, I'd been eating rice and salt and raw jungle turnips. I was so stunned that all I could say was, "Uh, fine sir."

"Have you been getting mail regularly?" inquired the General. All my mail was going to headquarters in Saigon so I said, "Oh yes sir."

"Good. Fine job, lad."

Lad? And with that he walked off. But the cameras were still whirring away. At that moment I lost any respect for that General I'd ever had.

General William Westmoreland (left) and US Army Maj. Norman Schwarzkopf (center) at Duc Co, a Special Forces camp near the Cambodian border.

During the 1997 conference in Hanoi, an exchange between Secretary McNamara and Gen. Vo Nguyen Giap, one of the chief architects of North Vietnamese military policy, revealed how deeply the two sides differed in their historical views of the war:

> McNamara: "We need to draw lessons which will allow us to avoid such tragedies in the future."

> Giap: "Lessons are important. I agree. However, you are wrong to call the war a 'tragedy.' Maybe it was a tragedy for you, but for us the war was a noble sacrifice. We did not want to fight the United States, but you gave us no choice."

Clark Dougan was a co-author of the original edition of The American Experience in Vietnam.

Looking Back

The Media

Of the several enduring myths attached to the Vietnam War, few are more persistent or frequently invoked as the media myth: "The media lost the war." In the aftermath of the Tet Offensive, General Westmoreland correctly claimed that the Communist offensive had ended in a massive military victory for the US; even his North Vietnamese counterpart, General Giap, agreed with that. But Westmoreland, who later said that he thought censorship should have been imposed on the media in Vietnam, blamed the American news media for portraying it as a defeat, and seemed to never understand why, to many Americans, the Tet attacks *appeared* to be a defeat. He seemed to overlook the fact that his command center in Saigon and the Johnson administration in Washington had been issuing optimistic reports about the war's progress for months, and the Tet attacks dramatically undermined those reports. Giap understood that even though his forces were thrashed on the battlefield, the attacks had dealt a major psychological blow to the United States.

For his book *The "Uncensored War": The Media and Vietnam*, Daniel Hallin carefully researched the coverage of the war in the *New York Times* from 1961 through 1965 and network television coverage from 1965 through the end of the war. He found that with few exceptions, the press reflected the military's and the administration's views. The exceptions resulted from reporters doing what the press is supposed to be doing, which is questioning authority and exposing government lies—the highest purpose of the First Amendment, whose authors saw the press as a watchdog over government.

Hallin also found in his analysis of the media coverage of the 1968 Tet Offensive that the reporting in fact rallied the public behind the war effort, and that the media later followed, rather than led, the shift of opinion against the war. Look back at the coverage of the antiwar movement and you will find very unflattering portraits, not of the soldiers in Vietnam but of the protesters, who were depicted as unkempt, long-haired, pot-smoking radicals.

Another myth is that Americans watched "live" coverage of the war in their living rooms every night on the evening news. In truth, there was virtually no live coverage. Satellites were a brand-new technology, and there was no "uplink" in Vietnam to send signals via satellite to the networks in

A CBS News camera crew interviews American soldiers on Tay Ninh Road, Vietnam, in 1967.

New York or Los Angeles. Footage shot in Vietnam was all on film—no video cameras were then in use—and the film had to be flown somewhere else to be processed and edited. Haney Howell, who was reporting for CBS News in the late stages of the war, explained:

> On breaking stories we'd carry or ship the film to Bangkok or Hong Kong for processing and editing. Bangkok was closer but Hong Kong easier. No uplink in Vietnam. In my desk drawer in Saigon was a proposal by the networks and other broadcasters to build an uplink in Vung Tao. New York lost interest as war wound down. When we'd alert Hong Kong we were headed in with good film on a breaking story, Don Webster, then the bureau chief, would head down the hall to the film processing company with a carton of blank film and tell them to keep processing. No one else could process their film until ours arrived and was processed. Made us first in line for the satellite!

Notable among the exceptions to the generally obsequious press were reporters like Neil Sheehan, Malcolm Browne, and David Halberstam, who widened the so-called "credibility gap" by reporting the differences between what the MACV briefers and Washington politicians were telling the public and what they learned from commanders in the field. The journalists had gone to Vietnam believing in and supporting the mission, but, as Halberstam put it in the 2003 documentary *Reporting America at War*: "We were finding out stuff we didn't want to find out. We were going against our own grain. We wanted the Americans to win. One of the interesting things was our own difficult re-education process, because we wanted it to work. And then it didn't work, so we started saying it didn't work. That's when they all started attacking us, saying, 'These are the guys who want us to lose.'"

March 2015 marks the fiftieth anniversary of the beginning of US combat operations in Vietnam, when the US Marines waded ashore onto the beaches of Da Nang. As journalist Joe Galloway put it, in the title of his wonderful book, "We were soldiers once, and young." Young, indeed; the average age of those who served in Vietnam, based on casualty records, was about twenty-two. Children of some Vietnam veterans are now in or nearing middle age, and the fathers of some of those children are among the 58,286 American servicemen and women whose names are etched into the polished black stone surface of the Vietnam Veterans Memorial Wall in Washington, D.C.

It is hard—and surprising, these many years later—to remember how controversial the Wall was when Maya Lin's design was first unveiled. Many veterans were outraged that "their war" was to be remembered with a black gash in the earth and not with a gleaming heroic monument. They did not understand how a twenty-one-year-old Yale undergraduate, and an Asian American woman at that, could be chosen to memorialize the hardships, the death, and the suffering—as well as the heroism—of the veterans of the Vietnam War. And yet, Maya Lin's design was selected and few veterans have been able to face that wall without their knees buckling, without tears flowing, when confronted with the power of that luminous, reflective memorial with its tens of thousands of names etched into the stone.

Many Vietnam War veterans returned to a nation that was deeply divided over the war, but reports of actual hostility toward returning veterans may have been exaggerated—there are no documented cases to support the rumor that some vets were spat upon by antiwar protesters. Many returning veterans encountered either mild curiosity or indifference—perhaps some people were afraid to ask for one reason or another. It is certain that many, many veterans who experienced deeply traumatic events in Vietnam did not want to talk, and as a result they kept their memories and feelings hidden well out of sight for years.

It took Frank Lee, a former Marine Corps combat photographer, many years to finally show his grown son, Alex, some of the motion picture film he had shot in combat. He told Alex about how he had been wounded and how he had to call in air strikes on a village when the platoon he was filming was caught in an ambush and the platoon leader had been badly wounded. The air strikes virtually wiped out the village and, as he told Alex in a scene broadcast on the History Channel: "I heard, in that event, women and children, crying and dying. And that clung on me forever."

Posttraumatic stress disorder, which wasn't recognized as an illness by the American Psychiatric Association until 1980, hit Frank hard when he reached his forties. He went through divorce, remarriage, frequent job

Above: Frank Lee and his son, Alex.

Left: Marine Sergeant Frank Lee served as a combat correspondent in Vietnam from November 1966 to December 1967. Lee was awarded the Bronze Star for his actions in Vietnam. Here, in the field in 1967, he signals for a roll of film.

changes, and a lot of depression. "Finally, a friend got me to go to the VA, where I was classified one-hundred percent disabled," Frank told me. "I said no, I still want to work, so they reclassified me as seventy percent." Alex, who was thirty-nine when he finally heard his father's story, was "very touched" by the discussion and by seeing Frank's films. "He is not a demonstrative guy," Frank said, "but he was very impressed and had seen something I had kept private, a side of me that he had never seen. Sharing my experience with my son was somewhat like a confession, relieving guilt and being exposed naked." The episode helped both father and son.

Daniel Ellsberg and the Pentagon Papers

The reporters who got it right in Vietnam, those whose reporting went beyond the "Five O'Clock Follies," as the MACV daily briefing was called, were ultimately vindicated by what is known as the Pentagon Papers, a massive document that revealed the full scope of the US government's deceptions and misrepresentations in Saigon and Washington. The official title of the document is "United States–Vietnam Relations, 1945–1967: A Study Prepared by the Department of Defense." The top-secret document (which is now available in its entirety on the Internet) was created at the order of Defense Secretary McNamara, who later claimed that he wanted to leave a record for future historians. The project employed a loosely knit team of some three dozen historians, headed by Assistant Secretary of Defense John T. McNaughton, who died soon after the study was begun. McNamara chose Defense Department official Leslie Gelb to replace McNaughton. Defense Department analyst Daniel Ellsberg had been working on the study at the Pentagon, and when he moved to the RAND Corporation, Gelb allowed him continued access to the papers. Ellsberg was a former Marine Corps company commander who had spent two years in Vietnam as a Defense Department analyst going out into the field with US and ARVN units, and that experience had left him increasingly skeptical about the war. In 1969, now fully opposed to the war based on his field experiences and his reading of the study papers, Ellsberg and colleague Anthony Russo photocopied the papers. In March 1971, Ellsberg gave forty-three volumes of the study to *New York Times* reporter Neil Sheehan. The *Times* put Sheehan up in a Manhattan hotel to read the papers and extract information for what would become one of the great blockbuster news stories of all time.

On Sunday, June 13, 1971, the *New York Times* began publishing excerpts from the papers. The first-day headline was a masterpiece of understatement and neutrality: VIETNAM ARCHIVE: PENTAGON STUDY

The scene after a federal judge dismissed the Pentagon Papers case against Daniel Ellsberg. He had been prosecuted for violating the Espionage Act by releasing the top-secret documents to the media.

TRACES 3 DECADES OF US INVOLVEMENT. The "archive" mentioned in the headline soon became known as the Pentagon Papers.

One revelation contained in the papers was that US policy was never about preserving freedom and democracy in South Vietnam—it was about containing China. In February 1965, shortly before the United States began its bombing campaign against North Vietnam, Defense Secretary McNamara sent a memo to President Johnson: "The February decision to bomb North Vietnam and the July approval of Phase 1 deployments makes sense only if they are in support of a long-run United States policy to contain China." The papers also acknowledged that "South Vietnam (unlike any of the other countries in Southeast Asia) was essentially the creation of the United States." A creation, it was noted, to serve that long-run goal of containing China.

The Nixon administration obtained a court injunction forcing the *Times* to cease publication of the material. It was the first time in US history, not counting official wartime censorship, that the government had invoked "prior restraint," preventing a newspaper from publishing freely.

On June 18, the *Washington Post* began publishing its own series based on portions of the papers, which Ellsberg had supplied. Again the Nixon administration went to court, but Federal District Court Judge Murray Gurfein refused to issue an injunction.

The *Times* case went quickly to the US Supreme Court, which ruled on June 30 in favor of the *Times* and lifted the two-week injunction, allowing the *Times* to continue publication of the papers. Each Justice wrote a separate opinion; Justice Hugo Black's reads, in part: "Only a free and unrestrained press can effectively expose deception in government. And paramount among the responsibilities of a free press is the duty to prevent any part of the government from deceiving the people and sending them off to distant lands to die of foreign fevers and foreign shot and shell."

Ellsberg and Russo were indicted and prosecuted, accused of violating the Espionage Act. After two years of legal proceedings, Federal District Court Judge Matthew Byrne declared a mistrial and dismissed all charges against the men.

In his 2002 book, *Secrets,* Ellsberg recalls walking out of the Boston courtroom that day into a "sea of TV cameras and flashbulbs." Someone in the crowd held up that morning's *Boston Globe*—the headline read, MITCHELL INDICTED. The US attorney general who had issued the indictments against Ellsberg and Russo was now himself facing trial, and ultimately served prison time, for his role in the Watergate affair.

David Halberstam

David Halberstam graduated in 1955 from Harvard University, where he was an editor of the *Harvard Crimson* student newspaper. In 1962, after covering the early days of the civil rights movement for the *Tennessean,* Halberstam went to Vietnam as a reporter for the *New York Times.* Halberstam's aggressive reporting, along with that of colleague Neil Sheehan and others, irritated the US military and the Kennedy administration so much that President Kennedy, who has been business editor of the *Crimson* when he attended Harvard, asked the *Times* publisher, Arthur Sulzberger, to remove Halberstam from Vietnam. Sulzberger refused. For his Vietnam reporting, Halberstam shared a Pulitzer Prize in 1964. In 1972, Halberstam published *The Best and the Brightest,* about

Left to right: reporters David Halberstam of the *New York Times*, AP Saigon correspondent Malcolm Browne, and Neil Sheehan of UPI chat beside a helicopter in Vietnam. Halberstam won a Pulitzer Prize for his hard-hitting reporting in Vietnam.

the Kennedy administration's foreign policy, which had been formulated largely by the corps of intellectuals and academics Kennedy recruited to his administration.

In 1997, Halberstam was presented with the Elijah Lovejoy Award at Colby College in Waterville, Maine. Lovejoy, an early graduate of the college that would become Colby, was an abolitionist newspaper publisher who was killed by a pro-slavery mob in Illinois in 1837. The Elijah P. Lovejoy Award "honors a member of the newspaper profession who continues Elijah Parish Lovejoy's heritage of fearlessness and freedom," according to the Colby College website.

The following is excerpted from Halberstam's acceptance speech, reprinted by permission of Jean Halberstam:

> It was, to let you in on a terrible secret, not that hard to cover Vietnam in those days. In some ways it was a very easy place to work. The evidence of failure was all around us. My colleagues and I had our most difficult struggle in trying to gain access to the battlefield. The only important journalistic ingredient was to me a simple one—an essential one, particularly for all of you young people out there: the ability to put loyalty to the truth above loyalty to a government of men.
>
> I would like to tell . . . about an incident which also took place in Vietnam in the fall of 1963 . . . at the height of the tension between the reporters and the American mission. We had already been identified as the only problem between that mission and, it was said, certain and

imminent victory. On this particular day there had been a major battle in the Mekong Delta, invariably an ARVN defeat, and the MACV commanders had tried to keep us out of the battle area. My impassioned young colleague Neil Sheehan and I had tried very hard to get down there but had been blocked at every attempt. We had finally called General Harkins, the American commander, and Ambassador Lodge, who was in charge of the embassy, to ask for help, but to no avail. Later that afternoon there had been a briefing scheduled at MACV headquarters, given by Maj. Gen. Richard Stilwell, a rising star in Saigon and the smoothest operator in MACV, a man who was already a master of what is now called spin.

General Stilwell began by giving us details of what the ARVN commander had had for lunch that day and how good his English was and which American Army training schools he had been to; but his information about what had actually happened in battle was predictably scant. That was bad enough. But then he segued into a highly condescending lecture to the reporters present, and particularly Neil Sheehan and me, whom he referred to by name—we were the two bad boys of Saigon—for daring to bother Ambassador Lodge and General Harkins. They were very busy men, he said, with a great deal on their minds and a lot of other things to do. We were not to bother them in the future, he added. It was as if he was giving us orders.

And without even thinking of it, I found myself on my feet. . . . And I heard my voice telling General Stilwell that American helicopters flown by American pilots had carried South Vietnamese units into battle that day, along with their American advisors. And therefore we had a right to be there. Perhaps some had been wounded or killed, but we did not yet know. And I said that the American people who were paying for this had a right to know what had happened and that they would in the long run . . . agree with me, since these were their sons. And therefore, unpleasant as it might seem, as busy as Ambassador Lodge and General Harkins were, we would continue to call them if we were blocked from access again. More, I said, we might be young, but we did not work for him, and we were not his privates and corporals; we were representatives of the *New York Times* and United Press and the Associated Press, and if he did not like our reporting, he had a perfect right to write to our employers and complain that we were being too aggressive in asserting our right to cover a story. He could even ask for replacements. . . . But until we were replaced, I said, we would continue with our historic obligation to those who had gone before us in this profession and to those who read our papers every day. I think it's a moment Elijah Lovejoy would have understood.

Going Back

Vietnam, now unified and at peace and striving for self-improvement, is a destination for millions of tourists, who are drawn by the warmth of the Vietnamese people, by the many temples, palaces, and pagodas that reflect Vietnam's ancient roots, and by its great natural beauty. Over the past thirty years, countless Americans, many of them Vietnam veterans, have traveled to Southeast Asia seeking to make their own private peace. Their

A dedication on Veterans Day of an infirmary that Soldier's Heart built for the Da Nang Street Children's Center. Standing at left is Stephen Priestoff, brother of a soldier killed in action during the war. His family donated much of the money to build the infirmary in his brother's memory. The children seated in front are all residents of the Center.

Captain Terry Bell on Hill 724 near Dak To, 1967.

stories represent not just their personal journeys to remember, reconcile, and heal but also the effort of a whole generation to come to terms with the Vietnam War.

Many of the veterans who have returned to Vietnam to revisit the places that haunted them had been shutting down their feelings for years. Some have never been able to uncork their bottled-up emotions and have matured from angry young men into angry old men. But once PTSD attained the status of illness, many vets were able to get psychotherapeutic treatment through the VA or privately and open themselves to real feelings and emotions. Dr. Edward Tick, a psychotherapist who has treated hundreds of traumatized Vietnam veterans and has taken a hundred or so of them back to Vietnam, says that "cutting off grief and anger also cuts off feelings of love and happiness," so unlocking the place in the psyche that has been harboring the dark side also allows the light back in. Older societies welcomed their warriors back. "Warriors are meant to share their stories," says Tick, to transfer their experiences to their tribe so that everyone carries their burdens and triumphs. Modern societies can be cold and uncaring, or fearful of knowing, so that the modern warrior often has no one to share with or feels that no one wants to hear his story.

Ed Tick and his wife, Kate Dahlstedt, founded the nonprofit organization Soldier's Heart, which offers veterans suffering from PTSD healing retreats and what Ed calls reconciliation journeys. Ed and Kate began taking small groups of veterans, often with their spouses, back to Vietnam to the very scenes of the vets' worst nightmares. He has taken more than a hundred men back. One of them was a former Army captain named Terry Bell.

Terry Bell

Terrence M. Bell was your quintessential gung-ho, all-American poster boy for military service—the kind of officer who was every field commander's dream. He never doubted that he would become a soldier. His military career began at the University of Michigan, where he enrolled in ROTC. When he graduated in 1964, he went straight into the Army infantry and reported to Fort Benning, Georgia, for officer training, Airborne, and Ranger schools. From there, he was assigned to a mechanized infantry unit in Germany, where he honed his leadership and training skills. By the time he got to Vietnam, in August 1967, he wore a captain's bars and was eager to do what he had trained for: command an infantry rifle company in combat.

Captain Bell was assigned to Delta Company, 3/8—3rd Battalion, 8th Brigade, 4th Infantry Division. The Division had arrived at Pleiku, on the western edge of the Central Highlands, in September 1966, and Bell arrived just in time for the division's heaviest fighting, in the fall of 1967 against the 66th Regiment of the NVA 1st Division.

"I had a ninety-day grace period," Bell said, "to train and organize my company before we went into battle, and to learn how to operate with Alpha Company. We ran joint patrols and worked on squad tactics. This was what I had done in Europe, and I was good at it by the time I got to Vietnam."

The brigade deployed to the Dak To Air Base on Bell's birthday, October 30, and less than a week later they were "in the shit," as the expression goes. Alpha and Delta Companies were airlifted from Dak To to Hill 724, one of several heavily wooded hills near the point where Vietnam, Laos, and Cambodia converge. The fight for Hill 724 was one of several hill battles in what became known jointly as the Battle of Dak To.

"On November 4 we ran into the NVA and for ten days we fought like hell," Bell said. "We were surrounded and taking heavy casualties. Alpha Company's commander, Capt. John Taylor, was killed on November 6. Bravo and Charlie Companies reinforced us on November 9 and 10, and Bravo's commanding officer, Capt. John Falcone, was killed on November 11. A platoon leader, Lt. Levie Isaacks, took command of Bravo." The NVA were right on top of the Americans by then, and Lt. Isaacks had to call in a napalm strike close to his own position—then another strike, even closer.

By the time Delta Company was airlifted off Hill 724, Bell said, "my company had gone from ninety-five men, enlisted and officers, to thirty-nine. Two of my lieutenants had been killed and two wounded. Two of the four company commanders on the hill had been killed in action."

When the battle was over, Bell and the rest of the battered battalion had a week at the Division base camp to get some sleep, welcome replacements into the units, and receive their awards and decorations.

"One Distinguished Service Cross, four Silver Stars, and lots of Purple Hearts," said Bell.

Then it was back to the war, this time on the highest piece of ground in the area, Rocket Ridge, which the NVA had been using to launch rocket attacks on Dak To. The Army established a string of firebases along the ridge to deny the enemy the use of the high ground. "Several times we resisted being overrun by ground assaults," Bell said.

On December 20, Bell's battalion commander, Col. Glenn Belknap, a man Bell greatly admired, was killed in a helicopter crash while trying to land with supplies during a routine search-and-destroy mission. Bell witnessed the crash, which also took the life of the battalion sergeant major.

"That was a long day for yours truly," Bell said.

It was also a day when Bell began to question his role—questioning that would eventually lead him back to Vietnam.

"I wanted to finish out my command," he said, "but my goal changed from killing as many of the enemy as I could to bringing home as many of my own men as I could. My attitude went from mission at all costs to men at all costs." During the last month and a half of his tour, in early 1968, "I lost no one," he said.

Bell stayed in the Army for ten more years. He had married right out of college, and he and his wife had two sons. It seemed that as long as he was in uniform, he was able to handle what later erupted into a classic case of PTSD; within a year of leaving the Army in 1979, his wife divorced him,

Dr. Ed Tick of Soldier's Heart comforts Terry Bell as he buries his Army dog tags in the soil at Dak To, the scene of Bell's most traumatic experiences in the Vietnam War.

and Bell began "a long slide of depression. When I left the Army, I thought, 'I'm free as a bird.' But I was not free—I couldn't face the anger within me. I denied that the war had affected me, but I had no idea who Terry Bell was."

Divorced and "free" of the Army, Bell became "Joe Seeker," as he described it. "I went to grad school, had a lot of women, finally smoked dope, and in my loss and grief started to become spiritually aware." In 1987, Bell remarried, settled into a career selling insurance to service members, and to most appearances was living a normal life. But in 2003, Bell's former Army RTO (radio-telephone operator), who was living in St. Petersburg, Florida, got so concerned about Bell's mental state that he drove him to a VA hospital for evaluation.

"Three hours later I was an inpatient," Bell said, "and began a journey of psychotherapy." He was hospitalized for several months.

Jump ahead to 2007. Bell, now living in Gulfport, Florida, read *War and the Soul: Healing Our Veterans from Post-Traumatic Stress Syndrome* by Ed Tick. "My soul may have been touched [by the book]," Bell said. "It resonated. I had an 'Aha!' moment." He attended a group workshop conducted by Ed in the Massachusetts Berkshires, but, Ed said, "Terry was numb, as hard as they come. What he had is called 'psychic numbness.' He was bitter and sardonic and showed no emotions at all."

Ed asked Bell if he would like to go on his next trip to Vietnam, planned for later that year. "Something in me wanted to go back," Bell said, so he and his wife, Anita, signed on. On October 24, the group—including Ed; Ed's wife, Kate; and four other veterans—flew to Ho Chi Minh City. There they rendezvoused with filmmaker Stephen Olsson, who had been hired by Ed to make a film of the going-back experience.

"Seeing Vietnam again was a 'Wow!'" Bell said. "All those areas we had defoliated with Agent Orange were now lush green fields. The people we met were friendly and caring and they recognized our need for personal peace."

Ed Tick took Bell to Dak To, and in the shadow of Rocket Ridge, Bell had his catharsis—or at least the start of it. He wept, he sobbed, he begged forgiveness for what he had done in the war. Ed had arranged a small ceremony with flowers and incense, and Bell got on his knees, weeping, and buried his Army dog tags in the stony earth of the Central Highlands as Ed comforted and encouraged him.

"I don't remember a word of what Ed Tick said," Bell told me. "The only thing I remember is his hand over my heart."

"Terry was crying, shaking his head, saying 'I'm bad, I'm bad, I couldn't bring all my men home,'" Ed said. "I told him, 'Say *sad*, not *bad*. And remember, *more came home because of you*. I reminded him that while some of his men were killed, he left no one on the field of battle. 'Because of you, there are no MIA families suffering.'"

Dr. Ed Tick left Terry Bell with a gift. "It was his inspiration to give me the mantra 'more came home because of me,' which has been a nourishing mantra for all of these years," said Bell. "What was at stake in my healing was my need to recover from the illusion that I was God—that I had the power of life and death over my soldiers. Although a false illusion, it gave me great power when it was needed to preserve the lives of men in our unit, and perhaps my own as well. God only knows. Amen."

Stephen Olsson's film of Terry Bell's return to Vietnam is called A Soldier's Heart and the Long Road Home.

Robert Hodierne

Robert Hodierne dropped out of college after his junior year in 1966 and went to Vietnam as a freelance photographer. He came home in the summer of 1967 and finished college. In the summer of 1968, after graduation, "I enlisted for OCS, but when they gave me Engineering OCS instead of Infantry I opted out." He was sent to Vietnam in January 1969 as an infantry private. Once in-country, he managed to get assigned to Stars and Stripes, *the military newspaper, where he worked until April 1970.*

Photographer Robert Hodierne at Duc Lap Special Forces camp near the Cambodian border in Quang Duc Province, November 1969.

On the morning of February 20, 1967, Danish newsreel photographer Ib Heller and I were hanging out at a 1st Cav medevac pad at An Khe. I was working as a freelance still photographer. 1st Cav medevac pads were a good place for combat photographers. If the pilots knew you and knew you'd get off no matter what was happening, they'd take you to where the action was.

This particular morning we flew to a small village on the Bong Son plain in the Central Lowlands about one hundred miles north of Saigon. Charlie Company, 1st Battalion, 8th Cavalry Regiment had been in a fierce firefight the night before. Fire had been so intense, medevacs couldn't get in. When Heller and I arrived early the next morning, the fight was over. But two troopers had been killed and another wounded. After the Cav troopers rounded up all the men in the village, the troopers set fire to the hootches. But though they set fires, they did little or nothing to keep the villagers from trying to put them out. And they didn't raise any objections to Heller and me making pictures.

I've always been careful through the years to make sure that anyone who publishes those photos include something of the context: The men had taken heavy fire from within the village. The two men killed had stepped on mines. It was, by the cruel logic of war, an understandable

Robert Hodierne took this picture of two Vietnamese women trying to douse flames by throwing dirt on a house that had been set on fire by US troopers in the village of Lieu An on the Bong Son plain during Operation Pershing. The night before, the soldiers had taken heavy fire from within the village, and two soldiers were killed when they stepped on mines.

act. But I had always wondered about that village. Were the villagers Viet Cong sympathizers? Or were they simple peasants caught in the crossfire? Those questions became more intense for me after two trips to cover the Iraq war. There I had watched our troops kicking in doors in the dead of night, and I had seen the same terrified looks I had seen in that faraway Vietnamese village.

In 2005, I set out to get the answers to that question. But what few notes I had from that day in 1967 did not include the name of the village. Hell, I probably never knew the name of the village. But say what you will about the military, it keeps great records. In the National Archives at College Park, Maryland, I found the actual typed sit-reps from battalion headquarters. The entries for the action included the six-digit military map reference. The Archives also had the map. I located the village: Lieu An.

But knowing the name of the village and getting to it are quite different things. For all I knew, the village had vanished. My nineteen-year-old film-maker son, Cutter, and I flew to Saigon.

We hired a van, driver, and translator and took a two-day drive to the Bong Son plain on roads clogged with traffic. As a little footnote: You are nearly three times as likely to die in a car crash in Vietnam as in America. But when I wasn't cringing in terror in the back of the van, it made me feel glad to look out and see that the fields along the road, which I remembered as largely barren and dry, were lush with green rice.

When we got near where the village was supposed to be, we found that we were going to need a police escort. I envisioned some sour Communist functionary determined to make our life difficult. Instead we got a charming young policewoman who seemed mostly interested in practicing her English than making trouble for us.

One of the most dramatic photographs I had taken in 1967 showed a young mother holding an infant, her burning house behind her. In my dream world I was going to find that woman and ask her about that day, but that would have been too much to hope for.

We found the village. It had changed. Concrete walls and tile roofs have replaced simple thatch roofs and bamboo walls. Each house has electricity. But some things had not changed: The woman from that photograph was still living there. Her name was Nguyen Thi Hoai. It's hard to know who was more astonished, me at finding her or she at having two Americans show up with photographs from that far-off February day.

I asked her what she thought of Americans. "We hated the American soldiers," she said. "We have to remind future generations about what they did. They burned everything. They killed the water buffalo. We hated the American soldiers."

Among the men that the American soldiers had rounded up that February day in 1967 was her husband, Vung Than. He spent three years in a POW camp. "Were you Viet Cong?" I asked him.

In a Communist-ruled country, I assume being a former Viet Cong would have social and political cache. But the man said firmly, "During the day, the American soldiers were in the village. At night, the Viet Cong came. I was not a Viet Cong."

Bottom left: Nguyen Thi Hoai (left) and daughter Lam Thi Tho, photographed in the village of Lieu An. Hoai holds a picture of herself taken in 1967 holding Tho in her arms while soldiers burned the village.

Bottom right: Nguyen Van Sic holds the picture of his mother (in foreground) throwing dirt on their burning house (see previous page). Sic said that after the troops burned his home, he joined the Viet Cong. He is pictured in his old uniform.

And then there was Nguyen Van Sic. He walked up to where my son and I were shooting interviews, decked out in a well-worn olive-green Viet Cong field jacket and a pith helmet. I showed him pictures of a burning house that turned out to belong to his mother.

"When did you join the Viet Cong?" I asked.

"I joined the Viet Cong three days after you burned our village," he said. And then he posed for a picture somberly holding a print of my photograph of his mother's burning house.

Robert Hodierne is a documentary filmmaker. He is chairman of the journalism department at the University of Richmond.

Ernie Washington

Ernest E. Washington Jr. was born and raised in the Roxbury section of Boston, Massachusetts. In September 1966, Ernie and his best friend, Sonny Davis, enlisted in the Marine Corps shortly after receiving their draft notices.

Sonny and I had grown up in the same neighborhood, and our families belonged to the same church. We didn't go to the same high school, but from junior high on we did a lot of hanging out together. I was proud to be Sonny's best friend because he was the kind of person everyone else looked up to, the kind of person who was good at everything he did—a real good athlete with a good mind who was also very sensitive to other people. A lot of that had to do with his upbringing. His father, who was a businessman, commanded respect, and his mother was the same way. They were models for a lot of black kids in the community. So it wasn't surprising that when we got our draft notices, Sonny and I decided to go in together.

William W. "Sonny" Davis stands at attention outside his parents' home in January 1967, shortly before his departure for Vietnam. He and Ernie Washington, best friends, went to Vietnam together.

Before we left for boot camp, we made plans. We knew that everybody didn't make it out of Parris Island. We knew that you had to be in good shape mentally and physically to make it in the Marine Corps. You had to show them something. So our attitude was that we were going to show them what Boston was made of, what Roxbury was made of. We were going to be the best. And Sonny was. He was named the outstanding Marine in our training battalion. He was good at everything—the rifle, hand-to-hand, the drill, the whole works. I did well, too. We both got our PFC stripes during training. But Sonny just stood out. He was an inspiration to everyone.

Although the recruiter had promised Ernie and Sonny they would be able to serve together in the Corps, when they arrived in Da Nang in February 1967, they were assigned to different units.

I was assigned to the 1/1—1st Battalion, 1st Marines—and Sonny was assigned to the 1/9. We bitched about it, but it didn't do any good. I got on a truck headed west into the boonies, and Sonny went up north to Quang Tri and the DMZ.

Four months later, during a battalion-sized sweep called Operation Brown, Ernie was wounded by shrapnel from 20mm cannon rounds fired by an American jet flying close air support.

My squad was sent out in front to scout this "ville" that was supposedly empty. I was a grenadier at the time, so I walked the tail end, carrying my M79 blooper. As soon as we all got into the village, which was surrounded on three sides by thick hedgerows, the enemy opened up and pinned us down. So one of the officers called in an air strike. Only he threw

Ernie Washington (second from left) and members of his company at a temporary field south of Da Nang in Quang Nam Province, April 1967.

the wrong smoke and gave the wrong coordinates so that when the cannons started firing they unloaded on us. The first rounds hit some of the hooches, and they just burst into flames. Even though we were still taking hostile fire, a couple of guys stood up and started yelling and waving their arms at the plane. But there was too much smoke, and he was flying too fast to see anything.

Eight guys in my squad were killed that day—eight out of fourteen. I was lucky. I saw this stone wall and ran to it and hugged it, so when this round hit the wall I took a big piece of shrapnel in the right shoulder and some smaller pieces in the back. But I survived.

A few weeks later, while I was in the hospital in Da Nang recuperating from my wounds, I got a letter from my sister telling me that Sonny Davis had been killed up at Con Thien. And I couldn't believe it. I wouldn't accept it. I thought, "No, not Sonny. It couldn't happen to Sonny." Then I managed to scrounge up an issue of *Stars and Stripes* to try and confirm it, hoping that I wouldn't see his name. But his name was there. And I cried. I'm still crying today.

After completing his tour in Vietnam and fulfilling his commitment to the Marines, Ernie returned to Boston and got on with his life. He got married and had a child, earned a B.S. degree at Bentley College, and gradually reconnected with his hometown community. But he never forgot about Sonny— or the other African Americans from Roxbury who had served in the war. And after attending the dedication of the Vietnam Veterans Memorial in Washington, D.C., in November 1982, he decided to do something to honor their service and sacrifices.

When I got back to Boston, I felt driven to do something I'd been thinking about doing for some time, and that was to make sure that Sonny Davis was not forgotten. I wanted to help produce a better understanding of the sacrifices of black men in the Vietnam War. I wanted to educate people about the legacy of black participation in all of America's wars, from Crispus Attucks in the Revolution to the Red Ball Express during World War II. In my mind, Sonny exemplified all of that, so I came up with the idea of creating a memorial in his name. The black veteran community in Boston got behind me, and we went to Governor Dukakis and to Mayor Ray Flynn, and they gave us their backing.

January 29, 1984, turned out to be the big day. Everybody was there. People from the commissioner's office, from the governor's office, from the mayor's office. Television people, newspaper people. Black veterans, white veterans, veterans from the western part of the state. They all came to the memorial service—standing room only in the church. Then we went down to the intersection of Tremont and New Dudley—to William W. Davis Jr. Memorial Square—for the tribute to Sonny. We had a very impressive Marine color guard from the naval air station. They did the ceremony, gun salutes, the whole works.

The dedication of Sonny's memorial might have closed the book on the Vietnam experience for me—not on my veteran's work but on the experience itself—except a year later, in August 1985, I was invited by a local TV station to take a trip back to Vietnam. Not many veterans had gone back by that time, but they were doing a program for Veterans Day, so I and two white vets were invited to go along.

It was good to go back. It was good to visit a lot of places I'd never been before, like Hanoi, as well as some places I had. It was good to be reminded of the special relationship a lot of black troops had with the Vietnamese people, and to hear someone say "Soul brother number one" again. And it was good, too, to talk with the men who had once been my enemies, even though I wasn't sure I was ready for that before we left. One of the interesting things was that everywhere we went, the Vietnamese veterans kept grabbing our belts to demonstrate how they fought us. "We were right up underneath you all the time," they said, "up tight, so that when you called in the goddamn air strikes they would drop the shit on you, too." And I thought about the day I got wounded, because that's just how he played the game.

The highlight of the trip for me, though, was our visit to Con Thien. The Vietnamese authorities didn't want us to go up there because it was dangerous. There's only one trail, the guides told us, and there were still a lot of undetonated explosives up there. They said, "Nobody goes up there." And I said, "But that's what we came for." I needed to see the place where Sonny had died. So we got special permission and we went up, film crew and all. The guides went up the trail first, and we were right behind. I walked the tail end.

We joked about that, but I was dead serious. I wasn't walking point this time.

When we got to the middle of that firebase, I could do nothing but cry. Because except for the death and the dying, everything else was still there. All the remnants of the war were still at Con Thien. Concertina wire. Sandbags. Hard hats cut in half and rusting. Bottoms of jungle boots. C-ration cans. Budweiser beer cans. Still there. Just standing there, looking at the place, you couldn't help but think of the sacrifices the men there had made and what happened to many of the men who did come home. I turned to the journalist who headed our party and said, "I thought one of the foundations of America was that you get back what you put in." Because it was evident that everybody there had put out. They had put out everything they had.

Ernie Washington related his experiences in Boston Publishing Company's A War Remembered, *Volume 16 of the twenty-five-volume series* The Vietnam Experience. *Adapted with permission.*

Bill Ehrhart

William Ehrhart joined the Marines as soon as he finished high school in Perkasie, Pennsylvania, in 1966. He was wounded in the battle for Hue in 1968 but completed his thirteen-month tour of duty in Vietnam. After three years in the Marine Corps, he went to college, eventually earning a doctorate. He is the author of Vietnam-Perkasie: A Combat Marine Memoir. *Ehrhart has also written several volumes of poetry, and he has been called "the dean of Vietnam War poetry." He teaches at The Haverford School in Pennsylvania.*

The weapon that got Ken Takenaga and me was an RPG, a rocket-propelled grenade. The RPG launcher is a long, thin tube the gunner rests on his shoulder like a bazooka, and the projectile sticks out the front of the tube like a bulbous, cone-shaped piece of nastiness. We didn't call them RPGs back

Marines Kazunori "Ken" Takenaga and Bill Ehrhart in Vietnam in 1968.

then. We called them B-40s. But a rose by any other name still has thorns, and whatever you call it, one B-40 can screw up your whole day. It certainly screwed up ours.

Ken got the worst of it: a huge gash in his scalp and a shattered right arm. He was evacuated immediately, first to Da Nang, then to Hawaii. I got some small shrapnel wounds a doctor cleaned out, slept for a few hours, then went back to the war, stone-deaf but otherwise reasonably functional. This was Hue during the Tet Offensive. If you could walk, see, and shoot, you stayed. There were guys a lot worse off than me.

It took me thirty-two years to find Kenny again. I didn't even know his real first name (Kazunori) or which country he lived in (Japanese-born, he was still a Japanese citizen in 1968). He'd come to the US in the midst of the Vietnam War, as a permanent alien resident was subject to the draft, got drafted, and chose to join the Marines instead, thinking he was joining the Navy. When he got to Parris Island, he asked the drill instructors, "Where are the ships?"

I finally tracked him down in 2000, and since then we've renewed our friendship as if no time at all had passed. These days, he shuttles between Japan and New York, so we get together several times a year. Ken has spent his entire adult life in the travel and tourism industry, so when he suggested a trip back to Vietnam, he didn't have to ask twice.

This would not be my first trip back to postwar Vietnam. I'd been back in 1985 and again in 1990. But this trip was special for two reasons: I'd be able to take my wife, Anne, with me this time, to share with her a place she had only—but endlessly—heard about during our thirty years of marriage. And I'd be traveling with my buddy, my comrade, who'd literally been where I'd been and knew what I knew and needed no explanations.

Our journey began, however, not in Vietnam, but in Japan. Ken spent the first fifteen years of his life in the city of Yatsushiro, Kyushu, where he was raised by his maternal grandparents. Having seen where I grew up in Perkasie, Pennsylvania, Ken wanted to show us where he'd come from.

We spent eight days in Japan, then it was on to Vietnam. After a night in Saigon (now called Ho Chi Minh City)—where the street scene can only be described as "motor-scooter madness"—we flew to central Vietnam, the area between Hoi An and the seventeenth parallel, where Ken and I had been stationed. We drove over the Hai Van Pass, a spectacular ride that had been charged with danger the first time we'd taken it in 1967. We climbed Marble Mountain, where throughout the war the Viet Cong had maintained a field hospital right under the noses of the Americans at Da Nang. We drove over the bridge that had once connected the rest of Hieu Nhon District to the small fishing village of Phuoc Trac, displaced now by a string of luxury beach resorts.

We drove up to the old DMZ and descended into the tunnels of Vinh Moc, where an entire village of seventy families had lived underground for six years to escape US bombardment.

In Hue, the old Imperial capital of the Nguyen Dynasty, we visited the Citadel, made famous by the Tet Offensive of 1968, and the Holy Lady Pagoda, where we saw the actual Austin automobile that the monk Thich Quang Duc rode to Saigon in before immolating himself in protest of Ngo Dinh Diem's suppression of Buddhists in 1963. (The car is visible in the iconic photo by Malcolm Browne.)

Ehrhart and Takenaga in front of the building where they were wounded during fighting in Hue in 1968. The building had been a mansion at the time; when Ehrhart and Takenaga found it in 2011, it had become a small luxury hotel.

But the most amazing experience was finding the very building Ken and I had been in when we were wounded. During the war, it had been some big-wig's mansion—the mayor or provincial governor—a two-and-a-half story house surrounded by a yard and a wall. The bigwig had skipped town when the shooting started, so we Marines had moved in and were using it as a battalion command post. We'd spent several days trying to dislodge some North Vietnamese from the houses across the street, and were just marking time that morning, waiting for flame tanks to come and burn the block down. Ken and I were posted in a second-story bedroom. I was making a cup of C-ration coffee and Ken was cleaning his rifle when a North Vietnamese soldier put an RPG through the window.

It took some work to find the building—a lot can and does change in forty-three years—but we found it. Completely renovated and refurbished, the house is now the business offices for the four-star Duy Tan Hotel. The yard is now a tiled driveway and parking area for the hotel with a motor scooter rental operation and an outdoor coffee shop. Only the configuration of the windows, and the location of the house itself, allowed me to be certain we had the right place. Later, I wrote this poem:

Cheating the Reaper

This is the building, Ken.
This is the place
where our lives nearly ended.
My fault. I got careless.
That NVA gunner was aiming at me,
but all I got was a hell of a headache,
permanent tinnitus,
and a cheap Purple Heart.
You got a gaping gash in your head
and nearly lost an arm.
Both of us a rice shoot away
from buying the farm.
But here we are in a vibrant city
forty-three years later:
two ex-Marines shaking our heads
in wonder at what we survived
and what we are seeing now:

a five-story four-star hotel,
scooter rental and coffee shop
instead of a house we'd commandeered
for a makeshift battalion CP,
cinderblock wall
enclosing a littered yard.
Who would have thought
the day that RPG exploded
we'd live to see this day,
this house, this city, this Vietnam.
Who would have thought
we'd ever want to come back
or be happy because we'd lost.
This is the very building, Ken.
This is where we almost died
for nothing that mattered,
but didn't.

One evening in Hue, we went for a boat ride on the River of Perfumes, accompanied by eight singers and musicians in traditional dress, performing traditional folk music. One can hardly imagine, let alone describe, the beauty, the profound tranquility, of such an experience, especially for two ex-Marines who had nearly died next to that river so many years ago.

Later that night, Ken and I stood on a hotel balcony overlooking Hue. We could see the university that had been used as a refugee center, the roof of the building we'd been in, now dwarfed by the hotel built around it, the roofs of what had been the MACV compound. But the streets were crowded with noisy, jostling, energetic people. The river flowed with

colorful tour boats. The bridge glowed yellow, then green, then blue. We did not speak. There was nothing to say. This is what we had come to see. A country. Not a war.

Bill Ehrhart's latest books are a collection of poems, The Bodies Beneath the Table *(Adastra, 2010), and a collection of essays,* Dead on a High Hill *(McFarland, 2012).*

Bill Braniff and Ron Owens

Bill Braniff didn't have to serve in Vietnam—he's a Canadian. But he, like thousands of other Canadians, came south to join the US military during the Vietnam War, and twelve thousand or more served in Vietnam. His parents had served in World War II, and some of his other relatives were in the military, so he thought it was the right and natural thing to do. He signed up, went through basic and AIT, and left for Vietnam on January 23, 1968—one week before the start of the Tet Offensive. He arrived at Bien Hoa Air Base and boarded an Army bus to the nearby 90th Replacement Depot, on the road between Bien Hoa and the huge Long Binh Army base a few miles north of Saigon. From there he was ticketed to the seaside city of Vung Tau and a "cushy" assignment with a support unit. That plan changed dramatically when the Viet Cong attacked Bien Hoa and Long Binh on the night of January 30–31, the start of the countrywide offensive.

"A VC battalion found themselves trapped in Long Binh, and the only way out was through the 90th," Braniff said. "VC were running through the barracks. We piled up mattresses as a defense, and those mattresses stopped quite a few rounds."

As the fighting raged around the country, the soldiers trapped in the 90th quickly ran out of food. "I volunteered to take a deuce-and-a-half truck and make a supply run to Long Binh," Braniff said, "but I was pinned down by sniper fire for hours in the hot sun."

Braniff's first few days in Vietnam caused him to change course. Instead of Vung Tau, he went to the 25th Infantry Division base at Dau Tien, near Cu Chi, as an Eleven Bravo—a rifleman. He saw action below ground as well as above, volunteering to be one of the "tunnel rats" who crawled into the vast network of VC tunnel complexes to lay explosives for blowing the tunnels up. He served in Vietnam for seven months and twenty-nine days before he was knocked out of action, not by enemy fire but by a bleeding ulcer. He was sent to Japan for medical treatment and didn't return to Vietnam until 1996.

"Going back to Vietnam was very strange," Braniff said. "I was very worried about how I would react, and how the Vietnamese would react to me." He was accompanied by a Vietnamese friend, who had escaped by boat at the end of the war.

Through his Vietnamese friend, Braniff made friends with former enemies and stayed in the homes of former soldiers. He located the site where he and his platoon had staged an ambush, near a monastery, a place that held a lot of meaning—and baggage—for Braniff.

"I felt as though I was peeling a heavy weight off," he said. "It was like coming out of the cold into a warm shower, a cleansing feeling. I had a lot of

Left to right: Bill Braniff with Vietnam veterans Tom Vacchino and Ron Owens, who accompanied Braniff on a Back to the Nam journey to Vietnam in 2010. The men are standing in front of a house in the village of Vinh Moc, on the North Vietnamese coast near the DMZ.

hatred inside that I lost by meeting people and talking with them. The most amazing thing was that my former enemies were so friendly. They held no grudge against me."

Braniff wanted to help other veterans to have the same experience he had, so he started Back to the Nam, an organization providing what he calls "healing journeys," and began taking groups of veterans back to Vietnam. He took five vets back with him each time. "I knew my way around by then, and I knew what to expect. It was the same every time," Braniff said. "I would take them to the places where they had been stationed, and that's when the flood gates opened. They would break down. But then things would get better." Braniff said he often got compliments from the vets' wives, who thanked him for helping their husbands heal.

One of the veterans who returned to Vietnam with Bill Braniff was Ron Owens, who had served as a rifleman with the 101st Airborne Division in 1968 and 1969. Owens, a Rhode Island native, enrolled in junior college after graduating from East Providence High, but then came the draft notice. He went through Basic at Fort Jackson, South Carolina, and Advanced Individual Training (AIT) at Fort Polk, Louisiana. After two weeks' leave, he shipped out to Vietnam. Landing at Tan Son Nhut, he flew north at night in a C-130 and reported for duty with Delta Company, 1st of the 501st at LZ Sally, near Hue. The company was in the field, camped in a cemetery near the village of Ap Su Thuong, which they called Eight Klick Ville. "I'll never forget that first night, sleeping in a cemetery!" he said. The next day he was on patrol, conducting a sweep of the village. "We took some sniper fire, but there was no serious combat," Owens said. But a few days later, his company entered a hamlet they had nicknamed Booby Trap Ville. There they ran into opposition, and they took some casualties. When the fighting stopped, the company stood down in the field and a chaplain made the rounds of the company, offering absolution. "I remember the chaplain shaking the hand of the guy next to me, a guy from another platoon that I knew, and saying 'Peace.' An hour later, that kid was killed by a booby trap," Owens said.

Owens's unit set ambushes "a lot," he said, and those ambushes often claimed civilian lives, something that haunted him more than he understood at the time. "Every soldier in the field had their My Lai," Owens said, referring to the massacre of Vietnamese civilians by American troops in March 1968. "I had a lot of bad days." He particularly remembered watching his platoon sergeant shoot and kill a wounded enemy soldier.

In August 1968, Owens earned an Army Commendation Medal with "V" (for Valor) for his actions near Eight Klick Ville. He was outside the wire, at an observation post, when he spotted a squad of enemy soldiers sneaking through a hedgerow. Owens, alone, engaged the VC with rifle fire, pinning them down until his unit could maneuver into position to fight, then calling in artillery on the hedgerow.

He left the Army in October 1969. In 2010, he heard about Bill Braniff and his Back to the Nam tours and signed up to go. "I wanted to see what it was about," he said. "As a kid in Vietnam, I didn't think, I just did. I needed to go back to see if we had done any good there, and for my own personal healing."

Specialist Ron Owens in Vietnam in 1968 at LZ Sally, his unit's base camp. Owens was a rifleman in Delta Company, 1st of the 501st.

He found the visit very emotional, especially revisiting LZ Sally and Eight Klick Ville, which was his "biggest bugaboo, because we swept that village so often and took so many casualties there. It helped me," he said. "And Bill was great, he helped me a lot. But I came back possessed with the need to reconnect with military stuff. I was on the Internet all the time looking up my unit, finding guys I knew, and it drove my wife crazy. She said 'This is consuming you! Snap out of it!'"

Owens did snap out of it, and while he still held some anger and suppressed memories when he returned, he said he has been able to "mellow out" much more. As he wrote in a letter to Bill Braniff, the trip was "just what I needed to understand what the hell we did accomplish while we were there. Although the war did not end the way we would have liked, I think the fact that the country is now at peace is a win for both sides."

Bill Braniff of Kitchener, Ontario, now lives in Bucksport, Maine. His website is backtothenam.org. Ron Owens retired in January 2013 as a market development manager with PepsiCo and lives in Kennebunk, Maine.

Giving Back

The story of the Vietnam veteran is not complete without an accounting of the many ways the veterans have drawn on their own wartime and postwar experiences to give back—to their country, to their brothers-in-arms, and to the younger veterans of other conflicts, notably Iraq and Afghanistan. Many Vietnam veterans have gone into public service and have fought new battles to ensure that veterans receive the benefits they are entitled to and the care they need. Others have reached out to the neediest, the most troubled, and the badly wounded and have found ways to give help and comfort. And still others have given back to the country that suffered the worst—Vietnam.

Soldier's Heart

Ed Tick's nonprofit Soldier's Heart, in addition to offering psychotherapy to troubled veterans and healing journeys back to Vietnam, also offers veterans an opportunity to help create something of lasting value in Vietnam: a

school for Vietnamese children or a home for a Vietnamese family—a Compassion House, which Ed describes as follows:

[A] single family, flood-proof, weatherproof home built and gifted to the most destitute of Vietnamese. Soldier's Heart has raised the money to build about six or eight of them around Vietnam. With the Vietnamese we research the most needy cases in a region, raise, and provide the money. The homes are built locally using local products. Our group gifts the homes to their recipients in a ceremony when we are there. We always have the vets who served in that region gift the home so they experience giving back and the re-creation of a positive identity. We have given homes

Left: Vietnam War veteran "Magoo" Philips surrounded by Vietnamese schoolchildren in a kindergarten built by Soldier's Heart for five villages in the Mekong Delta.

Below: An American veteran and a Montagnard Viet Cong veteran hug in reconciliation in the Central Highlands in 2010. The American vet traveled to Vietnam with Soldier's Heart.

to elderly with no survivors to care for them, disabled Vietnamese veterans, orphans, severe Agent Orange victims. We have built houses in the Central Highlands, the rural north, in Montagnard villages.

Soldier's Heart has also built a school near Vinh Long in the Mekong Delta and helped rebuild elementary schools in Da Nang and Tam Ky after typhoons.

"We also give many smaller individual gifts," Ed said, "donating water buffalos, sampans, cows, ducks, and chickens to needy families."

Everyone who travels to Vietnam with Ed and his wife, Kate, contributes a fee that goes toward a humanitarian project. Every project has a dual purpose, Ed says: "Helping Vietnam rebuild from our war and transforming the identities of our vets from destroyers to creators, preservers, restorers. Remember Isaiah? 'You shall be called the repairers of the breach, the restorer of paths to dwell in.'"

The Shelter

In 1990, in Boston, veterans Ken Smith, Mark Helberg, and Peace Foxx opened the New England Shelter for Homeless Veterans, the first shelter in the US specifically for veterans. Four years earlier, the three had made their first visit to the Vietnam Veterans Memorial in Washington, D.C., and had been shocked to find homeless veterans camping near the Washington Mall. They decided to do something about it. Two years later, they founded a workshop for veterans in Boston, and a year later they were able to acquire a long-term lease on a former VA facility on Court Street, near Boston City Hall, and NESHV was born. The shelter offered meals, drug and alcohol counseling, hot showers, and beds. Smith and the others ran the shelter in military style—beds had to be made, residents had to pull KP (kitchen duty) and other work details, and no one was allowed in for the night with booze on his breath. The shelter dispatched a detail to City Hall Plaza each day to raise and lower the American flag. As time went on, the shelter began offering a wider range of services, including health care and transitional housing, and established vocational training programs. It was honored as the 147th of President George H. W. Bush's "Thousand Points of Light." Now called the New England Center for Homeless Veterans, it is the largest facility in the country for homeless vets; hundreds of hot meals are served every day.

In 1996, the Center expanded its services to include homeless women veterans as the population of female vets grew. In 2014, there were about 1.8 million women veterans, of a total veteran population of around 21 million, who faced many of the same challenges as their male counterparts upon returning

Staff Sergeant Kenneth Overshown served in the Air Force during the Vietnam era. Having successfully completed the New England Center for Homeless Veterans (NECHV) transitional housing program, Ken was NECHV's 2010 "Battlefield Citation" award recipient.

A former US Marine serves meals at the New England Center for Homeless Veterans. The Center serves around four hundred meals per day to the homeless veterans who reside there.

to civilian life. Under the guidance of CEO Andy McCawley, a retired Navy captain, the center embarked on an ambitious program to reconfigure the existing space to add more permanent housing and services for veterans. Supported by a mix of federal, state, and city grants and contracts, the center works with numerous public agencies and private sector organizations to help homeless vets find jobs and housing. "The goal is to place at least one veteran a day in affordable housing," said McCawley, a goal that is usually exceeded. In a typical year, the center provides more than a thousand veterans with case-managed support and helps find secure employment for two hundred. On any given day, the center houses more than 330 veterans and serves more than four hundred hot meals.

The Milkshake Man

On April 26, 1969, an Army infantry grunt in Vietnam named Jim Mayer stepped on a land mine that took off both his legs at the knees. After months of rehab at Brooke Army Medical Center in San Antonio, Texas, Mayer wanted to go to college, and he applied to the Veterans Administration for veterans' benefits to pay for his education. He had to get his congresswoman to go to bat for him before he got what he was entitled to, and he decided that the VA needed some reforming. He moved to Washington, D.C., and started working for the VA in 1974 with the goal of making the VA work better for veterans.

In 1991, Mayer started volunteering at Walter Reed Army Medical Center, just outside of Washington, because he reckoned that Operation Desert Storm would result in American casualties, including amputations. Desert Storm was followed by the wars in Afghanistan and Iraq. In both conflicts, the signature weapon deployed against American soldiers was the IED, the improvised explosive device, and the signature wound was loss of limbs—arms or legs, or both. As a double amputee, Mayer understood what the new generation of wounded warriors had to endure; as a double amputee who had gone on to lead a productive life, he served as an example of the possible. He had been inspired by a veteran he had seen at Brooke during his own rehab, a guy who had lost both arms and visited the amputee ward when he came back for checkups. The man offered matter-of-fact, useful advice to the new amputees, and to Mayer that felt about right. He never sympathized—he didn't need to—and never told his own story unless someone asked. He was a quiet presence in Walter Reed's Ward 57, nicknamed "Amputee Alley," but in one way he stood out from the other Red Cross Volunteers: he brought milkshakes from McDonald's.

The milkshake run started with a request by one patient. But when Mayer thought about it, milkshakes seemed like the perfect thing, a cold, sweet, American treat—a milkshake tastes like home. Mayer started bringing milkshakes without being asked, an average of forty-five a week. He became the local McDonald's "Most Valued Customer," but more importantly, he became a most valued presence in the ward.

US Air Force Tech. Sgt. Adam Popp, an explosive ordinance disposal technician—the guys who disarm unexploded bombs, IEDs, and booby traps—lost his right leg to one of the latter in Afghanistan. Like many of the young wounded warriors at Walter Reed, Technical Sergeant Popp's introduction to Jim Mayer was via the milkshake route. "Yeah, he brought me a milkshake," Popp said with a smile. And while Adam Popp would be leaning on crutches for a while before he would be able to get the full use of his new prosthetic leg, he could also lean on Jim Mayer and another double amputee, US Marine Corps Vietnam veteran Bill Johnston.

Johnston, like Mayer, had stepped on a mine in Vietnam. It happened in 1970 when Johnston was about halfway through his thirteen-month tour of duty. He rehabbed in the Philadelphia Naval Hospital, where he met a Korean War veteran who occasionally visited the ward. And like the armless veteran whose visits at Brooke had inspired Jim Mayer, the Korean vet impressed Johnston with the same sort of approach—quiet, informative, matter-of-fact. After completing rehab, Johnston traveled the world for a couple of years, able to fly space-available for free on military planes. Then he went to college, earned a master's degree in rehab therapy, and went to work helping others. When he came to Walter Reed for additional therapy for himself, he started a wheelchair basketball program.

The Medical Center encouraged its amputee patients to challenge themselves physically, through sports like wheelchair basketball. Adam Popp said he had been skiing twice and was taking scuba lessons. The next day, vans rolled up to the Center and took a dozen or so wounded warriors out to the Virginia countryside to go fly-fishing.

Healing Waters

Bill Johnston loves trout fishing, but on this May day he was happy just watching the younger guys. He rolled his chair up to the edge of the bank of the Rose River and looked down into the cold, pristine mountain water, where maybe a dozen fat rainbow trout were holding in the gentle current. Johnston and a platoon of wounded warriors were guests of Doug Dear's Rose River Farm, a fly-fishing-only paradise in the Virginia Piedmont, and of Project Healing Waters Fly Fishing.

Vietnam veteran Ed Nicholson, a retired Navy captain, founded Project Healing Waters in 2005 after being treated for prostate cancer at Walter Reed Army Medical Center and seeing how the younger generation of wounded warriors faced adversity. Nicholson, an avid angler, thought that fly-fishing, an accessible, contemplative pastime, would help the men heal the psychic wounds of war. He started the first chapter of Project Healing Waters at Walter Reed, and, as good ideas do, it spread across the country and serves wounded warriors through VA hospitals and other facilities that treat the soldiers who return from combat with life-altering injuries. The organization works with local angling groups, such as Trout Unlimited, to arrange for one-on-one volunteer mentors, places to fish, transportation, and all the requirements for a fishing expedition that can be one day or several days long.

Project Healing Waters doesn't just lead the vets to water and hand them a fly rod. It offers basic training in fly-fishing; classes in fly-tying, rod building, and fly-casting; and the equipment and materials, at no cost to the veterans.

At the Rose River Farm on that day in May, the Walter Reed warriors and their mentor-guides were competing in a two-fly tournament. Each two-angler team started the day with only two trout flies, and if they lost them, too bad. Each fish caught was measured by one of the volunteer streamside observers and released back into the river; at the end of the day, the team that had landed the most fish-inches won a trophy. The day was sunny and warm, the mood mostly buoyant—except for nineteen-year-old Joe Devan, who had lost his right leg below the knee in Iraq when an IED smashed his Humvee. Joe was there with his equally young wife, Stephanie, but he was not enjoying himself. Would any nineteen-year-old, recently married and more recently wounded, be radiating happiness about life's prospects? But the stream, the casting, and the catching worked their magic. By the time the fishing ended, Joe was radiant, and he went off in search of Stephanie to tell her proudly, "I caught a rainbow!"

Opposite page: US Navy veteran Rusty Emmerton, who lost his right arm in a shipboard accident, uses his prosthesis to grip a fly rod at Rose River Farm on a fly-fishing trip sponsored by Project Healing Waters.

Jan C. Scruggs served with the 199th Light Infantry Brigade near Saigon in 1969 and 1970. Years after his return to the United States, he had a vision that dominated his life for several years—a national Vietnam memorial. Today, he has a new mission: to build the Education Center at The Wall.

When I first got home, it wasn't such a neat thing to be a Vietnam veteran. It wasn't as though I thought somebody should have bought me a new suit or anything, but I did think I deserved some appreciation. I was amazed at the fervent antiwar sentiment and the kind of scarlet letter one had for being a Vietnam veteran.

I went to college and then enrolled at American University in Washington to get my master's degree in psychology. I did research on Vietnam veterans' readjustment and even testified about my data before a US Senate subcommittee in 1977. I found out some amazing things. One of them was that the divorce rate of the Vietnam combat veterans was three times higher than that of the Vietnam noncombat veteran or the pre–Vietnam era veteran. Another was that combat veterans were significantly less trustful of people and authority.

From my research came the idea for a Vietnam memorial. I read all kinds of books on the psychiatry and psychology of trauma. From them I got the idea of collective states of mind: collective guilt, collective shame, collective pride. I thought that if a memorial could be built, and if indeed it had the names of those who had given their lives, it would be unifying for both veterans and the country. It would give the veterans who came back a kind of welcome, because it would be built and supported by everyone, regardless how they felt about the war. In terms of the collective psychology of America, it would provide the country with a shrine, a place that everyone could feel good about, in one way or another, and a place that could absolve a certain amount of guilt and bitterness about the war in both participants and nonparticipants.

But the design of the memorial itself was shrouded in controversy. In the spring of 1981, we staged the largest design competition ever held in the United States, and the winner was Maya Ying Lin's design of a wall bearing the names of the dead. Over the next several months, there were extraordinarily heated and emotional arguments against it, saying it was a "black gash of shame," asking why Vietnam veterans should be honored with a black ditch. After some negotiation, we agreed to add a traditional statue and flag to the memorial site.

It took three years, almost $9 million, and the support of many friends to build the Vietnam Veterans Memorial, commonly referred to as the Wall. During construction, we held a press conference at the site and called in the relatives of people we had identified from the panels. After the little ceremony, we noticed the way people reacted to the memorial: they wanted to touch the names, leave flowers and things there, and see their reflection in it. That's when it became obvious that the memorial was going to work. We knew that the memorial would be a success.

Over the past thirty years, Vietnam Veterans Memorial Fund has continued to heal the wounds of the Vietnam War. A traveling half-scale replica of the memorial, the Wall That Heals, has visited over 350 cities and towns throughout the nation. We host six annual ceremonies at the memorial and maintain an online database with photos and remembrances for every man and woman on the Wall. We develop and distribute education materials to teachers across the country.

But I believe that these efforts are no longer enough. Many of the visitors to the Wall weren't even alive when the memorial was dedicated. For them, the names etched in granite are faceless and lacking in historical context. They have no firsthand knowledge of the Vietnam War, the reason for the Wall, or the nation's reaction to this memorial. It is now my mission to build the Education Center at the Wall. Across the street from the Vietnam Veterans Memorial and in the shadow of the Lincoln Memorial, the Education Center will be a place where our heroes' stories and sacrifices will never be forgotten.

Here, visitors will come face to face with those who gave their lives in service to this country and explore a selection of the personal effects left so lovingly for them at the Wall. Visitors will learn about the politics and tactics of the Vietnam War, in the war zone and on the home front, while understanding its place in American history.

The Wall changed America in ways we couldn't have expected. It began a process of welcoming home the Vietnam veterans and giving them their just due—recognition and respect for the sacrifices they made. The memorial began an era of American culture in which service is honored and elevated. Today, we say "Welcome home" and "Thank you for your service" to every man and woman in a uniform.

Visitors at the Vietnam Veterans Memorial in Washington, D.C., on the day before its official dedication, November 12, 1982.

The Education Center will help the next generation of Americans to understand why this change is so important; it will teach them to never again allow what happened to the Vietnam veterans to happen to another American service member. The center will also display the photos of those Americans who have given their lives in service to the nation since September 11, 2001, until such a time as they have their own memorial.

There is so much that the Vietnam Veterans Memorial can still teach us, and I do not want to let those lessons fade away into obscurity. I hope to make the Education Center at the Wall a reality in the near future, ensuring that the legacy of those who answered America's call to duty will be preserved for generations to come.

EPILOGUE

The Vietnam War veterans came home to a nation that wanted nothing more than to put the war behind it. The veterans stayed low, kept their heads down, and tried to blend into the fabric of civilian life without calling attention to themselves. It took years of healing and reflection for Americans to open up to these veterans and for the veterans to open up to their country.

Not long after I returned from my service in Vietnam, I was asked to speak to a group of middle school students about Memorial Day. I told them that the soldiers who had fought in the Vietnam War were the same as the soldiers who had fought in other, more glorified wars. They did their duty. They fought bravely and with honor. Some fought heroically, "above and beyond," in the well-known words of the Medal of Honor citation. Many of them paid the ultimate price. You may not have thought well of the war, I told the students, but please do not think badly of the warriors.

Perhaps it was just the passage of time; perhaps it was the sight of a new generation of warriors going off to fight in foreign lands; perhaps the Vietnam Veterans Memorial—the Wall, which is one of the most popular memorials in a city that has many—touched the nation's collective heart. Maybe it was a combination of these things, and more, that made it possible for America to finally say to its Vietnam veterans:

"Welcome home."

—Nick Mills, Senior Writer

The Three Servicemen statue, with the Vietnam Veterans Memorial Wall in the distance, Washington, D.C. The sculpture, depicting Vietnam War servicemen in uniform, was designed to complement the Wall and was dedicated as part of the memorial two years after the Wall opened.

Senior writer Nick Mills traveled back to Vietnam in 2003 for the first time since his tour of duty.

From deep in the Mekong Delta to the sidewalks of Hanoi, from the bustling traffic of Saigon to the sandy beaches of Da Nang, the physical scars of war have mostly healed in Vietnam. Countryside that had been pocked with countless bomb craters is now smooth and green with ripening rice. Where the dusty, sprawling American bases once stood are modern industrial centers or entire new towns. It is difficult to spot traces of our once ubiquitous and very heavy bootprint.

Saigon

Saigon by any other name is still Saigon. That's one of the first things one realizes upon arrival in what has been called, since 1975, Ho Chi Minh City. Gone is the look of military occupation, but the heart of the city beats as strongly as ever. HCMC is a hustling, bustling, on-the-make capitalist metropolis, buzzing with motorbikes and swarming with street vendors, pedicabs, and pedestrians.

On the streets, two-wheeled traffic reigns. The major thoroughfares resemble vast schools of noisy fish migrating up- and downstream, and crossing these streets on foot seems a death-defying act—or at least an injury-defying one. Observe natives doing it and you think it's a conjurer's trick. They just wade into the school, unhurried, and miraculously make it to the other side unscathed. Finally summoning the nerve, you step off the curb to discover that the motorized fish swim gracefully around you. Don't hesitate, and don't make eye contact, and you will live to cross the next street.

Standing in the way of the traffic chaos are stern-faced young women in blue shirts and bush hats waving triangular red flags with military precision. They regulate the flow at intersections with grave authority and a book of traffic tickets. They tell the swarms of scooters when to stop—and they do stop, lest their names and license numbers be logged into the traffic warden's notebook for further action.

The vast, covered Ben Thanh Market is national treasure. I never saw it when I was in Saigon as a soldier, but when I returned as a civilian, I spent a happy couple of hours there, sampling cuisine from the food stalls and browsing through the myriad wares on offer. Everything has a price, and every price is negotiable. I was tempted to try to bring home a bottle of rice wine with a pickled cobra inside, but sanity won out. On the sidewalks around the market are countless vendors selling whatever they can—fruit, handicrafts, trinkets. Free-market economics are alive and well on the sidewalks of HCMC.

There's a lot that is new—there are new hotels, new apartment blocks, high-end shops and restaurants—but an old soldier knows immediately where he is. Old landmarks still stand: the Rex Hotel

with its rooftop bar where we could drink cold beer while listening to the sounds and watching the flashes of not-too-distant warfare, is still here; the Caravelle and the Continental Palace, too, remain, although all the hotels have been smartly upgraded. Tu Do Street is now Dong Khoi Street, and fancy shopping has replaced the bars.

Top: Ho Chi Minh City. Above: Statue of Ho Chi Minh in front of the former Saigon City Hall, now the Ho Chi Minh City People's Committee Head Office.

Traffic in Ho Chi Minh City may seem chaotic (below, right), but the flow is regulated by young women with red flags.

Ben Thahn Market.

In 1965, Marines waded ashore onto the beaches of Da Nang. Later in the war, many battle-weary soldiers landed on those same sands to work on their tans and play in the surf for a brief in-country R&R. Now, bikini-clad sunbathers from around the world relax on Da Nang's beautiful beaches alongside Vietnam's rising middle class. Luxury hotels line the beachfront, while further down the coast, old Vietnam still exists in shantytowns and fishing villages. Boats are made entirely by hand; at night, they will head out into the bay with lanterns to fish for squid.

Hue, utterly devastated in the Tet battles of 1968, has remarkably rebuilt itself, charm intact, along the soft banks of the Perfume River where boatloads of tourists glide along to the strains of Vietnamese folk music. The walls of the ancient Citadel, reduced to rubble in the Marines' epic struggle to recapture the city, have been rebuilt, and the capital of imperial Vietnam is a popular tourist attraction. In the palace within the Citadel, giggling young Vietnamese don facsimiles of imperial robes and pose for pictures on the Emperor's throne.

Marines splash ashore at Da Nang beach in 1965 as Vietnam War combat operations begin.

Marines help a wounded comrade from atop the Citadel in Hue, during a battle with Communist troops in 1968.

Hanoi

Hanoi, though it has greatly expanded, is more sedate than HCMC, and its parks, pagodas, and temples reflect its centuries of culture and scholarship. The French left Vietnam with bad memories but beautiful architecture and broad, tree-lined boulevards replete with stately homes, many of which have been repurposed as offices and schools. Much is modern, but the old way of sweeping the sidewalks with long straw brooms continues—a soothing contrast to the mechanized sweepers so common in American cities. The magnificent Hanoi Opera House has been fully renovated and hosts performances ranging from classical opera to traditional Vietnamese pageants.

The infamous "Hanoi Hilton," the Hoa Lo Prison, where captured American servicemen were held in brutal conditions, is now a quiet museum. Its focus is not the "American War," as it's called in Vietnam, but the longer, cruel occupation by the French, who built the site in the late 1800s to hold political prisoners. Near the Opera House is the new Hanoi Hilton—officially named the Hanoi Opera Hilton after veterans protested to the Hilton hotel chain—where large-screen TVs in the sports bar carry international soccer matches and you can hear a Vietnamese all-women guitar quartet play Latin American music in the lounge. One might well wonder, *Where am I?*

Nearly seven million tourists visit Vietnam annually. They find fascinating history, world-class hotels, wonderful food, efficient transportation, and very welcoming people, many of whom are too young to have any memory of the war we fought there. Many American veterans of that war say they will never go back, but many who do find a beautiful and forgiving country, and a place where scars can be healed.

Much is modern in Hanoi, but the practice of sweeping the sidewalks with long straw brooms continues.

A Hanoi sidewalk in 1967: a resident peers out from a bunker during a US air attack.

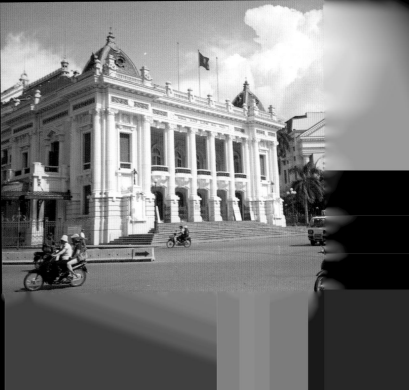

Above: The "Hanoi Hilton" (Hoa Lo Prison) today.
Right: The Hanoi Opera House.

Timeline

100 BC (approx.) — Chinese forces conquer and consolidate several northern provinces of what today is Vietnam. China dominates Vietnam for roughly a thousand years.

938 AD — Ngo Quyen defeats Chinese forces to win Vietnam's independence, and Vietnam begins a centuries-long southward expansion that envelopes the Mekong Delta region in the eighteenth century.

16th–17th c. — Civil wars between warlords divide Vietnam north and south.

1620 — French Jesuit missionary Alexandre de Rhodes arrives in Indochina, beginning centuries of French involvement in Vietnam.

1787–1789 — Nguyen Anh, with limited military assistance from France, captures Saigon and unifies Vietnam, ruling as Emperor Gia Long. This marks France's first military role in Vietnam.

1858–1859 — Napoleon III's forces attack and capture Da Nang and Saigon. The French are primarily interested in Vietnam's natural resources, especially rubber, coffee, and tea. They also hope to establish a base for trading with China.

1884–1885 — The Sino-French War. France drives China from northern Vietnam.

1887 — French Indochina is formed, encompassing modern Vietnam plus Cambodia. Resistance to French rule is already underway.

1890 — Ho Chi Minh is born in Quang Ngai Province.

1940 — Nazi Germany conquers France, and the Vichy government is given administrative power in Indochina. Japan, already fighting in China, enters Indochina in pursuit of the deep-water ports of Da Nang and Saigon to support its military expansion in the Pacific as it drives toward its objective, Australia. The Japanese allow the Vichy government to remain in a puppet role. Under Japanese occupation, millions of Vietnamese starve to death.

1941 — Ho Chi Minh returns to Indochina after decades of Communist organizing activities in France, the USSR, and Hong Kong, and establishes the Viet Minh, an anti-colonialist, nationalist independence movement.

The Viet Minh supply intelligence reports on the Japanese to the American Office of Strategic Services (OSS).

1942 — Ho Chi Minh goes to China to work with the anti-Japanese underground and is held there for two years by the *Kuomintang*, the Chinese Nationalist Party.

1945 — Events lead to Ho Chi Minh's declaration of independence:

April 12–President Roosevelt dies.

May 7–Germany surrenders.

August 6 and 9–Atomic bombs are dropped on Hiroshima and Nagasaki.

August 15–Japan surrenders and withdraws forces from China and Vietnam.

September 2–Ho Chi Minh declares Vietnam's independence, but within weeks a British-French force re-establishes French rule and the First Indochina War begins, between France and the Viet Minh.

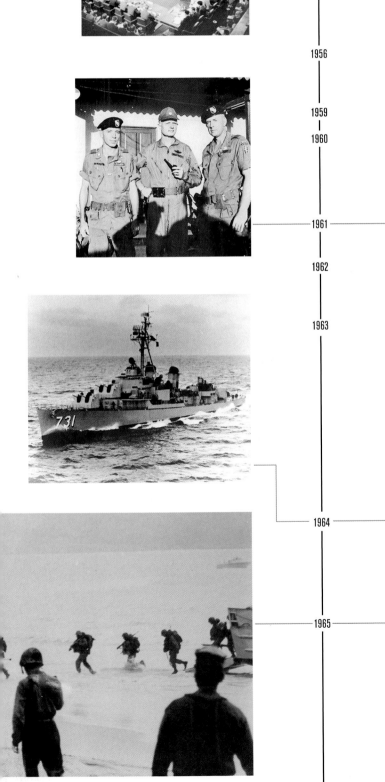

1946	Vietnam's first National Assembly elections are won in the northern and central provinces by the Viet Minh.
1950	President Harry Truman sends the first US Military Assistance Advisory Group (MAAG) to South Vietnam.
1954	The Viet Minh defeat the French at Dien Bien Phu.
	The Geneva Conference provisionally divides Vietnam, leaving Ho Chi Minh's Communist government in power in the north and the US-backed regime of Ngo Dinh Diem ruling the south. France is required to withdraw all armed forces from Indochina.
	The US increases financial aid to South Vietnam.
1956	Elections to unify Vietnam, mandated by the Geneva Conference, are rejected by the Saigon government, with encouragement from the US, due to the near certainty that Ho Chi Minh would win.
1959	Chester Ovnand and Dale Buis become the first two US casualties of the Vietnam conflict.
1960	The number of MAAG advisors in South Vietnam is more than doubled, to 685. US advisors are coming under more frequent attack by Communist guerrillas.
	The National Liberation Front is formed in South Vietnam; the NLF becomes known as the Viet Cong.
1961	President John F. Kennedy increases military aid to South Vietnam and sends four hundred Green Berets to train South Vietnamese soldiers.
1962	Operation Ranch Hand begins the widespread spraying of the herbicide Agent Orange in South Vietnam to defoliate the forests and deny cover to insurgents; the spraying will continue until 1971.
1963	Viet Cong defeat a large South Vietnamese military force at the battle of Ap Bac. Three American advisors are killed.
	South Vietnamese military officers stage a successful coup with the unspoken approval of the US; President Diem and his brother Ngo Dinh Thuc are killed.
	Gen. Duong Van "Big" Minh heads the military junta that rules South Vietnam after the assassination of Diem; Minh is ousted by another coup after three months.
	President Kennedy increases US military presence in South Vietnam from nine hundred to eighteen thousand.
	November 22—President Kennedy is assassinated.
1964	The US claims that the warship USS *Maddox* is attacked on August 2 and 4 by North Vietnamese gunboats in the Gulf of Tonkin. It is later determined that the August 4 claim was false.
	The US Congress passes the Gulf of Tonkin Resolution, giving President Lyndon Johnson broad powers to defend South Vietnam.
1965	The US Marine 9th Brigade comes ashore at Da Nang.
	Operation Rolling Thunder begins. The three-and-a-half-year bombing campaign would drop 864,000 tons of bombs on North Vietnam between March 1965 and November 1968.

Operation Starlight, the US's first major battle of the war, is launched at Chu Lai.

The 1st Air Cavalry fights three NVA regiments for thirty-five days in the battle of Ia Drang.

1966

Operation Birmingham, north of Saigon, finds few Viet Cong.

Operation Hastings, near the DMZ, pits the 3rd Marine Division against the NVA 324B Division in the battle of Dong Ha.

The battle of Con Thien leaves 1,300 NVA soldiers dead.

1967

NVA artillery bombards Khe Sanh and the Rockpile.

Operation Cedar Falls sends thirty thousand American and ARVN troops into the Iron Triangle.

Operation Junction City features a massive airmobile assault in Tay Ninh Province.

1968

The siege of Khe Sanh continues.

The Viet Cong launch the Tet Offensive.

The My Lai Massacre leaves hundreds of Vietnamese civilians dead.

Operation Pegasus ends the siege of Khe Sanh after seventy-seven days. The base is dismantled and abandoned.

Rolling Thunder is ended after three and a half years.

American troop strength in South Vietnam reaches 500,000, on its way to 550,000.

1969

President Richard Nixon takes office promising to achieve "peace with honor."

Nixon announces the withdrawal of twenty-five thousand US troops.

1970

US and ARVN forces push into Cambodia.

1971

Operation Lam Son 719 results in three ARVN divisions decimated in Laos.

Daniel Ellsberg leaks the Pentagon Papers to the *New York Times*, which goes on to publish excerpts.

The Nixon administration obtains a federal court injunction halting the *Times*' publication of the Pentagon Papers.

Daniel Ellsberg and Anthony Russo are indicted under the Espionage Act.

The US Supreme Court overturns the injunction and the *Times* resumes publishing excerpts from the Pentagon Papers.

1972

Only 133,000 US troops remain in South Vietnam, most in support roles.

The Paris Peace Accords break down.

Nixon orders Operation Linebacker, a new bombing campaign against North Vietnam.

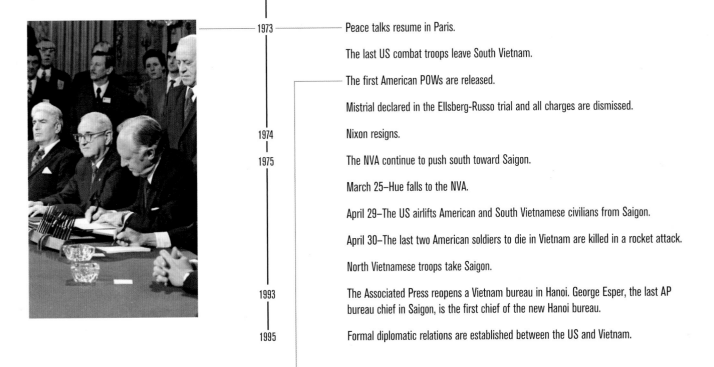

1973 — Peace talks resume in Paris.

The last US combat troops leave South Vietnam.

The first American POWs are released.

Mistrial declared in the Ellsberg-Russo trial and all charges are dismissed.

1974 — Nixon resigns.

1975 — The NVA continue to push south toward Saigon.

March 25–Hue falls to the NVA.

April 29–The US airlifts American and South Vietnamese civilians from Saigon.

April 30–The last two American soldiers to die in Vietnam are killed in a rocket attack.

North Vietnamese troops take Saigon.

1993 — The Associated Press reopens a Vietnam bureau in Hanoi. George Esper, the last AP bureau chief in Saigon, is the first chief of the new Hanoi bureau.

1995 — Formal diplomatic relations are established between the US and Vietnam.

Glossary

AFVN Armed Forces Vietnam Network, the radio service notably portrayed in the film *Good Morning, Vietnam*.

airburst Munitions designed to explode above the ground, such as anti-aircraft airbursts (or flak) and anti-personnel ground artillery designed to explode above the heads of opposing ground forces.

AK-47 The Kalashnikov military assault rifle, used by the Viet Cong and the North Vietnamese Army.

AO Area of Operations

APC Armored Personnel Carrier. The M113 APC was used extensively in Vietnam. It could carry a crew of two, plus eleven infantrymen, and could withstand small-arms fire. The APC carried a turret-mounted .50-caliber machine gun but could also be fitted with grenade launchers and antitank missiles.

arc light B-52 air strikes that generally involved a "cell" of three or more B-52s, which each dropped 108 500-pound bombs from high altitudes.

arty Artillery. The basic land-based artillery guns used in Vietnam include the 105mm howitzer, which had a firing range of about seven miles; and the 155mm howitzer, a bigger gun with a range of approximately eleven miles. Both weapons could be towed or airlifted. There was also a self-propelled version of the 155mm howitzer, a heavily armored tracked vehicle.

Naval artillery, fired from warships offshore, was also heavily used in Vietnam in support of troops in the field. The battleship USS *New Jersey* served one tour in Vietnam; her 16-inch guns could fire a 2,700-pound projectile about 25 miles.

ARVN Army of the Republic of Vietnam—the South Vietnamese army

BDA Bomb damage assessment following an air strike

Bouncing Betty An antipersonnel mine developed by the Germans in World War II and used by the Viet Cong during the Vietnam War. When activated by being stepped on, a preliminary explosion launched the device about three feet into the air, where it would detonate, spraying shrapnel in all directions.

CAP Civic Action Program. Part of the "hearts and minds" effort, these programs offered medical (MEDCAP), sanitation, agricultural, and other kinds of support for Vietnamese civilians.

CAV Army air mobile units

CIDG Civilian Irregular Defense Group. In the early 1960s, the US Special Forces recruited and trained Montagnard tribesmen and established camps along the Laotian border to monitor the Ho Chi Minh Trail.

Claymore mine A command-detonated, directional antipersonnel mine that fired metal balls into a killing zone.

COSVN Central Office for South Vietnam. The possibly mythical North Vietnamese military and political headquarters, believed to be operating somewhere inside South Vietnam or in Cambodia. Its existence was never fully confirmed.

C-rations Official designation: MCI ("Meal, Combat, Individual"). A packaged meal for troops in the field, usually called C-rats or Charlie Rats. The MCI came in a dozen varieties, each of which included a canned meat entrée such as beefsteak; chicken or turkey loaf; or the least favorite, ham and lima beans, often called "ham and motherfuckers." The package also included some combination of canned fruit, cookies or pound cake, crackers and cheese spread, and white bread and peanut butter. C-rations were replaced by MREs (Meals, Ready-to-Eat) in 1975.

CTZ Corps Tactical Zone. Vietnam was divided into four CTZs, known as I Corps, II Corps, III Corps, and IV Corps.

DEROS Date of Expected Return from Overseas. This is the date every short-timer counted down to.

DMZ The Demilitarized Zone that separated North and South Vietnam. The line between North and South was established at the Geneva Conference of 1954, when the French surrendered to the Viet Minh. The DMZ extended for three miles on either side of the line. Military forces were barred from the zone, though this was an often-violated protocol.

FAC Forward Air Controller. This person coordinated air strikes, usually from a light aircraft flying over a battle scene.

fighting hole A defensive fighting position, generally a foxhole for more than one person surrounded by sand bags; sometimes included a tin or wood roof.

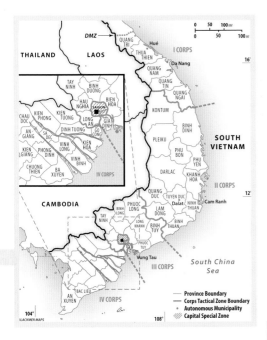

FO Forward Observer. A member of a field unit who coordinated the placement of artillery and other indirect or direct fire.

freedom bird The aircraft that took a soldier home from Vietnam

friendlies Friendly forces

friendly fire Fire mistakenly directed at friendly forces, often due to the "fog of war" confusion of the battlefield or mistaken identification of friendly troops as enemy forces.

FSB Fire Support Base. A sometimes-temporary base, often on a hilltop, for one or more artillery batteries to support troops in the field who were operating beyond the range of the artillery at their home base.

getting hosed Being fired at by automatic weapons; the tracers appear to wave through the air like water from a garden hose.

grunt An infantry soldier, sometimes called a "boonie-rat," whose primary job in Vietnam was to "hump the boonies," meaning to go into the field on foot in search of the enemy.

GVN Government of Vietnam

HE High-explosives weapons, such as bombs or artillery shells

Hmong A Laotian hill tribe, many of whom were recruited by US Special Forces to fight against the Communist forces in Vietnam and Laos.

Ho Chi Minh Trail The supply route from North Vietnam to South Vietnam, used by the Communists to bring troops, weapons, and other supplies to the south.

hootch Living quarters. GIs referred to all types of living spaces, from their own bunkers to Vietnamese huts, as hootches. At a base camp, hootches were often swept and cleaned by local Vietnamese "hootch girls."

Huey The UH-1 helicopter, the most ubiquitous aircraft in the Vietnam War. The Huey could be configured as a troop carrier or a gunship.

in-country/out-country In Vietnam/Outside Vietnam (e.g., Laos, Cambodia, or anywhere else)

KIA/WIA/MIA Killed in Action/Wounded in Action/Missing in Action. There were 1,643 Americans listed as MIA in Southeast Asia as of January 1, 2014. By comparison, 73,640 are listed as WWII MIA and 7,896 from the Korean War.

klick Kilometer

KP "Kitchen Police." New recruits and low-ranking enlisted men were assigned to work a shift (or several) in a mess hall doing menial work.

LZ Landing Zone. A predetermined area where helicopters could land to insert or recover troops in the field. Some LZs were semi-permanent, while others were temporary. A "hot LZ" was one that was under fire; a "cold LZ" was one that was not.

M16 The US military assault rifle that became the standard-issue weapon in Vietnam, replacing the World War II–era M14. The M16 was plagued with reliability problems when first issued and had a reputation for jamming in combat.

M60 The standard machine gun carried by infantry platoons. The M60 is a belt-fed 7.62mm gun that can be shoulder-fired, but it usually is set on its built-in bipod. The M60 generally required a crew of two or three men: the gunner; the assistant gunner (AG), who carried ammo and fed the ammo belts into the gun while it was being fired; and an occasional third crew-member to carry additional ammo.

MAAGV The US Military Assistance and Advisory Group, Vietnam, established in 1955 to coordinate the military assistance to South Vietnam by elements of the US Army, Marines, Navy, and Air Force. MAAGV was absorbed into MACV in 1964 as the United States' role began to expand into combat operations.

MACV Military Assistance Command, Vietnam. This was a joint-services command created in 1962 to oversee and direct MAAGV's advisory and assistance efforts; in 1964, MAAGV was disbanded and its personnel shifted to MACV as US military operations grew.

Montagnards Refers to several tribes or clans of Vietnamese mountain people

napalm Jellied petroleum, one of the war's most controversial weapons. Burning napalm clings to the skin and causes excruciatingly painful burns. Its use against civilians was banned internationally in 1980.

NLF National Liberation Front (the Viet Cong)

NVA North Vietnamese Army

number one An expression often used by Vietnamese to mean "the best." The opposite end of the scale was number ten–"the worst."

Psy Ops Psychological Operations, conducted by US (and enemy) forces, which included propaganda leaflets, radio broadcasts aimed at demoralizing enemy troops, and disinformation.

PTSD Posttraumatic stress disorder. An anxiety disorder that may affect a soldier for years after being in combat, resulting in nightmares, flashbacks, violent behavior, depression, and alcohol or drug abuse, among other maladies. PTSD is also common in civilian life after an individual experiences some sort of trauma. PTSD did not become a recognized disorder for years after the Vietnam War, delaying treatment for many veterans.

Punji sticks Sharpened wooden spikes, driven into the ground and concealed, meant to inflict a painful wound on an enemy. Punji sticks, or Punji stakes, were often used in Viet Cong booby traps (Punji pits). Sometimes the sticks were treated with poisons or feces. The wounds were usually not fatal, but they took a soldier out of combat and halted his unit's progress.

R&R Rest and Recreation. Every soldier who served in Vietnam was entitled to a one-week R&R "vacation" from the war in one of several destinations, including Hawaii; Sydney, Australia; Hong Kong; and Bangkok, Thailand.

RPG Rocket-Propelled Grenade. A high-explosive, shoulder-fired grenade directed against personnel, vehicles, or aircraft at close range.

RTO Radio-Telephone Operator. All units in the field had an RTO who carried a portable radio for communicating with other units and with headquarters. The RTO was often a target of enemy snipers; without a radio, a unit could not call in air or artillery support or call for reinforcements.

sapper A Viet Cong commando, usually carrying explosives, who would lead an attack by infiltrating barbed-wire perimeter defenses and blowing up bunkers or other structures in a base camp.

short-timer The closer a soldier got to his DEROS date, the "shorter" he got. Many short-timers kept track by notching a stick or filling in spaces on a calendar.

smoke Various types and colors of smoke were deployed to mark targets for air and artillery strikes or landing zones for helicopters. Troops on the ground would "pop smoke"–detonate a smoke grenade–to signal to an approaching aircraft where to land and whether it was safe to land. Artillery gunners fired white phosphorus, called "willie pete," as a marker for a forward observer to direct fire or to create a smokescreen to hide the movement of friendly forces.

SOG Studies and Observation Group, a clandestine unit controlled by the Pentagon to conduct cross-border reconnaissance and other classified operations, including "body snatches" in Laos, Cambodia, and North Vietnam.

SOP Standard Operating Procedures

Tet The Vietnamese New Year, the most important celebration of the year. The date of Tet is determined by the lunar cycle and marks the beginning of spring. The countrywide Communist attacks on the eve of Tet in 1968 marked a turning point in the war.

tunnel rats American soldiers who volunteered to crawl through the enemy's extensive tunnel complexes. Starting with the war against the French, the Communist guerrillas created large underground complexes where they would be relatively safe from bombing and artillery. The complexes held command headquarters, supplies, hospitals, training facilities, and more.

unit designations An Army or Marine *division* consists of 10,000 to 15,000 soldiers. Each Army division includes three or more *brigades* of 3,000 to 5,000 troops; the Marines call these units *regiments*. Brigades and regiments are each subdivided into three to five *battalions* of roughly 1,000 soldiers. A battalion usually consists of four *companies*, designated by letters and referred to as Alpha Company, Bravo Company, and so on. The companies are divided into *platoons* of roughly fifty soldiers, and the platoons are further subdivided into *squads* or *sections* and *fire teams*. A unit designator such as "the 2/12 Cavalry" signifies 2nd Battalion, 12th Cavalry Brigade.

Bibliography

Amter, Joseph A. *Vietnam Verdict.* Continuum, 1982.

Anderton, David A. *The History of the US Air Force.* Crescent Books, 1981.

Arlen, Michael J. *The Living Room War.* Viking Press, 1969.

Bain, Chester A. *Vietnam: The Roots of Conflict.* Prentice-Hall, 1967.

Baskir, Lawrence M., and William A. Strauss. *Chance and Circumstance.* Alfred A. Knopf, 1978.

BDM Corporation. *A Study of the Strategic Lessons Learned in Vietnam, Vols. 1–8.* National Technical Information Service, 1980.

Berger, Carl, ed. *The United States Air Force in Southeast Asia, 1961–1973.* Office of Air Force History, 1977.

Booher, Neil W. "President Johnson, Harrison Salisbury and the Contradictions of a Limited War," *The Fellows Review 2011–2012.* Center for the Study of the Presidency and Congress.

Bowman, John S., ed. *The Vietnam War Almanac.* World Almanac Publications/Bison Books, 1985.

Braestrup, Peter. *Big Story: How the American Press and Television Reported and Interpreted the Crisis of Tet 1968 in Vietnam and Washington.* Westview Press, 1977.

Burchett, Wilfred G. *Vietnam: The Inside Story of the Guerrilla War.* International Publishers, 1965.

Butler, David. *The Fall of Saigon: Scenes from the Sudden End of a Long War.* Simon & Schuster, 1985.

Butterfield, Fox. "In Hanoi, Leaders and the Public Seem Confident." *New York Times*, December 16, 1969.

Buzzanco, Robert. *Masters of War: Military Dissent and Politics in the Vietnam Era.* Cambridge University Press, 1996.

Campbell, W. Joseph. *Ten of the Greatest Misreported Stories in American Journalism.* University of California Press, 2010.

Caputo, Philip. *A Rumor of War.* Ballantine Books, 1977.

Casey, Michael, et al. *The Army at War.* Boston Publishing Company, 1987.

———. *Flags into Battle.* Boston Publishing Company, 1987.

Charlton, Michael, and Anthony Moncrieff. *Many Reasons Why: The American Involvement in Vietnam.* Hill & Wang, 1978.

Cooper, Chester L. *The Lost Crusade: America in Vietnam.* Fawcett Publications, 1972.

Dawson, Alan. *55 Days: The Fall of South Vietnam.* Prentice-Hall, 1977.

Dougan, Clark, and David Fulghum. *The Fall of the South.* Boston Publishing Company, 1986.

Dougan, Clark, and Stephen Weiss. *Nineteen Sixty-Eight.* Boston Publishing Company, 1983.

Doyle, Edward, and Samuel Lipsman. *America Takes Over.* Boston Publishing Company, 1982.

———. *Setting the Stage.* Boston Publishing Company, 1981.

Doyle, Edward, Samuel Lipsman, and Terrence Maitland. *The North.* Boston Publishing Company, 1986.

Doyle, Edward, Samuel Lipsman, and Stephen Weiss. *Passing the Torch.* Boston Publishing Company, 1981.

Doyle, Edward, and Stephen Weiss. *A Collision of Cultures.* Boston Publishing Company, 1984.

Draper, Theodore. *Abuse of Power.* Viking Press, 1967.

Drendel, Lou. *The Air War in Vietnam.* Arco Publishing Company, 1968.

Dylan, Bob. "Subterranean Homesick Blues," 1965.

Ehrhart, W. D. *Vietnam-Perkasie: A Combat Marine Memoir.* McFarland & Company, 1983.

Ellsberg, Daniel. *Secrets: A Memoir of Vietnam and the Pentagon Papers.* Penguin, 2003.

Emerson, Gloria. *Winners & Losers.* Harcourt Brace Jovanovich, 1976.

Fallaci, Oriana. *Interview with History.* Translated by John Shepley. Liveright, 1976.

Fallows, James. "What Did You Do in the Class War, Daddy?" *Washington Monthly*, October 1975.

FitzGerald, Frances. *Fire in the Lake: The Vietnamese and the Americans in Vietnam.* Vintage Books, 1973.

Fowler, Will. *The Vietnam Story.* Chartwell Books, 1983.

Fromson, Murray. "And That's the Way It Was . . ." *Huffington Post*, July 21, 2009

Frook, John. "Here's a New Crop—From Civilians to Sad Sacks." *Life*, August 20, 1965.

Fulghum, David, and Terrence Maitland. *South Vietnam on Trial.* Boston Publishing Company, 1984.

Gallup, George H. *The Gallup Poll: Public Opinion, 1935–1971.* Random House, 1972.

Gallup Organization. *Gallup Opinion Index.* Gallup, June 1965–January 1981.

Gelb, Arthur. *City Room.* Putnam, 2003.

Gitlin, Todd. *The Whole World Is Watching.* University of California Press, 1980.

Glasser, Ronald J., M.D. *365 Days.* George Braziller, 1980.

Gravel, Sen. Mike, ed. *The Pentagon Papers, Vol. I–IV.* Beacon Press, 1971.

Halberstam, David. *The Best and the Brightest.* Random House, 1972.

———. *The Making of a Quagmire.* Random House, 1964.

———. *The Powers That Be.* Alfred A. Knopf, 1979.

———. *The Unfinished Odyssey of Robert F. Kennedy.* Random House, 1968.

Hallin, Daniel. *The "Uncensored War": The Media and Vietnam.* University of California Press, 1989.

Hearts and Minds. Dir. Peter Davis, 1974.

Herr, Michael. *Dispatches.* Alfred A. Knopf, 1977.

Herring, George C. *America's Longest War: The United States and Vietnam, 1950–1975.* John Wiley & Sons, 1979.

Herrington, Stuart A. *Peace with Honor: An American Reports on Vietnam 1973–1975*. Presidio Press, 1983.

——. *Silence Was a Weapon: The Vietnam War in the Villages*. Presidio Press, 1982.

Hersh, Seymour. *My Lai 4: A Report on the Massacre and Its Aftermath*. Vintage Books, 1970.

Hodgson, Godfrey. *America in Our Time: From World War II to Nixon*. Doubleday, 1976.

Hoopes, Townsend. *The Limits of Intervention*. Revised edition. David McKay Company, 1973.

Hosmer, Stephen T. *Viet Cong Repression and Its Implications for the Future*. Heath, 1970.

Hosmer, Stephen T. et al., eds. *The Fall of South Vietnam: Statements by Vietnamese Military and Civilian Leaders*. Crane, Russak & Company, 1980.

Isaacs, Arnold R. *Without Honor: Defeat in Vietnam and Cambodia*. Johns Hopkins University Press, 1983.

Isaacs, Arnold R., and Gordon Hardy. *Pawns of War*. Boston Publishing Company, 1987.

Jennings, Patrick. *Battles of the Vietnam War*. Exeter Books, 1985.

Johnson, Lyndon Baines. Presidential Papers of Lyndon Baines Johnson (unpublished). White House Central File, National Security File, White House Aides File, Meeting Notes File, Declassified and Sanitized Documents, Oral History Interviews. Lyndon Baines Johnson Library, Austin, Texas.

——. *The Vantage Point*. Holt, Rinehart, & Winston, 1971.

Kahin, George McTurnan, and John W. Lewis. *The United States in Vietnam*. Dell Publishing Company, 1969.

Karnow, Stanley. *Vietnam: A History*. Penguin Books, 1983.

Kearns, Doris. *Lyndon Johnson and the American Dream*. Harper & Row, 1976.

Kerner Commission Report, Chapter 15, "The News Media and the Disorders." Quote appears on page 366 in *New York Times* edition, which includes an Introduction by Tom Wicker.

Kissinger, Henry A. *White House Years*. Little, Brown, 1979.

——. *Years of Upheaval*. Little, Brown, 1982.

Le Gro, Col. William E. *Vietnam from Cease-Fire to Capitulation*. US Army Center of Military History, 1981.

Lennon/McCartney, "Revolution 1," *The Beatles* ("The White Album"), 1968.

Lewy, Guenter. *America in Vietnam*. Oxford University Press, 1978.

Lifton, Robert J. *Home from the War*. Simon & Schuster, 1973.

Lipsman, Samuel, and Edward Doyle. *Fighting for Time*. Boston Publishing Company, 1983.

Lipsman, Samuel, and Stephen Weiss. *The False Peace*. Boston Publishing Company, 1985.

Maclear, Michael. *The Ten Thousand Day War: Vietnam, 1945–1975*. St. Martin's Press, 1981.

MacPherson, Myra. *Long Time Passing: Vietnam and the Haunted Generation*. Doubleday, 1984.

Maitland, Terrence, and Peter McInerney. *A Contagion of War*. Boston Publishing Company, 1983.

Maitland, Terrence, and Stephen Weiss. *Raising the Stakes*. Boston Publishing Company, 1982.

Manning, Robert, and Michael Janeway, eds. *Who We Are*. Atlantic-Little, Brown, 1969.

Matusow, Allen J. *The Unraveling of America: A History of Liberalism in the 1960s*. Harper & Row, 1984.

Millett, Allan R. *Semper Fidelis: The History of the United States Marine Corps*. Macmillan, 1980.

Morrocco, John. *Rain of Fire: Air War, 1969–1973*. Boston Publishing Company, 1985.

——. *Thunder From Above: Air War, 1941–1968*. Boston Publishing Company, 1984.

Moskin, J. Robert. *The US Marine Corps Story*. Paddington Press, 1979.

Murphy, Jack. *History of the US Marines*. Exeter Books, 1984.

Nalty, Bernard C. "Seventy-Seven Days: The Siege of Khe Sanh," from *The Vietnam War*. Salamander, 1980.

National Advisory Commission on Civil Disorders. *Report of National Advisory Commission on Civil Disorders*. Bantam Books, 1968.

Nixon, Richard. *RN: The Memoirs of Richard Nixon*. Grosset & Dunlap, 1978.

Oberdorfer, Don. *Tet!: The Turning Point in the Vietnam War*. Doubleday, 1971.

Palmer, Gen. Bruce, Jr. *The 25-Year War: America's Military Role in Vietnam*. University Press of Kentucky, 1984.

Parrish, John A., M.D. *12, 20 & 5: A Doctor's Year in Vietnam*. Penguin Books, 1972.

Pearson, Lt. Gen. Willard. *The War in the Northern Provinces 1966–1968*. Dept. of the Army, 1975.

Peatross, Brig. Gen. O. F., and Col. W. G. Johnson. "Operation Utah," *Marine Corps Gazette*, November 1966.

Perlstein, Rick. *Nixonland: The Rise of a President and the Fracturing of America*. Scribner, 2008.

Pike, Douglas. *Viet Cong*. The MIT Press, 1966.

Pimlott, John, ed. *Vietnam: The History and the Tactics*. Crescent Books, 1982.

Pisor, Robert. *The End of the Line: The Siege of Khe Sanh*. Norton, 1982.

Polenberg, Richard. *One Nation Divisible*. Viking Press, 1970.

Pratt, John Clark. *Vietnam Voices*. Penguin Books, 1984.

President's Commission on Campus Unrest. Report of President's Commission on Campus Unrest. GPO, 1970.

Pribbenow, Merle L. *Victory in Vietnam: The Official History of the People's Army of Vietnam, 1954–1975*. (Modern War Studies)

Race, Jeffrey. *War Comes to Long An: Revolutionary Conflict in a Vietnamese Province*. University of California Press, 1972.

Record, Jeffrey. *The Wrong War: Why We Lost in Vietnam*. Naval Institute Press, 1998.

"Renaissance in the Ranks," *Time*, December 10, 1965.

Sale, Kirkpatrick. *SDS*. Vintage Books, 1973.

Schandler, Herbert Y. *The Unmaking of a President: Lyndon Johnson and Vietnam*. Princeton University Press, 1977.

Schieffer, Bob. *This Just In: What I Couldn't Tell You on TV*. Putnam, 2004.

Schlesinger, Arthur M., Jr. *A Thousand Days: John F. Kennedy in the White House*. Houghton Mifflin Company, 1965.

Searle, John R. *The Campus War*. New World Publishing Company, 1971.

Shaplen, Robert. *The Lost Revolution: The US in Vietnam, 1946–1966*. Harper & Row, 1966.

Shawcross, William. *Sideshow: Kissinger, Nixon and the Destruction of Cambodia*. Simon & Schuster, 1979.

Shulimson, Jack. *US Marines in Vietnam, An Expanding War: 1966*. US Marine Corps, 1982.

Simmons, Brig. Gen. Edwin H. *The Marines in Vietnam, 1954–1973*. US Marine Corps, 1974.

———. *The United States Marines, 1775–1975*. Viking Press, 1976.

Smith, W. Thomas, Jr. "An Old Soldier Sounds Off," *George*. November 1998.

Snepp, Frank. *Decent Interval*. Vintage Books, 1977.

Stanton, Shelby L. *The Rise and Fall of an American Army: US Ground Forces in Vietnam, 1965–1973*. Presidio Press, 1985.

———. *Vietnam Order of Battle*. US News Books, 1981.

Summers, Harry G., Jr. *Vietnam War Almanac*. Facts on File Publications, 1985.

Sweetman, Jack. "Command of the Sea: The US Navy in Vietnam." Unpublished manuscript, 1987.

Szulc, Tad. *The Illusion of Peace: Foreign Policy in the Nixon Years*. Viking Press, 1978.

Tarr, Curtis W. *By the Numbers: The Reform of the Selective Service System, 1970–1972*. National Defense University, 1981.

Telfer, Maj. Gary L., Lt. Col. Lane Rogers, and V. Keith Fleming Jr. *US Marines in Vietnam: Fighting the North Vietnamese, 1967*. US Marine Corps, 1984.

The National Security Archive at George Washington University.

Thompson, Wayne. *To Hanoi and Back*. Smithsonian Institution Press, 2002.

Tilford, Earl H. *Setup: What the Air Force Did in Vietnam and Why*. Air University Press, 1991.

Tran Van Tra, Sr. Gen. *Vietnam: History of the Bulwark B-2 Theatre*. Vol. 5, Concluding the 30-Years War. GPO, 1983.

Tucker, Spencer C., ed. *Encyclopedia of the Vietnam War: A Political, Social, and Military History*. ABC-CLIO, 1998.

Van Staaveren, Jacob. Gradual Failure. Air Force History and Museums Program, 2002.

Van Tien Dung, Sr. Gen. *Our Great Spring Victory*. Translated by John Spragens Jr. Monthly Review Press, 1977.

Weiss, Stephen, et al. *A War Remembered*. Boston Publishing Company, 1986.

Welsh, Douglas. *The History of the Vietnam War*. Galahad Books, 1981.

Westmoreland, Gen. William C. *A Soldier Reports*. Dell Publishing Company, 1980.

White, Theodore H. *The Making of the President 1968*. Atheneum, 1969.

Online Sources

www.defencetalk.com/forums/air-force-aviation/us-aircraft-losses-over-vietnam-6485

www.history.com/this-day-in-history/us-marines-land-at-da-nang

www.historynet.com

IMAGE CREDITS

1888 photograph, reproduction in *La Royale* **by Jean Randier:** 316 (Sino-French War); **Abbie Rowe, White House Photographs, John F. Kennedy Presidential Library & Museum:** 23; **AFP/Getty Images:** 262; © **AP/Corbis:** 134, 191, 285; © **Associated Press:** 144, 171, 194 (bottom), 195, 204, 251, 256; © **Arthur Rothstein/Corbis:** 190; © **Bettmann/Corbis:** 18, 35, 64, 65, 96, 106, 120, 124, 125, 127, 158, 159, 162, 188, 193, 216, 220, 226, 227, 228, 230, 232, 235, 237, 244, 265, 270, 274, 283, 314 (top left), 314 (top right), 318 (Ellsberg); © **Bettmann/Corbis/AP Images:** 260; © **Bill Ehrhart:** 296, 297; © **Bob Adelman/Corbis:** 173 (bottom); © **Boston Publishing Company:** 48, 67, 109, 143, 321 (top), 321 (center); © **Burt Glinn/Magnum Photos:** 181, 185; © **Catherine Karnow/Corbis:** 57, 271; *Chronique de la Seconde Guerre Mondiale*: 316 (Vichy France); **Courtesy Clarence "Del" Williams:** 44, 45, 46; © **Corbis:** 20, 242, 319 (bottom); © **David Burnett 1987—Contact Press:** 233; **David M. Rubenstein Rare Book & Manuscript Library, Duke University:** 175; **Don North:** 278; **Dwight Carter:** 211; **Ed Tick:** 287 (top), 301, 302 (all); © **Eddie Adams/AP/Corbis:** 145 (bottom), 148; **Ernest E. Washington Collection:** 293, 294; **Fort Devens Museum:** 320 (C-rations); **Frank Lee Collection:** 282 (all); © **Gary Cameron/Reuters/Corbis:** 272; © **George Tiedemann/Corbis:** 33; **Getty Images:** 133 (top), 194 (top); © **Henri Huet/AP/Corbis:** 218; © **Henri Huet/Bettmann/Corbis:** 28; **Hiroji Kubota/Magnum Photos:** 192; © **Holloway/AP/Corbis:** 155; © **Hulton-Deutsch Collection/Corbis:** 225, 315 (center right); © **Jacques Pavlovsky/Sygma/Corbis:** 268; **Jean-Claude Francolon/Gamma-Liaison:** 259; © **John Filo/AP/Corbis:** 214 (top); © **John Stanmeyer/VII/Corbis:** 312 (top); © **Johner/AP/Corbis:** 145; © **JP Laffont/Sygma/Corbis:** 214 (bottom); © **Karen Kasmauski/National Geographic:** 314 (bottom left); **Kenneth George:** 6, 7 (bottom); **LBJ Presidential Library/Photo by Yoichi Okamoto:** 30, 114 (bottom), 141, 151, 153, 169; © **Leif Skoogfors/Corbis:** 61 (all); **Courtesy Leo Thorsness:** 243 (all);

Library of Congress: 17, 63, 310; © **Malcolm Browne/AP/Corbis:** 24; **Michael Ochs Archives/Getty Images:** 132, 133 (bottom); **NASA:** 135 (top); **National Archives:** 5, 22, 32 (top), 34, 40, 41, 42, 43, 49, 50, 56, 80, 78 (bottom), 71, 72, 73, 74 (all), 75 (all), 77, 81 (all), 94, 100, 99 (all), 101 (all), 102, 104, 105, 115 (all), 110, 111, 114 (top), 112–113, 118, 119, 123, 138, 139 (all), 147, 160, 161, 163, 166, 173 (top), 196, 198, 203, 205 (all), 205 (all), 206, 222, 223, 245, 246, 247, 263, 267 (all), 269, 309, 322 (top, bottom), 317 (Da Nang), 318 (Nixon), 319 (top); **Naval History & Heritage Command:** 37; **New England Center for Homeless Veterans:** 303, 304 (© 2010 Mark Davis); **Nick Mills:** 9, 210, 312 (bottom), 313 (all), 315 (top right, bottom left, bottom right); © **Nik Wheeler/Corbis:** 12, 257, 248; **Nina Berman:** 307; **Courtesy Richard Melis:** 164; © **Rob Whitworth/Corbis:** 314 (bottom right); **Robert George:** 7 (top), 10, 11, 36, 70, 98, 107 (all), 165, 224, 321 (bottom); **Courtesy Robert George:** 36; **Courtesy Robert L. Barker:** 47; **Robert Hodierne:** Cover, 58, 68–69, 78 (top), 79, 82, 83, 90, 91, 136, 200, 201, 208, 209, 290, 291, 292 (all); **Rolling Stone:** 135 (bottom); **Ron Owens:** 299, 300; **Courtesy Russell Burrows:** 52, 53, 54, 85, 86, 87, 88, 93, 92, 154, 217; **Skillman Library, Lafayette College:** 179 (all); **Stephen Olsson:** 289; © **Steve Stibbens/AP/Corbis:** 38; **Courtesy Terry Bell:** 287 (bottom); © **Tim Page/Corbis:** 280; **Time & Life Pictures/Getty Images:** 189; © **Tri Hieu/AP/Corbis:** 277; **Courtesy University Archives, Columbia University in the City of New York:** 186 ("Mark Rudd Speaking"), 187 ("The Bust"); **UPI/Corbis:** 238; **US Air Force:** 240, 320 (Claymore); **US Army:** 32 (bottom), 103, 128, 157, 317 (top two images), 318 (top two images), 320 (arty); **US Army Center of Military History:** 322 (center); **US Department of Defense:** 14, 16, 320 (AK-47, APC, Bouncing Betty); **US Marine Corps:** 25, 26; **US Navy:** 317 (USS *Maddox*); **Washington Post/Getty Images:** 172; © **White House/AP/Corbis:** 236; **White House Photograph Office:** 117, 252; **Wikimedia Commons:** 316 (de Rhodes, flag, top)

INDEX

The American
experience in
Vietnam.

5.15

$40.00

DATE			